AF834450

The Economic History of American Inequality

NATIONAL BUREAU *of* ECONOMIC RESEARCH

National Bureau of Economic Research
Conference Report

NBER
NATIONAL BUREAU *of* ECONOMIC RESEARCH

The Economic History of American Inequality

New Evidence and Perspectives

Edited by **Martha J. Bailey, Leah Platt Boustan, and William J. Collins**

The University of Chicago Press

Chicago and London

The University of Chicago Press, Chicago 60637
The University of Chicago Press, Ltd., London
© 2025 by National Bureau of Economic Research
All rights reserved. No part of this book may be used or reproduced in any manner whatsoever without written permission, except in the case of brief quotations in critical articles and reviews. For more information, contact the University of Chicago Press, 1427 E. 60th St., Chicago, IL 60637.
Published 2025
Printed in the United States of America

34 33 32 31 30 29 28 27 26 25   1 2 3 4 5

ISBN-13: 978-0-226-84064-2 (cloth)
ISBN-13: 978-0-226-84065-9 (e-book)
DOI: https://doi.org/10.7208/chicago/9780226840659.001.0001

Library of Congress Cataloging-in-Publication Data

Names: Bailey, Martha J., 1974– editor. | Boustan, Leah Platt, editor. | Collins, William J. (William Joseph), 1971– editor.
Title: The economic history of American inequality : new evidence and perspectives / edited by Martha J. Bailey, Leah Platt Boustan, and William J. Collins.
Other titles: National Bureau of Economic Research conference report.
Description: Chicago : The University of Chicago Press, 2025. | Series: National Bureau of Economic Research conference report | Includes bibliographical references and index.
Identifiers: LCCN 2024049880 | ISBN 9780226840642 (cloth) | ISBN 9780226840659 (ebook)
Subjects: LCSH: Income distribution—United States—History—19th century. | Income distribution—United States—History—20th century. | Equality—Economic aspects—United States—History—19th century. | Equality—Economic aspects—United States—History—20th century. | Economic security—United States—History—19th century. | Economic security—United States—History—20th century.
Classification: LCC HC110.I5 E26 2025 | DDC 339.2/20973—dc23/eng/20241121
LC record available at https://lccn.loc.gov/2024049880

♾ This paper meets the requirements of ANSI/NISO Z39.48-1992 (Permanence of Paper).

National Bureau of Economic Research

Officers

Peter Blair Henry, *Chair*
Karen G. Mills, *Vice Chair*
James M. Poterba, *President and Chief Executive Officer*
Robert Mednick, *Treasurer and Representative of the American Institute of Certified Public Accountants*
Kelly Horak, *Controller and Assistant Corporate Secretary*
Alterra Milone, *Corporate Secretary*
Denis Healy, *Assistant Corporate Secretary*

Directors at Large

Kathleen B. Cooper
Charles H. Dallara
Jessica P. Einhorn
Mohamed El-Erian
Diana Farrell
Helena Foulkes
Esther George
Peter Hancock
Karen N. Horn
Lisa Jordan
Karin Kimbrough
William M. Lewis Jr.
John Lipsky
Laurence C. Morse
Michael H. Moskow
Alicia H. Munnell
Douglas Peterson
Andrew Racine
John S. Reed
Hal Varian
Mark Weinberger
Martin B. Zimmerman

Directors by University Appointment

Timothy Bresnahan, *Stanford*
Alan V. Deardorff, *Michigan*
Benjamin Hermalin, *California, Berkeley*
R. Glenn Hubbard, *Columbia*
Samuel Kortum, *Yale*
George J. Mailath, *Pennsylvania*
Angelo Melino, *Toronto*
Joel Mokyr, *Northwestern*
John Pepper, *Virginia*
Richard Schmalensee, *Massachusetts Institute of Technology*
Christopher Sims, *Princeton*
Richard Steckel, *Ohio State*
Ann Huff Stevens, *Texas, Austin*
Lars Stole, *Chicago*
Ingo Walter, *New York*
David B. Yoffie, *Harvard*

Directors by Appointment of Other Organizations

Timothy Beatty, *Agricultural and Applied Economics Association*
Constance Hunter, *National Association for Business Economics*
Arthur Kennickell, *American Statistical Association*
Anne McCants, *Economic History Association*
Maureen O'Hara, *American Finance Association*
Dana M. Peterson, *The Conference Board*
Peter L. Rousseau, *American Economic Association*
Gregor W. Smith, *Canadian Economics Association*

Directors Emeriti

George A. Akerlof
Peter C. Aldrich
Jagdish Bhagwati
Don R. Conlan
George C. Eads
Ray C. Fair
Jacob Frenkel
Martin Gruber
Robert S. Hamada
Saul H. Hymans
Marjorie B. McElroy
Laurence H. Meyer
Robert T. Parry
Andrew Postlewaite
John J. Siegfried
Craig Swan
Marina v. N. Whitman

Relation of the Directors to the Work and Publications of the NBER

1. The object of the NBER is to ascertain and present to the economics profession, and to the public more generally, important economic facts and their interpretation in a scientific manner without policy recommendations. The Board of Directors is charged with the responsibility of ensuring that the work of the NBER is carried on in strict conformity with this object.

2. The President shall establish an internal review process to ensure that book manuscripts proposed for publication DO NOT contain policy recommendations. This shall apply both to the proceedings of conferences and to manuscripts by a single author or by one or more co-authors but shall not apply to authors of comments at NBER conferences who are not NBER affiliates.

3. No book manuscript reporting research shall be published by the NBER until the President has sent to each member of the Board a notice that a manuscript is recommended for publication and that in the President's opinion it is suitable for publication in accordance with the above principles of the NBER. Such notification will include a table of contents and an abstract or summary of the manuscript's content, a list of contributors if applicable, and a response form for use by Directors who desire a copy of the manuscript for review. Each manuscript shall contain a summary drawing attention to the nature and treatment of the problem studied and the main conclusions reached.

4. No volume shall be published until forty-five days have elapsed from the above notification of intention to publish it. During this period a copy shall be sent to any Director requesting it, and if any Director objects to publication on the grounds that the manuscript contains policy recommendations, the objection will be presented to the author(s) or editor(s). In case of dispute, all members of the Board shall be notified, and the President shall appoint an ad hoc committee of the Board to decide the matter; thirty days additional shall be granted for this purpose.

5. The President shall present annually to the Board a report describing the internal manuscript review process, any objections made by Directors before publication or by anyone after publication, any disputes about such matters, and how they were handled.

6. Publications of the NBER issued for informational purposes concerning the work of the Bureau, or issued to inform the public of the activities at the Bureau, including but not limited to the NBER Digest and Reporter, shall be consistent with the object stated in paragraph 1. They shall contain a specific disclaimer noting that they have not passed through the review procedures required in this resolution. The Executive Committee of the Board is charged with the review of all such publications from time to time.

7. NBER working papers and manuscripts distributed on the Bureau's website are not deemed to be publications for the purpose of this resolution, but they shall be consistent with the object stated in paragraph 1. Working papers shall contain a specific disclaimer noting that they have not passed through the review procedures required in this resolution. The NBER's web site shall contain a similar disclaimer. The President shall establish an internal review process to ensure that the working papers and the web site do not contain policy recommendations, and shall report annually to the Board on this process and any concerns raised in connection with it.

8. Unless otherwise determined by the Board or exempted by the terms of paragraphs 6 and 7, a copy of this resolution shall be printed in each NBER publication as described in paragraph 2 above.

Contents

Introduction

Martha J. Bailey, Leah Platt Boustan,
and William J. Collins

This volume is a collection of seven essays presented at a conference at the National Bureau of Economic Research (NBER) in April 2023 and subsequently revised from discussion at the conference and comments from reviewers. Sponsored by the NBER, Boston University, Princeton University, the University of California, Los Angeles, and Vanderbilt University, the conference was entitled Historical Labor Markets and Inequality. This introduction provides the context for the volume and summarizes its contributions.[1]

The core motivation for the NBER conference and its papers is straightforward: The measurement of economic inequality over the long run is essential to understanding the development of the American economy and the well-being of its population. Measures and interpretations of economic inequality deepen our understanding of how the economy operates and who benefits from economic shocks and policies. Economic inequality manifests in people's lives in various ways, including access to resources and security;

Martha J. Bailey is a professor of economics and director of the California Center for Population Research at the University of California, Los Angeles, and a research associate of the National Bureau of Economic Research.

Leah Platt Boustan is a professor of economics and director of the Industrial Relations Section at Princeton University, and a research associate and codirector of the Development of the American Economy Program at the National Bureau of Economic Research.

William J. Collins is the Terence E. Adderley Jr. Chair and Professor of Economics and a professor of history (by courtesy) at Vanderbilt University, and a research associate and codirector of the Development of the American Economy Program at the National Bureau of Economic Research.

1. The conference coincided with a dinner and evening event celebrating the academic career of Robert A. Margo, whose research and teaching have long shaped the scholarly debate on the subject matter of the volume. Funding for the dinner and event was contributed to by the College of Arts and Science at Boston University.

choices about education, migration, and family formation; and hopes for the future. In this context, people and policymakers often reference some earlier historical period as a benchmark for comparison or as a guide for policy prescriptions—but the past itself requires careful interpretation. At a fundamental level, different kinds of data become available in different periods, each with its own strengths and weaknesses, often complicating overarching stories. We convened this conference to discuss and refine new research on the economic history of American inequality with the broad goal of illuminating the past in a way that also sheds light on the present.

I Opening Remarks

Since Alexis de Tocqueville documented the living conditions he observed during his travels through the American countryside in the 1830s, there has been strong interest in understanding the patterns, sources, and consequences of income inequality in the United States. Given the dearth of data on wages and incomes from the early 19th century, historians have turned to Tocqueville's comments as one clue about economic inequality at the time. In comparison to Europe, Tocqueville found American society—at least among white men in the North—to be highly equal, extolling that "among a democratic people, where there is no hereditary wealth, every man works to earn a living."[2]

If one were to draw a straight line from Tocqueville's impressions in the 1830s to the high levels of income inequality today, one would infer that economic development in the United States over the past two centuries has been accompanied by a shift from a relatively equal distribution of resources to one of growing inequality. But these end points alone do not provide enough information to judge when and how the level and distribution of income changed, nor do they shed light on what might have caused these changes.

Filling in the gaps between these end points is where the painstaking work of economic historians comes in. Economic historians' work has focused largely on documenting and understanding changes in wage and income inequality. Income underpins consumption, builds wealth, and confers status. For most people, it derives primarily from the work they supply in labor markets or through self-employment. For the wealthy, income from rent, interest, dividends, and capital gains is also important. The ability to measure and analyze long-run changes in the income distribution depends first on the large-scale, systematic collection of data on wages and other sources of income, often by government entities, and then on scholars' ability to digitize, combine, and analyze this information.

Robert Margo's *Wages and Labor Markets in the United States, 1820–*

2. Tocqueville condemned the inequities of slavery in the South, writing: "At the present time the descendants of the Europeans are the sole owners of the land and the absolute masters of all labor; they alone possess wealth, knowledge, and arms. The black is destitute of all these advantages, but can subsist without them because he is a slave."

1860, published in 1999, is an important milestone on our path to understanding trends in American wages and inequality in the first half of the 19th century. Margo brought two historical data sources to bear on fundamental questions about the antebellum economy. From the *Reports of Persons and Articles Hired*, he compiled thousands of observations on civilians' wages paid by the army throughout the country. He gathered additional evidence from the 1850 and 1860 manuscripts of the *Census of Social Statistics*, including information on local average wages for various occupations and the cost of board. Through careful examination of these data, Margo illuminated nominal and real wage differences across regions, between occupations, and over time. He showed that workers' real wages increased at about the same pace as gross domestic product (GDP) per worker throughout the first half of the 19th century. But these gains did not accrue continuously or evenly: some periods entailed real wage declines; regional wage gaps between the South and North emerged; and highly educated workers gained ground faster than both artisans and unskilled laborers, with artisans having the slowest gains. This study placed our knowledge of antebellum wages and labor markets on firmer ground, which in turn has supported the development of a more nuanced narrative of long-run American economic development and its implications for workers and families.

For a view of the late 19th and early 20th centuries, more data sources are available to scholars. In large part this reflects the federal and state governments' increasing interest in labor markets and their resulting efforts to collect more data on employment and wages. Lebergott's *Manpower in Economic Growth* (1964) compiles, evaluates, and summarizes much of this evidence with references to the various original sources.[3] Because scholars do not have information on the full distribution of wages or income, they have often relied on comparisons of wages by occupation to capture trends in skill differentials and earnings inequality. These do not reveal a strong trend in the later part of the 19th century. Instead, "the best available evidence suggests slight upward trends in the wages of skilled artisans and white-collar workers relative to common labor from 1860 to 1900" (Margo 2000, 227).[4] Evidence from *within* the manufacturing sector, which underwent rapid changes in this period, reveals rising wage inequality across establishments (Atack et al. 2004), a topic that Atack, Margo, and Rhode revisit in chapter 1 of this volume.

3. The Aldrich and Weeks reports are prominent sources in studies of late 19th-century wage trends. Each report compiled retrospective wage data from manufacturing firms' payroll records, reaching back from 1880 (Weeks) or the early 1890s (Aldrich). See Margo (2006) for further description. The census of manufactures also routinely inquired about wages and the number of production workers. Establishment-level samples of these data are available from Atack et al. (2006).

4. See also Lindert and Williamson (2016)—which updates Williamson and Lindert (1980)—who summarize estimates of income shares accruing to top percentiles of the distribution circa 1870 and 1910. Their interpretation points to a "modest and mixed" rise in inequality but the evidence is "tentative" (173).

For studies of the early 20th century, federal income tax return data and the earliest micro-level income datasets shed light on new dimensions of American income inequality. With these sources, scholars rely less heavily on occupational income series or snapshots specific to the manufacturing sector, although such perspectives remain valuable and informative. Simon Kuznets used income tax returns to characterize trends in income shares accruing to the highest-earning households (Kuznets and Jenks 1953). Piketty and Saez (2003) extended this approach to the late 20th century. In their series, inequality in the 20th century started at and maintained a high level through the 1920s, declined in the midcentury decades, and then resurged in the late 20th century. Interpreting income tax data—given the incentive to underreport taxable income and sizable amounts of nontaxed income—requires great care, and debates are ongoing regarding the magnitude of shifts in inequality when viewed through this lens.[5]

An alternative and complementary view comes from census-based sources. Goldin and Katz (2008), for instance, collected micro-level data from Iowa's state census of 1915, one of the earliest to gather information on both income and education. They associated earnings differentials with varying levels of educational attainment, a form of human capital investment, because the market "returns to education" are a key component of overall wage inequality. After calculating educational earnings premia in Iowa in 1915, they compared these premia to those estimated in later federal censuses. They found a decline in the returns to high school and college attainment from 1915 to 1940, which they attribute to changes in the supply of better-educated workers, which was driven largely by the high school movement. Evidence from occupational differentials, in which a notable decline in the skill premium occurs before the early 1920s, offers additional support to the view that wage inequality declined in the early decades of the 20th century.[6]

The federal census of population in 1940 brought a major expansion in the sources available for the study of inequality. Following the economic collapse of the Great Depression, it was the first federal census that collected individual wage and salary data for every individual in the United States (although it did not cover self-employment earnings or other nonwage income from sources like agriculture). This enabled scholars to characterize the full distribution of wage earnings and to track changes in the cross-sectional distribution over time. By midcentury, the "size distribution of income" was well established as an important object of measurement and research interest.[7]

5. See Auten and Splinter (2023) and Piketty et al.'s (2003) reply.

6. Goldin and Katz (2008, chap. 2) review and refine much of this evidence and present new estimates for the manufacturing sector in 1890 and 1940.

7. See, e.g., the essays in the NBER's *An Appraisal of the 1950 Census Income Data* (1958) and Goldsmith et al. (1954).

As computing power increased, microdata samples from the censuses and comparable samples from the Current Population Survey and, more recently, the American Community Survey, formed the basis for a new literature in labor economics that documented changes in wage inequality and formulated explanations for those changes. A key advantage of the microdata samples is that individual scholars could partition the labor force by age, education, region, race, sex, and other characteristics, depending on their specific research questions. Goldin and Margo's paper "The Great Compression: The Wage Structure in the United States at Mid-Century" (1992) was the first to use midcentury microdata samples to offer a rich view of the earnings distribution in 1940 compared with later periods (1950–1990). They documented and decomposed a large decline in income inequality in the 1940s, the decade of World War II, which they named the "Great Compression." For three decades, income inequality remained low, anchored by institutional features of the midcentury labor market and an increasing supply of educated workers (Collins and Niemesh 2019; Farber et al. 2021; Goldin and Katz 2008). But since the 1970s, inequality has risen to and surpassed the level observed prior to the Great Compression.

In connecting the dots between the various data sources, economic historians have collectively pieced together a story of income inequality in the US over the past two centuries. This now-standard narrative is that earnings inequality within the free population of the US was comparatively low in Tocqueville's day but likely rose over the 19th century, as revealed by growing antebellum wage gaps between workers in jobs that required high levels of formal education and workers in other jobs. This pattern follows the classic "Kuznets curve," whereby economic development and technological change shift the population from relatively homogeneous and equal rural areas dominated by agricultural activity to more heterogeneous and unequal urban areas, where manufacturing and service jobs dominate. Within the manufacturing sector, the transition from artisan shops to steam-powered, and later electrified, factories resulted in the emergence of larger enterprises with a finer division of labor, more specialization and mechanization, and a larger role for management. As the divide between skilled and unskilled jobs in the labor force became ever more pronounced, so too did the gap in their respective wages. Workers in skilled and white-collar positions enjoyed relatively high pay around the turn of the century, and their status in the labor market was further cemented by the increase in managerial training provided to them during World War II (Giorcelli 2023).

Income inequality then fell in the early 20th century from this high point as parents encouraged children to spend more years in school rather than working on farms or in factories, and as localities invested in building public schools to prepare them for these more skilled jobs. The decline in inequality was particularly rapid in the 1940s given various policy features of the wartime economy. After World War II ended, veterans returned to a society transformed by federal activity, including programs rooted in the New Deal era, widespread unionization, and the GI Bill. Wage inequality remained low from 1950 to about 1970. At that point, inequality began rising again alongside tax cuts and changing compensation for executives, the decline of unions and the real minimum wage, as well as the spread of computerization, which made skilled labor even more productive. Particularly given the sharp rise in college tuition, parents' income became an increasingly important determinant of college enrollment, and many talented prospective students did not enter or complete college. Since the 1980s, the skill levels in the population have not kept pace with changes in technology. The college-to-noncollege wage ratio, one measure of inequality, has continued to rise, driven primarily by income gains at the very top of the distribution.

Income inequality has been described by various U-shaped patterns over specific periods of time: as an inverted U from 1850 to 1950 (rising and then falling, as associated with a traditional Kuznets curve) or as a U shape from 1920 to 2020 (falling and then rising again, what Piketty and Saez have called a second Kuznets curve). With a 200-year bird's-eye view, the trajectory of inequality has had multiple peaks and valleys.

II This Volume and Its Contributions

The chapters in this volume refine and extend the economic history literature on income inequality in the United States. Chapters in the first section provide fresh evidence about the income distribution during the 19th and early 20th centuries by using new data on wages and prices. The second set of chapters extends our thinking about inequality beyond wage and salary income to other dimensions of well-being. The third section considers the consequences of income inequality, beyond the effects on relative economic well-being. The volume concludes with an intellectual history of "human capital," a core concept in economists' thinking about the underpinnings of labor market inequality.

New Evidence on Historical Wage Inequality

The first contributions of this volume are the introduction of new wage data from the 19th and early 20th century and new data on price levels faced by households at different points of the income distribution over the 1940s.

In chapter 1, Jeremy Atack, Robert A. Margo, and Paul W. Rhode provide new data, adding richness and further evidence supporting the consensus view that wage inequality in American manufacturing increased over the 19th century and then decreased through 1940, following the canonical inverted-U shape. For the first half of this period, the chapter draws on new data from the US Department of Labor's 1899 *Hand and Machine Labor* study to argue that wage inequality within manufacturing establishments rose over the 19th century, primarily because of the increasing division of labor. A second data source from Massachusetts state reports allows the authors to extend their analysis to the 1930s. The new time series shows that wage inequality among production workers declined from the early 1890s to the late 1930s, mainly because of rising wages for the lowest-earning workers. The compression of the lower tail of the wage distribution in manufacturing is particularly strong in industries that adopted electrification, which facilitated the move into mass production.

The 1940s stand out as a unique period of substantive compression in wage inequality in the US. In their foundational paper, Goldin and Margo (1992) document a significant narrowing in nominal wage differences across the board—by education, job experience, and occupation. However, during this decade, the American economy also experienced unusually high inflation, which may have affected different types of households in markedly different ways. Consequently, it is important to consider how shifts in real wage inequality might have differed from shifts in nominal wage inequality during this period. In chapter 2, Carola Frydman and Raven Molloy calculate inflation rates for different groups of households during the 1940s to estimate changes in the distribution of real wage earnings. Using micro-level data from the 1935–1936 Consumer Expenditure Survey for a sample of about 2,000 urban families, they construct consumption baskets by education, occupation, and income. Then, they compute group-specific price indexes by matching the spending shares to price indexes for specific items published in various historical reports. Differences in inflation across groups in the 1940s turn out to be small because spending shares were similar across groups. Therefore, the real wage distribution compressed by about the same amount as the nominal wage distribution. In short, the Great Compression was "real" after all.

These contributions join a growing trend toward reexamining the first generation of data collection on income inequality. Some of these revisions aim to change important aspects of the broader narrative, whereas others refine and reinforce earlier interpretations. Getting the data right can have important implications for our understanding of key historical events. For example, Geloso et al. (2022) revise Piketty and Saez's data on the share of income earned by the top 10 percent of the distribution. These revisions, which are based on applying alternative assumptions for how to fill in inherent gaps and missing data in the income tax series, imply that inequality may not have been as high as we thought in the early 20th century, and thus, the decline in inequality was perhaps not as pronounced at midcentury. Work to sort out these questions is ongoing and underscores the challenges of measurement and the importance of clear and well-grounded assumptions.

Understanding how the prices of consumption baskets vary across the income distribution can likewise change our interpretation of wage inequality. Moretti (2013) argues that the rise in inequality after 1980 is not as extreme as often feared. Yes, high-skilled workers have enjoyed rising nominal pay, but they also tend to live in coastal cities that have been plagued by rising housing prices and cost-of-living increases. An alternative view of these rising coastal housing costs is that highly paid skilled workers are simply choosing to spend their expanding incomes on living in an attractive city with a wide basket of local amenities (Diamond 2016). In this view, high housing costs paid by the highly educated simply reflect the choice of the rich to buy luxury products. Jaravel (2021) summarizes a wider literature on inflation inequality for the full basket of consumer goods. In the modern data, prices are rising more slowly for basic consumer products purchased by the poor, whereas prices for luxury items are rising more rapidly.

Measuring Inequality in Well-Being Beyond Income

Cross-sectional data provide a snapshot of the level and dispersion of income at a given point in time. Repeated cross sections, when the data are sufficiently comparable, provide a sense of how the income distribution has trended over time. Yet these snapshots of income provide a limited understanding of differences and changes in lifetime resources, wealth, or intergenerational mobility. They also provide a narrow window on the population's economic security, the causes and consequences of household formation, and nonwage sources of income and wealth. The second contribution of the volume is, therefore, to move beyond economists' standard focus on wage and income inequality and shift attention to other dimensions of well-being and inequality.

In chapter 3, William J. Collins and Gregory T. Niemesh highlight the connection between changes in income during the Great Compression era and the unprecedented increase in homeownership rates between 1940 and 1960. This era was characterized by a narrowing of the income distribution and, just as importantly, a sharp increase in real wage levels across the distribution. Collins and Niemesh show that post-1940 wage changes varied substantially across space, and these differential changes in wages were strongly positively correlated with subsequent changes in homeownership. Economic theory, multiple specification checks, and an instrumental-variables approach harnessing variation in local income distributions before 1940 suggest that rising income causally affected homeownership. The chapter concludes that between one-third and one-half of the homeownership gains between 1940 and 1960 were attributable to the strong growth in income, complementing other changes in housing and financial markets that supported increases in homeownership. This relationship is vital to understanding American inequality because land- and homeownership have long been the primary component of most families' asset holdings, and, for some, they have supported the accumulation of additional net wealth. Moreover, housing consumption—both in terms of a housing unit's intrinsic quality and in terms of the access it provides to nearby goods, services, schools, and amenities—is a core aspect of material well-being and environmental conditions for adults and children.

In chapter 4, Laura Salisbury examines widows' participation in the US's first major income-support program: the pensions offered to Union Army veterans and their families. Standard wage-based measures of inequality tend to look only at income received for market work, which misses income that comes from rising government transfers, most famously with the advent of Social Security in the 1930s and other means-tested transfer programs.[8] Focusing on market work also tends to leave women outside the frame of study, reflecting married women's historically low labor market participation rates. Salisbury's chapter brings widowed women into the story of inequality in the postbellum period and assesses their take-up rate of pension benefits in an era when labor market opportunities for women were sharply limited. She shows that, although the pension program was well publicized and eligibility criteria were straightforward, the take-up rate was around 50 percent—low but similar to take-up rates for modern income-support programs. The far-from-universal take-up rate reflected the high administrative cost of applying for the program, including travel to appear in court and the assistance of an attorney. The take-up rate varied with the widow's age and number of children, likely reflecting opportunities for remarriage, which would terminate the pension benefit and thus reduce the expected benefit of applying. Providing income support for families that might otherwise be impoverished, especially when the heads of such families were viewed as "deserving" of public assistance, eventually became a core function of the federal government. By reducing poverty, these programs ameliorated inequality of material well-being in ways that snapshots of labor market earnings do not capture.

In chapter 5, Martha J. Bailey and Peter Z. Lin explore changes in well-being during the 19th- and early 20th-century US through the lens of marriage. Scholars have long noted that the dissimilarity of husbands and wives in terms of age, nativity, education, and family socioeconomic status strongly determines gender equity, bargaining power, and the allocation of resources within households (Calvo et al. 2024; Ciscato and Weber 2020; Eika et al. 2019; Fernandez and Rogerson 2001; Greenwood et al. 2014; Kremer 1997). Processes governing marital matching determine the intergenerational mobility of women and the level of investments made in children (Aiyagari et al. 2000; Chadwick and Solon 2002; Currie and Almond 2011; Ermisch et al. 2006). Bailey and Lin find that age homogamy changed very little for women born in the 19th century, making the rapid transition

8. Auten and Splinter (2023) and Meyer and Sullivan (2023) emphasize how our understanding of the income distribution changes when we include income from transfer programs.

to smaller within-couple age gaps in the 20th century a stark departure from the 100-year trend. In addition, they find that intercultural marriage (the likelihood that a woman had a father-in-law who was of different nativity to her father) increased and helped stir the US melting pot. As mass public education grew in the late 19th and early 20th centuries, assortative matching on education changed little, but women's relative intergenerational mobility increased between 1900 and 1940. They conclude that, even as the importance of a father's heritage and occupational standing fell, women's own educational attainment remained a powerful force in shaping their socioeconomic status. Bailey and Lin's approach to conceptualizing and measuring well-being and inequality through the lens of household structure complements a modern literature that is increasingly focused on the distribution of wealth and the importance of transfer income.

Consequences of Inequality

The third contribution of the volume is to consider the *consequences* of shifts in income inequality. There is mounting evidence in modern settings that income inequality can have deleterious effects on the political process, on social attitudes, and on health, stress and self-worth (Buttrick and Oishi 2017; Patel et al. 2018; Voorheis et al. 2015).

In chapter 6, Leah Platt Boustan, Jiwon Choi, and David Clingingsmith take a first step at studying the effects of rising inequality on social outcomes. They focus on a specific episode: rising inequality in the late 20th century due to factory computerization. One such technology—computer numerical control (CNC)—used programmable motors and sensors to automate a significant part of the machining tasks in metal manufacturing. The diffusion of CNC machine tools encouraged manufacturing firms to shed workers on the production floor, particularly in the nonunionized sector. In this volume, Boustan, Choi, and Clingingsmith trace out the effect of this new technology on trust in institutions and political partisanship. Since the late 1960s, Americans have been losing confidence in political and elite social institutions, and certain regional and demographic groups have turned away from the previously dominant Democratic Party. Scholars have highlighted the role of cultural factors in explaining these shifts. The chapter documents that workers who were more exposed to CNC technology reported declining confidence in American institutions and weakened identification with the Democratic Party. Exposure to the CNC shock at the commuting zone level reduced vote share for Democratic candidates in the South and decreased voter participation outside of the South.

The Human Capital Paradigm

The concluding chapter considers the broader underpinnings of inequality in the United States. Inequality in income, earnings, and other dimensions is to a significant extent determined by differences in human capital—the investment in human beings at a point in time in the form of education, training, health, job search, migration, or anything else that affects future productivity—and by the "returns" to these investments. This framework has guided research on the economic history of American inequality for decades, including applications to eras that long predate the concept's modern definition, as in landmark works like Margo's *Race and Schooling in the South* (1990) and others.

In chapter 7, Claudia Goldin and Lawrence F. Katz trace the emergence of the insights of human capital theory and the role of the National Bureau of Economic Research (NBER) in promoting this paradigm in economics today. Although the concept has roots going back to Adam Smith, the phrase "human capital" sparked some scholarly controversy when it first started to gain wide circulation. When Gary Becker published his influential volume *Human Capital* in 1964, he described his hesitation in using the term as the title, as it equated people with property. This intellectual history describes how the work of Gary Becker, Jacob Mincer, Theodore Schultz, and others played an important role in incubating human capital research during the 1950s and 1960s, followed by its stark ascendance in the 1970s and dominance as a paradigm in the decades beyond. With the explosion in the availability of microdata and the ability of human capital as a concept to link together macro- and microeconomists' approaches, today over 25 percent of NBER working papers and 20 percent of all economics papers reference human capital.

III Closing Remarks

The chapters in this volume, though varying in their focus, data, and methods, all point to economic historians' resourcefulness and determination in tracing out the path of American inequality and understanding its increases and declines. Ongoing debates and missing pieces of the story show both the limits of our knowledge and the possibilities for improvement and extension in light of better data and new theoretical and econometric perspectives. Generations of economic historians have engaged these important issues—some have done so for decades and trained others to do the same. We see this volume as evidence of that intergenerational transfer of insight and motivation, and as encouragement for future cohorts of scholars.

For acknowledgments, sources of research support, and disclosure of the authors' material financial relationships, if any, please see https://www.nber.org/books-and-chapters/economic-history-american-inequality-new-evidence-and-perspectives/introduction-economic-history-american-inequality-new-evidence-and-perspectives.

References

Aiyagari, S. R., J. Greenwood, and N. Guner. 2000. "On the State of the Union." *Journal of Political Economy* 108: 213–44.

Almond, Douglas, and Janet Currie. 2011. "Killing Me Softly: The Fetal Origins Hypothesis." *Journal of Economic Perspectives* 24: 153–72.

Atack, Jeremy, Fred Bateman, and Robert A. Margo. 2004. "Skill Intensity and Rising Wage Dispersion in Nineteenth-Century American Manufacturing." *Journal of Economic History* 64 (1): 172–92.

Atack, Jeremy, Fred Bateman, and Thomas Weiss. 2006. *National Samples from the Census of Manufacturing: 1850, 1860, and 1870*. Inter-University Consortium for Political and Social Research. https://doi.org/10.3886/ICPSR04048.v1.

Auten, Gerald, and David Splinter. 2023. "Income Inequality in the United States: Using Tax Data to Measure Long-Term Trends." *Journal of Political Economy* 132 (7): 2179–2227.

Buttrick, Nicholas, and Shigehiro Oishi. 2017. "The Psychological Consequences of Income Inequality." *Social and Personality Psychology Compass* 11 (3): e12304. https://doi.org/10.1111/spc3.12304.

Calvo, Paula, Ilse Lindenlaub, and Ana Reynoso. 2024. "Marriage Market and Labor Market Sorting." *Review of Economic Studies*: rdae010. https://doi.org/10.1093/restud/rdae010.

Chadwick, Laura, and Gary Solon. 2002. "Intergenerational Income Mobility Among Daughters." *American Economic Review* 92: 335–44.

Ciscato, Edoardo, and Simon Weber. 2020. "The Role of Evolving Marital Preferences in Growing Income Inequality." *Journal of Population Economics* 33: 307–47.

Collins, William J., and Gregory T. Niemesh. 2019. "Unions and the Great Compression of Wage Inequality in the US at Mid-Century: Evidence from Local Labor Markets." *Economic History Review* 72 (2): 691–715.

Currie, Janet, and Douglas Almond. 2011. "Human Capital Development Before Age Five." In *Handbook of Labor Economics*, edited by D. Card and O. Ashenfelter, 4B:1315–1486. North Holland.

Diamond, Rebecca. 2016. "The Determinants and Welfare Implications of US Workers' Diverging Location Choices by Skill: 1980–2000." *American Economic Review* 106 (3): 479–524.

Eika, Lasse, Magne Mostad, and Basit Zafar. 2019. "Educational Assortative Mating and Household Income Inequality." *Journal of Political Economy* 127: 2795–2835.

Ermisch, John, Marco Francesconi, and Thomas Siedler. 2006. "Intergenerational Mobility and Marital Sorting." *Economic Journal* 116: 659–79.

Farber, Henry S., Daniel Herbst, Ilyana Kuziemko, and Suresh Naidu. 2021. "Unions and Inequality over the Twentieth Century: New Evidence from Survey Data." *Quarterly Journal of Economics* 136 (3): 1–61.

Fernandez, Raquel, and Richard Rogerson. 2001. "Sorting and Long-Run Inequality." *Quarterly Journal of Economics* 116: 1305–41.

Geloso, Vincent, Phillip Magness, John Moore, and Philip Schlosser. 2022. "How Pronounced Is the U-Curve? Revisiting Income Inequality in the United States, 1917–60." *Economic Journal* 132 (647): 2366–91.

Giorcelli, Michela. 2023. "Creating the 'American Way' of Business: Evidence from WWII in the U.S." NBER Working Paper No. 31980. National Bureau of Economic Research.

Goldin, Claudia, and Lawrence F. Katz. 2008. *The Race Between Education and Technology*. Harvard University Press.
Goldin, Claudia, and Robert A. Margo. 1992. "The Great Compression: The Wage Structure in the United States at Mid-Century." *Quarterly Journal of Economics* 107: 1–34.
Goldsmith, Selma, George Jaszi, Hyman Kaitz, and Maurice Liebenberg. 1954. "Size Distribution of Income Since the Mid-Thirties." *Review of Economics and Statistics* 36: 1–32.
Greenwood, Jeremy, Nezih Guner, Georgi Kocharkov, and Cezar Santos. 2014. "Marry Your Like: Assortative Mating and Income Inequality." *American Economic Review* 104: 348–53.
Jaravel, Xavier. 2021. "Inflation Inequality: Measurement, Causes, and Policy Implications." *Annual Review of Economics* 13: 599–629.
Kremer, Michael. 1997. "How Much Does Sorting Increase Inequality?" *Quarterly Journal of Economics* 112: 115–39.
Kuznets, Simon, and Elizabeth Jenks. 1953. *Shares of Upper Income Groups in Income and Savings*. National Bureau of Economic Research.
Lebergott, Stanley. 1964. *Manpower in Economic Growth: The American Record Since 1800*. McGraw-Hill Co.
Lindert, Peter H., and Jeffrey G. Williamson. 2016. *Unequal Gains: American Growth and Inequality Since 1700*. Princeton University Press.
Margo, Robert A. 1990. *Race and Schooling in the South, 1880–1950: An Economic History*. University of Chicago Press and NBER.
Margo, Robert A. 1999. *Wages and Labor Markets in the United States, 1820–1860*. University of Chicago Press and NBER.
Margo, Robert A. 2000. "The Labor Force in the Nineteenth Century." In *The Cambridge Economic History of the United States*, edited by S. Engerman and R. Gallman, 2:207–43. Cambridge University Press.
Margo, Robert. 2006. "Wages and Wage Inequality." In *Historical Statistics of the United States*, millennial ed., Part B, *Work and Welfare*, edited by S. Carter, 40–46. Cambridge University Press.
Martin, Molly. 2006. "Family Structure and Income Inequality in Families with Children, 1976 to 2000." *Demography* 43 (3): 421–45.
Meyer, Bruce, and James Sullivan. 2023. "Consumption and Income Inequality in the United States Since the 1960s." *Journal of Political Economy* 131 (2): 247–84.
Moretti, Enrico. 2013. "Real Wage Inequality." *American Economic Journal: Applied Economics* 5 (1): 65–103.
National Bureau of Economic Research, Conference on Research in Income and Wealth. 1958. *An Appraisal of the 1950 Census Income Data*. Princeton University Press.
Patel, Vikram, Jonathan K. Burns, Monisha Dhingra, Leslie Tarver, Brandon A. Kohrt, and Crick Lund. 2018. "Income Inequality and Depression: A Systematic Review and Meta-Analysis of the Association and a Scoping Review of Mechanisms." *World Psychiatry* 17 (1): 76–89.
Piketty, Thomas, and Emmanuel Saez. 2003. "Income Inequality in the United States, 1913–1998." *Quarterly Journal of Economics* 118: 1–39.
Piketty, Thomas, Emmanuel Saez, and Gabriel Zucman. 2023. "Comment on Auten and Splinter." Technical Note 2023/09, World Inequality Lab.
Schwartz, Christine. 2010. "Earnings Inequality and the Changing Association Between Spouses' Earnings." *American Journal of Sociology* 115 (5): 1524–57.
Tocqueville, Alexis de. 1835. *Democracy in America*. Translated by Henry Reeve. https://en.wikisource.org/wiki/Democracy_in_America.

Voorheis, John, Nolan McCarty, and Boris Shor. 2015. "Unequal Incomes, Ideology and Gridlock: How Rising Inequality Increases Political Polarization" (August 21, 2015). SSRN. http://dx.doi.org/10.2139/ssrn.2649215.

Williamson, Jeffrey G., and Peter H. Lindert. 1980. *American Inequality: A Macroeconomic History*. Academic Press.

I

New Evidence on Wage Inequality

1

Wage Inequality in American Manufacturing, 1820–1940
New Evidence

Jeremy Atack, Robert A. Margo, and Paul W. Rhode

1.1 Introduction

At the start of the 19th century, over 80 percent of the American labor force was engaged in agriculture. Among those not in farming, only a small portion, perhaps 5 percent of the labor force, was engaged in manufacturing for the domestic market. Virtually all this production occurred in small-scale artisan shops, in which a highly skilled proprietor, either on his own or with apprentices, made goods using traditional hand tools. By the end of the 19th century, the share of the labor force in agriculture had been cut in half, to 40 percent, and the share of the labor force in manufacturing rose to 15 percent. While artisan shops remained numerically important, most manufacturing production circa 1900 came from large, mechanized factories, in which the typical production worker was a semiskilled operative using special-purpose, steam-powered machinery while other "nonproduction" workers reported on and managed the flow of output. Subsequently, over the next several decades before World War II, factory production continued to grow while

Jeremy Atack is professor emeritus and a research professor of economics at Vanderbilt University, and a research associate of the National Bureau of Economic Research.

Robert A. Margo is a professor of economics at Boston University and a research associate of the National Bureau of Economic Research.

Paul W. Rhode is a professor of economics at the University of Michigan and a research associate of the National Bureau of Economic Research.

An earlier version of this paper was presented at the NBER conference in Cambridge, MA, in April 2023. Comments from the conference volume editors, Hoyt Bleakley, Martin Fiszbein, conference participants, and workshop participants at the University of Michigan and the University of Groningen are gratefully acknowledged. For acknowledgments, sources of research support, and disclosure of the authors' material financial relationships, if any, please see https://www.nber.org/books-and-chapters/economic-history-american-inequality-new-evidence-and-perspectives/wage-inequality-american-manufacturing-1820-1940-new-evidence.

steam power was displaced by electricity. These developments greatly altered the absolute and relative demands for various occupational skills in manufacturing as well as the incentives for individuals to acquire and supply them, potentially altering the distribution of manufacturing wages and, therefore, of economic inequality. As Frederick C. Mills would remark in his introduction to Harry Jerome's famous NBER study, "Mechanization . . . in all its countless manifestations reacts upon the volume of employment, the skills and the working methods of the human factors of production" (1934, xxiii).

The consensus view from these changes is that wage inequality in American manufacturing followed an inverted-U path over our period of study (Lindert and Williamson 1976, esp. fig. 1.1, 2016; Williamson and Lindert 1980). The rising portion of this inverted U occurred from the early to the late 19th century, and the decreasing portion from the turn of the 20th century until just before World War II (Atack et al. 2004; Goldin and Katz 1999, 2008; Katz and Margo 2014; Margo 2000). The rising portion of the inverted U has been attributed to "hollowing out"—growing relative demand for factory operatives in the lower tail of the wage distribution and for white-collar nonproduction workers in the upper tail—at the expense of artisans in the middle (Atack et al. 2004; Goldin and Sokoloff 1984; Katz and Margo 2014). The falling portion is attributed to the rapid growth in the supply of skilled labor at the top end of the distribution due to the "high school movement" and to the emergence of "technology-skill complementarity" as electrification reorganized factory production, reducing the demand for low-paid factory jobs at the bottom (Goldin and Katz 1998, 1999, 2000, 2008; Gray 2013; Lafortune et al. 2019).

Since wage labor figures prominently in explanations for both the rise and fall, one might suppose that economic historians have documented the inverted U shape with comprehensive time series on the full distribution of manufacturing wages. Unfortunately, the previously available evidence falls short of the ideal, especially earlier in the 19th century. Instead, scholars have relied heavily upon occupation-specific average wages to produce time series of "skill differentials"—ratios of wages of skilled blue-collar or white-collar to unskilled or semiskilled workers—which broadly trace out an inverted U (Autor et al. 2020; Goldin and Katz 1999, 2008; Goldin and Margo 1992; Lindert and Williamson 1976; Margo 2000; Williamson and Lindert 1980). While such series are highly useful, their correlation with temporal movements in overall wage inequality cannot be established directly for the pre–World War II period. In recognition of that, there have been some attempts to go further using data from the federal censuses of manufacturing and related reports. For the rising portion of the inverted U shape, Atack et al. (2004) used data from samples of the 1850–1880 manufacturing censuses (Atack and Bateman 1999) to show that the distribution of the "establishment wage"—the average wage in individual establishments—became increasingly unequal over time, primarily because of an increase in the density of workers employed in establishments paying lower-than-average wages. While this pattern is consistent with rising wage inequality overall, it presumes that there were no offsetting changes in wage inequality within establishments, which cannot be tested with their data (Atack et al. 2004).

For the falling portion of the inverted U, Goldin and Katz (1999) estimate wage quantiles for a panel of 10 industries in 1890 and circa 1940, from which they construct standard inequality ratios (50–10, 90–50, and 90–10). These ratios are considerably smaller just before World War II than in 1890, consistent with a reduction in overall inequality. However, as they point out, this inference presumes no offsetting changes in interindustry wage differentials. Moreover, with just two end points, it is impossible to determine when the change occurred. In addition, existing studies provide, at best, limited direct evidence on the role of explanatory factors, such as the increasing division of labor and the declining importance of physical strength with increasing use of inanimate sources of power such as steam earlier in the period (Atack et al. 2004) and electricity later (Goldin and Katz 2008).

Our new evidence comes from two sources. The first is recently digitized data from the US Department of Labor's 1899 *Hand and Machine Labor* (hereafter, *HML*) study, which provides detailed data at the production operation level for two different production modes, "hand" (artisan) versus "machine" (mechanized factories) in the manufacture of hundreds of specific goods, called "units" in the study.[1] In previous work (Atack et al. 2019, 2022), we have shown that empirical differences between hand and machine labor in the *HML* study faithfully reflect changes over time in the evolution of labor productivity in 19th-century manufacturing from artisan to factory production. With this as (broad) validation, we use these data to explore the impact of these changes on wage inequality within manufacturing establishments, something not previously possible.

We begin our analysis of the *HML* study data by computing the time-weighted standard deviation of (ln) labor cost (wage of the worker per standardized unit of time) across all operations within the machine or hand labor unit, which becomes the main variable of interest.[2] Compared with hand

1. A unit in the *HML* study refers to two modes of production and the sequences of operations that each involved making a precisely defined (in terms of characteristics, quantity, and quality) product, one using the traditional, "hand" (i.e., artisan) methods, and the other the most advanced factory ("machine") methods then available. Within this unit, the *HML* staff traced and matched production steps across modes. While these data are not, strictly speaking, establishment level, they are sufficiently related to provide useful evidence on the differences in, for example, labor productivity and de-skilling that resulted from the long-term shift from the artisan shop to the factory system (Atack et al. 2022, 2024).

2. "Time-weighted" means that the ln (labor cost) of each operation is weighted by the amount of time needed to complete the operation. Note that if a single worker performs all operations, then *ln* (labor cost) is the same for all operations and therefore the standard deviation is identically zero. As we show, single worker units were disproportionately found in hand labor.

labor, machine labor production utilized a greater division of labor, which required more workers, as well as greater use of special purpose machinery, which was powered inanimately, mainly by steam (Atack et al. 2022). We sketch a simple framework under which greater division of labor will lead to increased dispersion of wages within establishments and hence a higher level of wage inequality. Wage inequality may increase further due to mechanization, as greater use of steam power raised the relative demand for unskilled—and hence low-wage—labor, since the machines being driven by steam required less operator skill than the use of traditional hand tools.

Our main empirical result from the analysis of the *HML* data is that wage inequality was approximately 90 percent higher, on average, within the machine labor units than the hand labor units, a difference that is economically and statistically significant. Regression analysis includes unit fixed effects and so is equivalent to differencing between machine and hand labor, holding the product (the unit) constant. We find that wage inequality was increasing in the use of inanimate power and in the division of labor. On average, use of inanimate power was much higher under machine labor, as was the division of labor. However, in terms of explanatory power, greater division of labor was the more important factor, accounting for approximately twice as much of the higher wage inequality in machine labor production compared with mechanization. Our analysis of the *HML* study data suggests, therefore, that the transition from the artisan shop to the mechanized factory over the 19th century was associated with an increase in wage inequality in manufacturing, due disproportionately to changes in the organization of production that occurred.

Our second source is newly digitized data from state government reports on manufacturing wages published as tables of so-called classified wages. These give the number of workers whose weekly earnings were categorized ("classified") into bins—for example, from $8.00 to $9.00 per week. These are the same type of data studied by Goldin and Katz (1999), except that our source and reference frame are different—the state versus the federal government, covering many years. Specifically, we use the most comprehensive such series, those for the state of Massachusetts, which cover from the late 1880s to the late 1930s.[3] We have also digitized data on electricity use in Massachusetts manufacturing, which the state collected for selected years.

3. The 1890 federal census of manufacturing (US Census Office 1895b) reported such distributions, by industry, for establishments in select cities, which Goldin and Katz (1999) used in their work. The Massachusetts data come from the state's "Annual Statistics of Manufactures" first taken in 1886 (Massachusetts Bureau of Statistics of Labor, [for the years 1886 and 1887] 1889, 135). It reported classified wage distributions beginning in the 1890 report. Because of how this serial of annual reports was issued, we reference the year of the specific issue in brackets and report its publication date in parentheses. In addition to the Massachusetts reports, we have located similar data in reports for nine additional states (California, Illinois, Iowa, Kansas, New Hampshire, Ohio, Rhode Island, Texas, and Wisconsin). Unlike the Mas-

Our main analysis of the Massachusetts data is based on estimates of the 10th, 25th, 50th, 75th, and 90th quantiles of the classified distribution of weekly earnings for production workers. The quantile estimates are made following the general procedure outlined in Blalock (1960, 55; also used by Goldin and Katz 1999). We present the actual series along with smoothed estimates derived from nonparametric regressions.

Our estimates show a marked reduction in wage inequality in Massachusetts manufacturing over the study period. This was present in the lower tail (50–10 ratio), upper tail (90–50), and the interquartile range (75–25) but, quantitatively, was largest in the lower tail. The compression in lower-tail inequality was modest in the 1890s but accelerated after the turn of the century.

In explaining the decrease in inequality between their 1890 observation and their circa 1940 one, Goldin and Katz (1999) emphasize two factors: the "high school" movement, which compressed the top half of the wage distribution (by reducing the returns to skill, as embodied in education), and electrification, which eliminated many of the low-wage jobs that were associated with the use of steam power, such as shoveling coal (see also Jerome 1934). We use our Massachusetts data to shed further light on the role of electrification. First, we generate a time series of the percentage of horsepower used in Massachusetts manufacturing derived from electricity. While this series is not sufficiently frequent to use for time-series regression, it conclusively shows electrification began in earnest after the turn of the 20th century, accelerating after 1910. In 1895, just 1.5 percent of horsepower used by Massachusetts manufacturing was provided by electric motors. This share had increased to a third in 1920 and then to over 60 percent by 1938.

To examine the impact of electrification on wage inequality, we have compiled an industry-level panel for Massachusetts for two years (1895 and 1920), which covers 42 industries. For each industry-year pair, and following Goldin and Katz (1999), we estimate the 50–10 ratio, which becomes the dependent variable. There are three independent variables—male share of workers, electric horsepower per worker, and nonelectric horsepower per worker. We estimate the regression in first differences, which is equivalent to two-way fixed effects (industry dummies and a year dummy for 1920). We find a statistically significant, negative effect of electric horsepower per worker on the 50–10 ratio, consistent with Goldin and Katz's argument. The

sachusetts reports, however, these cover much shorter periods of time (e.g., New Hampshire's is just for 1916). In discussing the state of information regarding wages in the United States, Nearing (1914, 14) lamented "of the 10 leading industrial states, but three—Ohio, Massachusetts, and New Jersey,—furnish wage data, which merits . . . comment. The statistics for Ohio are excellent, but very diffuse and unconcentrated. The statistics for Massachusetts and New Jersey are, on the other hand, scientifically classified, accurately presented, and in every sense satisfactory and reliable."

effect is large—at the sample means, we can account for nearly all (80 percent) of the decrease in the 50–10 ratio between 1895 and 1920.

1.2 Literature Review: Wage Inequality in Manufacturing, 1820–1940

Less than 5 percent of the American labor force in 1800 was engaged in manufacturing. By the middle of the 19th century, the manufacturing share had reached 15 percent, and it rose to 20 percent by 1900 (Atack et al. 2004, p. 172). The share continued to rise over the first half of the 20th century, reaching slightly more than a quarter of the labor force in 1950. It has declined since, so much so that by 2010, the share (10 percent) was lower than in 1850.

The initial shift of labor into manufacturing coincided with massive changes in industrial organization. At the start of the 19th century, almost all manufacturing took place in artisan shops (see, e.g., US Department of the Treasury 1791; Sokoloff 1982). In such shops, the owner worked either alone or with a partner, and perhaps with a few apprentices. Except for a few industries such as lumber and gristmills that used waterpower, capital was limited to basic, general-purpose hand tools, plus the building. In terms of numbers, these artisan shops would remain dominant at midcentury, but increasingly, production shifted toward larger establishments—places termed factories (US Census Office et al. 1883). These differed from artisan shops in three fundamental ways—a greater use of division of labor; more capital per worker; and, relative to the artisan shop, substantially greater use of inanimate power. Initially the power source was water, but as the century progressed, waterpower was displaced by steam power (Hunter 1979, 1985).

By the end of the 19th century the factory system was dominant, and it continued to grow in importance during the first half of the 20th century as steam was replaced by electricity as the inanimate power source (Devine 1983; Hunter and Bryant 1991). Overall, the consensus view is that these changes in industrial organization dramatically increased output per worker in manufacturing such that, by World War I, the United States was the leading industrial economy in the world (Bairoch 1982; Broadberry and Irwin 2006).

Although the success of American manufacturing in overtaking early industrializers like the British is undeniable, there is less evidence of how the shift from the hand labor of the artisan shop to the machine labor of the factory affected wage inequality in manufacturing.[4] There are two strands to the literature. The first strand measures changes in manufacturing wage inequality using time series of skill differentials—ratios of wages of skilled

4. This question is distinct from the general equilibrium impact of the growth of manufacturing on overall inequality in the economy. The general equilibrium impact would include the effect on inequality between manufacturing and the rest of the economy, including agriculture. The general equilibrium impact is beyond the scope of our analysis.

to unskilled workers—which are interpreted through the lens of (relative) demand and supply. There is a substantial body of work documenting the evolution of skill differentials over the 19th century (Autor et al. 2020; Goldin and Katz 2008; Margo 2000; Williamson and Lindert 1980). The consensus view is that, relative to unskilled labor, the wages of skilled artisans were roughly stable from the early to late 19th century, while the relative wages of white-collar workers increased modestly.

Katz and Margo (2014) document that, over the same period, the share of artisans in manufacturing declined, while the shares of operatives (including unskilled labor) and white-collar nonproduction workers increased. They interpret these shifts as evidence of "hollowing out"—a shift in labor demand in manufacturing toward operatives and managerial or clerical labor and away from artisans. However, if this were the case, one might have expected the relative wage of artisans to have declined relative to unskilled labor, but it did not. Katz and Margo point out that, while relative demand decreased in manufacturing, the construction sector, which was intensive in the use of artisan labor, grew over the century and took up the slack.

Although one can craft a sensible narrative around the evolution of skill differentials, such time series offer, at best, a limited window on overall movements in wage inequality in manufacturing. Because of this limitation, research has turned to evidence from the various 19th-century federal censuses of manufacturing, several of which collected data sufficient to compute the "establishment wage"—the average wage of workers employed in the establishment. Establishment-level samples from the original manuscript records are available for 1820, and for 1850–1880 (Atack and Bateman 1999; Sokoloff 1982). Unfortunately, samples are unavailable for other years either because relevant data were not collected (1830, 1840) or because the original returns have not survived.[5]

Atack, Bateman, and Margo (Atack et al. 2004; hereafter ABM) used samples for 1850 and 1880 to construct measures of inequality in monthly establishment wages. In table 1.1, we expand their original figures by providing inequality statistics for 1860 and 1870 (monthly) and for annual wages in 1820, 1870, and 1880.

These statistics are the 10–50 and 50–90 differentials in the natural logarithm of the establishment wage, the coefficient of variation, and (the closely

5. The 1810 census is generally judged to be too poor in quality to be useful and, in any case, most of the original records were destroyed by the British in 1814 (Fishbein 1973). For 1820 we use the digital file originally created by Sokoloff (1982), which is a complete count of all establishments in 45 randomly chosen counties in the Northeast; this is compared with observations from the Northeast in 1870–1980 (see table 1.1). No census was taken in 1830 and the Census of 1840 collected no data on wages. The Treasury Department's McLane Report for 1832 (US Congress, House 1833) contains wage information for manufacturing and were digitized by Sokoloff and Villaflor (1992) to estimate establishment wages in the Northeast, but their computer file is no longer extant. Records of the 1890 and 1900 censuses were destroyed in the early 20th century.

Table 1.1 Establishment wage inequality in American manufacturing, 1820–1919

A. Monthly establishment wage in manufacturing, inequality statistics

Sample screens	Full sample	Full sample	Full sample	Urban & Brissenden industries	Urban
Type	Ln(50/10)	Ln(90/50)	COV	COV	COV
1850	**0.62**	**0.50**	**0.467 {0.45}**	**0.506**	**0.498**
N, establishments	5,214	5,214	5,214	941	1,291
N, workers	43,093	43,093	43,093	16,145	19,105
1860	**0.72**	**0.41**	**0.481 {0.46}**	**0.487**	**0.468**
N, establishments	5,172	5,172	5,172	1,265	1,671
N, workers	47,994	47,994	47,994	21,222	26,377
1870	**0.70**	**0.58**	**0.507 {0.53}**	**0.451**	**0.474**
N, establishments	3,641	3,641	3,641	600	863
N, workers	43,467	43,467	43,467	13,930	20,518
1880	**0.94**	**0.56**	**0.571 {0.60}**	**0.544**	**0.542**
N, establishments	6,904	6,904	6,904	2,075	3,397
N, workers	83,613	83,613	83,613	44,177	60.585

B. Annual establishment wage in manufacturing, 1820, 1870–1880, and 1919: Coefficient of variation

Sample screens	Full sample	Northeast, 10% trim	Urban & Brissenden industries	Urban
1820		0.403		
N, establishments		801		
N, workers		8,620		
1870	0.521	0.406	0.435	0.470
N, establishments		1,451		
N, workers		25,966		
1880	0.596	0.516	0.570	0.563
N, establishments		2,767		
N, workers		43,819		
1919 (Brissenden)			0.335	

Note: Full sample: to be included, establishments must report positive values of total labor (males + females in 1850 and 1860, males + females + children in 1870 and 1880), capital invested, and \$500 of gross output; \$4.76 < average monthly wage in 1850 < \$190.5; \$4.93 < average monthly wage in 1860 < \$197.33; \$7.20 < average monthly wage in 1870 < \$314.67; \$5.20 < average monthly wage in 1880 < \$208. See Atack et al. (2004, table 1) for explanation of sample screens on average monthly wages in 1850 and 1880; 1860 and 1870 are similarly calculated. Panel A: Monthly wages in 1850 and 1860 are total monthly wages divided by total labor; monthly wages in 1870 = (Annual wage bill/months of operation)/number of workers; monthly wages in 1880 = (Annual wage bill/full-time equivalent months)/number of workers. COV: coefficient of variation of average monthly wage. {}: standard deviation of *ln* (average monthly wage). Panel B: Northeast, 10% trim: restricted to establishments in the Northeast, observations with annual establishments wages between 10th and 90th percentiles in the full distribution, among establishments reporting positive annual wage bill. Sources: 1820: Sokoloff (1982); 1850–80: Atack-Bateman-Weiss national samples (see description in Atack and Bateman 1999, 2004; Atack, Bateman et al. 2006); 1919: (Brissenden 1929).

related) standard deviation of the (ln) establishment wage. It is important to note that all measures in the table are weighted by the number of workers at the establishment, as was the case in the original ABM study. Sample sizes (number of establishments and number of workers) are also shown. As a further point of comparison, we also show the coefficient of variation of annual establishment wages for 1919, based on a proprietary sample from the 1920 census analyzed by Brissenden (1929) that is otherwise unavailable.[6]

As can be seen in table 1.1, in the columns labeled "Full sample" (which have the largest sample sizes), there was a steady upward trend in inequality in monthly establishment wages from 1850 to 1880, most of which occurred due to a rise in the 10–50 differential, that is, a rise in inequality below the median wage. The evidence is more limited for annual establishment wage inequality, but the general pattern is consistent with an inverted U, rising from 1820 to 1880 and then falling at some point after this, as indicated by the (much) lower level of inequality in 1919 than in 1880.

To understand the increase in establishment wage inequality between 1850 and 1880, ABM analyzed the establishment wage data in a two-step procedure. In the first step, ABM estimated regressions of the log of the establishment wage on establishment characteristics. Their main findings were twofold—first, that the establishment wage was a negative function of the number of employees; and second, that the establishment wage was a positive function of the log of capital per worker and of the use of steam power. ABM interpreted these patterns using a simple framework borrowed from Goldin and Katz (1999)—the negative correlation with the number of workers is consistent with a lower average skill level as the number of workers increases—de-skilling—whereas the positive effect of capital intensity and use of steam power can be read as both variables boosting the demand for skilled labor in these establishments.

In the second part of their paper, ABM used the data to compute a decomposition of the overall change in establishment wage inequality between 1850 and 1880. This decomposition is performed on the 10–50, 50–90, and 10–90 differential in the log establishment wage, in terms of the portion explained by changes in the distribution of the independent variables in the regressions, the regression coefficients, and residual wage inequality. The regressions used for this purpose contain just establishment-size dummies. The results show that, overall, establishment wage inequality increased substantially between 1850 and 1880 because of a growing concentration of employment in establishments with below-average wages. These were

6. Brissenden's (1929) estimates did not claim to be a nationally representative random sample of establishments but instead are for a sample of 8 cities and approximately 20 industries. Due to sample size limitations the best match we can make to Brissenden for 1850–1880 is to restrict the analysis to urban observations in the two-digit SIC industries which contain those studied by Brissenden (for a definition of "urban," see Atack and Bateman 1999). It is not possible to match Brissenden to 1820 because several of the cities in his sample did not exist in 1820 and because the available sample size for the rest is too small.

relatively large establishments in terms of the number of workers, and the reason they were low wage on average is that the establishment wage was a decreasing function of the number of workers. ABM argue that this is consistent with a relative demand shift in favor of less-skilled operatives, who increasingly dominated manufacturing employment as the factory system grew in importance.

There are three significant limitations to ABM's analysis. First, none of the extant samples from the federal censuses of manufactures provides direct evidence of the division of labor; the presumption is that such division was an increasing function of the number of workers employed by the establishment, but the census cannot be used to verify this directly because of the way that the original data were collected and reported. Second, while the increase in establishment wage inequality is clear enough, for wage inequality to have also increased across workers—as opposed to across establishments on average—it is also necessary that wage inequality within establishments did not decrease. ABM argue this was so but have no direct evidence of the evolution of wage inequality within manufacturing establishments. Third, while ABM show that average establishment wages were increasing in the use of steam power, the effect of the shift to steam on wage inequality remains unclear.

The second component of the consensus view is that wage inequality in manufacturing decreased from the turn of the century to 1940. Here, the main analyses are provided by Goldin and Katz (1999, 2008). Specifically, Goldin and Katz (1999) compare adjusted wage distributions for manufacturing operatives in particular industries reported in the census of manufacturing data for 1890 (US Census Office 1895b) with similar distributions from Bureau of Labor Statistics surveys in the late 1930s. These comparisons show a decrease in wage inequality within the given industries over the period.

Goldin and Katz attributed some of the decrease in wage inequality to electrification, which reduced the demand for very low-skilled workers in manufacturing. Annual time series of skill differentials over the period suggest that the bulk of the decrease in wage inequality occurred prior to 1920, which is consistent with the timing of electrification. There are, however, two limitations to Goldin and Katz's argument. First, they acknowledge that their evidence on wage inequality is within industry. It is possible that overall wage inequality in manufacturing was rising (or stable) if interindustry wage differences were increasing, although they discount this explanation. Rather more importantly, the precise timing of changes in wage inequality cannot be determined from Goldin and Katz's analysis of wage inequality with just a starting and ending date. Relatedly, Goldin and Katz present no evidence directly linking the rising use of electricity within manufacturing to decreases in wage inequality across manufacturing workers. The analyses in the next two sections are our proffer addressing the limitations of both ABM and Goldin and Katz.

1.3 The *HML* Study and Wage Inequality Within Manufacturing Establishments

The student of American manufacturing who wishes to document the evolution of wage inequality within establishments in the 19th century has limited choices for evidence. The so-called Weeks and Aldrich reports (US Congress 1893; Weeks 1886), which have been previously used to construct wage series, are one possibility, as both are establishment based. However, while these reports do contain some within-establishment information on wages, the evidence is limited to occupational averages and thus does not fully capture the variation at issue.[7] Another possibility is the 1900 census report on "Employees and Wages" (US Census Office and Dewey 1903), which provides so-called classified wage distributions (see section 1.4) at the establishment level in the late 19th century for a subset of industries in groups of states. However, this report, as well as either the Aldrich or the Weeks data, provides no direct evidence on the underlying causal factors at issue, such as the division of labor or mechanization.

The source that we use, the US Department of Labor's *Hand and Machine Labor* study (1899), is quite different. This source contains information on wage inequality pertaining to production workers in large, mechanized factories—all from the late 1880s to the mid-1890s– as well as wage inequality among production workers within small nonmechanized artisan shops. These were the typical production entities earlier in the century, although about a quarter of the observations in the *HML* study were from businesses still in operation in the 1890s. Differences in wage inequality between these two types of production—"machine" (factory) versus "hand" (artisan) labor—provide important insights, we argue, into changes in wage inequality within establishments over the 19th century, as well as the factors behind them.

Published in two volumes totaling almost 1,600 pages, the *HML* study detailed the production operations involved in the manufacturing of what the study termed "units"—specific quantities of precisely defined goods such as "50 dozen regular taper, triangular saw files, 4 inches long, tapering 23/64 inch" (US Department of Labor 1899, 1:241–46, 2:1026–29). The overall report covered 672 units in various economic sectors including 626 (units 28–653) in manufacturing. The units from manufacturing covered almost the entire range of broadly defined manufactured goods (i.e., two-digit SIC codes 20–39 (US Executive Office of the President, 1987), including those common in both the first Industrial Revolution and the second.[8]

7. Wesley Mitchell (1903) reported an 1860 classified wage distribution in manufacturing. However, this distribution—based on underlying data from the Aldrich report pertaining to establishment-occupation averages—fails to capture fully the within-establishment variance.

8. An important exception were products that were introduced late in the 19th century, such as bicycles, that were never produced by hand methods.

The *HML* data, however, should not be viewed as a representative sample of manufacturing industries at the time—a limitation of our analysis that should be kept in mind when extrapolating our findings to the whole of the manufacturing sector (Atack et al. 2022, table A1). We stress that the *HML* data pertain solely to wage inequality among production workers. The observed difference in wage inequality between machine and hand labor units in the *HML* from this comparison, however, will understate the true difference in the establishments from which the original data were collected because the share of nonproduction labor was higher for factories than artisan shops, and white-collar wages, on average, were higher than for skilled blue-collar workers.

For each unit, the *HML* staff actually collected production data from four establishments, two each that were using hand labor or machine labor methods, selecting "the better and more complete" accounting of each mode for publication (US Department of Labor 1899, 1:1). To maintain confidentiality, the *HML* staff anonymized the information in the published report so that we do not know the names of the establishments or their location.[9] The *HML* staff was clearly aware of the widely held belief that the machine methods yielded a lower-quality product than the hand methods, and they expended great efforts to find units producing factory goods that were *not* of inferior quality to artisan products so this argument cannot be used to impeach our results.[10] Our procedures in making these data amenable for econometric analysis are described in Atack et al. (2019, 2022, 2023, 2024).

In two previous papers, we used the operations-level data in the *HML* study to evaluate modern models of automation (Atack et al. 2019) and to estimate the impact of inanimate power use on the study's measure of labor productivity, which is the amount of time that it took to complete the same operation—for example, polishing a piece of metal—in the production of the same product by hand and machine labor, but where, under machine labor, inanimate power powering a specific machine might have been used (Atack et al. 2022). Specifically, Atack et al. (2022) demonstrate that the average difference in labor productivity between the hand and machine methods was of a magnitude that accurately tracks the evolution of productivity growth in manufacturing over the century due to the long-term shift from one type of production to the other.

The empirical analysis in Atack et al. (2022, 2024) focuses on the subset of production operations that overlapped between hand and machine labor, thus excluding operations under hand labor that were abandoned as well as those novel operations specific to machine labor. Here, instead we focus

9. A small number (15) of hand units were located outside the United States and identified as such in the published *HML* study. These are excluded from our analysis.

10. The text of the *HML* study discusses quality differences, from which we were able to categorize whether the staff thought the quality was better for product when made by hand or vice versa; or no difference was detected, or no opinion was expressed; see Atack et al. (2022).

primarily on the unit, and the outcome of interest is the standard deviation of the natural logarithm of "labor cost" across operations within the unit by production mode. For each operation we know the wage of the worker(s) performing the activity, as well as the amount of time the activity took; labor cost is the wage per standardized unit of time. Using this information, we can compute the standard deviation of *ln* (labor cost), where each operation is weighted by its completion time. The operative assumption is that differences in wage inequality between hand and machine labor can inform the debate over the course of wage inequality within establishments as manufacturing shifted from the artisan shop to the factory, analogous to our previous analysis of labor productivity differences.

A key advantage of the *HML* study for this paper is the information that it contains on potential explanatory factors. Of these, the two of greatest interest are division of labor and use of inanimate power. To motivate our use of this information in the regression analysis, we sketch a simple framework linking both factors to within-establishment wage inequality.

As a point of departure, imagine an artisan shop engaging in hand labor in which all production operations are performed by a single worker; that is, the artisan is both sole worker and proprietor (i.e., providing managerial direction). There are $N + 1$ such operations—N of which are actual production operations and a single overall task of "management" (nonproduction). We will assume that the opportunity cost of the artisan's time, say a day's worth of labor, is w. Because there is only one worker, observed wage inequality in these firms is, by definition, zero.

Although the artisan is skilled by virtue of being able to complete all the myriad production operations, the artisan—like everyone else—will have a comparative advantage at some operations, and a disadvantage at others. Now, imagine that, instead of doing all tasks himself, the artisan specializes in one task—"management"—and hires N workers, each of whom performs a single operation. Array tasks in increasing terms of the skill required to perform them, and let $w(n)$ be the wage for task $n = 1, \ldots N$. So long as at least some of the skill levels are strictly increasing, wage inequality within the establishment will increase through division of labor.

In addition, wage inequality may have been affected by the shift to steam power. Here, there are two possible effects. First, the shift to steam may have induced greater division of labor (Atack et al. 2008, 2024) among existing tasks. Second, and likely more important, the shift to steam would have created new tasks associated with the operation of steam engines. Some of these tasks—for example, installation and maintenance of steam engines—were highly skilled, while others—moving raw materials (e.g., coal to fuel it) and transferring intermediate inputs around the shop floor—were unskilled. Indeed, not surprisingly, there is a sharp increase in the need to move intermediate product between production "stations" as the division of labor increased. In either case, wage inequality should have risen.

Table 1.2 **Sample statistics: *Hand and Machine Labor* study observations ($N = 496$)**

Type	Standard deviation of *ln* (labor cost)	Fraction of time devoted to mechanized operations	*Ln* (# of different workers)	*Ln* (# of different operations)	One worker unit
Hand labor	0.142	0	1.202	1.853	0.270
Machine labor	0.282	0.553	2.806	2.495	0.010
Difference, machine – hand	0.140	0.553	1.604	0.642	–0.260

Source: *Hand and Machine Labor* study (US Department of Labor 1899, as described in Atack et al. 2019).

1.3.1 Regression Analysis

Table 1.2 reports sample statistics for our regression analysis of the *HML* study data. We restrict attention to those units in which no inanimate power was used at any point in hand labor and where steam or waterpower was used in machine labor.[11]

On average, the standard deviation of *ln* labor cost was about twice as high in machine labor production than in hand labor production, a level difference of 0.140 that is highly significant (s.e. = 0.013). About 55 percent of the production time under machine labor used inanimate power. On average, machine labor production employed more workers, allocated over many operations, implying a much higher degree of division of labor (Atack et al. 2022).[12] Twenty-seven percent of the hand labor units employed a single worker, compared with hardly any (1 percent) of the machine labor units. As noted, in single worker units, there was no division of labor by definition and, therefore, the standard deviation was identically zero.

Regression results are reported in Table 1.3. All regressions include unit fixed effects.

For comparison purposes, the second column reports the coefficient of a dummy variable for machine labor, $\beta = 0.140$. This is the mean difference in the standard deviation of ln labor cost. In column 3, we include the share of labor time devoted to operations that were mechanized using either steam or waterpower, the natural log of the number of workers, and the natural log of the number of operations. Collectively, these three variables "over-explain" the mean difference (by about 29 percent), as the coefficient on the machine labor dummy is now negative—$\beta = -0.040$—although statistically insignificant.

The signs of the variables are as expected and two of the three—the fraction of labor time in powered, mechanized operations and the number of workers—are highly significant. An increase in the fraction of production

11. This sample restriction approximates the comparison that the *HML* study was attempting to make; see Atack et al. (2022). There are 496 units that meet these sample criteria.

12. We include the natural logarithms of the number of workers and the number of operations separately as flexible controls for the division of labor.

Table 1.3 **Regression and decomposition analysis: Standard deviation of *ln* (labor cost)**

Variable	Coefficient	Coefficient	Percentage explained	Coefficient	Percentage explained
Machine labor = 1	0.140	–0.0400	–28.5	–0.030	–21.4
	(0.013)	(0.029)		(0.028)	
Fraction of time devoted to mechanized operations		0.107	42.3	0.086	34.3
		(0.043)	[32.8]	(0.042)	[28.3]
Ln (# of different workers)		0.061	69.8	0.046	52.7
		(0.009)	[54.2]	(0.009)	[43.4]
Ln (# of different operations)		0.035	16.1	0.036	16.1
		(0.020)	[12.5]	(0.020)	[13.3]
One worker unit				–0.100	18.3
				(0.025)	[15.1]
Adjusted R^2	0.296	0.448		0.474	

Note: In brackets: relative percent explained excluding the percent explained by the machine labor dummy (relative percentages within the brackets sum to 100 down a column).

Source: See table 1.2.

time using inanimate power is associated with greater wage inequality, as is greater division of labor—more workers and more operations. In column 5, we include a dummy variable for units in which a single worker performed all operations; in effect, this tests for a spline at exactly one worker. This coefficient is highly significant, which has the effect of reducing the magnitudes of the coefficients of the fraction of production time that was mechanized and the *ln* (# workers), although the reductions are relatively small.

Column 4 computes the "percentage explained" of each variable, which is the coefficient multiplied by the difference between machine and hand labor in the mean value of the independent variable, divided by the mean difference in the standard deviation of ln labor cost. As noted, collectively the variables overexplain the difference; however, if we scale each variable's contribution by the overall percent explained, mechanization accounts for about 28 percent to 32 percent of the higher average wage inequality within machine labor units, depending on the inclusion of the dummy variable for single worker units. It follows that the division of labor variables were relatively more important (68 percent to 72 percent). In sum, while mechanization contributed to greater wage inequality, the growing division of labor associated with the ascendancy of the mechanized factory was more important quantitively.

1.4 The Evolution of Wage Inequality in Manufacturing, 1890–1940: State Reports on Classified Wages

In this section we make use of state government reports on so-called classified wages for manufacturing in Massachusetts. Wages are said to be "classified" because these reports give the number of workers whose labor earnings—typically measured on a weekly basis—fell within given intervals. The first reporting of such statistics appeared in 1888 as a part of the 1885 Massachusetts Census (Massachusetts Bureau of Statistics of Labor, 1888, 233–62 on towns, 1115–26 on industries). What (or who) motivated this initial inquiry is unclear; however, it would subsequently become a regular feature of the Massachusetts "Annual Statistics of Manufactures," beginning with the state's fifth report for 1890 but also covering 1889 (Massachusetts Bureau of Statistics of Labor 1890, 142–61).[13] These annual statistics were intended to "fully portray the conditions of the industries" and "accurately show the trend of business from year to year" (Massachusetts Bureau of Statistics of Labor 1890, xiii).[14]

In all, Massachusetts reported classified wages for 43 individual years between 1885 and 1938, although the regular annual reporting of the data was eventually discontinued. Instead, in 1940, the bureau published a retrospective synopsis, with annual data from 1920 to 1924 and biennially thereafter to 1938 (Massachusetts Department of Labor and Industries 1940, table 6, 75ff.). This line of inquiry appears to have inspired periodic emulation by sister agencies in other states.[15] It also seems plausible (but not certain) that

13. Data collection was authorized by the Massachusetts legislature (see Massachusetts. Bureau of Statistics of Labor, [for the years 1886. 1887] 1889, 135–37) beginning April 29, 1886. Data on 12 specific topics (stipulated in section 1 of the act) were to be collected by mail of every manufacturing establishment in the state by mid-December with returns due before the end of the year. While the bureau complied with the law, the first data collected under it were not reported until 1889. Reasons for the delay were spelled out by Commissioner Wadlin (Carroll D. Wright's successor at the Massachusetts Bureau) in his introduction to his first report where he also provides a summary history of the collection of statistical data by the state (Massachusetts Bureau of Statistics of Labor [for the years 1886, 1887] 1889, xi–xix). The first classified wage series appeared in 1890 with a column comparing the same establishments in 1889 and 1890. As noted in the text, it is unclear what motivated their collection—or even their precise source as the data that they represent was not among the authorized and stipulated questions. Furthermore, Massachusetts law authorized destruction of the underlying returns on a regular basis—see, e.g., chapter 31 of 1889 Acts and Resolves (https://archive.org/details/actsresolvespass1889mass, p. 1365). The commissioner indicated the intent was to simplify the reporting burden on manufacturers by superseding the state's census in years ending in "5," although these too continued. The *Annual Statistics of Manufactures* volumes used for this study may be found either at https://archive.org or https://hathitrust.org.

14. The Chief of the Massachusetts Bureau of Statistics of Labor, Horace G. Wadlin, reported that the data collection excluded the smallest (and most numerous) establishments (i.e., it was not a census despite being called that in the law) because "the condition of manufacturing in the commonwealth can be accurately portrayed by returns that do not include the small and comparatively unimportant concerns" (Massachusetts Bureau of Statistics of Labor [for the year 1890] 1890, xix). His claim was apparently based on a (unreported) comparison between the restricted Massachusetts data and that collected at the Eleventh Census. Access to these data presumably reflected the close collaboration that had long existed between personnel at the Massachusetts Bureau of Statistics and federal census officials beginning with the Bureau of Labor Statistics' second commissioner, Carroll D. Wright, who played a leading role in the 10th Census before becoming the first US commissioner of labor (North 1909). We note that the data were to be collected during the week of maximum employment during the year and, therefore, comparisons across years should not reflect short-run fluctuations within years in hours worked per week.

15. Indeed, New Jersey explicitly adopted the Massachusetts Annual Statistics of Manufactures model in 1896 (New Jersey Bureau of Statistics 1897, 50).

the 1885 Massachusetts inquiry prompted inclusion of such a query as a part of the 11th Federal Census in 1890, appearing as item 6 of "General Schedule No. 3" of the Census of Manufactures to be asked of all respondents (US Census Office 1895a, 13; Wright 1900, 362). The federal census, however, made little use of these data. No summary tabulation of them by state was ever published and they only appear in the volume of statistics on cities (US Census Office 1895b). The federal data did, however, provide the starting point from which Goldin and Katz (1999) estimated wage inequality statistics among adult males at the industry level for 10 industries in 1890. These are matched by industry to analogous statistics reported by the US Bureau of Labor Statistics in its *Monthly Labor Review* (1999, 31).

For our purposes there are three advantages of the Massachusetts data. First, and foremost, their temporal coverage far exceeds that of any other state—effectively, the same timeframe, the 1890s to the late 1930s, covered by Goldin and Katz (1999), but on an annual or biannual basis. Second, contemporaries such as Nearing (1914) thought very highly of the quality of the Massachusetts data, which was not the case for all states that attempted to collect information on classified wages. Third, the data refer to production workers only, allowing a cleaner comparison over time, compared with Goldin and Katz's (1999) use of federal census data.[16] Fourth, we can construct an industry panel (see below) that allows us to explore the empirical impact of changes in electrification on wage inequality, as hypothesized by Goldin and Katz (1999).

Against these advantages one must keep in mind certain limitations. The Massachusetts industrial structure differed from that of the rest of the nation in that it had more of the "first Industrial Revolution" staple industries (e.g., textiles, boots, shoes) and less of those in the second, such as automobiles, although its industry data cover a broad swath of activities. While Massachusetts experienced electrification like the rest of the country in its broad contours and timing, the extent of coverage in manufacturing by the late 1930s fell somewhat below that of the rest of the country. Third, and related, a variety of factors local to Massachusetts—for example, the nature of its labor legislation, immigration, and labor strife, among others—may have affected wage inequality in the state's industries in ways that could have differed from elsewhere.[17]

The Massachusetts data give the number of workers whose nominal

16. As Goldin and Katz (1999) discuss extensively in their paper, the federal census data from the 1890 census cover all production and nonproduction workers. Goldin and Katz make certain assumptions to eliminate the latter from the 1890 distribution, allowing an "apples-to-apples" comparison with the Department of Labor reports from the 1930s, which pertain to production workers. The assumptions are plausible, but ideally it would be better to not have to adjust the data.

17. As we point out in the text, the Massachusetts reports, while very detailed, do not contain sufficient information to allow us to construct a continuous time series for adult males (Goldin and Katz's 1999 calculations of wage inequality pertain to adult males). That said, we do control for the male percent of workers in our analysis of the industry panel.

TABLE III. CLASSIFIED WEEKLY WAGES: BY INDUSTRIES—1907.

Industries and Sex.	Total Number of Wage-earners	Classified Weekly Wages (For Week of Employment of Greatest Number of Wage-earners) Under $3	$3 but under $5	$5 but under $6	$6 but under $7	$7 but under $8	$8 but under $9	$9 but under $10	$10 but under $12	$12 but under $15	$15 but under $20	$20 but under $25	$25 and Over
THE STATE.	**604,390**	**5,876**	**31,021**	**39,924**	**54,509**	**59,472**	**60,951**	**69,046**	**88,176**	**88,040**	**78,187**	**20,494**	**8,684**
Adults (21 years of age and over):													
Males,	371,156	1,713	4,154	6,594	12,898	23,835	32,076	45,653	64,759	76,313	74,664	19,980	8,517
Females,	147,677	2,149	8,816	15,122	23,301	23,788	21,512	18,546	20,086	10,507	3,214	472	164
Young persons (under 21 years of age),	85,557	2,014	18,051	18,208	18,310	11,849	7,373	4,847	3,331	1,220	309	42	3
Agricultural Implements.	*929*	*4*	*13*	*10*	*34*	*90*	*122*	*136*	*196*	*197*	*107*	*16*	*4*
Adults (21 years of age and over):													
Males,	878	2	9	7	24	78	110	130	194	197	107	16	4
Females,	–	–	–	–	–	–	–	–	–	–	–	–	–
Young persons (under 21 years of age),	51	2	4	3	10	12	12	6	2	–	–	–	–
Arms and Ammunition.	*3,756*	–	*106*	*168*	*219*	*250*	*206*	*416*	*549*	*873*	*766*	*124*	*79*
Adults (21 years of age and over):													
Males,	2,973	–	–	26	50	83	138	351	499	860	763	124	79
Females,	213	–	–	46	64	50	8	16	26	3	–	–	–
Young persons (under 21 years of age),	570	–	106	96	105	117	60	49	24	10	3	–	–
Artisans' Tools.	*5,776*	*23*	*109*	*166*	*239*	*279*	*392*	*624*	*970*	*1,308*	*1,225*	*276*	*170*
Adults (21 years of age and over):													
Males,	4,954	4	28	67	108	146	285	513	896	1,252	1,214	271	170
Females,	148	–	13	16	26	18	15	29	18	12	1	–	–
Young persons (under 21 years of age),	674	19	68	83	105	115	92	82	56	39	10	5	–

50 MANUFACTURES — 1907. [Pub. Doc.

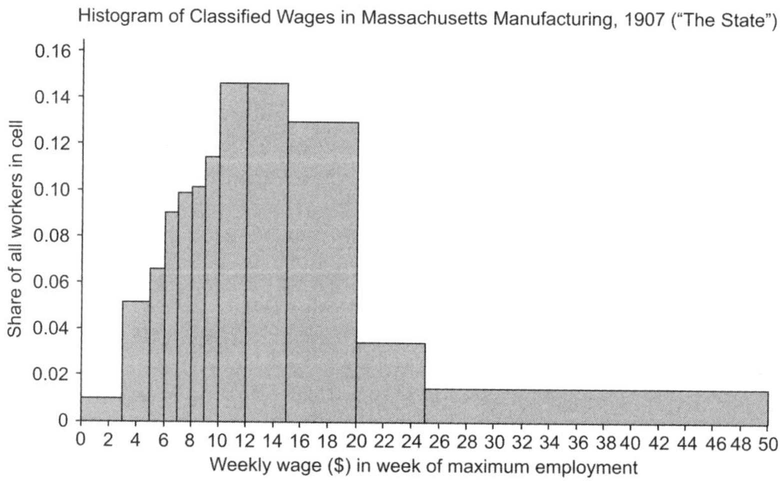

Figure 1.1 Extract from table 3, "Classified weekly wages: By industries—1907": Massachusetts manufacturing

Source: Massachusetts Bureau of Statistics of Labor [for the year 1907] (1908), 50. Courtesy of the State Library of Massachusetts Digital Collections. https://archives.lib.state.ma.us/server/api/core/bitstreams/393f6f0c-9569-4565-9002-3b82e2d59009/content.

weekly wages fall (i.e., are "classified") into specified wage intervals. The first interval is always bounded below at zero (e.g., "Under $3.00"), while the top interval is open; that is, for wages that exceed a certain amount there is no specified upper bound (e.g., "$25.00 or more"). In between, there are closed intervals of a specified but not identical absolute width—for example, $8.00–$8.99 ($1 width) or $12–$14.99 ($3 width). Figure 1.1 shows an extract from the table in the 1907 report and a histogram of the same (Massachusetts Bureau of Statistics of Labor 1908).

The classified wage tables are of a kind found in numerous government documents, historical to the present, in which observational units are categorized into bins. Blalock (1960) is a standard reference for methods applied to binned data to estimate distributional statistics, such as the mean or variance, and quantiles. The approach used by Goldin and Katz (1999) follows Blalock, and so we have also used it, although it is not perfect. In particular, it assumes that the distribution of observations within bin intervals is uniform as opposed to, say, being distributed within them in a way that more closely approximates the distribution across bins (see, e.g., von Hippel et al. 2017). Using Blalock's approach, however, it is straightforward to calculate the cumulative distribution function because the total number of observations in the table is always known and the resulting inequality metrics usually compare favorably with those derived from more complex processes (von Hippel et al. 2017).[18]

Once we know the cumulative distribution function, we can determine which bin intervals include the various quantiles. If the interval containing the quantile is closed at both ends with a nonzero lower bound, the uniform assumption implies that we can calculate the quantile using linear interpolation within the bin.

For the 10th quantile, there is the possibility that it will fall into the first interval, which is bounded below by zero. This, in fact, is the case for all years prior to 1906, for which the first interval is "$5.00 or below." Strictly speaking, we could use linear interpolation between 0 and 5, but it is not credible to assume that the support of the distribution is bounded from below by zero weekly earnings. Instead, we assume that the lower bound of the support is $3.00 per week for 1890–1905—that is, we treat the first interval as $3.00–5.00.[19] For the 90th quantile, the estimated values fall into a closed interval in all years except for 1919 and 1920 (where wartime and postwar inflation almost certainly played a role); for these two years we assume that the upper bound of the support is $50 per week.

For our base estimates, we focus on the distributions for all production workers, as these are reported for all years covered in the Massachusetts data, unlike for adult males. Figures 1.2–1.4 show our estimates of the 50–10 (fig. 1.2), 90–50 (fig. 1.3), and 75–25 (fig. 1.4) ratios, each indexed at 100 to its respective value in 1890. Also shown are nonparametric polynomial smoothing regressions of the indexed ratios on observation year, along with the associated 95 percent confidence intervals around them.

18. Von Hippel et al.'s (2017) analysis shows a clear advantage to these other approaches only if the true mean of the distribution is known—which it is not the case with the Massachusetts data.

19. In 1906 the first interval became "$3.00 and below" and the second interval was "$3.00–5.00". For the pre-1906 observations, the true lower bound of the support is less than $3.00, implying that our estimates of the 50–10 ratio are biased downwards—and, therefore, we are understating the downward trend in the 50–10 ratio from the 1890s to the 1930s. We have experimented with switching to a first interval of $2.00–$5.00 for the pre-1906 observations, which has only a modest effect on the estimated values of *q10*.

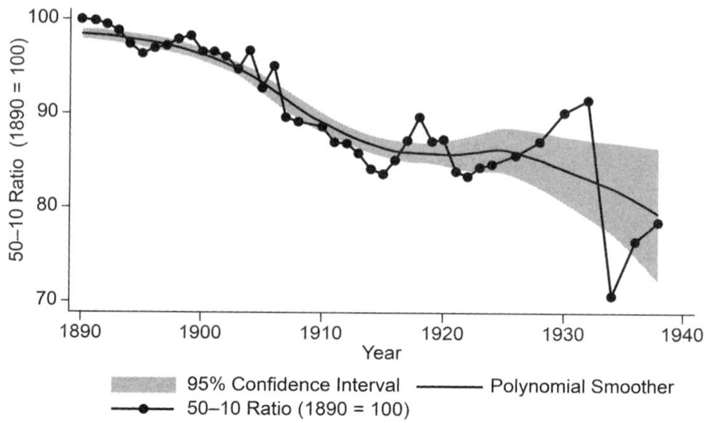

Figure 1.2 50–10 ratio: Weekly earnings in Massachusetts manufacturing, 1890–1938 production workers

Source: Computed from annual data for 1890–1919 from Massachusetts Bureau of Statistics of Labor and the available data for years from 1920–38 in Massachusetts Department of Labor and Industries (1940).

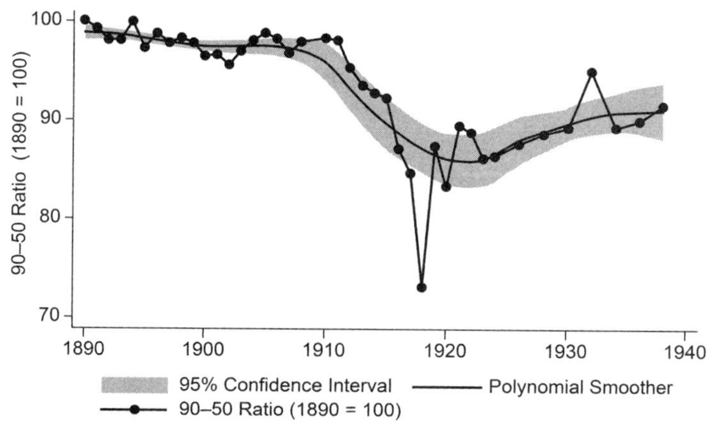

Figure 1.3 90–50 ratio: Weekly earnings in Massachusetts manufacturing, 1890–1938 production workers

Source: Computed from annual data for 1890–1919 from Massachusetts. Bureau of Statistics of Labor and the available data for years from 1920–38 in Massachusetts Department of Labor and Industries (1940).

These figures provide clear and compelling evidence of statistically significant, declining wage inequality. The data suggest modest compression in the 1890s, which then accelerates after the turn of the century. There is also evidence that period effects during World War I and the onset of the Great Depression appear to disrupt the broader secular forces at work. By the late 1930s, the 50–10 ratio—the left tail of the distribution—had narrowed by

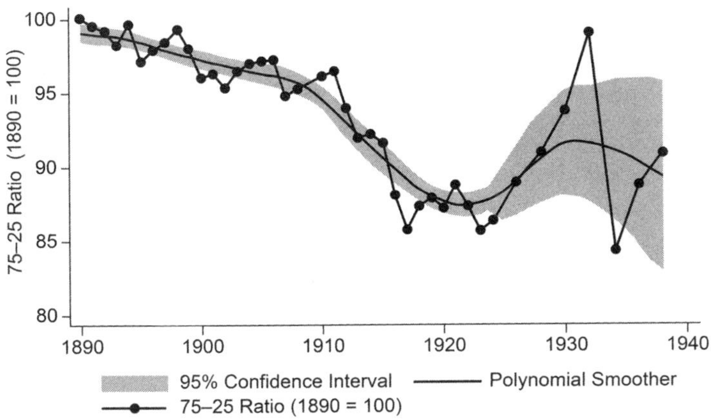

Figure 1.4 75–25 ratio: Weekly earnings in Massachusetts manufacturing, 1890–1938 production workers

Source: Computed from annual data for 1890–1919 from Massachusetts Bureau of Statistics of Labor and the available data for years from 1920–38 in Massachusetts Department of Labor and Industries (1940).

approximately 20 index points, or about –0.22 log points. The narrowing in the 90–50 ratio and the interquartile range was smaller, about 0.10 log points, or about 10 index points (from 100 to 90).

1.4.1 The Role of Electrification: Panel Estimates

The shift to steam-powered production (from hand or water) was one of the central features of the transformation of manufacturing over the second half of the 19th century and is, of course, captured in the *HML* study. Beginning in the late 19th century, the source of inanimate power began to shift from steam to electricity. The 1890 Census, for example, reported the use of over 15,500 electric horsepower in manufacturing with Massachusetts (#2), New York (#1 by a small margin), and Pennsylvania (#3) leading the way (US Census Office 1895a, 759). The shift began in earnest the 1890s and then accelerated swiftly after the turn of the 20th century (Du Boff 1966, 1979, esp. table 3, 427). As figure 1.5 shows, Massachusetts manufacturing followed this general pattern. By 1910 about 10 percent of horsepower used in Massachusetts manufacturing was generated by electricity. The electricity began rising steeply thereafter, reaching 60 percent in the late 1930s.

One of Goldin and Katz's (1999) main hypotheses is that electrification reduced wage inequality in the lower tail of the distribution. Shop floors were reorganized in response to electrification, reducing the demand for a wide array of low-wage jobs on the factory floor (Devine 1983), as materials handling was more easily electrified and as the production process was "linearized" (Jerome 1934). They were unable, however, to test for an effect of electrification directly because they did not have an annual time series of

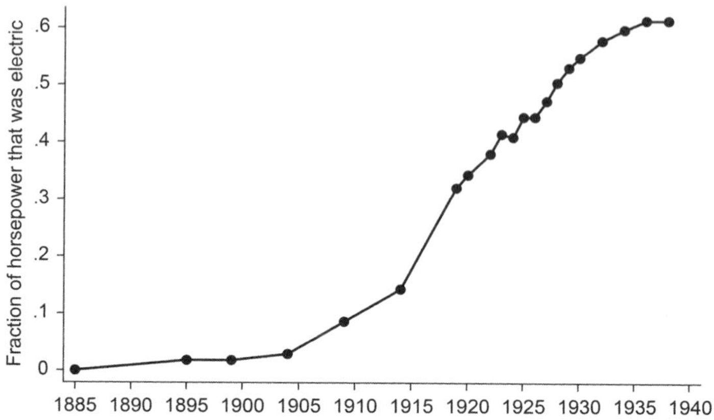

Figure 1.5 Electric Power as Share of Total Primary Horsepower, Massachusetts Manufacturing, 1885–1938

Source: 1885, 1895: Massachusetts and Wadlin (1898, 342–43). 1889–1919: US Bureau of the Census (1923, table 219, 471). 1920–38: Massachusetts Department of Labor and Industries (1940, 132).

wage inequality statistics matched to a similar time series on electrification, nor did they have an industry panel of classified wages matched to power use.

Following Goldin and Katz's (1999) lead, we estimate wage inequality at the industry level using the Massachusetts classified wage distributions. For two years, 1895 and 1920, we also have corresponding industry figures on power use (Massachusetts and Wadlin 1898, 575–84; US Bureau of the Census 1920, 636–47). The industries are identified at the three-digit SIC level, and we have constructed a matched panel of 41 observations for 1895 and 1920. We follow the same protocols regarding cut-offs and procedures with these industry-level data as for the aggregate data to estimate *q10* and *q50*.

We specify a two-way fixed effects model, with fixed effects for year (1920) and industry. Because there are only two years, we estimate the model in first differenced form. The regression specification is

$$\Delta\ Ln(q50/q10) = \alpha + \beta^{*}\Delta\ Elecwkr + \gamma^{*}\Delta\ Non\text{-}Elecwkr + \delta^{*}\Delta Pct\ Male + \varepsilon,$$

where *Elecwkr* = electric horsepower per worker, *Non-Elecwkr* = nonelectric horsepower (e.g., steam) per worker, and *Pct Male* = percentage of male workers. Because the industries differ greatly in employment, we weight observations by the average number of workers in the two years.

The regression results are shown in table 1.4. The hypothesis at issue is the sign of β. If it is negative, then electrification contributed to the compression in the lower half of the wage distribution. As can be seen, the coefficient is negative. It is also quite stable across the three columns, which add the other two independent variables. The magnitude of the coefficient, –0.128 in the

Table 1.4 **Regression analysis of Massachusetts industry panel, 1895 and 1920**

Variable	Sample means	Coefficients	Coefficients	Coefficients
Elecwkr	1.204	–0.127*	0.132*	–0.128*
		(0.034)	(0.036)	(0.038)
Non-Elecwkr	–0.486		–0.019	–0.017
			(0.032)	(0.033)
Pct Male	–0.028			–0.070
				(0.240)
Adjusted R^2		0.242	0.229	0.210

Note: Mean value of dependent variable (weighted by average employment) = –0.192. *Significantly different from zero at the 1% level. Source: Panel of 41 industries constructed from data in Massachusetts 1895 Census (Massachusetts and Wadlin 1898, 575–84) and data for Massachusetts in the Fourteenth Federal Census (US Bureau of the Census 1920, 636–47).

last column, is quite large. If we multiply this coefficient by the mean value of *Elecwkr*, the predicted change in the dependent variable is –0.154, which accounts for 80 percent of the change (–0.192) in the dependent variable. This result supports Goldin and Katz's (1999) argument that electrification contributed to the decrease in wage inequality in manufacturing before World War II.

1.5 Concluding Remarks

According to the conventional narrative, wage inequality in US manufacturing followed an inverted-U pattern from the early 19th century to just prior to World War II, a period that encompassed the transition from the artisan shop to the steam-powered factory and then electrification. This chapter fills in two important gaps. For the rising portion of the inverted U, the previous literature (see, e.g., Atack et al. 2004) was unable to measure changes in wage inequality within establishments, while for the falling portion, the precise time-series pattern of change from 1890 to 1940 could not be documented (Goldin and Katz 1999). For both parts of the evolution, a role for mechanization has been hypothesized, but previous work could not examine the role directly.

Here, we show that for the rising portion of the inverted U, we can use operations-level data from the US Department of Labor's 1899 *Hand and Machine Labor* study to study differences in wage inequality between "hand" (artisan) and "machine" (factory) production of specific manufactured goods. We show that wage inequality was much higher across operations in machine production than in hand production. In terms of explanatory power, the greater division of labor in machine production was responsible for about twice as much of the higher level of wage inequality than mechanization. We again emphasize that the evidence from the *HML* study pertains solely to the direct effect of mechanization on wage inequality among production workers. There is little doubt that the diffusion of steam power directly increased establishment scale, leading to an increased demand for nonproduction workers (Atack et al. 2008; Katz and Margo 2014) and, therefore, increased overall inequality in manufacturing. Steam power had an indirect effect on wage inequality by facilitating the transportation revolution, which increased market access and, therefore, the division of labor (Atack et al. 2011; Donaldson and Hornbeck 2016), a pathway that cannot be assessed with the *HML* data (because we lack information on where the units were produced).

Second, by digitizing and analyzing data from reports produced by the Massachusetts Bureau of Statistics of Labor, documenting so-called classified wages in manufacturing as well as the extent of electrification, we confirm a substantial narrowing of wage inequality across production workers, starting in the 1890s and accelerating after the onset of electrification. More concretely, we construct an industry panel for two years that allows us to estimate the impact of electrification on wage inequality directly, focusing on the lower half of the wage distribution. Consistent with Goldin and Katz (1999), we find a strong negative effect of electrification—as the use of electric power increased, absolutely and relative to other sources of power, wage inequality in the lower tail compressed significantly.

References

Atack, J., and F. Bateman. 1999. "Nineteenth-Century U.S. Industrial Development Through the Eyes of the Census of Manufactures." *Historical Methods* 32 (4): 177–88.

Atack, J., and F. Bateman. 2004. *National Sample from the 1880 Census of Manufacturing*. Inter-University Consortium for Political and Social Research (ICPSR).

Atack, J., F. Bateman, and R. A. Margo. 2004. "Skill Intensity and Rising Wage Dispersion in Nineteenth-Century American Manufacturing." *Journal of Economic History* 64 (1): 172–92.

Atack, J., F. Bateman, and R. A. Margo. 2008. "Steam Power, Establishment Size, and Labor Productivity in Nineteenth Century American Manufacturing." *Explorations in Economic History* 45 (April): 185–98.

Atack, J., F. Bateman, and T. Weiss. 2006. *National Samples from the Census of Manufacturing: 1850, 1860, and 1870*. Inter-University Consortium for Political and Social Research (ICPSR).

Atack, J., M. Haines, and R. A. Margo. 2011. "Railroads and the Rise of the Factory: Evidence for the United States, 1850–1870." In *Economic Evolution and Revolution in Historical Time*, edited by P. W. Rhode, J. Rosenbloom, and D. Weiman, 162–79. Stanford University Press.

Atack, J., R. A. Margo, and P. W. Rhode. 2019. "'Automation' of Manufacturing in the Late Nineteenth Century: The Hand and Machine Labor Study." *Journal of Economic Perspectives* 33 (2): 51–70.

Atack, J., R. A. Margo, and P. W. Rhode. 2022. "'Mechanization Takes Command?': Powered Machinery and Production Times in Late Nineteenth-Century American Manufacturing." *Journal of Economic History* 82 (3): 663–90.
Atack, J., R. A. Margo, and P. W. Rhode. 2023. "Digitizing Carroll D. Wright's 'Hand and Machine Labor' Study." *Jahrbuck für Wirtschaftsgeschichte* 64 (1): 9–30.
Atack, J., R. A. Margo, and P. W. Rhode. 2024. "De-skilling: Evidence from Late Nineteenth Century American Manufacturing." *Explorations in Economic History* 91: Art. 101554.
Autor, D., C. Goldin, and L. F. Katz. 2020. "Extending the Race Between Education and Technology." *AEA Papers and Proceedings* 110: 347–51.
Bairoch, P. 1982. "International Industrialization Levels from 1750 to 1980." *Journal of European Economic History* 11 (Fall): 269–334.
Blalock, H. M. 1960. *Social Statistics*. McGraw-Hill.
Brissenden, P. F. 1929. *Earnings of Factory Workers, 1899 to 1927: An Analysis of Pay-Roll Statistics*. US Government Printing Office.
Broadberry, S. N., and D. A. Irwin. 2006. "Labor Productivity in the United States and the United Kingdom During the Nineteenth Century." *Explorations in Economic History* 43 (2): 257–79.
Devine, W. D. 1983. "From Shafts to Wires: Historical Perspective on Electrification." *Journal of Economic History* 43 (2): 347–72.
Donaldson, D., and R. Hornbeck. 2016. "Railroads and American Economic Growth: A 'Market Access' Approach." *Quarterly Journal of Economics* 131 (2): 799–858.
Du Boff, R. B. 1966. "Electrification and Capital Productivity: A Suggested Approach." *Review of Economics and Statistics* 48 (4): 426–31.
Du Boff, R. B. 1979. *Electrical Power in American Manufacturing 1889–1958*. Arno Press.
Fishbein, M. H. 1973. "Censuses of Manufactures 1810–1890." Reference Information Paper No. 50. National Archives and Records, General Services Administration.
Goldin, C., and L. F. Katz. 1998. "The Origins of Technology Skill Complementarity." *Quarterly Journal of Economics* 113 (3): 693–732.
Goldin, C., and L. Katz. 1999. "The Returns to Skill in the United States Across the 20th Century." NBER Working Paper No. 7126. National Bureau of Economic Research.
Goldin, C., and L. F. Katz. 2000. "Education and Income in the Early Twentieth Century: Evidence from the Prairies." *Journal of Economic History* 60 (3): 782–818.
Goldin, C., and L. F. Katz. 2008. *The Race Between Education and Technology*. Belknap Press of Harvard University Press.
Goldin, C., and R. A. Margo. 1992. "Wages, Prices, and Labor Markets Before the Civil War." *Strategic Factors in Nineteenth Century American Economic History: A Volume to Honor Robert W. Fogel*, edited by C. D. Goldin and H. Rockoff, 67–104. University of Chicago Press.
Goldin, C., and K. Sokoloff. 1984. "The Relative Productivity Hypothesis of Industrialization: The American Case, 1820 to 1850." *Quarterly Journal of Economics* 99 (3): 461–87.
Gray, R. 2013. "Taking Technology to Task: The Skill Content of Technological Change in Early Twentieth Century United States." *Explorations in Economic History* 50 (3): 351–67.
Hunter, L. C. 1979. *A History of Industrial Power in the United States, 1780–1930: Water Power*. University Press of Virginia.

Hunter, L. C. 1985. *A History of Industrial Power in the United States, 1780–1930: Steam Power*. University Press of Virginia.
Hunter, L. C., and L. Bryant. 1991. *A History of Industrial Power in the United States, 1780–1930*. Vol. 3 *The Transmission of Power*. MIT.
Jerome, H. 1934. *Mechanization in Industry*. National Bureau of Economic Research.
Katz, L., and R. A. Margo. 2014. "Technical Change and the Relative Demand for Skilled Labor: The United States in Historical Perspective." In *Human Capital in History: The American Record*, edited by L. P. Boustan, C. Frydman, and R. A. Margo, 15–57. University of Chicago Press.
Lafortune, J., E. Lewis, and J. Tessada. 2019. "People and Machines: A Look at the Evolving Relationship between Capital and Skill in Manufacturing, 1860–1930, Using Immigration Shocks." *Review of Economics & Statistics* 101 (1): 30–43.
Lindert, P., and J. Williamson. 1976. "Three Centuries of American Inequality." *Research in Economic History* 1: 69–123.
Lindert, P. H., and J. G. Williamson. 2016. *Unequal Gains: American Growth and Inequality Since 1700*. Princeton University Press.
Margo, R. A. 2000. *Wages and Labor Markets in the United States, 1820–1860*. University of Chicago Press.
Massachusetts and H. G. Wadlin. 1898. *Census of the Commonwealth of Massachusetts: 1895*. Vol. 5, *Manufactures*. Wright.
Massachusetts Bureau of Statistics of Labor. *Annual Report on the Statistics of Manufactures for the* [*year*] . . . Wright & Potter, State Printers.
Massachusetts Bureau of Statistics of Labor. 1888. *Census of Massachusetts: 1885*. Vol. 2, *Manufactures, the Fisheries and Commerce*. Wright & Potter.
Massachusetts Department of Labor and Industries. 1940. *Statistics of Manufactures in Massachusetts, 1920–1938*. Wright & Potter, State Printers.
Mitchell, W. C. 1903. *A History of the Greenbacks, with Special Reference to the Economic Consequences of Their Issue: 1862–65*. University of Chicago Press.
Nearing, S. 1914. *Wages in the United States, 1908-1910; A Study of State and Federal Wage Statistics*. Macmillan Co.
New Jersey Bureau of Statistics. 1897. *Nineteenth Annual Report of the Bureau of Statistics of Labor and Industries of New Jersey for the Year Ending . . . 1896*. Bureau of Statistics of Labor and Industries.
North, S. N. D. 1909. "The Life and Work of Carroll Davidson Wright: Fifth President of the American Statistical Association." *Publications of the American Statistical Association* 11 (86): 447–66.
Sokoloff, K. L. 1982. "Industrialization and the Growth of the Manufacturing Sector in the Northeast, 1820–1850." PhD diss., Harvard University.
Sokoloff, K. L., and G. C. Villaflor. 1992. "The Market for Manufacturing Workers During Early Industrialization: The American Northeast, 1820 to 1860." In *Strategic Factors in Nineteenth Century American Economic History: A Volume to Honor Robert W. Fogel*, edited by C. Goldin and H. E. Rockoff, 29–65. University of Chicago Press.
US Bureau of the Census. 1920. *Fourteenth Census of the United States Taken in the Year 1920*. Vol. 9, *Manufactures 1919—Reports for States with Reports for Principal Cities*. Government Printing Office.
US Bureau of the Census. 1923. *Abstract of the Census of Manufactures, 1919*. Government Printing Office.
US Census Office. 1895a. *Report on Manufacturing Industries in the United States at the Eleventh Census: 1890*. Pt. 1, *Totals for States and Industries*. Government Printing Office.

US Census Office. 1895b. *Report on Manufacturing Industries in the United States at the Eleventh Census: 1890*. Pt. 2, *Statistics of Cities*. Government Printing Office.
US Census Office and D. R. Dewey. 1903. *12th Census 1900: Employees and Wages*. Government Printing Office.
US Census Office, F. A. Walker, and C. W. Seaton. 1883. *Report on the Manufactures of the United States at the Tenth Census*. Government Printing Office.
US Congress, House. 1833. *Documents Relative to Manufactures in the United States* [*collected and transmitted by . . . the Secretary of the Treasury . . .*]. Duff Green.
US Congress, Senate. 1893. *Wholesale Prices, Wages and Transportation, 1840–1891*. 4 vols.
US Department of Labor. 1899. *Hand and Machine Labor (Thirteenth Annual Report)*. Government Printing Office.
US Department of the Treasury. 1791. *Report of the Secretary of the Treasury of the United States, on the Subject of Manufactures. Presented to the House of Representatives, December 5, 1791*. Printed by Childs and Swaine.
US Executive Office of the President, Office of Management and Budget. 1987. *Standard Industrial Classification Manual*. For sale by National Technical Information Service.
von Hippel, P., D. Hunter, and M. Drown. 2017. "Better Estimates from Binned Income Data: Interpolated CDFs and Mean-Matching." *Sociological Science* 4: 641–55.
Weeks, J. D. 1886. *Department of the Interior, Census Office. Report on the Statistics of Wages in Manufacturing Industries; with Supplemental Reports on the Average Necessaries of Life and on Trades Societies, and Strikes and Lockouts*. Government Printing Office.
Williamson, J. G., and P. H. Lindert. 1980. *American Inequality: A Macroeconomic History*. Academic Press.
Wright, C. D. 1900. *History and Growth of the United States Census*. Government Printing Office.

2

A Real Great Compression
Inflation and Inequality in the 1940s

Carola Frydman and Raven Molloy

2.1 Introduction

Most countries experienced substantial reductions in income inequality in the first part of the 20th century, especially during the wars and the Great Depression (Atkinson et al. 2011; Chancel and Piketty 2021). In their seminal paper, Goldin and Margo (1992) document a "Great Compression" in the distribution of wages in the United States from 1940 to 1950 across the board—by education, job experience, and occupation. This era stands out as the only period of substantive increase in wage equality in America in almost a century.

Yet during the 1940s, the American economy also experienced an unusually large increase in prices (Rockoff 1984). Recent research has shown that in the 21st century, inflation has tended to be higher for lower-income households (Argente and Lee 2021; Jaravel 2019, 2021; Kaplan and Schulhofer-Wohl 2017). If the same were true for the 1940s, then real wage inequality would not have compressed as much as nominal wage inequality, thereby

Carola Frydman is the Harold L. Stuart Professor of Finance and the Faculty Director of the John L. Ward Center for Family Enterprises at the Kellogg School of Management of Northwestern University and a research associate of the National Bureau of Economic Research.

Raven Molloy is a deputy associate director of the Division of Research and Statistics of the Board of Governors of the Federal Reserve System.

We thank Reeves Coursey and Sungho Park for excellent research assistance and seminar participants at NBER Historical Labor Markets and Inequality Conference, and also NYU Stern. Any opinions and conclusions expressed herein are those of the authors and do not indicate concurrence with other members of the research staff of the Federal Reserve or the Board of Governors. For acknowledgments, sources of research support, and disclosure of the authors' material financial relationships, if any, please see https://www.nber.org/books-and-chapters/economic-history-american-inequality-new-evidence-and-perspectives/real-great-compression-inflation-and-inequality-1940s.

potentially changing the implications of the Great Compression in nominal wages documented by Goldin and Margo. Yet the effect of differential inflation on income inequality early in the 20th century has been largely unexplored. In this chapter, we fill this gap by calculating inflation rates for different groups of households and assessing the effects of changes in prices on the distribution of real incomes during the 1940s.

A small but growing body of literature studies differential inflation experiences across various socioeconomic and demographic groups primarily since the 1980s. A main approach within this literature consists of leveraging expenditure surveys to construct group-specific spending shares. For inflation to differ across groups, there must be significant differences in expenditure shares between groups, and prices must have varied significantly for these expenditure categories. For example, food inflation was particularly high in the 1940s, averaging more than 7 percent per year. In recent decades, lower-income and less educated households have tended to spend a larger fraction of their budget on food. If this were also the case in the 1940s, then this item would have contributed to higher inflation for lower-income and less educated workers. Other types of goods and services might also have contributed to differences in inflation across groups. Most modern evidence based on spending shares finds, at most, modest differences in inflation by income, though cumulative inflation over long periods of time may have differed across the income distribution (Jaravel and Lashkari 2024).[1] Ultimately, whether inflation varied significantly by household characteristics in the 1940s remains an unanswered question.

The Bureau of Labor Statistics (BLS) has been conducting expenditure surveys to understand workers' spending habits since the late nineteenth century. Most of the evidence from early surveys is available only at an aggregate level in published tables. However, constructing group-specific inflation rates requires information on expenditures by household characteristics. We base our main estimates on household expenditures from the 1935–36 Consumer Expenditure Survey (CEX), which was administered to 61,000 families by the BLS. Researchers at the Inter-University Consortium for Political and Social Research (ICPSR) selected samples of urban and rural families and converted the files to machine-readable form. We use the urban sample, which covers 31 cities, and further restrict the data to the 1,918 families for which we have complete information on all components of spending.

Using the micro-level data from the 1935–36 CEX allows us to construct consumption baskets by detailed categories of education, occupation, and income. We then match a group's basket to price indexes for specific item categories from 1939 to 1949 published in various historical BLS reports. One

1. See, e.g., Michael (1979) and Hagemann (1982) for the 1970s, Garner et al. (1996) and Cage et al. (2002) for the early 1980s and early 1990s, McGranahan and Paulson (2006) for 1983–2005, and Klick and Stockburger (2021) for 2003–2018.

important concern is whether spending patterns in the mid-1930s, which was in the midst of the Great Depression, are a reasonable approximation for consumption baskets during the 1940s. Unfortunately, there are no similar household-level data available for the 1940s. Reassuringly, we show that the spending shares we compute from the 1935–36 data are broadly similar to aggregate shares reported in national consumer expenditure surveys undertaken in 1941 and 1950.

We start by comparing spending shares for 15 broad item categories across socioeconomic groups. When we contrast households by educational attainment of the husband, we find that the category with the largest difference across groups is food. Families in which the husband has less education tend to spend a larger fraction of their budget on food, which is not surprising, since lower-income families spend a larger fraction of their budget on necessities (Orchard 2022). The higher spending share for food is offset by lower spending shares on automobile purchases, household operation, and reading and recreation. Despite these differences, our key finding is that spending shares are not different enough across groups to imply material differences in inflation. Even for food, the category with the most significant heterogeneity in shares, the contribution to the difference in inflation across groups amounts to less than 0.2 percentage points per year.

Next, we calculate group-specific inflation rates based on the 15 broad item categories. Limited variation in spending shares across groups translates into small differences in estimated inflation rates. For example, inflation for families where the husband has 8 or less years of education was only 0.2 percentage points higher per year than inflation for families where the husband has 16 or more years of education, a rather small difference given that the average inflation across all families in the sample is 5.3 percent per year. Converting these estimates to cumulative growth rates from 1939 to 1949, the price level faced by families in the least educated group rose by 70 percent over this period, whereas the price level faced by families in the most educated group rose by 67 percent.

It is possible, however, that focusing on a limited set of aggregate categories masks substantial variation in prices. Jaravel (2021) shows that inflation differences across groups can become significantly larger when using a larger number of more detailed item categories. By combing through historical BLS reports, we are able to construct inflation estimates for 89 specific item categories. These estimates suggest smaller differences across education groups than when using broad item categories. One reason is that inflation for domestic service was quite high during the 1940s, and the higher spending share on these services among families with a college-educated husband raises inflation differentially for these families, roughly offsetting the smaller contributions from many food items. Inflation estimates by occupation of husband are also quite similar across groups. When we split families by income, we find that inflation was 0.3 percentage points higher for the top quintile of families than for the bottom quintile, largely because of their higher spending shares on domestic service and food away from home.

Despite our best efforts, it is possible that the 89 item categories that we use to compute group-specific price indexes may still be too aggregated to elicit significant variation in prices. Our methodology assumes that all households face the same changes in prices for each item category. This is a limitation shared with modern work utilizing expenditure shares to assess inflation experiences between population groups. These studies also tend to find relatively limited variation in inflation across groups even though they are able to consider a much larger number of categories than what is available for earlier decades.[2] But estimates based on differences in expenditures across groups cannot capture other potentially important sources of heterogeneity, such as differences in product quality or differences in prices paid for the same item. A second line of research addresses these limitations by using scanner data, which can help uncover heterogeneity in consumer preferences and allow for analysis of variation in prices across consumers for the exact same good as defined by a bar code. Scanner data tend to show more variation in price changes across households than estimates based on broader item categories. Specifically, scanner data show that during the 2000s, inflation was higher for lower-income consumers (Jaravel 2019; Kaplan and Schulhofer-Wohl 2017), though it is possible that this pattern is partly driven by the Great Recession (Argente and Lee 2021). An important limitation of bar-code-level data on expenditures and prices is that they cover only a subset of consumer goods and exclude many other goods and services, such as gasoline, rent, and health expenditures, that constitute a significant portion of a household's consumption.[3] In our context, such data would have missed expenditures on domestic service, which was a large contributor to price increases for high-income families. Nevertheless, evidence from scanner data points to the importance of variation in product type and quality across different types of households. Our ability to address this issue using data for the 1940s is fairly limited, but we provide some evidence based on automobiles suggesting that differences in product quality across education groups were fairly small.

In sum, our main finding is that inflation experiences were rather similar across groups during the 1940s. Thus, it is not surprising that utilizing group-specific inflation rates to adjust Goldin and Margo's estimates of relative wages by education, experience, and occupation has an almost negligible effect on those estimates. We show that the significant narrowing of wage inequality during the 1940s was slightly more pronounced after taking differ-

2. For example, Klick and Stockburger (2021) have price data for 243 items across 32 distinct geographic areas.

3. Jaravel (2019) shows that scanner data cover products that account for only about 15 percent of total expenditures measured in the CEX surveys.

ences in inflation across groups into account. Thus, America experienced a "Great Compression" in real wages as well as nominal wages during this era.

Our chapter contributes to the literature on the historical trends in income inequality by considering the importance of differential inflation across groups, an issue that has been largely ignored both in the historical and in the modern context. Given the difficulties of constructing consistent estimates of group-specific inflation over time, most of the work studying income and wealth inequality over the long run or in a historical context is not adjusted for inflation (see, e.g., Goldin and Katz 2007; Goldin and Margo 1992; Piketty and Saez 2003). Notably, Williamson (1977) studies the impact of prices on inequality for certain periods during the 20th century using similar consumer expenditure data, albeit based only on a small number of item categories. Another important exception is Moretti (2013), who finds that accounting for inflation differences between people with a college education and people with a high school education leads to a material reduction in the relative wage increase across groups from 1980 to 2000.[4] By contrast, we assess differences in real wage inequality in a period of high inflation. While adjusting for inflation is unlikely to make much of an impact over a short time span at times when inflation is low, it has the potential to be a more significant factor during inflationary periods.

Our chapter also adds to our understanding of the Great Compression. Given the uniqueness and magnitude of the narrowing of the wage distribution during the 1940s, it is surprising that the groundbreaking work by Goldin and Margo (1992) has not led to more widespread efforts to understand this period. Related work has focused on further evaluating differences across other groups of workers (Frydman and Molloy 2012; Margo 1995; Margo and Finegan 2002), assessing the role of unions (Collins and Niemesh 2019; Frydman and Molloy 2012), and reassessing the basic facts by exploiting the more comprehensive Census data that are now available to researchers (Jarowski and Niemesh 2018). We add to this literature by showing that this compression did not result from differences in inflation experiences across groups.

We also contribute to a small but growing literature studying the heterogeneity in inflation experiences across socioeconomic and demographic groups. The findings in this literature vary by methodology—specifically, whether papers use expenditure shares matched to published price indexes or scanner data to calculate inflation for specific items—and period of analysis (see Jaravel 2021 for a review of this literature). Most of this work has focused on modern (post-1970s) data, and therefore it largely ignores periods of high inflation. We know much less about inflation patterns earlier in

4. See also Costa (1999), who uses historical consumer expenditure surveys to estimate the trend in inequality in recreational expenditures from 1888 to 1991 to get insights into the evolution of living standards for poor and rich households over time.

the century. Our chapter takes a first step to fill in this gap by focusing in the 1940s, a period when the American economy experienced a rapid increase in prices. At a time when inflation is again relatively high, and debates on who will pay its costs have resurfaced, it becomes ever more important to learn from past experience.

2.2 Data Sources and Sample

2.2.1 Consumer Expenditure Surveys over Time

Since the late 19th century, the BLS has been conducting expenditure surveys to understand the spending patterns of American households. The content, design, and geographic coverage of these survey instruments have varied significantly over time (Jacobs and Shipp 1990). The first two surveys, in 1888–91 and 1901, for example, had limited coverage and focused primarily on blue-collar workers' spending patterns. Starting with the third survey, conducted between 1917 and 1919, these data became the basis to estimate weights for the Consumer Price Index (CPI).

A fourth survey focusing on urban wage and clerical workers was conducted during the Great Depression. The BLS collaborated with other government agencies to pursue the first-ever nationwide survey of consumer purchases in 1935–36 to study family consumption patterns of about 300,000 urban and rural families.[5] This survey was titled the "Study of Consumer Purchases in the United States," but since later surveys were titled "Consumer Expenditure Survey" we refer to this survey as the 1935–36 CEX. A subset of 61,000 families—25,000 urban and 36,000 rural—were then selected for a series of extended questionnaires. The urban sample is the main basis of our analysis. We do not use the rural sample because the price data collected by the BLS cover only urban areas, and price changes could easily have differed in rural areas.

To be included in the 1935–36 CEX, native-born nonfarm families must have included a husband and wife and had at least one wage earner in a clerical, professional, or business occupation. Also, families with income below a nominal cutoff (which varied by city size) and those that received relief were excluded, as were recently married couples and families residing in hotels, institutions, and lodging houses. In the 1990s, researchers at the ICPSR selected samples of urban and rural families and converted the files to machine-readable form. We use the urban sample, which covers 2,480 families in 31 cities.[6] Two-thirds of the sample completed the survey in 1936, while one-third completed the survey in 1935. The amounts of spending

5. The surveys were conducted in 30 states, covering a total of 51 cities, 140 villages, and 66 farm counties.

6. See the documentation for ICPSR collection 8908 for more details on the survey and digitalization process, available at https://www.icpsr.umich.edu/web/ICPSR/studies/8908

reported generally refer to the prior 12 months, except for a module on food expenditures that records detailed categories of spending for the prior week.

While data on most categories of spending are available for all households in the ICPSR sample, the variable reflecting total spending on furniture is missing. We are able to get information on furniture spending from a detailed module that covers spending on furniture, furnishing and household equipment. However, this module is available for only 77 percent of families. Moreover, detailed food expenditure data are only available for the 70 percent of families that filled out a supplement covering food expenditures in the prior week. Therefore, our main sample is based on the 1,743 urban families for which we have complete information on all components of spending. This smaller sample has a similar distribution of income, husband education and occupation, and location as the full sample of families. Results are similar when we use the full sample of families and omit the information from the food and furniture modules (results not shown).

In their sampling of the microdata, the ICPSR researchers decided to make it representative of the broader CEX survey rather than reweighting the data to be representative of the US population. Therefore, we start by showing that the families in the ICPSR sample are indeed representative of the original 1935–36 CEX. Table 2.1 compares expenditure shares by item category in our sample to published estimates from several BLS reports. In columns 1 and 2, we compare expenditure shares in our sample with estimates from a BLS report based on the full 1935–36 survey, which reports shares for urban families with income above $500 and earnings between $300 and $2,000.[7] When we restrict our sample to these levels of income and earnings (in column 1), we find that the spending shares for each category are quite similar except for spending on food, which is a few percentage points lower in our sample, and spending on transportation and entertainment, which is a few percentage points higher. Despite these differences, it seems that our main microdata are a representative sample of the full 1935–36 survey.

Since our strategy is to use 1935–36 expenditure shares to study differential price inflation from 1940 to 1950, one important concern is that spending patterns during the Great Depression may not be a good proxy for consumption shares in the 1940s. While no comprehensive survey was run during the 1940s, a much smaller project covering only 1,300 urban families was undertaken in 1941–42 to obtain information on expenditures separately for all of 1941 and for the first three months of 1942. The family-level records from this effort, which we refer to as the 1941 survey, are not available

7. "Money Disbursements of Wage Earners and Clerical Workers 1934–36," by Faith M. Williams and Alice C. Hanson, BLS Bulletin No. 638. Roughly half of the ICPSR sample fits the income and earnings restrictions used in the published report. One-quarter of the ICPSR sample is excluded because at least one family member had earnings of more than $2,000, and one-quarter is excluded because no family members earned at least $300.

Table 2.1 **Comparison of expenditure shares in ICPSR sample of 1935–36 CEX to published BLS reports**

	Household income > 500 300 ≤ Earnings ≤ 2000		All Urban Families		
	ICPSR Sample (1)	1935–36 Published (2)	ICPSR Sample (3)	1941 Published (4)	1950 Published (5)
Food	31.2	34.6	30.0	30.8	31.1
Housing and utilities	25.4	25.0	20.4	18.5	15.1
Housing	18.6	17.6	14.1	—	11.1
Utilities	6.8	7.4	6.3	—	4.0
Household operation	4.7	3.9	5.6	5.2	4.7
Furniture, furnishing, equipment	3.2	4.1	3.6	5.3	7.1
Clothing	9.7	10.9	10.9	12.1	11.5
Transportation	9.9	8.5	11.4	12.1	13.8
Automobile related	—	—	10.0	9.7	12.1
Other transportation	—	—	1.3	2.3	1.7
Personal care	2.2	2.0	2.2	2.2	2.2
Medical care	4.7	4.0	5.0	4.7	5.2
Entertainment	7.4	5.6	8.3	7.5	7.2
Recreation	—	—	5.4	4.4	4.5
Reading	—	—	1.1	1.0	0.9
Tobacco	—	—	1.9	2.1	1.8
Education	0.6	0.5	1.2	0.8	0.6
Other	1.0	0.9	1.4	0.8	1.5

Note: Columns 1 and 3 authors' calculations from ICPSR collection 8908. Column 2 from BLS Bulletin 638 "Money Disbursements of Wage Earners and Clerical Workers 1934–36," table 1. We exclude spending on community welfare and gifts. Column 4 from BLS Bulletin 822 "Family Spending and Saving in Wartime" table 5, families of 2 or more persons in urban areas. Column 5 author calculations from 1956 BLS report "Study of Consumer Expenditures Incomes and Savings: Statistical Tables Urban US 1950," table 2 in vols. 2, 5, 9, and 10.

in machine-readable form and the published tables in BLS reports do not report spending differences by education or occupation. Consequently, we cannot use this survey to calculate inflation for these subgroups. But we can use the aggregate published data to compare spending shares in the 1930s with the early 1940s. In columns 3 and 4 of table 2.1, we compare our sample of urban families with spending shares in 1941 from the 1941 survey.[8] We find that spending shares were broadly similar in 1935–36 and 1941, although spending on "housing and utilities" and recreation was slightly

8. "Family Spending and Saving in Wartime," BLS Bulletin 822, 1945. For consistency with the earlier survey, we exclude the value of items received "in kind." For consistency with the 1935–36 sample we report data from table 5 of the report, which includes only families with two or more persons.

higher in our sample, while spending on clothing and food was a bit lower.[9] Therefore, it seems that spending patterns in 1935–36 were fairly similar to those seen in the beginning of the 1940s.

The war may have substantially altered consumption patterns. Many goods were in short supply, and a variety of price and quantity controls affected the types of goods that could be purchased. Consumption patterns may have shifted again after the war once most of the controls were lifted (Higgs 1999). Unfortunately, there were no large-scale surveys of family expenditures during the 1940s. The next large-scale survey was conducted in 1950, covering 12,000 urban families. While the family-level data from this survey are not available in machine-readable form, detailed tables were published in a BLS report.[10] In column 5, we report spending shares from this survey.

From 1935–36 to 1950, spending on housing had fallen somewhat, while spending on food, transportation, and furniture, furnishings, and household equipment had increased. The decline in housing expenditures was concentrated among renters (see table 2A.1). Rent growth during the 1940s was much lower than inflation for most other item categories, which can probably explain why rental expenditures became a smaller fraction of total spending. A significant increase in homeownership over this 14-year period also contributed to the decline in the housing expenditure share, since housing expenditures tend to be a smaller fraction of total spending for owners than for renters. However, we estimate that the rise in homeownership reduced the aggregate housing expenditure share by only 0.7 percentage points, about 25 percent of the observed decline in the aggregate (see table 2A.1). Turning to other expenditure categories, the increase in spending on food and transportation may have been because price inflation for these categories was relatively high. Despite these differences, table 2.1 shows that spending patterns were fairly similar on aggregate at the beginning and end of the decade, which supports our decision to use the 1935–36 spending shares to calculate inflation for the entire decade. This assumption seems reasonable since the main focus of this paper is to study inflation over the entire decade, rather than year-to-year variation in prices within the 1940s. We return to this issue in section 2.4.4, where we analyze how spending shares shifted from 1935–36 to 1950 by education of the husband. And in section 2.3.2,

9. To be consistent with the definitions used in each BLS report, to compare with the published 1935–36 data, we define housing expenditures for owner-occupants as their estimated rental value of their home, while to compare with the published 1941 data, we define housing expenditures for owner-occupants as their expenditures for repairs, replacements, insurance, mortgage interest, taxes, refinancing charges and special assessments. In section 2.4.1, we present more information on these two methods of measuring housing expenditures.

10. "Study of Consumer Expenditures, Incomes and Savings; Statistical Tables: Urban US 1950" tabulated by the Bureau of Labor Statistics, US Department of Labor, for the Wharton School of Finance and Commerce, University of Pennsylvania.

we describe the evolution of price controls and rationing and their potential for temporary shifts in spending patterns within the decade.

2.2.2 Representativeness of the 1935–36 CEX Microdata

Since our analysis focuses on comparing spending shares and inflation estimates across various socioeconomic groups, it is important to understand whether the 1935–36 CEX microsample is representative of the population. Though the CEX survey was designed to cover a wide array of areas and families, it was not constructed as a probability sample of the US population at that time. In table 2A.2, we compare the demographic and socioeconomic characteristics of our sample to data on urban families from the 1940 census.[11]

We find that the distributions of husband's age, race and housing tenure are fairly similar in the two data sources. However, the husbands of the families in the ICPSR sample tend to have more schooling and are more likely to be in a white-collar occupation. Correspondingly, mean and median earnings (adjusted to 1936 dollars using the headline CPI) are somewhat higher in the ICPSR sample than in the 1940 census. This difference is likely attributable to three reasons. One is that the 1935–36 CEX did not sample families receiving relief, therefore omitting many families at the lower end of the income distribution. In addition, the 1935–36 CEX aimed to only cover families with at least one worker in a clerical, professional, or business occupation, and therefore did not include as many blue-collar workers. A third reason may be that the geographic distribution of the ICPSR sample differs from the 1940 census: the ICPSR sample has a larger fraction of families in midsize cities relative to very large metropolises or very small cities, and it also has a larger fraction of families in the South and West.[12]

In table 2A.3, we compare the distribution of income in the ICPSR sample to the distribution of income among the 18,500 families included in the full 1935–36 survey. The latter distribution was reported in appendix B of a report by the National Resources Committee titled "Consumer Expenditures in the United States, Estimates for 1935–36." The distribution of income in the ICPSR sample is quite similar to the distribution in the

11. The 1935–36 CEX recorded the age, educational attainment, race and occupation of the husband. The occupation is reported in text form, so we use string cleaning and machine learning techniques to match the text strings to 1950 occupation codes. See Appendix A for details. The 1940 data are from the 1 percent 1940 IPUMS sample (Ruggles et al. 2022).

12. The ICPSR sample includes data from both metropolises included in the 1935–36 CEX (New York and Chicago) as well as all of the large and midsize cities in the full survey. However, it covers only about half of the small cities that were included in the full survey. At the same time, its coverage of New York City is much lower than we would expect based on the 1940 census data. Since coverage is low for the smallest and largest cities, implications for socioeconomic characteristics of the families are unclear. However, when we calculate average wages, median wages, and the distribution of educational attainment in the 1940 census using the geographic distribution of the ICPSR CEX sample, we can't explain much of the difference in these outcomes between the 1940 census and the ICPSR sample.

full sample, suggesting that the geographic differences between the ICPSR sample and the 1940 census are attributable to the geographic coverage of the full 1935–36 survey rather than an issue with the ICPSR's sample.

2.2.3 Price Data

We obtain price data for specific item categories from BLS price indexes published in several sources. Many of the indexes for broad item categories are available electronically at the BLS website. To obtain prices for more detailed item categories, we hand-collect information from various published sources. Indexes for 41 detailed food items are from the 1967 Handbook of Labor Statistics, table 109. Indexes for many other detailed item categories are from a 1962 report titled "Price Indexes for Selected Items and Groups 1935–61."[13] Other sources include the 1967 Handbook of Labor Statistics and BLS Bulletin 966. Table 2A.4 provides a list of sources for the broad item categories, and table 2A.5 provides a list of sources for detailed item categories.

For three of the detailed item categories (those from BLS Bulletin 966), we have price indexes only through 1947. In these cases, we estimate the growth rate from 1947 to 1949 using the growth rate of a broader category from 1947 to 1949 multiplied by the ratio of the 1939–47 growth rate for the specific category to the 1939–47 ratio of the broader category.

2.3 Results

2.3.1 Heterogeneity in Consumption Patterns

We begin our analysis by studying differences in consumption patterns across household types. As a starting point, we focus on differences by education since education was one of the main types of heterogeneity studied by Goldin and Margo (1992). Table 2.2 reports spending shares for each major item category by educational attainment of the husband.

For most item categories, spending shares are fairly similar across groups. The category exhibiting the largest difference by education levels is food. Families in which the husband has less education tend to spend a larger fraction of their budget on food, which is not surprising, as lower-income families tend to spend a larger fraction of their budget on necessities (McGranahan and Paulson, 2006; Orchard, 2022). The higher spending share for food is offset by lower spending shares on automobile purchases, household operation (which includes domestic services, laundry services, and cleaning supplies), and reading and recreation. Their lower spending on automobile purchases reflects a lower propensity to purchase a car: in this sample only

13. See the Online Books page, http://onlinebooks.library.upenn.edu/webbin/book/lookup id?key=ha001887682.

Table 2.2 Expenditure shares by education of husband in 1935–36

	8 years or less	9 to 11 years	12 years	13 to 15 years	16 years or more	Price change 1939–49 (annual rate)
Food	32.7	30.3	28.2	27.1	23.7	7.8
Housing	17.5	17.0	18.3	16.9	16.7	1.9
Electricity	1.9	1.9	2.0	1.8	1.8	–0.6
Other utilities	5.1	4.3	4.1	3.7	3.6	6.7
Household operation	4.1	5.3	5.2	6.2	7.1	3.9
Furniture, furnishing, equip.	3.0	4.0	3.4	4.3	3.7	6.4
Clothing	10.0	10.2	10.6	10.7	10.9	6.6
Automobile purchase	3.2	4.3	4.0	3.8	5.2	6.7
Gasoline	2.6	3.1	3.4	3.6	3.4	4.0
Other transportation	3.4	3.8	3.8	4.2	4.2	3.3
Personal care	2.2	2.2	2.1	2.1	2.0	5.4
Medical care	4.9	4.6	4.7	4.4	4.5	3.7
Reading & recreation	5.1	5.6	6.3	6.7	7.5	5.2
Tobacco	2.1	1.9	1.7	1.6	1.5	3.9
Other	2.0	1.5	2.2	2.9	4.3	3.9
Share of sample	39.1	18.8	17.5	10.7	13.9	—

Note: Housing expenditures are rent for renters and the owner's estimate of rent for owners. Other expenditures include education and occupation-related expenses. The price index for "other" excludes food, housing, apparel and upkeep, transportation, medical care, personal care, and reading and recreation. The price index for housing is the index for rent of primary residence.

16 percent of the families in the lowest-education group had purchased a car in the survey year, compared with 25 percent in the highest-education group. Conditional on having purchased a car in the schedule year, the price of the car was about 15 percent of total household spending for all five groups.[14]

Housing expenditures in 1935–36 were a much smaller fraction of total expenditures than in recent decades (McGranahan and Paulson 2006). For our baseline results, we follow the CPI methodology in defining housing expenditures as rent for renter households and the owner's estimate of rent for their home for owner-occupied households.[15] In section 2.4.1, we show that results are similar when we use owner expenditures on mortgage interest, taxes, insurance, etc. instead of the owner's estimate of rent.

Table 2A.6 reports spending shares for each quintile of the income distribution and by occupation. As with educational attainment, differences across groups are the most pronounced for the food category. Housing expenditure shares differ more across income groups than across education or occupation groups, with higher-income families having lower expenditure shares. Clothing expenditure shares also differ more across income groups,

14. Following the BLS methodology for the CPI, we subtract any trade-in amounts from the purchase price of the car.

15. We exclude lodging away from home because we do not have a price index for this category. Spending in this category was 1.7 percent of total spending, on average.

with higher-income families having higher expenditure shares. In general, differences between blue-collar and white-collar families are minor, consistent with a study conducted by the National Resources Committee, which found that spending patterns across occupation groups were similar in the 1935–36 survey data (National Resources Committee 1939, 17).

2.3.2 Price Changes from 1939 to 1949

In the last column of table 2.2, we report the price change that we use for each broad item category. (See table 2A.4 for the exact mapping between categories of spending and price indexes.) We focus on the price changes from 1939 to 1949 since our ultimate goal is to assess implications for changes in income inequality between the 1940 census and 1950 census, and incomes reported in the census reflect incomes in the prior year.

Price changes from 1939 to 1949 were largest for food. Since families with less-educated husbands spent a larger fraction of their budget on food, we would expect this component of spending to boost general inflation for this group. However, this boost is modest: Families in the lowest category of educational attainment spent 8.4 percentage points more of their budget on food than families in the highest category, but food inflation was only 2.3 percentage points higher than the growth rate of the published CPI for all items, which was 5.5 percent on average over the decade. Thus, differences in food spending across households should have raised inflation for the least-educated group by only about 0.2 percentage points on average over this 10-year period relative to the most-educated group. Categories with relatively low price growth include rent, electricity, medical care, and tobacco. Spending shares for these groups were fairly similar across categories, so we would not expect them to create a material difference in general inflation across groups.

2.3.3 Group-Specific Inflation Estimates

We calculate headline inflation for each socioeconomic group as the weighted average of price changes for each item category, where the weights are the spending shares calculated using the 1935–36 family-level spending data. Thus, these inflation estimates assume that all households face the same changes in prices for each item category. Research using data from the 2000s has found that price changes do vary across households within these broad item categories (Argente and Lee 2021; Jaravel 2019; Kaplan and Schulhofer-Wohl 2017). We return to this issue shortly.

It is important to note that our methodology does not allow for any change in spending shares over time. Therefore, it is similar in spirit to a Laspeyres index, which uses spending shares in time period t as weights for price changes from period t to $t + 1$.[16] The Consumer Price Index also uses

16. The difference is that we use shares not from time t but from a few years prior to time t.

Table 2.3 **Inflation by group, 1939–1949**

	Number of observations	Percentage of observations	Inflation (percentage change, annual rate) 15 categories	89 categories
All families	1,743	100	5.28	5.33
Education of husband				
≤8 years	682	39.1	5.39	5.34
9 to 11 years	327	18.8	5.35	5.38
12 years	305	17.5	5.22	5.26
13 to 15 years	187	10.7	5.23	5.35
≥16 years	242	13.9	5.14	5.34
Occupation				
Blue collar	646	37.6	5.39	5.35
White collar	1072	62.4	5.24	5.37
Craft	271	15.8	5.40	5.36
Operative	195	11.4	5.36	5.35
Laborer	57	3.3	5.48	5.35
Service	123	7.2	5.35	5.32
Professional	628	36.6	5.21	5.40
Clerical	444	25.8	5.30	5.33
Household Income				
Bottom quintile	386	22.1	5.37	5.24
Second quintile	366	21.0	5.34	5.30
Middle quintile	337	19.3	5.30	5.28
Fourth quintile	340	19.5	5.29	5.33
Top quintile	314	18.0	5.21	5.51

a Laspeyres-type method. In table 2.1, we showed that aggregate spending shares were fairly similar in 1935–36 and 1950, suggesting that inflation estimates would be similar if we used expenditure shares from 1950. In section 2.4.3, we show that our results are indeed similar when we calculate alternate inflation estimates that use spending shares by education of husband from the 1950 survey. This evidence suggests that keeping the consumption basket fixed over time is unlikely to significantly bias our main results.

Table 2.3 presents estimates of headline inflation by education, occupation and income group.[17] Column 3 reports inflation estimates based on the 15 broad item categories covered in table 2.2. The average across all families is 5.28 percent per year, only slightly lower than the 5.52 percent growth rate of the published CPI index.[18] The inflation estimates are quite similar

17. Note that we define income quintiles based on the full sample of 2480 families. Thus, there are not exactly 20 percent of families in each income group when we restrict the sample to those households with complete spending data.

18. One reason for this difference is that prior to 1952, the BLS used a shelter expenditure weight equal to zero for owner-occupants (since they did not have cash expenditures on rent). Because owner-occupants have a positive expenditure share in our analysis and rent growth was lower than for other goods and services, our estimate is lower than the published estimate. If we

Figure 2.1 Spending differences across education groups and relative inflation by item

Note: The x-axis presents the difference in expenditure shares between families where the husband had 17 or more years of education relative to families where the husband had 8 or less years of education. The y-axis displays the difference between price growth for each item category and headline inflation. Expenditure shares are defined over 15 broad item categories.

across groups, with inflation tending to be slightly higher for families with lower income and for which the husband has less education or works in a blue-collar occupation.

Figure 2.1 illustrates why the estimates are similar across groups. In this figure, each dot reflects the contribution of an item category to headline inflation. Specifically, the x-axis shows the difference in expenditure shares between families in the highest and lowest education groups, and the y-axis shows the price change of that item relative to headline inflation. The category of food reduces inflation of the more-educated group relative to the less-educated group because families with a more-educated husband have a lower food expenditure share and food inflation was higher than average. For the other item categories with large relative price differentials (shelter and electricity), expenditure shares were not that different across groups. Other item categories had relatively small relative price differentials as well as relatively small differences in expenditure shares.

Research using data from the 2000s has found that using a larger number of more detailed item categories can generate larger differences in inflation across income groups. Jaravel (2019) finds that inflation differences between the top and bottom quartiles of income are almost 4.7 times larger when

use a shelter expenditure weight equal to zero for owner-occupants, we calculate an aggregate inflation rate of 5.57 percent per year.

he studies 256 distinct categories than when he uses only 22 spending items, based on CEX-CPI data from 2004 to 2015. Similarly, he finds more variation in inflation by income using barcode-level information from scanner data than when aggregating information to product groups.

The level of detail can matter if price trends differ within broad item categories and if different types of households tend to purchase items with different price trends. For example, consider the category of clothing. If the prices of high-quality fashion-brand clothing increase at a different rate from the prices of low-quality clothing, inflation would differ for families depending on the type of clothing that they tend to purchase. But an inflation estimate based only on the average price change for all clothing would not capture these differences and would therefore understate inflation inequality.

We are able to expand our analysis to 89 item categories: 44 categories of food, 5 categories of spending on household operations, 7 categories of personal care, 9 categories of medical care, 10 categories of spending on transportation, and 3 categories of tobacco-related expenses. We are also able to separate spending on movies and newspapers from spending in other reading and recreation, and we are able to separate furniture from household furniture, furnishings and equipment.[19] The full list of items is in table 2A.5. The categories are detailed enough that one might expect spending differences across groups for many of these items. For example, one might expect differences across groups in the propensity to purchase various types of fresh fruits and vegetables versus canned or processed fruits and vegetables. Other item categories where one might expect differences across groups include different types or cuts of meat, spending on domestic service, and spending on beauty salon services.

Column 4 of table 2.3 shows that even using these much more granular data, inflation estimates remain very similar across groups. The largest difference across groups is a 0.27-percentage-point gap between the top and bottom income quintiles.[20] It turns out that the spending shares tend to be fairly similar, even for items that one might expect to differ more across groups such as movie admissions, beauty salon services, and cigars. To illustrate this fact, figure 2.2 shows the contributions to headline inflation by detailed items. The figure shows these contributions for high-income families

19. We are not able to create detailed categories of spending for clothing because the ICPSR data sample did not record these detailed expenditures, even though they were included in the survey. The dataset includes variables for these detailed categories, but the values are equal to zero for all observations. Nor are we able to create detailed categories of spending on furniture or furnishings because the ICPSR sample is too small to measure purchases of specific durable goods accurately. We are unable to create detailed categories of recreation other than movie admissions because we do not have price indexes for other items in this category.

20. The difference across groups becomes larger when we look at the extreme tails. Average inflation for the bottom 5 percent of the income distribution was 5.16, while average inflation for the top 5 percent was 5.74. However, these estimates are based only on about 75 families per group and are therefore not estimated very precisely.

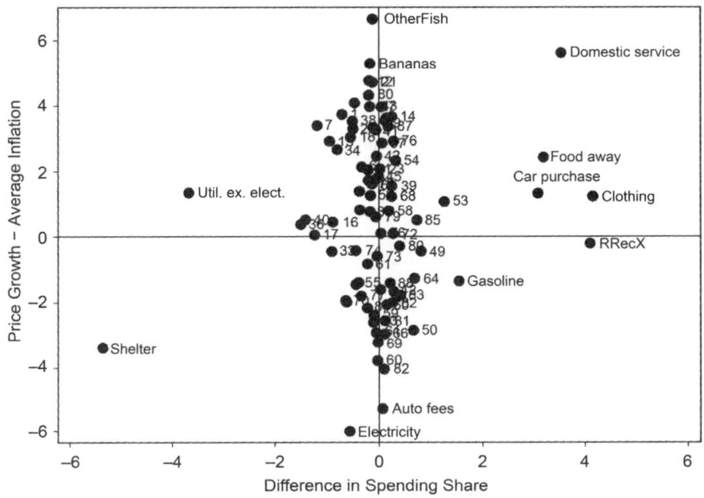

Figure 2.2 Spending differences across income groups and relative inflation by item

Note: The x-axis presents the difference in expenditure shares between families in the top quintile of the income distribution relative to families in the bottom income quintile. The y-axis displays the difference between price growth for each item category and headline inflation. Expenditure shares are defined over 89 item categories.

relative to low-income families, since the difference across income groups is larger than differences across education or occupation categories. While many items have large relative price differences, most of these items have fairly small differences in expenditure shares.

Our results differ materially from Jaravel (2019) in that inflation increases by more for high-income, high-education families when we use a larger number of item categories. By contrast, in his results using more item categories increased inflation more for low-income households. In the 1940s, inflation increases more for higher-income families when a finer level of disaggregation is used primarily because these families had larger expenditure shares on domestic service and food away from home, and these items had high relative price inflation during that decade.[21]

We have focused on groups defined by income, education and occupation because these groups are the most relevant to the Goldin and Margo (1992) analysis, but other household characteristics are of relevance as well. When we group families by race, average inflation was 5.42 percent for White families and 5.27 percent for Black families, a smaller difference than the gap between the top and bottom income quintiles.[22]

21. The BLS did not publish a price index for food away from home in the 1940s, so we use the aggregate food index for this category.

22. For this analysis, we limit the sample to cities where Black families were included in the ICPSR sample: Atlanta, GA; Columbus, OH; and Mobile, AL.

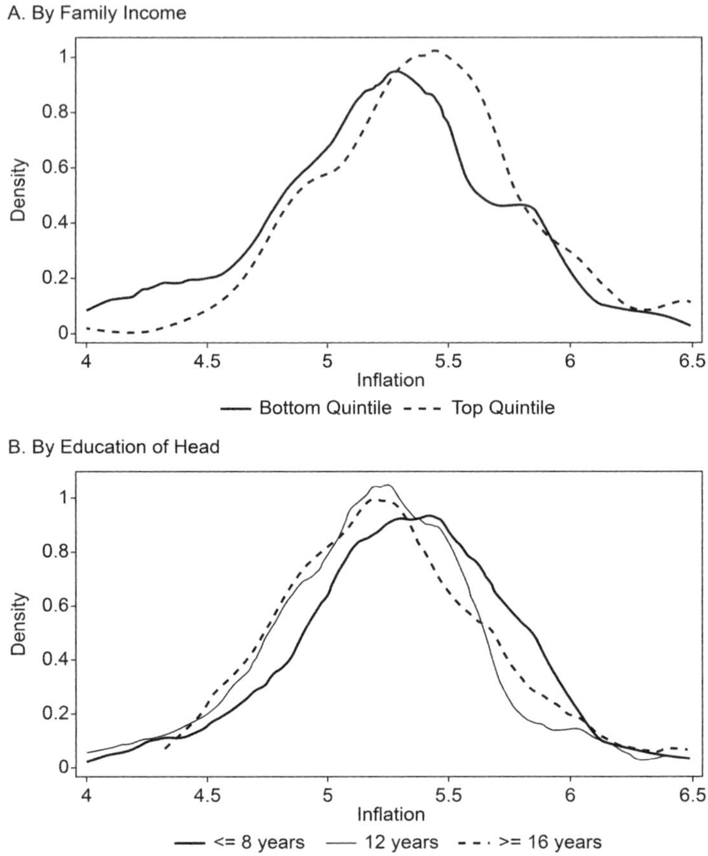

Figure 2.3 Distribution of inflation across families

Thus far our results have focused on the difference in average inflation for each group. It is possible that these averages mask important heterogeneity within groups. To investigate this possibility, we calculate inflation for each family using its expenditure shares. Panel A of figure 2.3 plots the distribution of inflation rates for families in the highest- and lowest-income groups. Although a Kolmogorov-Smirnov test rejects that the two distributions are the same, there is a fair amount of overlap, especially at the top of the distribution. For example, 12 percent of families with low income have an inflation rate more than 0.5 percentage points above 5.3 (the mean of the aggregate distribution), and 11 percent of families with high income have this high inflation rate. There is a larger difference between groups at the lower tail: 17 percent of families with low income have an inflation rate more than 0.5 percentage points below 5.3, while only 7 percent of families with high income experience an inflation rate this low.

Panel B of figure 2.3 shows similar results across education groups. While average inflation is the lowest for the middle education group (heads with 12 years of schooling), the distribution is statistically indistinguishable from the distribution of inflation for the highest education group. Both distributions are statistically different from the distribution of inflation for families in lowest education group, which is clearly shifted to the right. The lowest education group has 4 percent fewer families with low inflation and 4 percent more families with high inflation relative to the other two groups shown.

Another advantage of calculating family-specific inflation rates is that we can test how different the means of the distributions are. While we can reject that the means of the highest and lowest education groups are the same, we can also reject that they are more than 0.2 percentage points apart. Similarly, we can reject that the means of the highest and lowest income groups are the same, and we can also reject that the means are more than 0.3 percentage points apart.

In sum, the differences in means across groups are small relative to the heterogeneity in family-specific inflation rates, similar to Kaplan and Schulhofer-Wohl (2017) and Hobijn and Lagakos (2005). These differences are also small relative to the average inflation rate during this time period. For example, the difference between the highest and lowest income groups is only 1/20th of the average inflation rate. Converting these estimates to cumulative growth rates from 1939 to 1949, the price level faced by families in the lowest income group rose by 67 percent over this period, whereas the price level faced by families in the highest income group rose by 71 percent.

2.3.4 Annual Inflation Estimates

Our main analysis focuses on cumulative inflation from 1939 to 1949, and therefore averages periods of very high inflation with periods of lower inflation. This inflation volatility was largely related to wartime inflationary pressures combined with government price (and wage) controls. The coverage and strength of the federal government's price controls varied substantially over time (Rockoff 1984). Though there were some discussions to introduce price controls as early as 1939, price controls started in earnest only in May 1940. This early phase, which lasted until April 1942, was relatively permissive. Many goods and services were excluded from controls altogether, and while some controls were formal, others were based on informal agreements. The enactment of the General Maximum Price Regulation in 1942 led to a four-year period of much broader and stricter controls. While the initial set of rules were relatively ineffective at curbing inflation, the "hold the line" order passed in April 1943 essentially prohibited most price increases.

The strong enforcement of this order resulted in moderate inflation until the controls began to relax in February 1946. Prices began to increase at that time, and inflation picked up even further in late 1946, when most price controls were removed. By November of that year, controls for only sugar,

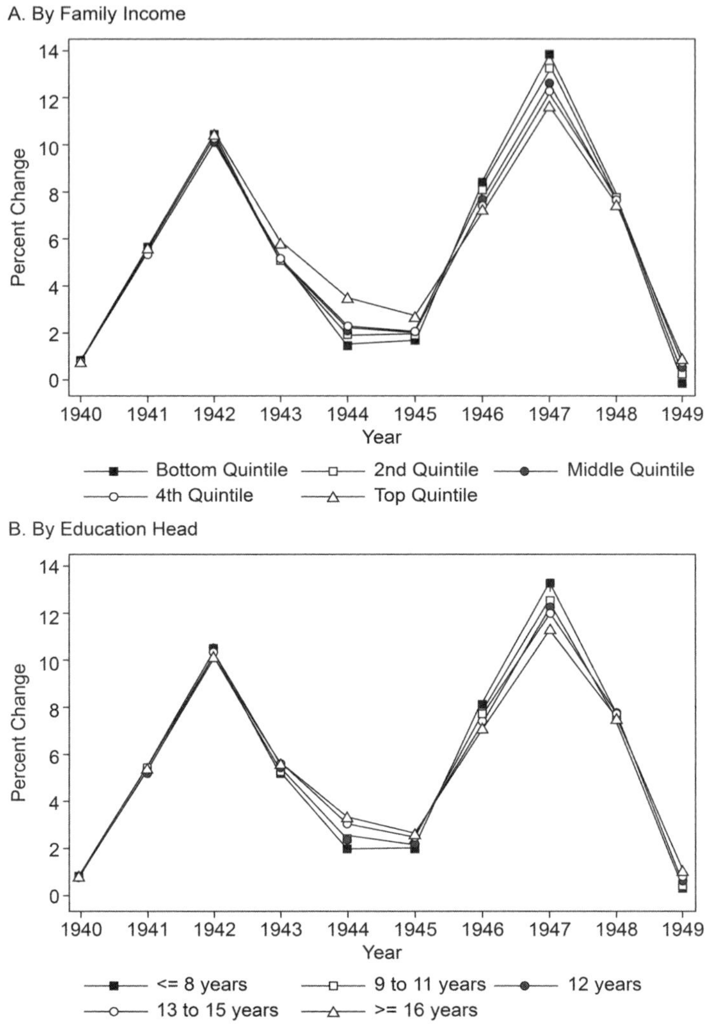

Figure 2.4 Annual inflation, 1940–1949

Note: Estimates of annual inflation are calculated based on consumption baskets by family income (panel A) and education of husband (panel B) from the 1935–36 CEX and detailed price indexes for specific item categories from 1939 to 1949 published in various historical BLS reports.

rice, and rent remained. Of these, only rent controls persisted long after the war ended (Fetter 2016). Inflation moved down in 1948 and 1949 as many of the supply constraints that had pushed up inflation during the war eased.

In figure 2.4 we show annual inflation estimates by income and education group, which we calculate using annual price changes for the 89 items and expenditure shares from 1935–36.[23] The baseline result that average inflation from 1939 to 1949 was higher for higher income groups is mostly driven by the war years. During that time, the price increases for domestic service and reading and recreation were much higher than average, and these items have a larger weight for higher-income families. By contrast, inflation was higher for lower-income, less educated families in 1947 due to large price increases for a variety of food items such as beef, pork, flour, and sweets.

One issue with using 1935–36 expenditure patterns to measure inflation throughout the 1940s is that expenditure patterns could have shifted materially during the war. In section 2.2.1, we showed that expenditures in 1935–36 were fairly similar to those in 1941 and 1950. This is reassuring when the objective is to calculate inflation inequality on average for the entire decade, but it is not informative of year-to-year changes in consumption patterns across groups within the decade. While no large-scale expenditure surveys were conducted during this time, the BLS did survey a handful of cities in each year from 1944 to 1948. Published aggregates from these surveys suggest that expenditures on food and clothing increased during the war, while expenditures on automobiles and reading and recreation decreased (see table 2A.8). Expenditure shares had mostly returned to their pre-war patterns by 1948. Because these expenditure surveys were small and there is only limited published information on how shares differed across types of households, it is difficult to assess the implications for inflation inequality. Therefore, we view the patterns in figure 2.4 as only suggestive and focus on the average inflation rate from 1939 to 1949. That said, since much of inflation during the 1940s was attributable to war-related constraints, it is important to note that the patterns we document in this chapter may not be more broadly representative of changes in prices during other periods of early US history.

2.3.5 Revisiting Goldin and Margo's Estimates

Given the relatively small differences in inflationary experiences across groups we documented thus far, our analysis suggests that changes in nominal and real relative incomes must have been fairly similar. For completeness, we utilize the estimates of inflation over the entire 1939–49 period to assess their implications for changes in relative wages between the 1940 and 1950 census. The first two columns of table 2.4 replicate estimates of relative wages by education and occupation as reported in tables 2 and 3 of Goldin and Margo (1992). The relative wages by education are reported separately for different groups of labor market experience because wages rise with experience and less-educated workers tend to have more labor market experi-

23. Because vehicle production was shifted to military vehicles during World War II, automobile prices are not available for 1942 to 1946. For these years we set the expenditure share for auto purchases to zero and renormalize the spending shares for all other categories. This assumption is fairly extreme since some families could have purchased used cars during this period, but we do not have data on used car prices during this period.

Table 2.4 Relative wages in 1940 and 1950

	Relative nominal wage			Relative real wage
	1940	1950	Relative inflation	1950
College – high school				
1 to 5 years experience	1.742	1.357	—	—
6 to 10 years experience	1.728	1.369	1.000	1.369
11 to 15 years experience	1.777	1.461	1.005	1.454
16 to 20 years experience	1.652	1.421	1.019	1.395
21 to 25 years experience	1.408	1.449	1.013	1.430
26 to 30 years experience	1.475	1.466	0.994	1.475
31 to 35 years experience	1.393	1.367	1.023	1.336
36 to 40 years experience	1.357	1.189	—	—
Some college – high school				
1 to 5 years experience	1.195	1.029	—	—
6 to 10 years experience	1.184	1.151	0.988	1.165
11 to 15 years experience	1.219	1.147	1.005	1.141
16 to 20 years experience	1.316	1.215	1.010	1.203
21 to 25 years experience	1.164	1.276	1.008	1.266
26 to 30 years experience	1.126	1.063	0.992	1.072
31 to 35 years experience	0.989	1.084	1.041	1.041
36 to 40 years experience	0.999	1.204	—	—
High school – 8th grade				
1 to 5 years experience	1.376	1.442	—	—
6 to 10 years experience	1.463	1.322	—	—
11 to 15 years experience	1.377	1.299	0.978	1.328
16 to 20 years experience	1.385	1.267	0.992	1.277
21 to 25 years experience	1.371	1.221	0.990	1.233
26 to 30 years experience	1.427	1.286	1.014	1.268
31 to 35 years experience	1.354	1.250	0.978	1.278
36 to 40 years experience	1.283	1.326	0.978	1.356
White collar – average	1.256	1.177	0.999	1.178
Blue collar – average	0.860	0.891	1.001	0.890
Professional	1.474	1.254	1.003	1.250
Clerical	0.988	0.940	0.997	0.943
Craft	1.039	1.023	1.000	1.023
Operative	0.856	0.861	0.999	0.862
Laborer	0.630	0.750	0.999	0.751
Service	0.737	0.779	0.996	0.782

ence. The third column reports relative inflation for each group. Due to the small sample size of the ICPSR data, we do not have sufficient information to construct reliable estimates for all categories of labor market experience in the Goldin and Margo paper. When possible, we use our estimates of group-specific inflation to adjust the nominal relative wages. Specifically, the fourth column presents relative wages in 1950 adjusted for relative inflation over the decade—that is, relative real wages.

The estimates of relative real wages are very similar to the estimates of relative nominal wages. For example, relative nominal wages of workers with a college education and 16 to 20 years of labor market experience fell from 1.65 times the wage of a worker with a high school education and the same amount of labor market experience in 1940 to 1.42 times in 1950. After adjusting for the fact that inflation was slightly higher for families with a more-educated husband, real wages in 1950 were 1.40 times the real wage of the less-educated group. Thus, the narrowing of wage inequality was generally more pronounced after taking differences in inflation across groups into account, but only slightly.

2.4 Robustness

We have found that inflation differed little across types of families from 1940 to 1950, despite the high rate of inflation during this period and the material differences in inflation across broad categories of item types. In this section we explore the robustness of this baseline result to various alternative methods.

2.4.1 Housing Expenditures

Housing is one of the main components of household spending, amounting to about 15 percent of spending for the average household in the sample. It is also one of the most difficult categories to measure appropriately. Ideally, a measure of inflation faced by consumers would use the price of shelter for its housing component because shelter is the service consumed by the residents living in a home. Estimating the price of shelter is relatively straightforward for renters because it can be measured using rents. However, the price of shelter is not observed for owner-occupants. In our baseline results, the expenditure share for owner-occupants is based on the rent that the owners think they would have to pay if they were to rent the home where they reside. This is the same way that expenditure shares are calculated for owner-occupants in the modern CPI. To measure changes in the price of shelter, the modern CPI uses an index called "owners' equivalent rent," which is based on rents paid by tenants. Since this index is not available for the 1940s, in our baseline results we use a price index for rent of primary residence to measure the change in the price of shelter for owner occupants as well as for renters.

In short, our baseline results are based on two assumptions: that the owners' estimate of the rent for their home is a good proxy for their cost of shelter, and that the growth in the price of shelter for owner-occupants was the same as the growth in the price of shelter for renters. Since 40 percent of families in the 1935–36 survey were owner-occupants, our baseline estimates could be biased by a substantial amount if either of these assumptions are flawed. Importantly, since homeownership rates differed across groups, as

Table 2.5 **Housing expenditure shares and inflation by socioeconomic group**

		Housing expenditure share				
		All households		Owners only		Headline inflation
	Percentage owners (1)	Using rent for all (baseline) (2)	Using owner expenses (3)	Using rent (4)	Using owner expenses (5)	using owner expenses (6)
Education of head						
≤8 years	40.2	17.5	14.2	20.3	11.0	5.55
9 to 11 years	33.0	17.0	14.4	20.1	11.4	5.55
12 years	38.4	18.3	14.7	20.5	10.2	5.47
13 to 15 years	38.0	16.9	13.9	19.8	11.2	5.53
≥16 years	47.5	16.7	13.3	18.5	10.7	5.56
Occupation						
Blue collar	37.6	17.6	14.6	20.7	11.9	5.54
White collar	40.2	17.6	14.3	20.1	10.9	5.58
Craft	37.6	17.5	14.4	20.8	11.7	5.56
Operative	37.9	17.2	14.6	20.2	12.3	5.53
Laborer	38.6	18.6	15.0	22.5	12.0	5.57
Service	36.6	18.2	15.2	20.6	11.3	5.51
Professional	44.3	17.3	13.6	19.5	10.4	5.62
Clerical	34.5	18.1	15.5	20.4	11.5	5.50
Household income						
Bottom quintile	30.1	21.0	17.3	25.6	11.2	5.45
Second quintile	34.2	19.2	15.8	22.2	10.6	5.49
Middle quintile	40.4	18.1	14.8	19.7	10.5	5.48
Fourth quintile	43.8	17.4	14.1	19.3	10.9	5.54
Top quintile	50.6	15.7	12.8	16.1	9.8	5.71

shown in column 1 of table 2.5, any bias imparted by these assumptions would also differ across groups.

An alternative way to measure the cost of shelter for owner-occupants is to add up all of their direct expenditures related to owning the home: mortgage interest, repair and replacement costs, property taxes, insurance, special assessments, and mortgage refinancing charges.[24] Column 3 of table 2.5 reports housing expenditure shares using this direct measure for owners and rent for renters. For comparison, column 2 reports housing expenditure shares from our baseline specification. The direct ownership expenditures tend to be lower than the owner's estimate of the rental value of their home, causing the housing expenditure share to be lower when this alternate measure is used. However, as with the owner's estimate of rental value there is relatively little variation across groups. We find similar patterns when we

24. In keeping with the definitions used in the 1941 and 1950 surveys, we exclude expenditures on mortgage principal and structural additions because they are considered investment.

calculate housing expenditures using both methods for homeowners only, shown in columns 4 and 5 of the table.

In order to assess the assumption that the change in the price of shelter was the same for owner-occupants as it was for renters, a natural strategy would be to calculate our own estimate of owners' equivalent rent and compare it to the index for tenants' rent. The BLS calculates owners' equivalent rent as a weighted average of rent growth for different Census block groups, with locations where owner-occupants are more likely to live getting a larger weight. We cannot follow this strategy because there is no detailed data on rent growth for different neighborhoods in the 1940s. Instead, we calculate the change in direct ownership costs.[25] Specifically, using a BLS report published in 1956 that summarizes results from the 1950 consumer expenditure survey, we calculate average expenditures for owner-occupied dwellings as the average expenditures on owner-occupied dwellings among all families of two or more persons divided by the fraction of families reporting expenditures for owner-occupied dwellings.[26] We find that owner expenses were about $385 in 1950, whereas they were $219 in the 1935–36 survey. Therefore, owner expenditures increased by 4.13 percent per year over this roughly 14-year period. When we do a similar calculation for renters, we find that renter expenses increased by 2.31 percent per year, quite similar to the growth rate of the CPI for tenants' rent of 2.22 percent per year over this period. If we assume that the ratio of the growth rate for owners' expenses to the growth rate for rent was the same from 1939 to 1949 as it was from 1936 to 1950, we find that owner expenditures increased by 3.45 percent per year from 1939 to 1949. Column 6 of table 2.5 shows estimates of headline inflation using this estimate for the change in the price of shelter for owner-occupants instead of rent growth. This alternate inflation measure also uses the direct owner expenditures instead of the owner's estimate of rent. The alternate inflation estimate is higher than our baseline estimate for two reasons: the increase in owner costs was larger than the increase in rent, and the smaller housing expenditure share for owners puts less weight on an item category for which price growth was relatively low. Nevertheless, differences across groups remain quite small since the alternate housing expenditure shares do not differ much across groups.

Another way in which our baseline analysis has oversimplified the housing component of inflation is that we use a national rent index for all house-

25. Another strategy could have been to calculate the change in the owner's estimate of rent, but the 1950 survey did not ask owners to estimate the rental value of their home.

26. "Study of Consumer Expenditures, Incomes and Savings; Statistical tables: Urban U.S.-1950" tabulated by the Bureau of Labor Statistics, US Department of Labor, for the Wharton School of Finance and Commerce, University of Pennsylvania, vol. 4, table 2. Expenditures are reported separately for nine classes of city size and location, so we take a weighted average across groups using the number of owner-occupied families in each group as weights.

Table 2.6 **Distribution of families by region and education of husband and implications for inflation**

	8 years or less	9 to 11 years	12 years	13 to 15 years	16 years or more	Rent growth 1940–49
Percentage of families by region						
New York City	21.3	13.6	12.3	12.5	17.5	1.03
Northeast Region excl. New York City	22.0	21.0	18.0	13.9	17.5	2.04
Chicago	8.3	7.1	6.7	6.7	6.1	2.98
Midwest Region excl. Chicago	25.5	28.2	28.5	26.2	25.1	2.36
South	14.8	17.2	17.4	21.4	19.5	2.65
West	8.1	13.0	17.0	19.3	14.4	2.75
Shelter component of inflation						
Using aggregate rent growth	0.40	0.39	0.39	0.38	0.37	—
Using regional rent growth	0.37	0.39	0.39	0.40	0.38	—

holds. If rent growth varied materially across locations and different types of families lived in different locations, then our baseline analysis would be missing an important source of inflation heterogeneity.

To assess this possibility, we need data on rent growth for various locations. We use data reported in BLS Bulletin 1165, which reports indexes from 1940 to 1952 for 34 cities.[27] Most of the cities in the 1935–36 CEX are not included in this report so we cannot include city-specific rent measures directly in our inflation calculation. Instead, we use the city-specific indexes for New York City and Chicago and calculate population-weighted average rent growth for the four Census regions excluding these two cities.[28] Table 2.6 reports the distribution of families by education of husband across these six locations and average rent growth in each location. Because the geographic distribution of families in the 1935–36 CEX does not line up well with the 1940 census, the table shows the geographic distribution of families from the 1940 census.

We find noticeable differences in rent growth across locations. Rent only rose by 1 percent per year in New York City, whereas it rose 3 percent per year in Chicago. Rent growth in the rest of the Northeast was higher than in New York City, but still lower than in the other three regions. Although the geographic distribution of families was fairly similar across these locations, families with a husband with eight or fewer years of education were more likely to live in New York City and less likely to live in the West than other families.

27. We include one additional city (St. Louis, MO) that is not included in Bulletin 1165 but for which the rent index posted on the BLS website extends back to 1940.

28. We separate New York City and Chicago because otherwise they would have a very large weight in the region averages, whereas most of the families in the 1935–36 CEX do not live in these two cities.

The bottom two rows of the table report estimates of the shelter component of inflation. These estimates use the geographic distribution of families in the 1940 Census and average housing expenditure shares by location and family type from the 1935–36 CEX. Using location-specific rent growth reduces shelter inflation for the least-educated group because of the heavier concentration of families in New York City, where rent growth was relatively low. However, this effect is small, only 0.04 percentage points. Effects on other groups are even smaller. Therefore, allowing for regional heterogeneity in rent growth does not lead to material differences in inflation across groups. In table 2A.7, we show that the distribution of families by income quintile was also quite similar across these six locations.

The cities included in BLS Bulletin 1165 were among the largest in the country. Only four had a population smaller than 100,000 (Manchester, NH; Portland, ME; Savannah, GA; and Mobile, AL). By contrast, nearly half of the families in the 1935–36 lived in cities with a population smaller than 100,000, and rent growth could have been different in these smaller cities. We are not aware of any rent indexes for small cities, so instead we examine this possibility by comparing average rental expenditures by city size in the 1935–36 CEX and the 1950 CEX. Specifically, the report covering expenditure data from the 1950 CEX includes rent expenditures for cities in the North, South and West with populations over 50,000 and those with populations less than 50,000.[29] When we calculate the increase in rent expenditures between the two survey periods, the increases seen in small cities were fairly similar to the larger cities in the same region (results not shown).

2.4.2 Car Prices

Another significant item where we may be underestimating heterogeneity across households is automobile purchases. Our baseline estimates assumed that car prices increased by the same amount for all households, regardless of the characteristics of the car they purchased, or whether they purchased a new or used vehicle. However, among families in the 1935–36 CEX that purchased a car in the schedule year and had only one car, 66 percent of those with a husband with an eighth-grade education or less bought a used car, while only 19 percent of those with a husband with 16 or more years of education bought a used car.[30] Thus there were substantial differences across groups in the propensity to buy a new versus used car.

The BLS does not publish a price index for used cars from the 1940s, so in our baseline estimates, we use the new automobile price index for all car purchases. The only aggregated data on used car prices that we have been

29. In this report, some cities in the Midwest are included in the North, while the remaining cities are included in the West.

30. For this analysis we must limit to families with only one car because for families with multiple cars we cannot distinguish which car was purchased in the schedule year. Among families that purchased a car in the schedule year, 8 percent owned more than one car.

able to find are from a figure reporting average used car prices by age of car from the 1950 volume of *Automobile Facts and Figures* (14). Based on estimated values from the figure, we calculate that the prices of used cars rose by 12, 12, 14, and 25 percent (annual rate) for cars that were one year old, two years old, three years old, and seven years old, respectively.[31] These increases are much larger than the increase in the BLS price index for new cars, which was 6.7 percent per year from 1939 to 1949. However, the increase in the price of a used car of a given age will reflect the quality difference between cars produced in different years as well as pure price changes, so it is important to keep in mind that these estimates overstate the pure price change for used cars. Nevertheless, these calculations suggest that price increases for used cars were likely larger than price increases for new cars. This factor would tend to increase inflation for lower income or lower education groups relative to our baseline estimates, although the exact magnitude is difficult to gauge with the limited data available.

Even conditional on buying a new or used car, different types of households may purchase different makes of cars, or different models within a particular car make. In the 1935–36 survey, we can identify 10 different car makes with enough purchases to reliably estimate an average price of a new car.[32] Table 2.7 shows the distribution of families by socioeconomic group that purchased low-priced cars, medium-priced cars, and high-priced cars. There is a modest amount of sorting by group, with 79 percent of families in the lowest-education group purchasing a low-priced car make, compared with only 57 percent of families in the highest-education group. Since we also know the price paid by each family, we can examine the price paid given the car make for five makes for which we have enough observations. We find little difference across groups in prices paid given the make of the car. Specifically, when we regress the log of the car's purchase price on indicators for make and education of the husband, the coefficients on the family-type indicators are small and insignificantly different from zero.

It is difficult to assess the implications of different types of cars purchased for inflation since we do not have much data on changes in car prices in the 1940s. The BLS Bulletin 966 includes price indexes for three car makes: Ford, Chevrolet, Plymouth. All of these makes are in the "low priced" category in Table 2.7—their average prices in the 1935–36 CEX were $700, $730, and $770, respectively. The BLS price indexes for each of these car makes rose at similar rates from 1939 to 1948—at 7.0, 5.7, and 6.6 percent, respectively. We don't know whether more expensive car makes might have undergone materially different price trends over the 1940s.

In summary, the biggest difference in car purchase patterns across socio-

31. The figure does not show car prices in 1949 for cars that are four to six years old because passenger cars were not produced during World War II.

32. For this analysis we use the full sample of 2,450 families since we want to have the largest possible sample size.

Table 2.7 **New car purchases by price of car make**

	$900 or less (Ford, Chevrolet, Plymouth, Terraplane, Pontiac)	$900 to $1,100 (Dodge, Oldsmobile)	More than $1,100 (Chrysler, Buick, Studebaker)
Education of husband			
≤8 years	79.2	13.2	7.5
9 to 11 years	79.5	13.6	6.8
12 years	64.8	20.4	14.8
13 to 15 years	58.8	29.4	11.8
≥16 years	57.3	20.0	22.7
Occupation			
Blue collar	80.4	13.7	5.9
White collar	64.1	19.9	16.0
Craft	74.1	18.5	7.4
Operative	86.7	6.7	6.7
Laborer	100	0	0
Service	8.75	12.5	0
Professional	59.1	19.1	21.7
Clerical	78.0	22.0	0.0
Household Income			
Bottom quintile	71.4	14.3	14.3
Second quintile	88.9	11.1	0
Middle quintile	87.9	9.1	3.0
Fourth quintile	76.7	16.7	6.7
Top quintile	49.5	25.3	25.3

economic groups (conditional on purchasing a car at all) appears to be whether the family chose to buy a new or used car. It seems likely that used car prices rose by more than new car prices, which would have boosted inflation for families with lower incomes and husbands with less education and in blue-collar occupations. If we assume that used car prices rose by 10 percent per year, which is likely an overestimate given the data on used car prices cited above and the assumption that auto quality increased over time, then our estimate of the difference in inflation between the lowest and highest income groups only decreases from 0.27 percentage point to 0.25 percentage point.

2.4.3 Shifts in Spending Patterns from 1935–36 to 1950

Our baseline results used spending patterns in 1935–36 to weight each category of spending. We have already shown that aggregate spending patterns were fairly similar in 1941 and 1950 as they were in 1935–36. However, these similarities might mask important shifts in spending patterns for particular socioeconomic groups. In this section we calculate spending shares by education of husband from the 1950 consumer spending survey to assess this possibility.

Table 2.8 Expenditure shares in 1950 by education of husband in 1950

	8 years or less	9 to 12 years	13 to 16 years	17 years or more	Price Change 1939–49 (annual rate)
Food	34.4	30.8	28.2	25.5	7.8
Housing	10.5	11.7	12.5	12.8	1.9
Utilities	4.8	3.8	3.3	3.2	3.3
Household operation	3.9	4.5	6.0	7.5	3.9
Furniture, furnishing, and equip.	6.4	7.0	7.2	8.4	6.4
Clothing	11.2	11.4	11.9	11.8	6.6
Automobile purchase	6.1	7.0	7.1	6.5	6.7
Automobile operation	4.5	5.5	5.3	5.0	4.0
Other transportation	2.0	1.7	1.7	1.7	3.3
Personal care	2.3	2.3	2.2	1.9	5.4
Medical care	5.3	5.2	5.1	4.9	3.7
Reading, recreation & education	5.3	6.0	6.5	7.6	5.2
Tobacco	2.0	1.8	1.4	1.1	3.9
Other	1.5	1.3	1.5	2.0	3.9
Headline inflation	5.73	5.63	5.55	5.47	—
using 1935–36 spending patterns	5.43	5.32	5.28	5.14	—

Note: Housing expenditures are rent for renters and the owner's expenditures for owners.

Table 2.8 reports expenditure shares by education of husband from the 1950 consumer spending survey. We draw these estimates from the tables published in the 1956 BLS report mentioned earlier.[33] Estimates are reported separately for nine combinations of city size and location, so we average across these categories using the number of families in each category as weights. It is important to note a few distinctions across surveys that may affect comparability. Unlike the 1935–36 CEX, which focused solely on families, the 1950 survey included single consumers as well as families with at least two people. Also, the report uses a slightly different set of education categories, as it combines those with 12 years of education with those with 9 to 11 years, and it includes those with 16 years of education with the 13 to 15 category rather than the 17+ category. The reported categories of spending are also slightly different from the ones that we used for our baseline results: electricity is included with other utilities, and expenses for automobile operation like insurance and maintenance are included with gasoline.[34]

Despite the slightly different categories of families and items, the patterns across groups are quite similar to those found in the 1935–36 survey. The item category with the largest difference across groups is still food, with a

33. Most estimates are from vol. 2, table 7. We supplement these estimates with detail on transportation expenditures from vol. 10, table 7.

34. We still use the price index for motor fuel for this category since the majority of expenses in this category will be gasoline.

9-percentage-point difference between the families with the most-educated husbands and the least-educated husbands. When we calculate expenditure shares in the 1935–36 survey using the same education categories as the 1950 survey, we find a difference in food expenditure shares across groups of 9.6 percentage points. One might have expected food expenditure shares to have risen more for less-educated families, since food price inflation was higher than average and food is a necessity, but this was not the case. The food expenditure share for families with 8 years or less increased by 1.8 percentage points from 1935–36 to 1950, while for those with 17 years or more it increased by 2.5 percentage points.

The last row of the table reports an estimate of headline inflation using the 1950 expenditure shares as weights. The results are quite similar to our baseline results using the 15 broad item categories, with inflation for the lowest education category being 0.26 percentage points higher than inflation for the highest education category. When we calculate inflation using these same education groups but expenditure shares from the 1935–36 survey, we find a difference of 0.29 percentage points.[35]

2.5 Conclusions

The 1940s were a unique period of significant narrowing in the wage distribution in America. It was also a decade of high inflation rates, yet the potential impact of unequal inflationary experiences on the distribution of income during this era has been unexplored so far.

In this chapter, we combine detailed data on expenditures by socioeconomic group with price changes by item category to estimate group-specific inflation rates from 1940 to 1950. We find that differences in spending patterns across groups were small for most item categories, leading to similar estimated inflation rates for all groups. The differences across groups ranged between 0.1 and 0.25 percentage points per year, only about 1/20th of the average inflation rate over this period. Differences across groups were also small relative to the large compression in wage inequality from 1940 to 1950 documented by Goldin and Margo (1992). We conclude that the compression in nominal wages documented by Goldin and Margo (1992) across the board—by education, income, and occupation—is essentially unchanged when one considers real wages.

Although our results are robust to various alternate assumptions and specifications, the sparseness of historical data is an impediment to measuring inflation inequality with as much specificity as research using modern data. These studies tend to find larger differences across groups when using price and expenditure data for very detailed item categories. Despite our

35. For this estimate we use the item categories from our baseline estimates.

efforts to include as much detailed data as available, it is still possible that our estimates may understate the true differences in inflation across groups.

Keeping these concerns in mind, it is also possible that the supply constraints imposed by the wartime economy on the variety of available goods and price controls may have served to limit differences in consumption patterns and inflationary experiences across groups. Whether our findings are specific to the war period, or more broadly representative of the early 20th-century economy is a remaining open question.

The variation in consumption patterns across groups may have also been limited by a narrower choice set of consumption goods in the early 20th century than it is today. Rising incomes, increasing returns to scale, and technological changes that allow for highly customized products may have contributed to increased product variety over time, by favoring innovation and entry for high-end products (Jaravel 2019; see Jaravel 2021 for a review of this literature). Thus, inflation may have a larger impact on the income distribution today than it did in the past. Assessing this possibility empirically is a promising avenue for future research.

Appendix

Table 2A.1 Housing expenditure shares in 1935–36 and 1950

	1935–36	1950
All Families	13.8	11.1
Renters	16.5	13.6
Owner-occupants	10.0	9.8
Counterfactual using 1950 homeownership rate	13.1	—
Homeownership rate	39.5	52.6

Note: The sample used to calculate the housing expenditure shares for renters and owners in 1950 includes single consumers in addition to families of at least two people. The homeownership rate of this sample is 48.7 percent and the aggregate housing expenditure share is 11.7 percent. The counterfactual housing expenditure share in 1935–36 is calculated as the average of housing expenditure shares for renters and owners, using the 1950 homeownership rate to weight each component.

Table 2A.2 Comparison of ICPSR Sample of 1935–36 CEX with 1940 census

	ICPSR sample	1940 census
Age		
Less than 30	13.9	14.6
30 to 39	33.0	28.0
40 to 49	27.4	27.1
50 to 59	16.3	19.6
60 or older	9.4	10.7
Education		
8 years or less	39.1	55.2
9 to 11 years	18.8	16.9
12 years	17.5	15.4
13 to 15 years	10.7	6.0
16 years or more	13.9	6.5
Occupation		
White collar	62.4	35.5
Blue collar	37.6	64.5
Professional and managerial	36.6	17.3
Clerical and sales	25.8	18.2
Craft	15.8	22.5
Operative	11.4	22.2
Laborer	3.3	11.0
Service	7.2	8.8
Housing tenure		
Homeowner	39.3	33.0
Renter	60.7	67.0
Race		
White	90.5	93.3
Black	9.5	6.7
Annual earnings of husband (1936 dollars)		
Mean	1678	1443
Median	1500	1296
City size		
Metropolis (pop. >2 million)	14.3	25.4
Large (pop. 100k–2 million)	41.8	50.6
Midsize (pop. 25k–100k)	35.7	4.5
Small (pop. 10k–25k)	8.1	19.4
Region and city		
New York City	3.3	17.8
Northeast region excl. New York City	13.3	20.4
Chicago	11.0	7.6
Midwest region excl. Chicago	14.7	26.5
South	24.2	16.3
West	33.5	11.4

Note: 1940 Census includes white and black male heads of household, married with spouse present, in cities with a population greater than 10,000 and with family earnings of at least $300. We could not find city size definitions used in the 1935–36 survey, so we guessed at the population cutoffs based on the city sizes in the sample and which category each city was assigned to. In the 1940 census, only cities with population greater than 25,000 are identified. Column 2 includes all of these cities plus families in urban areas with a population greater than 10,000.

Table 2A.3 **Distribution of income in full 1935–36 survey of consumer purchases compared with ICPSR's sample of this survey**

Income level	Number of families in urban communities	Percentage of families (calculated by authors)	Percentage of families in the full ICPSR sample	Percentage of families in the ICPSR sample used for analysis
Under $250	62	0.3	0.5	0.4
$250–$500	354	1.9	2.4	3.1
$500–$750	780	4.2	5.1	5.6
$750–$1,000	1,216	6.6	7.1	8.0
$1,000–$1,250	1,607	8.7	9.6	10.0
$1,250–$1,500	1,965	10.6	9.8	10.0
$1,500–$1,750	1,882	10.2	10.5	11.2
$1,750–$2,000	2,043	11.0	11.3	10.6
$2,000–$2,500	3,528	19.1	18.4	18.0
$2,500–$3,000	1,704	9.2	8.0	7.5
$3,000–$4,000	1,756	9.5	9.1	8.2
$4,000–$5,000	824	4.5	3.5	3.3
$5,000–$10,000	670	3.6	3.9	3.4
$10,000–$15,000	77	0.4	0.6	0.6
$15,000–$20,000	15	0.1	0.1	0.1
$20,000+	13	0.1	0.2	0.0

Source: Column 1, table 1B, section 3 of appendix B in "Consumer Expenditures in the United States, Estimates for 1935–36" by the National Resources Committee.

Table 2A.4 **Linkage of spending categories to price indexes**

Spending category	Price index name	Price index source
Food	Food	BLS website: CUUR0000SAF1
Housing	Rent of primary residence	BLS website: CUUR0000SEHA
Electricity	Electricity	BLS website: CUUR0000SEHF01
Other utilities	Fuel oil and other fuels	BLS website: CUUR0000SEHE
Household operation	Household operation, total	BLS report "Price Indexes for Selected Items and Groups" table 1
Furniture and furnishing	House furnishings	BLS report "Price Indexes for Selected Items and Groups" table 1
Clothing	Apparel	BLS website: CUUR0000SAA
Automobile purchase	New vehicles	BLS website: CUUR0000SETA01
Gasoline	Motor fuel	BLS website: CUUR0000SETB
Other transportation	Transportation services	BLS website: CUUR0000SAS4
Personal care	Personal care	BLS website: CUUR0000SAG1
Medical care	Medical care	BLS website: CUUR0000SAM
Reading and recreation	Reading and recreation	Handbook of Labor Statistics 1967, table 105
Tobacco	Tobacco and smoking products	BLS website: CUUR0000SEGA
Other	Other goods and services	Handbook of Labor Statistics 1967, table 105

Note: The price index for "other goods and services" excludes food, housing, apparel and upkeep, transportation, medical care, personal care and reading & recreation. The price index for "housefurnishings" includes textiles, floor coverings, furniture, bedding, appliances and miscellaneous household items like dinnerware, paper napkins, and electric lightbulbs.

Table 2A.5 Linkage of detailed item categories to price indexes and sources

Item category	Price index	Source
Food		
Beef steak round	Steak, round	1967 HLS
Pot roast chuck	Chuck roast	1967 HLS
Beef rib roast	Rib roast	1967 HLS
Veal cutlets	Veal cutlets	1967 HLS
Other beef and veal	Beef and veal	1967 HLS
Pork chops	Pork chops	1967 HLS
Whole ham	Whole ham	1967 HLS
Bacon	Bacon	1967 HLS
Other pork	Pork	1967 HLS
Other meat	Meats	1967 HLS
Poultry	Poultry	1967 HLS
Fresh fish	Fish, fresh or frozen	1967 HLS
Canned salmon and other fish, cured fish, canned seafood, other seafood	Fish (includes fresh or frozen fish, canned fish and frozen seafood)	1967 HLS
Eggs	Eggs	1967 HLS
Sugar, molasses, corn syrup, jellies, jams, preserves, candy, other sweets, chocolate, cocoa, packaged desserts	Sugar and sweets	1967 HLS
Butter	Butter	1967 HLS
Vegetable shortening	Margarine	1967 HLS
Salad and cooking oil, mayonnaise, cod liver oil, lard	Fats and Oils	1967 HLS
Apples	Apples	1967 HLS
Bananas	Bananas	1967 HLS
Oranges	Oranges	1967 HLS
Carrots	Carrots	1967 HLS
Lettuce	Lettuce	1967 HLS
Cabbage	Cabbage	1967 HLS
Potatoes, white and sweet	Potatoes	1967 HLS
Onions	Onions	1967 HLS
Other fresh fruit and vegetables	Fresh fruit and vegetables	1967 HLS
Dried beans: navy, lima, peas, lentils	Dried beans	1967 HLS
Canned peas	Canned green peas	1967 HLS
Canned tomatoes	Canned tomatoes	1967 HLS
Other processed fruit and vegetables	Processed fruit and vegetables	1967 HLS
Flour: white, graham, rye	Flour	1967 HLS
White bread	White bread	1967 HLS
Corn flakes	Corn flakes	1967 HLS
Other grain products	Cereals and bakery products	1967 HLS
Milk: whole (bottled and loose), buttermilk	Unweighted average of fresh grocery milk and fresh delivered milk	1967 HLS
Evaporated milk	Evaporated milk	1967 HLS
Cheese	Cheese	1967 HLS
Ice cream, cream, skimmed milk, dry milk, other milk	Dairy products	1967 HLS
Coffee	Coffee, can and bag	1967 HLS
Tea, fruit juice, soft drinks and other drinks	Nonalcoholic beverages	1967 HLS

(*continued*)

Table 2A.5 (cont.)

Item category	Price index	Source
Other food at home	Total food	BLS website
Food away from home	Total food	BLS website
Household operation		
Household help: cook, cleaner, laundress	Domestic services	PISIG
Laundry services	Laundry bundle services	PISIG
Telephone services	Residential telephone services	PISIG
Cleaning supplies	Cleanser and scouring powder	Bulletin 966
Other household operation	Household operation	PISIG
Furniture, furnishing and household equipment		
Household furnishing and equipment	Housefurnishings	PISIG
Furniture	Furniture	PISIG
Personal care		
Husband's personal care services	Men's haircuts	PISIG
Wife's personal care services	Beauty shop services	PISIG
Toothpaste	Toothpaste	PISIG
Shaving cream	Shaving cream	Bulletin 966
Toilet soap	Toilet soap	PISIG
Cold cream, powder, rouge, nail polish, perfume, brushes, combs, razors, files, other toilet articles	Toilet goods	PISIG
Other personal care	Personal care	PISIG
Medical care		
Physician office visits	General practitioners' fees, office visits	PISIG
Physician home visits	General practitioners' fees, house visits	PISIG
Dentist	Dentists' fees	PISIG
Medical specialists	Surgeons' and specialists' fees	PISIG
Optical: Oculist and glasses	Optical services	PISIG
Hospital room or bed	Hospital rates	PISIG
Private nurse in hospital	Hospital rates, private nurse	Bulletin 966
Medicines and drugs	Prescriptions and drugs	PISIG
Other medical expenses	Medical care, excluding drugs	PISIG
Recreation and reading		
Movies, adults	Motion picture admissions, adults	PISIG
Movies, children	Motion picture admissions, children	PISIG
Newspapers: daily and weekly	Newspapers	PISIG
Other recreation and reading	Reading and recreation	PISIG
Tobacco		
Cigarettes	Cigarettes	PISIG
Cigars	Cigars	PISIG
Other tobacco and smokers' supplies	Tobacco products	PISIG
Transportation		
Automobile purchase (new and used)	New automobiles	PISIG
Gasoline	Gasoline	PISIG
Motor oil	Motor oil	PISIG
Tires and tubes	Tires	PISIG
Auto repairs, replacement and service	Auto repairs	PISIG
Auto license and registration fees	Auto operations' licenses and fees	PISIG
Automobile insurance	Automobile insurance	PISIG

Table 2A.5 **(cont.)**

Item category	Price index	Source
Other auto-related (garage rent, parking, fines and damages, tolls, auto accessories, other auto)	Total transportation	PISIG
Bus, trolley, taxi, train, ferry boat, rent of automobile, interurban bus	Streetcar and bus fares	PISIG
Railroad fare, including Pullman	Railroad fares, coach	PISIG

Note: 1967 HLS is the 1967 *Handbook of Labor Statistics*, table 109. PISIG is the 1962 BLS Report "Price Indexes for Selected Items and Groups," table 1. Bulletin 966 is the BLS Bulletin 966, appendix tables F and G. All data were hand-collected by the authors. The price indexes reported in Bulletin 966 only cover 1939 to 1947, so we estimate the growth rate for 1939–49 using the growth rate of a broader category from 1939–49 and the ratio of the growth rate of the detailed category 1939–47 to the broader category 1939–47.

Table 2A.6 **Expenditure shares by income and occupation in 1935–36**

	Income quintile					Occupation	
	1st	2nd	3rd	4th	5th	Blue collar	White collar
Food	35.5	32.3	29.4	28.0	23.9	31.6	26.8
Housing	20.7	18.9	17.7	16.8	14.6	17.0	16.7
Electricity	2.1	2.1	2.0	1.9	1.5	1.9	1.8
Other utilities	6.7	5.2	4.4	4.0	2.9	4.8	3.9
Household operation	3.5	4.1	4.6	4.8	7.1	4.1	5.8
Furniture, furnishing, equip.	2.4	3.4	3.5	3.2	3.9	3.1	3.6
Clothing	8.2	9.3	9.3	10.3	11.7	9.5	10.6
Automobile purchase	2.7	3.7	6.0	7.3	7.3	5.3	6.4
Gasoline	2.0	2.6	3.3	3.3	3.3	2.7	3.2
Other transportation	2.6	3.1	3.5	3.9	4.4	3.3	3.9
Personal care	2.3	2.2	2.1	2.1	2.0	2.2	2.1
Medical care	4.4	4.7	4.5	4.5	4.9	4.9	4.6
Reading & recreation	4.0	5.0	5.6	5.9	7.4	5.5	6.3
Tobacco	2.0	2.0	1.9	1.8	1.5	2.1	1.7
Other	1.1	1.4	2.1	2.2	3.6	2.0	2.6

Note: Housing expenditures are rent for renters and the owner's estimate of rent for owners. Other expenditures include education and occupation-related expenses. Income quintiles are defined over the distribution of households in the ICPSR 1935–36 data.

Table 2A.7 **Distribution of families by region and income and implications for inflation**

	Income quintile					Rent growth, 1940–49
	1st	2nd	3rd	4th	5th	
New York City	18.0	16.2	17.1	18.0	20.0	1.03
Northeast Region excl. NYC	20.2	21.6	22.4	20.0	17.9	2.04
Chicago	6.5	7.0	8.0	7.9	8.7	2.98
Midwest Region excl. Chicago	23.3	25.4	29.3	28.8	25.3	2.36
South	22.0	20.3	12.0	12.8	14.6	2.65
West	10.1	9.6	11.2	12.5	13.6	2.75
Shelter component of inflation						
Using aggregate rent growth	0.57	0.47	0.44	0.41	0.35	—
Using regional rent growth	0.56	0.45	0.43	0.40	0.35	—

Table 2A.8 **Aggregate Expenditure Shares during the 1940s**

	1935–36	1941	1944	1945	1946	1947	1948	1950
Food	29.3	30.9	35.9	34.8	34.5	32.7	30.4	31.1
Housing, fuel, light & refrigeration	20.2	18.7	17.5	15.7	15.5	16.5	14.9	15.1
Household operation	5.5	5.3	5.3	6.0	4.5	5.5	5.0	4.7
Furnishing and equipment	3.6	5.0	3.3	4.5	5.2	5.9	7.1	7.1
Clothing	10.6	12.0	16.0	15.6	16.2	14.7	13.6	11.5
Automobile	12.0	9.6	3.9	4.7	6.3	7.0	10.2	12.1
Other transportation	1.3	2.4	2.4	2.2	1.9	2.1	1.8	1.7
Medical care	4.8	4.7	5.5	6.1	4.7	5.0	5.7	5.2
Personal care	2.2	2.2	2.4	2.5	2.4	2.4	2.3	2.2
Recreation	5.2	4.4	2.8	2.9	3.9	4.1	4.5	4.5
Reading	1.0	1.0	1.1	1.1	0.9	0.9	0.9	0.9
Education	1.1	0.9	0.6	0.7	0.6	0.5	0.6	0.6
Tobacco	1.8	2.1	2.0	1.7	1.9	1.7	1.7	1.8
Other	1.4	0.8	1.3	1.6	1.5	1.0	1.4	1.5

Note: Spending shares in 1941 and 1944 are from "Consumer spending in World War II: the forgotten consumer expenditure surveys," *Monthly Labor Review* August 2015. Spending shares in 1945 to 1948 are author calculations from the Handbook of Labor Statistics 1950 table D7. The 1945–48 surveys covered three cities in each year. We take an unweighted average of spending in each city.

References

Argente, David, and Munseob Lee. 2021. "Cost of Living Inequality During the Great Recession." *Journal of the European Economic Association* 19 (2): 913–52.

Atkinson, Anthony B., Thomas Piketty, and Emmanuel Saez. 2011. "Top Incomes in the Long Run of History." *Journal of Economic Literature* 49 (1): 3–71.

Cage, Robert A., Thesia I. Garner, and Javier Ruiz-Castillo. 2002. "Constructing Household Specific Consumer Price Indexes: An Analysis of Different Techniques and Methods." Working Paper 354. Bureau of Labor Statistics.

Chancel, Lucas, and Thomas Piketty. 2021. "Global Income Inequality, 1820–2020: The Persistence and Mutation of Extreme Inequality." *Journal of the European Economic Association* 19 (6): 3025–62.

Collins, William J., and Gregory T. Niemesh. 2019. "Unions and the Great Compression of Wage Inequality in the US at Mid-century: Evidence from Local Labour Markets." *Economic History Review* 72 (2): 691–715.

Costa, Dora. L. 1999. "American Living Standards: Evidence from Recreational Expenditures." NBER Working Paper No. 7148. National Bureau of Economic Research.

Fetter, Daniel K. 2016. "The Home Front: Rent Control and the Rapid Wartime Increase in Home Ownership." *Journal of Economic History* 76 (4): 1001–43.

Frydman, Carola, and Raven Molloy. 2012. "Pay Cuts for the Boss: Executive Compensation in the 1940s." *Journal of Economic History* 72 (1): 225–51.

Garner, Thesia I., David S. Johnson, and Mary F. Kokoski. 1996. "An Experimental Consumer Price Index for the Poor." *Monthly Labor Review* (September): 32–42.

Goldin, Claudia, and Lawrence F. Katz. 2007. "Long-Run Changes in the U.S. Wage Structure: Narrowing, Widening, Polarizing." Brookings Papers on Economic Activity No. 2. Brookings Institution.

Goldin, Claudia, and Robert A. Margo. 1992. "The Great Compression: The Wage Structure in the United States at Mid-Century." *Quarterly Journal of Economics* 107 (1): 1–34.

Hagemann, Robert P. 1982. "The Variability of Inflation Rates Across Household Types." *Journal of Money, Credit and Banking* 14 (1): 494–510.

Higgs, Robert. 1999. "From Central Planning to the Market: The American Transition, 1945–1947." *Journal of Economic History* 59 (3): 600–23.

Hobijn, Bart, and David Lagakos. 2005. "Inflation Inequality in the United States." *Review of Income and Wealth* 51 (4): 581–606.

Jacobs, Eva, and Stephanie Shipp. 1990. "How Family Spending Has Changed in the U.S." *Monthly Labor Review* (March): 20–27.

Jaravel, Xavier. 2019. "The Unequal Gains from Product Innovations: Evidence from the U.S. Retail Sector." *Quarterly Journal of Economics* 134 (2): 715–83.

Jaravel, Xavier. 2021. "Inflation Inequality: Measurement, Causes, and Policy Implications." *Annual Review of Economics* 13 (1): 599–629.

Jaravel, Xavier, and Danial Lashkari. 2024. "Measuring Growth in Consumer Welfare with Income-Dependent Preferences: Nonparametric Methods and Estimates for the United States." *Quarterly Journal of Economics* 139 (1): 477–532.

Jaworski, Taylor, and Gregory T. Niemesh. 2018. "Revisiting the Great Compression: Wage Inequality in the United States, 1940–1960." *Historical Methods: A Journal of Quantitative and Interdisciplinary History* 51 (1): 39–48.

Kaplan, Greg, and Sam Schulhofer-Wohl. 2017. "Inflation at the Household Level." *Journal of Monetary Economics* 91: 19–38.

Klick, Josh, and Anya Stockburger. 2021. "Experimental CPI for Lower and Higher Income Households." Working Paper 537. Bureau of Labor Statistics.

Margo, Robert A. 1995. "Explaining Black-White Wage Convergence, 1940–1950." *ILR Review* 48 (3): 470–81.

Margo, Robert A., and T. Aldrich Finegan. 2002. "The Great Compression of the 1940s: The Public versus the Private Sector." *Explorations in Economic History* 39 (2): 183–203.

McGranahan, Leslie, and Anna Paulson. 2006. "Constructing the Chicago Fed Income Based Economic Index—Consumer Price Index: Inflation Experiences by Demographic Group: 1983–2005." Working Paper 2005–20. Federal Reserve Bank of Chicago.

Michael, Robert T. 1979. "Variation Across Households in the Rate of Inflation." *Journal of Money, Credit and Banking* 11 (1): 32–46.
Moretti, Enrico. 2013."Real Wage Inequality." *American Economic Journal: Applied Economics* 5 (1): 65–103.
National Resources Committee. 1939. *Consumer Expenditures in the United States Estimates for 1935–36*. Government Printing Office.
Orchard, Jacob. 2022. "Cyclical Demand Shifts and Cost of Living Inequality." Working Paper.
Piketty, Thomas, and Emmanuel Saez. 2003. "Income Inequality in the United States, 1913–1998." *Quarterly Journal of Economics* 118 (1): 1–41.
Rockoff, Hugh. 1984. *Drastic Measures: A History of Wage and Price Controls in the United States*. Studies in Economic History and Policy: The United States in the Twentieth Century. Cambridge University Press.
US Department of Labor, Bureau of Labor Statistics, Cost of Living Division; US Department of Agriculture, Bureau of Home Economics, Economics Division; US National Resources Committee, Consumption Research Staff, Industrial Section; US Central Statistical Board; and US Works Progress Administration. *Study of Consumer Purchases in the United States, 1935–1936*. Inter-University Consortium for Political and Social Research. https://doi.org/10.3886/ICPSR08908.v3.
Williamson, Jeffrey G. 1977. "'Strategic' Wage Goods, Prices, and Inequality." *American Economic Review* 67 (2): 29–41.

II

Measuring Inequality in Well-Being

3

Income Gains and the Geography of the US Homeownership Boom, 1940–1960

William J. Collins and Gregory T. Niemesh

3.1 Introduction

Between 1940 and 1960, workers' earnings surged in the United States, with median annual real wage and salary income nearly doubling and with widespread gains across the age and income distributions.[1] Over the same decades, there was an unprecedented rise in the rate of homeownership, by more than 20 percentage points, by far the largest gains of the 20th century. The coincidence of these changes is clear and readily observed in aggregate data, and extensive bodies of literature in economics study each trend. But empirical evidence on the strength of the causal link running from changes in income to changes in homeownership is thin relative to the importance of this era in shaping the trajectory and geography of American economic development.

William J. Collins is the Terence E. Adderley Jr. Chair and Professor of Economics and a professor of history (by courtesy) at Vanderbilt University, and a research associate and codirector of the Development of the American Economy Program at the National Bureau of Economic Research.

Gregory T. Niemesh is an associate professor of economics at Miami University and a research associate of the National Bureau of Economic Research.

This chapter benefited from participants' feedback at the NBER conference on Historical Labor Markets and Inequality (March 2023), especially Richard Baker's comments as the paper's discussant. The authors also acknowledge helpful input from participants in Vanderbilt's Economic History seminar and from conversations and correspondence with Jeremy Atack, Dan Fetter, Bob Margo, Sarah Quincy, and Ken Snowden. For acknowledgments, sources of research support, and disclosure of the authors' material financial relationships, if any, please see https://www.nber.org/books-and-chapters/economic-history-american-inequality-new-evidence-and-perspectives/income-gains-and-geography-us-home-ownership-boom-1940-1960.

1. The sample is restricted to men who worked at least 17 weeks in the prior year, who reported being wage and salary workers, and who earned wage and salary income of more than $100 in 1939 dollars (Ruggles et al. 2021, 2023).

In this chapter, we focus on the hypothesis that the widespread and sustained increase in the level of income allowed more people to afford and select into owner-occupied housing than in previous generations. In doing so, we turn our attention from the causes of midcentury income changes, a focus of much prior research, to one potentially important ramification—the boom in homeownership. Many things happened between 1940 and 1960 that could confound efforts to measure the strength of the connection between the era's income and homeownership gains. We take advantage of the fact that although gains in income and ownership were widely shared, they were not evenly spread over space. Differential changes in income and ownership across localities are the basis of our ordinary least squares (OLS) and IV measurement strategies.

We find that at the local level—defined by groups of adjacent and similar counties—the rise in homeownership was strongly correlated with changes in income. This relationship is evident and similar in magnitude even when conditioning on a rich set of prewar local characteristics, regional trends, and wartime shocks.[2] Between 1940 and 1960, a 10 log-point difference in the increase in average real wages for nonfarm male workers was associated with a 2- to 3-percentage-point difference in homeownership gains. Although we are cautious about adopting a strongly causal interpretation of the OLS coefficient estimates, this approach can account for many potential confounders, and we test the robustness of the baseline results at length. If taken at face value, the OLS estimates would attribute approximately half the gains in ownership from 1940 to 1960 to gains in income.

It appears that the baseline results are not driven by the sorting of households by income across localities, given that adding ("bad") controls for post-1940 changes in population characteristics does not greatly alter the key point estimate. Moreover, we conclude that the results are not attributable to geographic variation in shocks from the wartime economy because the estimated coefficient of interest is similar whether or not the regression includes the value of wartime contracts per capita, controls for local age structure in 1940 (a proxy for draft-eligible men), and state-level military mobilization rates. Although the baseline results are robust from many perspectives when using the full national sample, we do find some evidence of heterogeneity when we split the sample by region and locality size, with larger point estimates in larger localities (above the 75th percentile) and in the Northeast, especially relative to the West.

To complement the OLS results, we develop an instrumental variable approach following Borusyak et al. (2022). This relies on a shift-share instrument that interacts 1940 shares of local workers at each percentile of the

2. We focus on men's earnings here because changes in women's labor force participation between 1940 and 1960 may complicate the interpretation of changes in observed wages at the local level. We do not focus on household income because household formation is endogenous to changes in labor and housing markets.

national wage distribution and post-1940 changes in wages at each percentile. This approach yields smaller but still strongly positive coefficient estimates linking income and homeownership gains, such that about one-third of the ownership gains would be attributed to changes in income.

Our findings contribute to several strands of literature. Studies of mid-century changes in wages tend to focus on uncovering the sources of the decline in income inequality.[3] Studies of the homeownership boom, on the other hand, tend to focus on changes in mortgage markets, including the expanding use of long-term self-amortizing mortgages and the GI Bill's support for World War II and Korean War veterans (see, e.g., Chambers et al. 2014; Fetter 2013; Grebler et al. 1956; Klaman 1961; Saulnier et al. 1958;). The likely importance of rising income is widely acknowledged in this literature, but consideration of the effects of income gains tends to fall into the background as institutional change and policy interventions take center stage. Our findings clarify the connection between post-1940 labor market gains, a period of widely shared and rapid improvements, and the unprecedented surge in homeownership. In characterizing the potential connection, Fetter (2014, 344) emphasizes the dearth of research "that attempts to isolate quasi-experimental variation in income for the purpose of estimating its causal relationship with homeownership at either the beginning or end of the period." We attempt to develop evidence in that direction, and in doing so, bring the role of income gains back into the forefront of discussions of the American homeownership boom.

The findings also provide a partial view of changes in the composition of Americans' wealth. Homeownership is one of the few census variables that provides a long-run view of a major component of wealth in nationally representative samples (Collins and Margo 2001, 2003). Throughout the 20th century, equity in housing has been the most important component of the median household's wealth. In 1960, in the Survey of Consumer Finances sample (University of Michigan, ICPSR 7440), relatively few households owned stocks or savings bonds, but most had at least some home equity. Home equity, in turn, reflects the ownership rate, the value of what is owned conditional on being an owner, and the debt-equity ratio. In this chapter, we focus on the first component, and specifically on how large changes in income supported large gains in ownership—the first step in building home equity—during the post-Depression decades.

This chapter is also closely related to the economic history of suburbanization (Baum-Snow 2007; Boustan and Margo 2013; Jackson 1985, Margo 1992). Much of the new, post-1940 owner-occupied housing came in the form of single-family housing units that were located outside of central

3. Contributing factors include wartime labor market conditions and wage setting polices, the shifting supply of well-educated workers, and labor market institutions such as the rise of unions. See Miller (1958), Goldin and Margo (1992), Juhn (1999), Goldin and Katz (2008), Jaworski and Niemesh (2018), Collins and Niemesh (2019), and Collins and Callaway (2018).

cities. Our main analysis is conducted using broad geographic areas as the units of analysis (groups of counties), with the idea of capturing spillovers within localities and avoiding results driven largely by city-to-suburb sorting by higher-income households.[4] Nonetheless, new housing in suburban areas was, in practice, an important mechanism through which ownership gains occurred. In turn, suburbanization shaped American economic geography, culture, and politics in profound ways. From this perspective, homeownership per se is just one of many potential ramifications of the midcentury change in income and its distribution.[5] We encourage additional explorations of how midcentury labor market gains translated into other forms of social and economic change.

3.2 Background and Context

3.2.1 Changes in Wages and Homeownership, 1940–1960

We begin by establishing some important facts about changes in earned income in the mid-20th century. As in previous studies in this literature, we are somewhat constrained by the available data. The 1940 census of population was the first to inquire about wage and salary income in the previous year, but it omitted self-employment income. For comparability, we focus on the wage and salary component of earnings in both the 1940 and 1960 censuses, restricting the samples to men, ages 18 to 64, who reported being wage and salary workers at the time of the census. We omit 1950 because that year's microdata sample does not report homeownership status, which limits its usefulness in our analyses.

Figure 3.1 plots the distributions of real weekly wages reported in the 1940 and 1960 censuses, for samples of nonfarm men.[6] The strong rightward shift is obvious, with median wages rising from $23.53 to $46.72. In a longer time series, which pertains to manufacturing workers, the real weekly wage gains from 1940 to 1960 stand out as historically large, much larger than the gains registered over the 20-year spans from 1920 to 1940 or from 1960 to 1980.[7]

4. The 1960 census microdata do not reveal suburban status for a large number of observations, and so our place-based regression analysis does not attempt to parse out this distinction.

5. For instance, income gains may be connected to the baby boom (Easterlin 1961), and it is plausible that economic prosperity and lower inequality influenced American politics and policymaking.

6. The 1940 and 1960 censuses inquired about income in the previous calendar year, referencing 1939 and 1959. We focus on men because their consistently high rates of labor force participation throughout this period makes interpreting their earnings more straightforward, albeit with the caveat about missing self-employed workers who might be differentially selected over time. We do not focus on household income because household formation is endogenous to changes in labor and housing markets.

7. These calculations are based on data from Margo (2006, series Ba4362) for nominal wages and Lindert (2006, series Cc1) for a consumer price index. The ratio of real earnings in 1960 vs. 1940 is 1.7, whereas the ratios for 1940 vs. 1920 and 1980 vs. 1960 are 1.37 and 1.16, respectively.

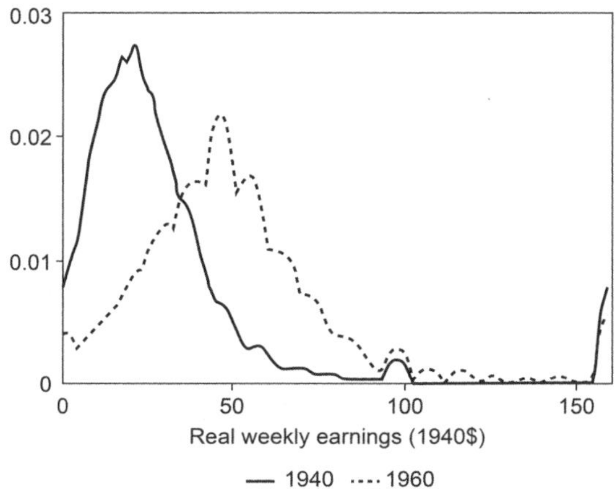

Figure 3.1 Change in real earnings distribution between 1940 and 1960

Note: The earnings sample includes men not residing or working on a farm and reporting wage and salary employment in the reference week, age 18 to 64 years who reported positive wage and salary income in the year prior to the census, worked more than 39 weeks, and earned more than half the minimum wage at a full-time basis (weekly wages of $6 in 1940 and $9.52 in 1960). Earnings in 1960 are deflated using the CPI.

Source: Earnings data from decennial census microdata provided Ruggles et al. (2021) and Ruggles et al. (2023), Integrated public use microdata series, 1940 complete count (100 percent), and 1960 5 percent sample.

Figure 3.2, which is also based on samples of microdata from the 1940 and 1960 censuses, shows that these wage gains were widely shared. All regions experienced sizable increases in wages, as did all education groups, racial categories, and broad occupational groups. At the same time, inequality fell in what Goldin and Margo (1992) termed the "Great Compression." This narrowing is reflected in figure 3.2 in the relatively large gains that accrued to laborers, southern residents, and nonwhite workers.

Figure 3.3 graphs the changes in real earnings relative to age. The key insight from this figure is that income gains after 1940 were large throughout the age distribution. This is important because the literature on midcentury ownership gains emphasizes the sizable increase in ownership for younger households, especially in their 30s. This is often presented as evidence that changes in mortgage markets facilitated access to credit early in the life cycle, and we agree that such innovations must be an important part of the story. But the pattern is also consistent with changes in young men's income having a direct effect on demand for owner-occupied housing and, thus, for the financial instruments that enabled their increased ownership.

Figure 3.4 shows that the midcentury surge in real income was accompanied by an unprecedented jump in homeownership rates (Collins and Margo 2001, 2011). We present ownership series for all men (18–64), male heads of household, and all heads of household including women (Ruggles et al.

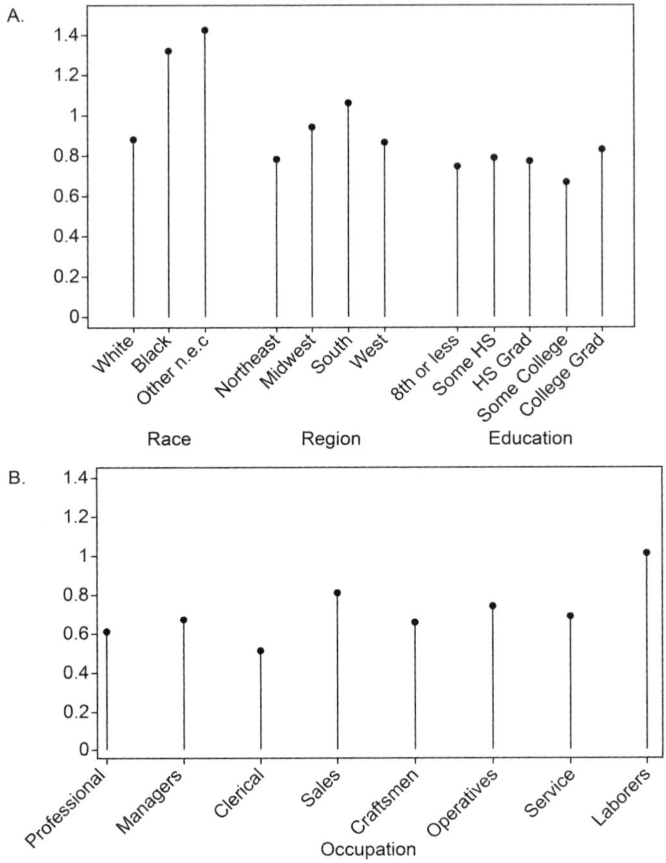

Figure 3.2 Percentage gains in real wages between 1940 and 1960 by groups

Note: Graphs show the percentage gains (1 = 100 percent) in real weekly earnings. The earnings sample includes men not residing or working on a farm and reporting wage and salary employment in the reference week, age 18 to 64 years who reported positive wage and salary income in the year prior to the census, worked more than 39 weeks, and earned more than half the minimum wage at a full-time basis (weekly wages of $6 in 1940 and $9.52 in 1960). Earnings in 1960 are deflated using the CPI.

Source: Earnings data from decennial census microdata provided Ruggles et al. (2021) and Ruggles et al. (2023), Integrated public use microdata series, 1940 complete count (100 percent), and 1960 5 percent sample.

2023). We code an observation as "owner" if he was recorded as the head of household and resided in owner-occupied housing.[8] Prior to 1960, the series for all household heads is nearly identical to the series for male household

8. There is some room for error here in that census data do not record exactly who owns the home. We assume that the head and/or spouse do.

C.

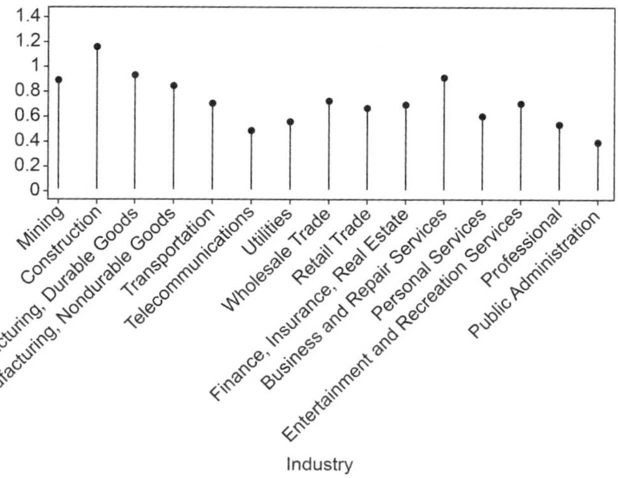

Figure 3.2 (cont.)

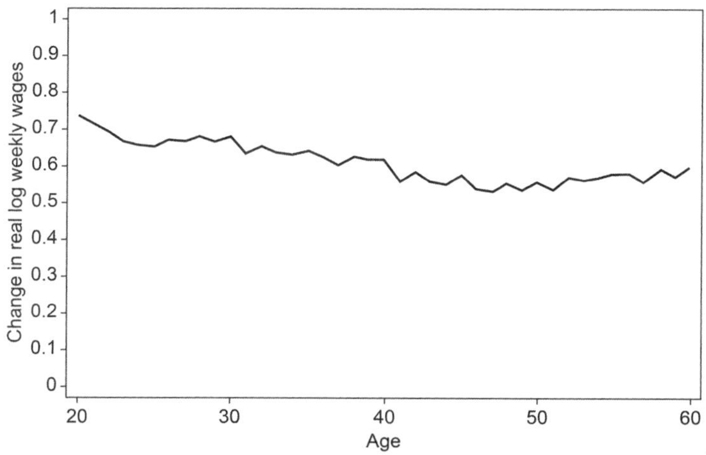

Figure 3.3 Changes in real earnings relative to age

Note: The earnings sample includes men not residing or working on a farm and reporting wage and salary employment in the reference week, age 18 to 64 years who reported positive wage and salary income in the year prior to the census, worked more than 39 weeks, and earned more than half the minimum wage at a full-time basis (weekly wages of $6 in 1940 and $9.52 in 1960). Earnings in 1960 are deflated using the CPI.

Source: Earnings data from decennial census microdata provided Ruggles et al. (2021) and Ruggles et al. (2023), Integrated public use microdata series, 1940 complete count (100 percent), and 1960 5 percent sample.

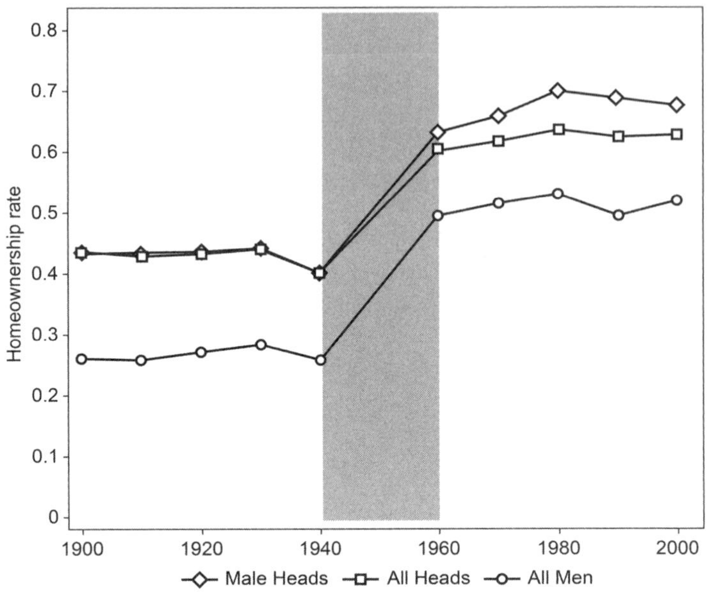

Figure 3.4 National homeownership rates, 1900–2000

Note: The sample for "All men" includes men age 18 to 64; "Male heads" includes only male household heads (18–64); "All heads" includes female heads, as well. We define homeownership if the head or spouse of the head reports residing in owner-occupied housing. Adult-male non-household heads are recorded as renting.

Source: 1900 through 2000 IPUMS 1 percent census samples provided by Ruggles et al. (2023).

heads.[9] The series for "all men" is of particular interest because many adult men did not form independent households—some lived with parents or other family members, others as boarders or in group quarters. This shift of perspective is important, as the ownership rate for all men is at least 10 percentage points lower than for the series for all heads or male heads.[10]

The aggregate homeownership rates depicted in figure 3.4 were flat from the turn of the 20th century to 1930, before dipping slightly during the Great Depression. The sudden and sustained increase in the 1940s and 1950s—by more than 20 percentage points for all heads and by even more for all men—is striking in retrospect. As with income, large increases in ownership occurred in all regions and for all racial groups. Ownership gains were espe-

9. Census enumerators recorded men as household heads in the majority of cases up to 1960 (nearly 90 percent of heads ages 18–64 years old). Among female heads up to 1960, a large share were widows, who were more likely to own homes than other female heads. Before 1970, enumerators were instructed to list men as the heads of married households: https://usa.ipums.org/usa-action/variables/RELATE#comparability_section.

10. This gap is somewhat smaller if the sample is restricted to the 25–64 age range, but it is still large (e.g., slightly under 10 percentage points in 1940 and 1960).

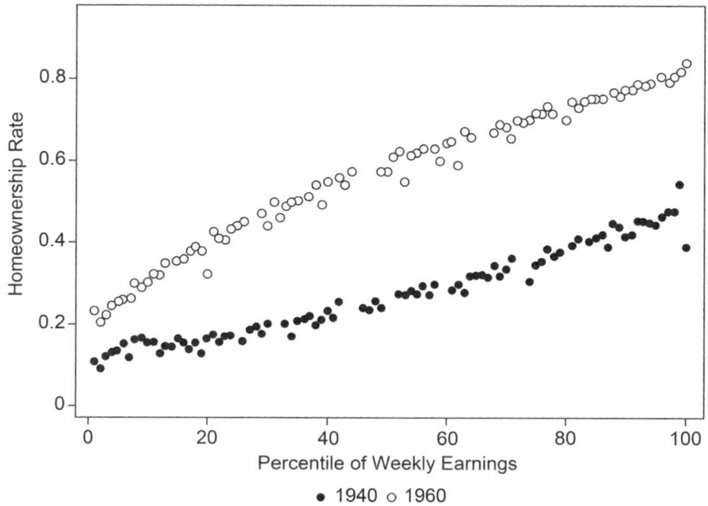

Figure 3.5 Ownership gains throughout the income distribution, 1940–1960
Note: The sample includes men not residing or working on a farm and reporting wage and salary employment in the reference week, age 18 to 64 years who reported positive wage and salary income in the year prior to the census, worked more than 39 weeks, and earned more than half the minimum wage at a full-time basis (weekly wages of $6 in 1940 and $9.52 in 1960).

Source: Earnings data from decennial census microdata provided Ruggles et al. (2021) and Ruggles et al. (2023), Integrated public use microdata series, 1940 complete count (100 percent), and 1960 5 percent sample.

cially pronounced among younger households, who entered homeownership earlier in the life cycle than in the previous generation (Fetter 2014). Not only did most American household heads reside in owner-occupied housing in 1960 for the first time since at least 1870, but the lion's share of the entire increase in homeownership that occurred in the 20th century happened between 1940 and 1960.[11]

Finally, figure 3.5 shows that the increase in homeownership between 1940 and 1960 was spread throughout the income distribution. Gains were smaller at the bottom than at the middle and top of the income distribution, but they were sizable by historical standards throughout the distribution.

We acknowledge that our reliance on census data limits our ability to distinguish between the wartime and postwar periods. By spanning 1940 to 1960, our analyses combine periods with quite different labor and housing market conditions. During the war, labor markets were tight and wages increased, but housing construction was limited due to the resource demands

11. The 1870 census reports the value of real estate wealth. In the 1870 1 percent IPUMS sample, assigning "ownership" status to all household heads in with greater than zero real property yields an ownership rate of about 48 percent.

for supporting the war effort. That said, it is likely that income gains and savings accrued during the war carried over into strong demand for new, owner-occupied housing when residential construction resumed in earnest after the war.[12] Thus, combining the war and postwar periods, as we do in this chapter, may obscure the timing of change and distinctions between the periods, but may capture empirical connections that could be missed by analyzing the periods as separate eras.

3.2.2 Income and Tenure Decisions in Midcentury Context

The cross-sectional correlation of income and nonfarm homeownership is strongly positive in the United States, and it has been so for a long time. This is difficult to see directly in pre-1940 data due to the lack of nationally representative income data, but in 1920, for instance, a linear regression of homeownership on occupational status (*occscore*) for white men, ages 18–64, who did not live on a farm or hold an agricultural occupation reveals a strongly positive relationship. A 10 log-point increase in *occscore* (roughly 1 standard deviation) was associated with a 5-percentage-point increase in ownership.[13] Comparable regressions reveal similar (1940) or somewhat stronger (1960) positive relationships in later years.

Although these cross-sectional patterns are clear in the data, it is not self-evident from a theoretical perspective that households with higher income would be more likely than others to choose to own their home rather than rent it. In a life cycle context, homeownership typically occurs after leaving the parents' home and acquiring enough savings to purchase a home outright or, more likely, to provide a down payment in conjunction with a mortgage to be paid out of future earnings.[14] Higher and more stable income makes it more feasible to establish an independent household, accumulate savings, qualify for credit, and acquire property ownership if so desired.[15] An optimally diversified asset portfolio may include real estate. It is, however, possible to invest in real estate without living in one's own property. This additional step—choosing to live inside one's own property and "rent to oneself"—may reflect principal–agent considerations, as described by Henderson and Ioannides (1983) and Glaeser and Shapiro (2003). Because

12. See Fetter (2016) for an examination of wartime increases in ownership driven by conversions from rental to owner-occupied units. See Brunet (2019) on how wartime savings may have led to postwar housing investment.

13. The sample is restricted to men who are in the labor force and have occupation scores above zero. The correlation is strong for Black men too, but the IPUMS *occscore* variable is not a good proxy for Black men's earnings within occupations. *Occscore* is an IPUMS variable that is available for all years and that is derived from the 1950 census; its value equals the median annual income of workers holding a particular occupation.

14. Inheritance would be another channel and would not require the accumulation of savings.

15. Along these lines, Grebler et al. point out that "the number of social units who may demand separate dwelling space is not solely a function of the distribution by age and marital status of the population but is also a function of prevailing economic conditions and social attitudes" (1956, 80).

renters are less likely to care for a property conscientiously and do not internalize the full costs of utilization and "wear and tear," owners might find it advantageous to live in the property themselves. Other potential motivations for ownership might come from "pride of ownership," a form of consumption that is more readily indulged at higher income levels, or perhaps tax incentives associated with itemized deductions of mortgage interest and the treatment of capital gains (Aaron 1972; Fetter 2013, app. 2; Poterba 1992; Rosen and Rosen 1980).

The connection between income and ownership is mediated by housing markets, which on the supply side include builders, financial institutions, and government agencies. The context within which housing markets functioned changed over time, especially in the wake of the Great Depression (Fishback et al. 2013; Klaman 1961). Starting in the 1930s, the federal government influenced nonfarm mortgage markets through agencies such as the Home Owners Loan Corporation (HOLC) and Federal Housing Administration (FHA), the first of which refinanced distressed mortgages during the Depression and the second of which began insuring mortgages.[16] Mortgages that entailed longer-term, self-amortizing loans and low down payments became more prevalent, even in the "conventional" (uninsured) segment of the market (Grebler et al. 1956, 257–60; Rose and Snowden 2013). In the postwar period, Veterans Administration (VA) loans provided even more generous terms to large cohorts of veterans (Fetter 2013).

Another consequence, and indeed a primary goal, of the FHA is that builders were encouraged to undertake new construction projects, often at large scale (Saulnier et al. 1958, 336–48).[17] This may have increased the elasticity of housing supply and lowered costs for home buyers relative to a counterfactual without federal involvement. Among other channels, Saulnier et al. emphasize that, "by giving the builder assurance that the mortgages he generates will (provided all standards of construction, land use, credit, etc. are satisfied) be insured, and thus virtually guaranteeing the financing . . . this system encourages the planning and construction of very large developments" (1958, 348). Since many new developments were located outside city centers, there is likely a strong connection between these institutional changes and the pace and extent of suburban growth. In addition, Grebler et al. claim, "The automobile . . . has been the main initiator of the recent era of suburban sprawl with its emphasis on the single family house" (1956, 8), implying that exogenous changes in transportation technology and endogenous changes in car ownership and road construction likely reinforced the shift toward the construction of a type of hous-

16. Snowden (2014) reviews the NBER's extensive research program on residential capital formation in this period, including major contributions such as Harriss (1951), Grebler et al. (1956), Klaman (1961), Saulnier et al. (1958), and several others.

17. We thank Ken Snowden for pointing this out in conversation.

ing—single-family detached—that has typically been owner occupied in the United States.

The influence of the federal policies mentioned here is commonly at the forefront of discussions of the rise in homeownership after 1940, which is understandable since they were direct manifestations of specific policy decisions. However, contemporaries understood that such policy effects are not easily separated from the effects of rising income. As Grebler (1953, 20) observed: "It would be rash to assume that all the new construction financed by FHA and VA loans represents additional volume that would not have been produced without those aids . . . for the two facilities operated largely in a period of rising or high incomes conducive to an expanding demand for new residential construction. It would be equally rash to deduce that these programs had no influence on the volume of residential construction." As Fetter (2014) emphasizes, income gains and changes in access to credit were likely complementary in this period. Higher income not only increased demand for housing directly, perhaps especially for owner occupancy, but also increased the likelihood of qualifying for credit in an era where lower down payments entailed higher loan-to-value ratios.

3.2.3 The Housing Stock in 1960

How did the housing stock evolve in the wake of the income and institutional changes discussed above? New housing unit starts had fallen to historic lows during the Great Depression before recovering in the later 1930s and then plunging again during World War II (National Bureau of Economic Research, macrohistory database). The postwar years entailed a much more robust era of home building, and of course this timing coincided with the homeownership boom we study in this chapter.[18]

The 1960 census microdata are particularly helpful in seeing the midcentury housing stock because for each household it includes information on tenure status, location, and the building's age (Ruggles et al. 2023). Table 3.1 splits all households into one of four groups depending on tenure (own or rent) and the age of the housing unit (built before 1940 or later). A large share of the owner-occupied housing stock in 1960 was relatively new. Among home-owning households in 1960, approximately 50 percent resided in units that had been built since 1940 (i.e., of the 62 percent of heads who owned homes, half were in units built since 1940). Among renters, the share in new housing units was much lower, at approximately 29 percent. Focusing on the newer housing, units built after 1940 were disproportionately owner occupied, such that 73 percent of all households residing in newer units were owners (31 of 42).

18. In addition, Fetter (2016) shows that many housing units were converted from rental to owner-occupancy during World War II. These conversions occurred inside the scope of our 1940 to 1960 investigation, and they will be reflected in observed homeownership levels, but they cannot be separately identified in our analysis.

Table 3.1 **Age of housing stock and tenure in 1960**

	Rent	Own	Total
Old stock	14,210,660	16,312,220	30,522,880
	26.9	30.9	57.8
New stock	5,941,440	16,382,580	22,324,020
	11.2	31.0	42.2
Total	20,152,100	32,694,800	52,846,900
	38.1	61.9	100.0

Note: "Old stock" refers to housing units built before 1940. "New stock" was built in 1940 or later. This is based on the IPUMS variable "builtyr." The sample includes all household heads and omits group quarters. Interior cells with percentages show the distribution of households over four tenure and housing unit age cells and sum to 100. Household weights are used.

Source: 1960 5 percent IPUMS sample (Ruggles et al. 2023).

An important and related trend is that much, though certainly not all, of the new building took place in suburban and nonmetro areas where ownership rates were high. Among households identified as residing in central cities in 1960, the overall ownership rate was only 43 percent, and only 15 percent of all central-city households owned new housing units.[19] For those identified as residing in metro areas but not central cities (henceforth "suburbs"), the ownership rate was 72 percent, and 45 percent of all suburban households owned new housing units. Although much of the housing literature on this era is centered on metropolitan areas, it is important to acknowledge that a large share of the housing stock at midcentury was located outside of metropolitan areas. Ownership rates were nearly as high in nonmetro areas (67 percent) as in suburbs, but only 29 percent of all nonmetro households owned newer housing in 1960. Sorting the data differently indicates that approximately 40 percent of new housing units (built after 1940) were in suburbs, 40 percent were in nonmetro areas, and 21 percent were in central cities.

3.2.4 Counterfactual for Motivation

The econometric analysis in the next section attempts to shed light on the role of income gains in driving the homeownership boom. For the sake of motivation, we start with a simple Blinder-Oaxaca decomposition to clarify the potentially large role of income gains in driving the rise of homeownership. We base the decomposition on the empirical relationship between income and ownership in the 1960 data; implicitly, this approach "bakes in" mortgage market reforms, tax policies, and everything else that is embedded in 1960's cross-sectional data.

19. These tabulations pertain to households for which the year built and metro *and* central city status are reported (*builtyr* > 0 and *builtyr* < 5 and *metro* > 0 and *metro* < 4). Unfortunately, approximately 22 percent of households with known building age reside in areas for which metro/central city status is not definitive.

We begin with a dataset of all men, ages 18–64, who were wage and salary workers, in the labor force, worked at least 27 weeks in the previous year, and earned more than $100 (in 1939 dollars). "Owners" in this framework are men who resided in owner-occupied housing and were identified as the head of household. Those who resided in owner-occupied housing but were not the head of household are coded as "nonowners" along with all those who resided in rental units. The idea is that all such men had the potential for forming a household and entering into ownership—they were in a sense "at risk" of ownership.

Ownership (0–1) is regressed on a quartic in real wage and salary income (expressed in 1939 dollars), an indicator variable for real income above $5,000 (the topcode value in 1939), and a quartic in age in the 1960 sample.[20] Given these parameter estimates, differences in real income between the 1940 and 1960 samples may "account for" 15 percentage points of the change in ownership out of a total of 28. This suggests a counterfactual ownership rate of 39 percent in 1960 (with no income gains) compared to an actual rate of 54 percent. This is roughly consistent with Chevan (1989), despite using different census datasets and decomposition methods. Like any such decomposition, this perspective is not causal, does not take account of general equilibrium effects, and depends on which year's coefficients are chosen. Even so, the magnitude of the difference between the actual and counterfactual ownership rate helps to motivate a closer examination of how labor market changes and income gains after 1940 may have contributed to the homeownership boom.

3.3 Data and Empirical Approach

Our analysis builds on micro-level census of population data from 1940 and 1960. Because the 1940 census recorded wage and salary income only, we focus on samples of nonfarm men between the ages of 18 to 64 who reported being wage and salary workers.[21] The census homeownership question per-

20. The population in 1960, even within the 18–64 range, was slightly older than in 1940. Age differences account for about 2 percentage points of the change in ownership. Because 1940's relationship between ownership and income is flatter than in 1960, a decomposition would attribute less explanatory power to changes in income if using coefficients for 1940 (about half as much). We use 1960's coefficients since they reflect important changes in mortgage and housing markets. The decomposition was undertaken with 1 percent samples from 1940 and 1960 (Ruggles et al. 2021) and was implemented using Stata's *oaxaca* command (Jann 2008).

21. Calculating weekly income involves dividing the annual income from wage and salary work by the total number of weeks worked. However, it is important to note that the 1940 census did not report self-employment income or capital income, and to maintain consistency, we do not include these sources of income in 1960. Weeks worked is recorded as a continuous value in 1940 (*wkswork1*). In 1960, weeks worked is recorded as an interval value (*wkswork2*), which we convert to the midpoint of the interval. Our analysis is limited to males aged 18 to 64 who were employed for at least 40 weeks in the previous year and reported positive wage and salary earnings of more than half of the implied weekly minimum wage. This approach focuses on individuals who worked most of the year, allowing us to characterize the local weekly wage

tains to whether the housing unit in which a person resides is owner occupied, but it does not specify who actually owned the unit. We assume that the household head owns the unit. Therefore, as described earlier, we coded men who lived with relatives and were not household heads as "nonowners." We coded men who lived in owner-occupied housing and were household heads as "owners," although in principle it is possible that another household member owned the unit.

We aggregate the micro-level data to local-level measures of ownership rates, income levels, and other local observables, and then we analyze variation in changes in ownership rates at the local level. In 1940, each household's "state economic area" (SEA) is identified in the microdata. A state economic area is a set of contiguous counties with similar economic and demographic characteristics, as determined and discussed in Bogue (1951). In 1960's microdata, SEA is not directly reported, and the dataset's mini-PUMAs do not map seamlessly to counties or SEAs. We assigned households to SEAs with the assistance of a crosswalk provided by IPUMS staff and, when necessary, using fractional weights as in Autor and Dorn (2013).[22]

Gains in homeownership and earnings across SEAs mirror those at the national level. Table 3.2 reports summary statistics for our main variables and controls. From 1940 to 1960, the mean change in homeownership from 1940 to 1960 across SEAs was 28 percentage points, with meaningful variation across SEAs with a range from 7 to 48 and a standard deviation of 5 percentage points. Likewise, the mean change in real log weekly earnings had a range of 34 to 98 log points and a standard deviation of 8 log points over the same period. The potential for gains in homeownership, as measured by the 1940 homeownership rate, also varied across SEAs. The mean homeownership rate was 32 percent with a standard deviation of 7 percent.

Figures 3.6 and 3.7, which map local income and ownership gains respectively, show that the national-level aggregates (figs. 3.1–3.4) mask a great deal of variation across space. This geographic variation is central to our identification strategy. In our regression framework, described in detail shortly, local fixed effects are differenced out by design, as are national-level changes that affect places similarly. Spillovers across households within localities will be

structure and omitting those whose computed weekly earnings are implausibly low. It is also worth noting that topcoding of annual wage and salary income affects a small percentage of men in each census year. We multiply topcoded values by 1.4 in each year, following Goldin and Margo (1992). We further limit the sample to observations not residing on a farm or working in a farm occupation (IPUMS variables: *farm* = 2, and *occ1950* equal to 100, 123, and 810–840.)

22. Each observation in a mini-Public Use Micro Area (PUMA) is probabilistically allocated to an SEA based on the fraction of the population in a mini-PUMA that maps into an SEA. For example, suppose a mini-PUMA is evenly split over two SEAs. In that case, each observation in the mini-PUMA is weighted by one-half in the first SEA and by one-half in the second SEA. Out of 2,765 mini-PUMAs in the 1960 sample, 1,873 (68 percent) are contained within a single SEA, 654 (24 percent) are split over two SEAs, 198 (7 percent) are split over three SEAs, and 40 (1 percent) are split over four SEAs. For more details, see the supplemental appendix to Collins and Niemesh (2013).

Table 3.2 Summary statistics

	Mean	S.D.	Min.	Max.
Change in homeownership (1940–60) (in p.p.)	0.28	0.05	0.07	0.48
Change in real log weekly earnings (1940–60)	0.63	0.08	0.34	0.98
Percent urban 1940	0.42	0.24	0.0	1.0
Homeownership rate in 1940	0.32	0.07	0.13	0.52
Change in homeownership (1930–40) (in p.p.)	0.015	0.045	–0.16	0.24
Change in homeownership (1920–30) (in p.p.)	0.023	0.036	–0.09	0.12
Change in homeownership (1910–20) (in p.p.)	0.021	0.026	–0.08	0.10
Median log weekly earnings in 1940	3.01	0.25	2.45	3.56
Log 90–10 weekly earnings gap in 1940	1.42	0.18	0.90	1.84
Share of men that are HS grads	0.25	0.05	0.11	0.39
Observations	467			

Note: Unweighted summary statistics over SEAs. All variables are constructed on a sample of nonfarm male workers age 18–64. Household heads and spouses are considered homeowners if the head reports owning the home. Other adult male members of the home are coded as renting.

Source: Median log weekly earnings, log 90–10 weekly earnings gap in 1940, and share of men that are high school grads and above are from Collins and Niemesh (2019). All other variables are derived from the 1910–40 complete-count (Ruggles et al. 2021) and 1960 5 percent IPUMS samples as described in the text and provided by Ruggles et al. (2023).

reflected in the conditional correlation. For instance, suppose there are positive spillovers through a "keeping up with the Joneses" channel or through scale economies in building new housing developments; if so, income gains to some households might increase observed ownership rates both directly (for those households) and indirectly (through spillovers to others). Finally, by aggregating to the local level over a relatively long span of time, we might achieve a clearer view of changes in earnings while still retaining a sizable number of cross-sectional units for comparison. Individual-level reports of earnings—even if accurate for a given year—might be a noisy indicator of a household's economic resources or "permanent income" (Reid 1962).

3.3.1 Regression Framework

We begin by investigating whether places with differential increases in average real wages had differential increases in homeownership between 1940 and 1960, conditional on region (or state) and observable economic characteristics. The identifying assumption for a causal interpretation is that, conditional on observables, places with different gains in wages after 1940 would have had similar trends in homeownership were it not for those differential changes in wages. There are reasons to be skeptical of this assumption in any nonexperimental setting, and so we interpret the conditional correlation between ownership and income with caution, explore robustness and sensitivity to additional covariates, and finally present an instrumental variable approach.

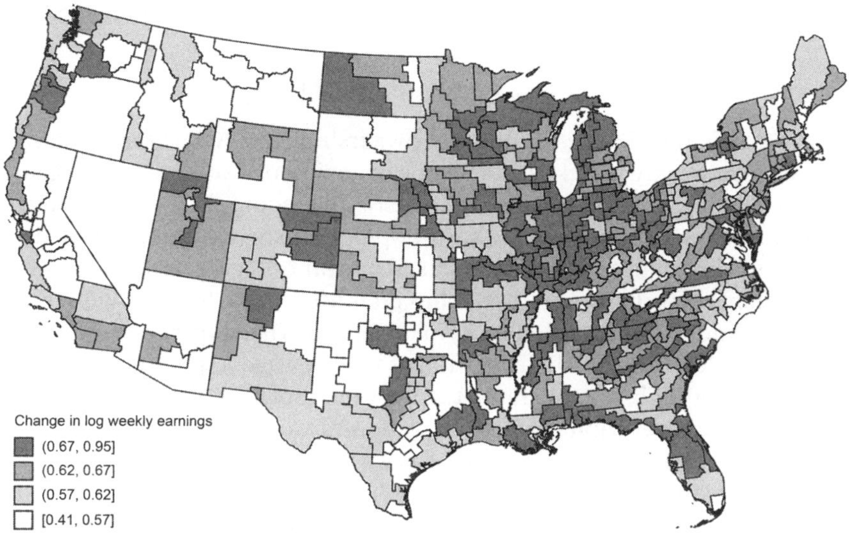

Figure 3.6 SEA-level changes in log average earnings, 1940–1960

Note: This map displays the geographic variation in the gains in log average weekly earnings between 1940 and 1960 across State Economic Areas (SEAs).

Source: SEA-level average log weekly earnings are derived from the 1940 complete-count (Ruggles et al. 2021) and 1960 5 percent (Ruggles et al. 2023) IPUMS census samples as described in the text.

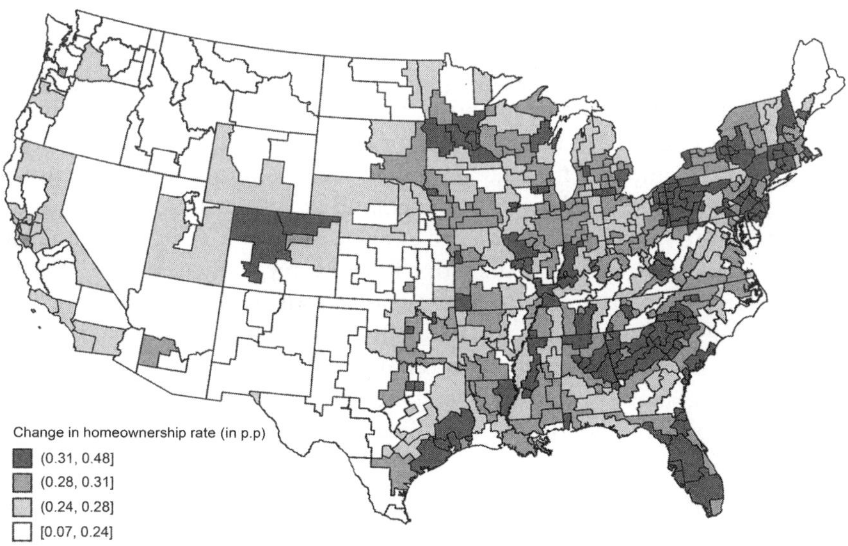

Figure 3.7 SEA-level changes in homeownership, 1940–1960

Note: This map displays the geographic variation in the gains in homeownership rates between 1940 and 1960 across State Economic Areas (SEAs).

Source: Homeownership rates are derived from the 1940 complete-count (Ruggles et al. 2021) and 1960 5 percent (Ruggles et al. 2023) IPUMS census samples as described in the text.

We estimate the following baseline regression equation spanning the 1940 to 1960 period:

$$\Delta O_i = \alpha + \beta \Delta W_i + \gamma_r + X_i \Gamma + e_i,$$

where ΔO_i is the change in the local ownership rate, ΔW_i is the change in log average weekly wages, γ_r is a vector of region or state fixed effects, and X_i is a vector of prewar local characteristics including the 1940 homeownership rate, urban and foreign-born population shares, and a set of nine age bins. Thus, places with differences in prewar observables are allowed to have differential changes in ownership rates after 1940. Subsequent regressions expand X_i to include changes in the homeownership rate before 1940; the median level and 90–10 dispersion of weekly wages reported in 1940; the 1940 share of high-school graduates, wartime shocks to the local economy (war contracts per capita and mobilization rates), and more. We find that estimates of β change relatively little as we change the specification.

Local productivity shocks, exogenous human capital gains, or local institutional changes (e.g., unionization) that raised local wages might have led to increased demand for owner-occupied housing, along the lines described earlier. If this demand shift was met by an elastic supply of owner-occupied housing, perhaps encouraged by midcentury policy support for new construction and vast suburban areas awaiting development, then the cross-place change-in-income and change-in-ownership correlation would reflect a causal mechanism, at least in part.

If, however, unobserved shocks to local ownership were correlated with changes in local average wages, then the correlation would be confounded and difficult to interpret. Consider, for instance, a hypothetical exogenous shock to a local consumer amenity that is especially attractive to high-income households.[23] In this case, we might see a correlation between ownership changes and income changes due to the in-migration of households that happen to have a relatively high demand for owner-occupied housing. It is difficult to rule out such scenarios. Our use of groups of counties as the unit of analysis should limit the scope for movement from central cities to nearby suburbs to drive results. And we do investigate whether β is sensitive to including contemporaneous (1940–60) controls, including local population growth and sample composition changes, that would be consistent with such a channel being open and driving the estimates of β.[24] This mechanism does not appear to underpin our baseline findings.

23. Our example in the text supposes an amenity that is especially attractive to higher-income households, leading to income-specific sorting and rising local ownership. However, in a Rosen-Roback framework, a new consumer amenity would raise land values and reduce wages. This could lower local homeownership if new construction skews to higher-density, multifamily construction.

24. We are mindful that these may be "bad controls" and interpret results accordingly.

3.4 Results and Interpretation

3.4.1 Baseline Results

Estimates of β are reported in table 3.3. Each column presents an estimate from a separate regression of the change in the homeownership rate on the change in log average weekly earnings between 1940 and 1960. All regressions cluster standard errors at the state level. The first column shows the raw positive correlation between ΔO_i and ΔW_i. A 10-log-point (0.10) increase in the change in average income is associated with a 2.02-percentage-point increase in the change in homeownership.

The strong positive association remains in specifications with an extensive set of control variables that allow for differential trends in ownership according to prewar observables. Column 2 adds census region fixed effects, as both the changes in homeownership and weekly wage gains were uneven across regions, as seen in the maps discussed earlier. Column 3 adds the 1940 homeownership rate, a set of age bins, and the urban and foreign-born population shares. Localities with high ownership rates in 1940 would have less room for growth in ownership than others (though the highest rates in 1940 were just above 50 percent). The prewar age structure is relevant for two reasons: First, it is well known that changes in ownership rates after 1940 were largest for relatively young household heads (e.g., in their 30s); second, likelihood of service in World War II and, therefore, eligibility for postwar GI Bill support was also closely associated with birth year. We view this as our baseline specification, which is parsimonious while allowing for differences in key prewar economic characteristics. Estimates of β are robust to these additional control variables and remain statistically significant at the 1 percent level.

The magnitude of the β estimate is sizable: a 1-standard-deviation increase in ΔW_i(0.08) is associated with a 1.8-percentage-point increase in homeownership, equivalent to 6 percent of the mean increase in the homeownership rate over the 1940s and 50s. All areas experienced sizable increases in log real weekly earnings, and the mean change to 1960 (0.63) dwarfs the standard deviation of the change. Evaluated at the mean change in weekly earnings, the baseline estimates imply an increase in homeownership of 14 percentage points, approximately 51 percent of the actual mean increase in ΔO_i.

The OLS results are stable across the remaining specifications in table 3.3 and remain statistically significant. In each column we add variables to the baseline regression to account for differences across places that might have affected post-1940 homeownership gains and been correlated with average wage gains. Column 4's specification adds two variables to characterize the 1940 local wage structure: median log earnings and the 90–10 log earnings differential. It also includes the share of the sample that had completed high

Table 3.3 Baseline OLS results

	(1)	(2)	(3)	(4)	(5)	(6)	(7)
Change in real log weekly earnings (40–60)	0.202***	0.196***	0.226***	0.275***	0.278***	0.240***	0.259***
	(0.048)	(0.047)	(0.040)	(0.042)	(0.045)	(0.042)	(0.037)
Percent urban 1940			0.060***	0.018	0.015	0.008	0.004
			(0.014)	(0.016)	(0.017)	(0.017)	(0.021)
Homeownership rate, 1940			–0.249***	–0.326***	–0.350***	–0.371***	–0.369***
			(0.061)	(0.055)	(0.063)	(0.077)	(0.061)
Share sample foreign-born, 1940			–0.088	–0.127	–0.116	–0.223	–0.049
			(0.068)	(0.073)	(0.077)	(0.129)	(0.076)
Median log weekly earnings, 1940				0.084***	0.081***	0.117***	0.064**
				(0.019)	(0.018)	(0.024)	(0.021)
Log 90–10 weekly earnings gap, 1940				–0.036	–0.034	–0.044	0.006
				(0.018)	(0.019)	(0.024)	(0.017)
Percent males HS grads				–0.080	–0.076	–0.161	0.007
				(0.080)	(0.084)	(0.096)	(0.083)
Change in homeownership rate, 1930–40					0.036	–0.114	–0.024
					(0.104)	(0.111)	(0.107)
Change in homeownership rate, 1920–30					–0.024	–0.029	0.088
					(0.139)	(0.134)	(0.106)
Change in homeownership rate, 1910–20					0.174*	0.122	0.238***
					(0.075)	(0.099)	(0.063)
Per capita WWII contracts (1,000s 1940$)							0.371
							(1.265)

State WWII mobilization rate							–0.022
							(0.146)
Region fixed effects		X	X	X	X		X
State fixed effects						X	
Age controls			X	X	X	X	X
1940 industry mix controls							X
Observations	467	467	467	467	467	467	466
R^2	0.10	0.28	0.44	0.50	0.51	0.65	0.58
Oster- δ			6.7	6.4	5.6	2.7	4.4
Mean change in homeownership (in p.p.)	0.28						0.28

Note: $***p < 0.01$. $**p < 0.05$. $*p < 0.1$. Each column in the table is from a separate regression of change-in-homeownership variable on the change-in-earnings. The top row reports the estimated coefficient (β) on the change-in-earnings variable. Standard errors are clustered at the state level. Column 1 includes no controls. Region fixed effects are added in column 2. Our base specification, column 3, adds controls for the share foreign-born, share urban, initial level of homeownership, and a set of six age category controls, all measured in 1940. Column 4 adds the initial 1940 median earnings, the log 90–10 gap in earnings, and the share of the sample that graduated high school. Pretrends in the change in homeownership are included in column 5. State fixed effects replace region fixed effects in column 6. Finally, column 7 includes controls for wartime shocks: World War II contract spending per capita, state-level mobilization rates, and a set of six industry mix controls. We lose one SEA observation in column 7 because Washington, DC, did not report a war mobilization rate. The Oster-δ statistic reports the degree of selection on unobservables relative to the observables that would be required to explain away the coefficient of interest. The Oster-δ statistic is calculated using a maximum R^2 of $1.3 \times R^2$ in the fully controlled regression in column 6, as suggested in Oster (2019).

Source: Median log weekly earnings, log 90–10 weekly earnings gap in 1940, and share of men that are high school grads and above are from Collins and Niemesh (2019). Per capita war expenditure is calculated with data from Haines and ICPSR (2010). War mobilization is from Acemoglu et al. (2004). All other variables are derived from the 1910–40 complete-count (Ruggles et al. 2021) and 1960 5 percent IPUMS samples as described in the text and provided by Ruggles et al. (2023).

school or more. This addresses the concern that places with different initial levels of income, inequality, or human capital might have been poised for different post-1940 gains in homeownership and, coincidentally, different changes in earnings. In column 5, we add variables for pre-1940 changes in homeownership rates over the three previous decades (1910–20, 1920–30, and 1930–40) to allow for different trajectories in ownership. Column 6 replaces the region-level fixed effects with state fixed effects. This substantially narrows the geographic scope for confounding shocks and trends by basing identification on within-state variation rather than within-region. The results are similar to those in the baseline regression. In sum, conditional on wide range of prewar observables and regional or state indicators, the correlation between local wage gains and local homeownership gains is sizable.

Finally, column 7 adds variables to see whether events or policies related to World War II might be driving the baseline results. The variables include mobilization of men into the armed forces at the state level, local labor market shocks from war contract spending per capita, and a set of control variables for shares of local workers in nine industry categories to capture the prewar local industry composition. Wartime mobilization required the movement of millions of men into the armed forces and drew many women into the labor market. At the same time, federal expenditures on manufactured goods to support the war effort shocked local economies, and federal subsidies attempted to expand housing stocks to better accommodate workers in key industries. The extent of mobilization and war production varied considerably across locations in ways that might have affected trends in income and homeownership. In a sense, these are "bad controls" because local wartime shocks might have driven the differential post-1940 income gains that we seek to evaluate; if so, such regressions would reveal whether the conditional correlations described above largely reflect the wartime economy's lasting effect on homeownership via income.[25] In practice, the estimates of β are quite stable, and the coefficients on the wartime variables are statistically insignificant. (Later in the chapter, we discuss the correlation between local veterans in 1960 and homeownership rates.)

The stability in the coefficient of interest across columns is informative only to the extent that selection on the observables that we capture is informative about selection on the remaining unobservables. For reference, we report the Oster δ statistic to provide evidence of robustness with respect to the unobservables (Oster 2019). From this perspective, selection on unobservables would need to be 2.7 to 6.7 times larger than the selection on

25. Because the regressions already control for local prewar age structure, some of the war's direct effects on homeownership via GI Bill eligibility may already be accounted for.

observables to drive the estimate of β to zero, increasing our confidence in the positive OLS results.[26]

3.4.2 Additional Robustness: Changes in Variable Definitions, Estimation, and Sample

The gains in homeownership associated with increases in average weekly earnings documented above may be sensitive to the choice of specification or underlying samples. We address a number of these concerns in table 3.4 and show that the baseline results are robust. Column 1 reprints the baseline coefficient from column 3 of table 3.3 for reference. Column 2 uses weighted least squares (WLS) with 1940 SEA observation counts as weights. The coefficient estimate of 0.327 is 45 percent larger than our baseline estimate of 0.226, suggesting some unmodeled heterogeneity (Solon et al. 2015), which we explore later in the chapter. In column 3, the estimate of β from a median regression (0.224) is indistinguishable from the baseline estimate, suggesting that the baseline OLS result is not driven by extreme values.

In column 4 we drop all SEAs in California and New York, coastal states with some of the largest and densest population centers, where perhaps the supply of housing was less elastic than elsewhere. Dropping the two states does not substantially alter the coefficient estimate.

Next, in column 5, we use the change in log annual earnings rather than the change in log weekly earnings as the key independent variable. One might argue that annual income is more relevant for an individual's homeownership decision; however, the change in weekly earnings may better capture the local productivity or distributional shocks leading to increased lifetime income and homeownership. Using the annual income measure yields an estimate of β (0.229), which is similar to our baseline estimate.

The baseline regressions limit the sample to nonfarm observations. This is due to the difficulty of assessing farmer and farm laborer income, especially in 1940, and to the literature's traditional distinction between the nonfarm housing market and the market for farms. The results are robust to changing this restriction, as shown in column 6, where we include men residing or working on a farm as long as they satisfy the other sample selection criteria (including being wage and salary workers) in the calculation of both the local homeownership and change-in-earnings variables.

The period we study was one of pronounced changes in the relative income of Black Americans (Maloney 1994; Margo 1995), as well as large gains in Black homeownership despite their increased concentration in central cities (Collins and Margo 2001, 2011). Moreover, changes in income and ownership in the South stand out in the maps shown earlier. We defer a

26. We calculate the Oster-δ statistic using a maximum R^2 of $1.3 \times R^2$ in the fully controlled regression in table 3.3 column 5, as suggested in Oster (2019).

Table 3.4 **Robustness to changes in specification and sample restrictions**

	Base (1)	Weighted (2)	Median regression (3)	Drop CA & NY (4)	Log annual earnings (5)	Full sample (6)	White nonfarm (7)
Change in real log weekly earnings, 1940–60	0.226***	0.327***	0.224***	0.237***		0.224***	0.227***
	(0.0396)	(0.0833)	(0.0388)	(0.0406)		(0.0360)	(0.0442)
Change in real log annual earnings, 1940–60					0.229***		
					(0.0373)		
Observations	467	467	467	433	467	467	467
R^2	0.440	0.437	0.427	0.452	0.446	0.411	0.468

Note: ***$p < 0.01$. **$p < 0.05$. *$p < 0.1$. Each entry represents the estimated coefficient (β) on the change-in-earnings variable from a separate regression of change-in-homeownership variable on the change-in-earnings variable. All regressions include the same controls as the base specification from column 3 of table 3.3: census region fixed effects, the share foreign-born, share urban, initial level of homeownership, and a set of six age category controls, all measured in 1940. Standard errors are clustered at the state-level. Column 1 reprints the baseline result from column 3 of table 3.3. Column 2 estimates the regression with weighted least squares where weights are the number of observations in the sample in 1940 for each SEA. Column 3 reports an estimate of β from a median regression. All SEAs in California and New York are dropped from the sample in column 4. The change in real log annual earnings replaces the variable of interest (change in real log weekly earnings) in column 5. Restrictions on the sample are relaxed in column 6 to include men residing or working on farms. Column 7 tightens the sample restriction to include only white nonfarm men.

Source: Median log weekly earnings, log 90–10 weekly earnings gap in 1940, and share of men that are high school grads and above are from Collins and Niemesh (2019). All other variables are derived from the 1940 complete-count (Ruggles et al. 2021) and 1960 5 percent IPUMS census samples as described in the text and provided by Ruggles et al. (2023).

deeper examination of local-level Black–White differences in homeownership to future research. For now, to see whether our baseline results hinge on changes in income and homeownership among Black men, we estimate the baseline regression based on variables derived from a sample of White men (column 7). Again, the coefficient estimates are indistinguishable from the baseline.

3.4.3 Extensions: Contemporaneous Variables

The cross-place conditional correlation of ΔO_i and ΔW_i may represent a causal relationship. However, the interpretation is not straightforward since it could work through multiple channels with different implications, such as the differential sorting of high-income households into certain SEAs. This would tend to drive a positive estimate of β, assuming that the relative supply of owner-occupied housing would adjust by 1960.[27] This mechanism is causal, in a sense, because changes in local income drive changes in owner-occupancy. But the correlation would ultimately reflect changes in local population composition rather than intrinsic changes in local wages. We do not know of a nationally representative dataset that would allow us to recover income-specific migration patterns across SEAs over this period. However, we can observe how local population characteristics changed between 1940 and 1960 and whether the OLS estimates are sensitive to the inclusion of such variables.

We incorporate three measures of changing local characteristics to gauge the potential importance of such sorting in response to unobservable local shocks: the change in the share of the sample that has completed high school or more, the change in the log of population between 1940 and 1960, and the veteran share of the sample in 1960. The first captures the idea that people with higher levels of productivity may have sorted into certain locations and driven ownership gains there. The second captures the idea that unobserved local shocks should affect total population through migration. The third captures the idea that men were positively selected into the military (Bound and Turner 2002), and then surviving veterans benefited from policies designed to support their homeownership through the GI Bill (Fetter 2013); thus, differential shares of veterans might be associated with differential changes in income and homeownership.

Table 3.5 reports results from including these measures as controls in the base specification. Column 2 adds the change in the share of the sample that is a high school grad or above. The estimate for β remains similar to the baseline result in column 1, suggesting a limited role for differential sorting based on education and human capital driving the baseline results. Column

27. Movement from central cities to suburbs in the same SEA would be "within locality" in our framework and would not drive estimates of β. Our identifying variation is from differential changes in average income and ownership across SEAs.

Table 3.5 Sensitivity to potential endogenous sorting

	(1)	(2)	(3)	(4)	(5)
Change in real log weekly earnings, 1940–60	0.226***	0.242***	0.226***	0.196***	0.211***
	(0.040)	(0.042)	(0.040)	(0.038)	(0.040)
Change in share HS and above, 1940–60		–0.107			–0.074
		(0.054)			(0.050)
Change in log population, 1940–60			0.000		–0.005
			(0.010)		(0.009)
Share veteran in 1960 sample				0.415***	0.414***
				(0.056)	(0.055)
Observations	467	467	467	467	467
R^2	0.44	0.44	0.44	0.52	0.52

Note: ***$p < 0.01$. **$p < 0.05$. *$p < 0.1$. Each column in the table is from a separate regression of change-in-homeownership on change-in-earnings. The top row reports the estimated coefficient (β) on the change-in-earnings variable. All regressions include the same controls as the base specification from column 3 of table 3.3: census region fixed effects, the share foreign born, share urban, initial level of homeownership, and a set of six age category controls, all measured in 1940. Standard errors are clustered at the state-level. Column 1 reprints the baseline result from column 3 of table 3.3. Column 2 adds the change in the share of the sample that graduated high school from 1940–60. Column 3 includes the change in log population from 1940–60 as a control. Column 4 includes the share of the sample in 1960 made up by veterans. Finally, column 5 includes all of the three previously discussed variables jointly.

Sources: The change in share high school and above and change in log population are from Collins and Niemesh (2019). All other variables are derived from the 1940 complete-count (Ruggles et al. 2021) and 1960 5 percent IPUMS census samples as described in the text and provided by Ruggles et al. (2023).

3 includes population growth; again, the estimate of β is unchanged from the baseline. Column 4 includes the share of the 1960 sample that is a veteran in each SEA. The estimate of β is reduced somewhat to 0.196 and remains statistically significant. The coefficient on the veterans variable (0.415, s.e. 0.056) is positive as we would expect—areas where veterans made up a higher share of the population had higher homeownership rates in 1960. We include all three contemporaneous variables simultaneously in column 5. The coefficient estimate for β is slightly smaller than the baseline, but it is similar in magnitude and remains statistically significant. Taken together, the evidence does not suggest that differential changes in sample composition due to sorting drive the baseline regression results.

3.4.4 Heterogeneity

We investigate whether the impact of ΔW_i on ΔO_i depended on characteristics that varied across locations. Table 3.6 presents results from running separate OLS regressions on split samples. Columns 1 and 2 of panel A divide the sample into SEAs that are below or above the 75th percentile in initial 1940 population. As alluded to above in the discussion about weighting, we find suggestive evidence that the effect of increases in income is larger in areas with more population. This is consistent with the idea that scale

Table 3.6 **Heterogeneous effects**

Panel A: Heterogeneity by population and initial 1940 earnings

	<75th percentile population (1)	≥75th percentile population (2)	<75 percentile earnings (3)	≥75th percentile earnings (4)
Change in real log weekly earnings (40–60)	0.222***	0.335**	0.226***	0.455***
	(0.037)	(0.104)	(0.042)	(0.121)
Observations	351	116	351	116
R^2	0.47	0.48	0.45	0.60

Panel B: Heterogeneity by region

	Northeast (5)	Midwest (6)	South (7)	West (8)
Change in real log weekly earnings (40–60)	0.356***	0.248***	0.246**	0.116
	(0.041)	(0.046)	(0.065)	(0.084)
Observations	68	146	186	67
R^2	0.63	0.33	0.40	0.27

Note: ***$p < 0.01$. **$p < 0.05$. *$p < 0.1$. Each entry represents the estimated coefficient (β) on the change-in-earnings variable from a separate regression of change-in-homeownership variable on the change-in-earnings variable. All regressions include the same controls as the base specification from column 3 of table 3.3: the share foreign-born, share urban, initial level of homeownership, and a set of six age category controls, all measured in 1940. All regressions in panel A include census region fixed effects. Standard errors are clustered at the state level. Columns 1 and 2 of panel A split the sample into SEAs with below and above the 75th percentile of population (in reality we use the sample size in 1940 as a proxy for population). Columns 3 and 4 of panel A split the sample into SEAs with below and above the 75th percentile of the 1940 earnings distribution. Panel B reports estimates from separate regressions by census region.

Source: Median log weekly earnings, log 90–10 weekly earnings gap in 1940, and share of men that are high school grads and above are from Collins and Niemesh (2019). All other variables are derived from the 1940 complete-count and 1960 5 percent IPUMS census samples as described in the text and provided by Ruggles et al. (2023).

effects in the construction of housing may have played a role in translating the midcentury gains in income into increased homeownership rates. In a regression on the pooled sample, the estimated coefficient on the interaction of ΔW_i with an indicator for population at or above the 75th percentile is 0.149 (s.e. = 0.117) with a p-value of 0.211.[28]

Columns 3 and 4 of panel A split the sample into below and above the 75th percentile of the 1940 average weekly earnings distribution across SEAs. Here, we find suggestive evidence that the subset of SEAs above the 75th percentile of initial wages experienced larger increases in homeownership for a given increase in average earnings. Again, the difference in the OLS

28. We include only the main effects of control variables, not the interactions with group indicators, in this case for population at or above the 75th percentile.

estimates of β across columns is sizable but only marginally significant. In a pooled regression, the estimated coefficient on the interaction of ΔW_i with an indicator for average earnings at or above the 75th percentile is 0.179 (s.e. = 0.135) with a *p*-value of 0.193.

Finally, the estimated impact of changes-in-earnings also varies across census regions. Panel B of Table 3.6 reports results from regressions on separate samples by census region. The effect of a 10-log-point differential increase in the change in log weekly earnings was largest in the Northeast region at a 3.6-percentage-point increase in the homeownership rate, followed by the Midwest and the South at 2.4 percentage points. The West had the smallest estimated effect at 1.2 percentage points.[29] It is not clear to us, from the data we have assembled, why the relationship appears weaker in the West than elsewhere. Apart from the large cities of the Pacific coast, the West was relatively sparsely settled in 1940, and it is possible that this limited positive spillovers within localities, but this is speculation on our part. A deeper dive into regional heterogeneity is beyond the bounds of this chapter but may illuminate regional differences in economic development and provide a more nuanced understanding of the midcentury homeownership boom.[30]

3.4.5 Instrumental Variable Approach

Concerns about bias may remain despite the robustness of the OLS regressions, the limited room for unobservables suggested by analysis using Oster's δ, and the lack of direct evidence that cross-SEA sorting drives the estimates. Next, we complement the OLS results reported in the previous section with a shift-share IV (SSIV) strategy. The type of bias this strategy addresses is from an unobserved *local* shock that influences both local earnings gains and local homeownership rates. For example, bias from endogenous sorting might remain in the OLS estimates from a shock that causes differential migration patterns by income level, such as a positive consumer or productive amenity shock to high-earning households. Alternatively, reverse causality could drive the association in OLS through sorting. Areas with potential for rapid homeownership gains coming out of the Depression era housing crisis might have drawn in more high-earning migrants.[31] Our IV strategy limits the potential for endogenous sorting to affect estimates of β by fixing the local shares of men over income percentiles at the 1940 earnings distribution.

The basic idea is that some local labor markets were more exposed than

29. In regressions on a combined full sample, the estimated effect of change-in-earnings in the West is statistically different from the Northeast at the 1 percent confidence level, and the Midwest at the 10 percent confidence level. The *p*-value of the difference between the Northeast and the Midwest is 0.122, and between the Northeast and the South is 0.128.

30. Chapter 14 in Grebler et al. (1956) provides a discussion of regional differences in mortgage debt.

31. Reverse causality would have to occur within region, as our main specifications include a set of region indicators that capture any differential trends across regions.

others to national shocks specific to different parts of the earnings distribution due to their preexisting composition of workers in terms of their location in the national earnings distribution. These national-level shocks are plausibly unrelated to unobservable local shocks. By interacting the 1940 local shares of workers across the national earnings distribution with the exogenous national shifts in earnings at each percentile of the distribution, we create a potential instrument for average earnings changes for local labor markets.[32] Specifically, we construct the instrument Z_i as a weighted average of 1940–60 changes in earnings at the national level by earnings percentile (G_j), where the weights (s_{ij}) are local sample shares across earnings percentiles measured from the full-count 1940 census data:

$$Z_i = \sum_{j=1}^{J} s_{ij} \times G_j.$$

The identifying assumption is that the instrument is orthogonal to omitted local characteristics that are correlated with changes in homeownership, which occurs when either the shares or the shocks, or both, are exogenous. In our setting, the local earnings percentile shares, though lagged, might capture a local labor market's exposure to any number of shocks. Thus, we follow the approach of Borusyak et al. (2022) and assume the income-percentile shocks are as good as randomly assigned to provide identification in our use of the SSIV.[33] Adão et al. (2019) show that standard geographic clustering of standard errors may lead to overrejection in significance tests in applications using shift-share instruments. We address this issue by estimating standard errors with a shock-level regression as suggested by Borusyak et al. (2022). Specifically, we regress the shock-level change-in-homeownership on the shock-level change-in-earnings instrumented with the national growth in earnings for individual earnings percentiles.

32. Boustan et al. (2013) developed this strategy interacting changes in income across a set of income bins at the national level with the initial local composition of households across the income bins. They calculate a predicted change in a Gini coefficient, whereas we create a standard shift-share IV predicting the change in average earnings.

33. Borusyak et al. (2022, 182) show that orthogonality between a shift-share instrument and an unobserved shock in the residual in our local labor market regression is equivalent to orthogonality between our national earnings percentile shocks and an unobservable from a shock-level regression. This shock-level unobservable "captures the average unobserved determinants of the original outcome among observations most exposed to a given shock." Thus, an SSIV regression at the local labor market level only identifies the causal impact of changes in average earnings on changes in homeownership at the local-local if and only if the shock-level unobservable is uncorrelated with the national earnings percentile shocks. Moreover, they provide an equivalence result that the standard SSIV regression coefficients are numerically equivalent to those from an IV regression estimated at the level of the shocks, in our case earnings percentiles. We obtain shock-level aggregates for each earnings percentile, by first averaging the change-in-homeownership and change-in-earnings variables, as well as all controls in the baseline specification. The dataset now consists of an observation for each earnings percentile. The SSIV regression coefficients can be recovered from a regression at the percentile shock-level of the change-in-homeownership on change-in-earnings instrumented by the national changes in earnings for that earnings percentile.

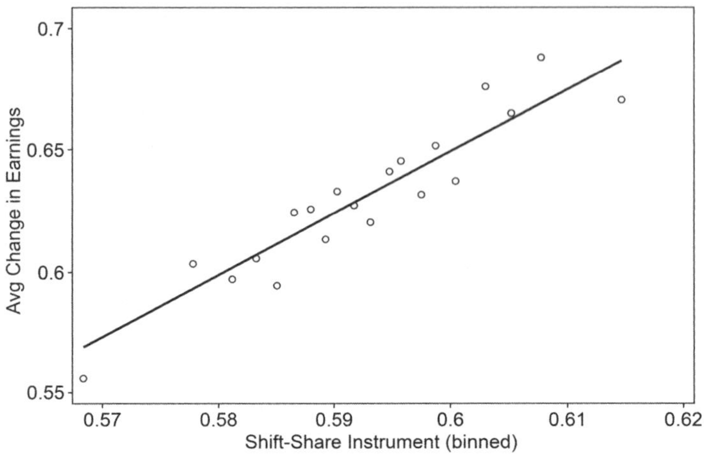

Figure 3.8 First stage on change in average earnings

Note: This binned scatterplot shows the relationship between the actual change in average log weekly earnings between 1940–1960 across State Economic Areas (ΔW_i) and the instrument—the predicted change in average log weekly earnings using the 1940 SEA earnings percentile composition and the national-level changes in earnings by percentile (Z_i). Both variables have been residualized on the controls in the baseline specification (column 3 of table 3.2): region fixed effects, a set of six age category controls, the share foreign-born, the share urban, and the initial 1940 homeownership rate.

Source: 1940 complete-count (Ruggles et al. 2021) and 1960 5 percent (Ruggles et al. 2023) IPUMS census samples as described in the text.

The shift-share instrument shows relevance and is strongly associated with the local changes-in-earnings variable. Figure 3.8 shows a binned scatterplot of the relationship between ΔW_i and Z_i, where both variables have been residualized on census region fixed effects and the set of controls in the baseline OLS regression specification. The average change-in-earnings within a bin increases along the *y*-axis and the *x*-axis plots the value of the predicted change in average earnings (shift-share IV). The estimated slope of the regression line suggests that a 1-log-point increase in the predicted change in average earnings is associated with a 2.51-log-point increase in the actual change in average earnings. The estimated coefficient is reported in column 1 of table 3.7. The first-stage *F*-statistic is 92.0.[34]

The SSIV estimates of β are positive and statistically significant, although smaller in magnitude than our baseline estimates. Column 3 of table 3.7 reports the SSIV coefficient, which suggests that a 10-log-point increase in the change-in-earnings variable causes a 1.7-percentage-point increase in homeownership at the local level. While somewhat smaller than

34. The first-stage *F*-statistic comes from squaring the *t*-statistic ($9.59 \times 9.59 = 92.0$) from an earnings percentile shock-level regression of the log change-in-earnings on the shift-share IV instrumented with the national growth in earnings for the specific earnings percentile as suggested in Borusyak et al. (2022).

Table 3.7 **Shift-share IV estimates of effect of change-in-average-earnings on change-in-homeownership**

	First stage (1)	Reduced form (2)	Shift-share IV (3)
Coefficient	2.51***	0.441***	0.175**
	(0.262)	(0.149)	(0.071)
No. of SEAs	467	467	467
No. of percentiles	79	84	84
SSIV first stage F-statistic	92.0		

Note: This table reports a shift-share IV analysis of changes in homeownership rates on local changes in average earnings, instrumented with the predicted change in average log weekly earnings using the 1940 SEA earnings percentile composition and the national-level changes in earnings by percentile (Z_i). Exposure robust standard errors are estimated using the shock-level regressions from Borusyak et al. (2022). The number of observations used in the SEA-level regional regressions is 467. The number of earnings percentiles used in the equivalent percentile shock-level regressions is 84. Column 1 reports the first-stage results, where the F-statistic comes from squaring the t-statistic ($9.59 \times 9.59 = 92.9$) from an earnings percentile shock-level regression of the log change-in-earnings on the shift-share IV instrumented with the national growth in earnings for the specific earnings percentile. Column 2 reports results from a reduced form regression. The shift-share IV estimates of the coefficient (β) on the change-in-earnings variable are reported in column 3. All regressions include the same controls as the base specification from column 3 of table 3.3: census region fixed effects, the share foreign-born, share urban, initial level of homeownership, and a set of six age category controls, all measured in 1940.

Sources: Median log weekly earnings, log 90–10 weekly earnings gap in 1940, and share of men that are high school grads and above are from Collins and Niemesh (2019). All other variables are derived from the 1940 complete-count (Ruggles et al. 2021) and 1960 5 percent IPUMS census samples as described in the text and provided by Ruggles et al. (2023).

the OLS estimates, the SSIV estimates of β remain economically important: a 1-standard-deviation increase in ΔW_i (0.08) is associated with a 1.36-percentage-point increase in homeownership. Evaluated at the mean change in weekly earnings (0.63), the baseline estimates imply an increase in homeownership of 10.7 percentage points, approximately 38 percent of the actual mean increase in ΔO_i.

There are various reasons estimates from OLS and SSIV may differ, including measurement error in the change-in-earnings variable and the presence of a small amount of endogenous sorting. However, one should exercise caution when attempting to attribute this difference to specific causes, especially in the presence of suggestive evidence of heterogeneity in effects that require a local average treatment effect (LATE) interpretation of the SSIV estimates.

3.5 Conclusions

In retrospect, the mid-20th century's widely shared gains in income supported a boom in homeownership and, more broadly, a sense that a new "middle class" was enjoying a wave of post-Depression, postwar prosperity.

In this chapter, we assess the role of post-1940 income gains in driving the unprecedented boom in homeownership alongside institutional and policy innovations in housing and mortgage finance. We do so by leveraging variation across places in wage gains and ownership gains, thereby differencing out local fixed effects and national-level changes that affected ownership rates similarly across places. Whether with or without extensive sets of control variables, including prewar characteristics and trends, wartime shocks, and post-1940 changes in population composition, there is a strong correlation between local income gains and homeownership gains. This is consistent with theory, as higher income allows more people to form independent households, afford down payments, secure financing, and select into owner occupancy if so desired.

The baseline OLS estimates suggest that income gains made large contributions to the rise in homeownership, accounting for half of the total gains in homeownership observed in our samples of men, ages 18 to 64. Instrumental variable estimates, based on relatively new shift-share techniques, are smaller in magnitude, but still indicate economically significant ownership gains due to income gains. We also uncover some evidence of heterogeneity by region, with stronger effects apparent in the Northeast relative to the West, and by local population size.

In earlier research, extending estimates based on eligibility for veterans' benefits, Fetter (2013) suggested that about 40 percent of the 1940–60 ownership boom might be attributed changes in mortgage terms. Chambers et al. (2014), relying on a dynamic general equilibrium model, estimate that about 21 percent of the era's homeownership gains are attributable to changes in mortgage markets. Thus, our findings, although based on a different kind of variation and approach to measurement, complement earlier work that has focused on innovations in mortgage finance in accounting for the rise of homeownership.

The chapter's findings are closely connected to American suburban growth. Although that story remains in the background of our regression analyses, it is clear from 1960's cross-sectional data that new, single-family housing in the suburbs was an important vehicle for gains in homeownership. The chapter's findings are also connected to changes in the level and distribution of home equity, a key component of Americans' wealth in 1960 and beyond. Few families held stocks or bonds in 1960's Survey of Consumer Finances, but most owned housing. Both aspects—midcentury suburban development and the accumulation of housing wealth—are important for our understanding of the changing geography of US economic activity and prosperity, including our understanding of how homeownership interacted with group disparities and residential segregation by race and income.

Finally, we would argue that homeownership is just one of many potential ramifications of the rapid and widespread gains in midcentury income. Effects from the rise in labor market earnings, on which we focus here, or the compression of the income distribution, which is featured in the "Great Compression" literature, may have been widespread. We encourage more research on how midcentury income gains affected American consumption patterns, demographic outcomes, public finance decisions, urban planning choices, and political economy.

References

Aaron, Henry J. 1972. *Shelter and Subsidies: Who Benefits from Federal Housing Policies?* Brookings Institution.

Acemoglu, Daron, David H. Autor, and David Lyle. 2004. "Women, War, and Wages: The Effect of Female Labor Supply on the Wage Structure at Midcentury." *Journal of Political Economy* 112 (3): 497–551.

Adão, Rodrigo, Michal Kolesar, and Eduardo Morales. 2019. "Shift-Share Designs: Theory and Inference." *Quarterly Journal of Economics* 134 (4): 1949–2010.

Autor, David H., and David Dorn. 2013. "The Growth of Low-Skill Service Jobs and the Polarization of the US Labor Market." *American Economic Review* 103 (5): 1553–97.

Baum-Snow, Nathaniel. 2007. "Did Highways Cause Suburbanization?" *Quarterly Journal of Economics* 122 (2): 775–805.

Bogue, Donald J. 1951. *State Economic Areas: a Description of the Procedure Used in Making a Functional Grouping of Counties in the United States*. Department of Commerce, Bureau of the Census. Government Printing Office.

Borusyak, Kirill, Peter Hull, and Xavier Jaravel. 2022. "Quasi-Experimental Shift-Share Research Designs." *Review of Economic Studies* 89 (1): 181–213.

Bound, John, and Sarah Turner. 2002. "Going to War and Going to College: Did World War II and the GI Bill Increase Educational Attainment for Returning Veterans?" *Journal of Labor Economics* 20 (4): 784–815.

Boustan, Leah, and Robert A. Margo. 2013. "A Silver Lining to White Flight? White Suburbanization and African-American Homeownership, 1940–1980." *Journal of Urban Economics* 78: 71–80.

Boustan, Leah, Fernando V. Ferreira, Herman Winkler, and Eric M. Zolt. 2013. "The Effect of Rising Income Inequality on Public Expenditures: Evidence from US Municipalities and School Districts." *Review of Economics and Statistics* 95 (4): 1291–1302.

Brunet, Gillian. 2019. "After the War: Wartime Saving and Postwar Housing Investment, 1946–1950." Unpublished working paper.

Chambers, Matthew, Carlos Garriga, and Don E. Schlagenhauf. 2014. "Did Postwar Housing Policies Cause the Postwar Boom in Home Ownership?" In *Housing and Mortgage Markets in Historical Perspective*, edited by P. Fishback, K. Snowden, and E. White, 351–85. University of Chicago Press.

Chevan, Albert. 1989. "The Growth of Home Ownership, 1940–1980." *Demography* 26 (2): 249–66.

Collins, William J., and Brant Callaway. 2018. "Unions, Workers, and Wages at the Peak of the American Labor Movement." *Explorations in Economic History* 68: 95–118.

Collins, William J., and Robert A. Margo. 2001. "Race and Home Ownership: A Century-Long View." *Explorations in Economic History* 38 (1): 68–92.

Collins, William J., and Robert A. Margo. 2003. "Race and the Value of Owner-Occupied Housing." *Regional Science and Urban Economics* 33: 255–86.
Collins, William J., and Robert A. Margo. 2011. "Race and Home Ownership from the End of the Civil War to the Present." *American Economic Review: Papers and Proceedings* 101 (3): 355–59.
Collins, William J., and Gregory T. Niemesh. 2019. "Unions and the Great Compression of Wage Inequality in the US at Mid-Century: Evidence from Local Labor Markets." *Economic History Review* 72 (2): 691–715. https://doi.org/10.1111/ehr.12744.
Easterlin, Richard A. 1961. "The American Baby Boom in Historical Perspective." *American Economic Review* 51 (5): 869–911.
Fetter, Daniel K. 2013. "How Do Mortgage Subsidies Affect Home Ownership: Evidence from the Mid-Century GI Bills." *American Economic Journal: Economic Policy* 5 (2): 111–47.
Fetter, Daniel K. 2014. "The Twentieth Century Increase in US Home Ownership: Facts and Hypotheses." In *Housing and Mortgage Markets in Historical Perspective*, edited by P. Fishback, K. Snowden, and E. White, 329–50. University of Chicago Press.
Fetter, Daniel K. 2016. "The Home Front: Rent Control and the Rapid Wartime Increase in Home Ownership." *Journal of Economic History* 76 (4): 1001–1043.
Fishback, Price, Jonathan Rose, and Kenneth Snowden. 2013. *Well Worth Saving: How the New Deal Safeguarded Home Ownership*. University of Chicago Press.
Glaeser, Edward, and Jesse Shapiro. 2003. "The Benefits of the Home Mortgage Interest Deduction." *Tax Policy and the Economy* 17: 37–82.
Goldin, Claudia, and Robert A. Margo. 1992. "The Great Compression: The Wage Structure in the United States at Mid-Century." *Quarterly Journal of Economics* 107 (1): 1–34.
Goldin, Claudia, and Lawrence F. Katz. 2008. *The Race Between Education and Technology*. Harvard University Press.
Grebler, Leo. 1953. "The Role of Federal Credit Aids in Residential Construction." Occasional Paper No. 39, NBER.
Grebler, Leo, David M. Blank, and Louis Winnick. 1956. *Capital Formation in Residential Real Estate*. NBER and Princeton University Press.
Haines, Michael R., and Inter-University Consortium for Political and Social Research. 2010. Historical, Demographic, Economic, and Social Data: The United States, 1790–2002 [computer file]. ICPSR02896-v3. Ann Arbor, MI: ICPSR 2010.
Harriss, C. Lowell. 1951. *History and Policies of the Home Owners' Loan Corporation*. NBER.
Henderson, J.V., and Y.M. Ioannides. 1983. "A Model of Housing Tenure Choice." *American Economic Review* 73 (1): 98–112.
Jackson, Kenneth T. 1985. *Crabgrass Frontier: The Suburbanization of the United States*. Oxford University Press.
Jann, Ben. 2008. "The Blinder-Oaxaca Decomposition for Linear Regression Models." *Stata Journal* 8 (4): 453–79.
Jaworski, Taylor, and Gregory T. Niemesh. 2018. "Revisiting the Great Compression: Wage Inequality in the United States, 1940–1960." *Historical Methods: A Journal of Quantitative and Interdisciplinary History* 51 (1): 39–48.
Juhn, Chinhui. 1999. "Wage Inequality and Demand for Skill: Evidence from Five Decades." *Industrial and Labor Relations Review* 52 (3): 424–43.
Klaman, Saul. 1961. *The Postwar Residential Mortgage Market*. Princeton University Press.
Lindert, Peter H. 2006. "Consumer Price Indexes for All Urban Consumers, for

Selected Items and Groups: 1935–1997." In *Historical Statistics of the United States*, edited by S. Carter, S. Gartner, M. Haines, A. Olmstead, R. Sutch, and G. Wright, table Cc6–48. Cambridge University Press.
Margo, Robert A. 1992. "Explaining the Postwar Suburbanization of Population in the United States: The Role of Income." *Journal of Urban Economics* 31: 301–10.
Maloney, Thomas N. 1994. "Wage Compression and Wage Inequality Between Black and White Males, 1940–1950." *Journal of Economic History* 54 (2): 358–81.
Margo, Robert A. 1995. "Explaining Black-White Wage Convergence, 1940–1950." *Industrial and Labor Relations Review* 48 (3): 470–81.
Margo, Robert A. 2006. "Hourly and Weekly Earnings of Production Workers in Manufacturing: 1909–1995." In *Historical Statistics of the United States*, edited by S. Carter, S. Gartner, M. Haines, A. Olmstead, R. Sutch, and G. Wright, table Ba4361–4366. Cambridge University Press.
Miller, Herman P. 1958. "Changes in the Industrial Distribution of Wages in the United States, 1939–1949." In *An Appraisal of the 1950 Census Income Data*, Studies in Income and Wealth 23, Conference on Research in Income and Wealth, 355–420. NBER and Princeton University Press.
National Bureau of Economic Research. Number of New Private Nonfarm Housing Units Started, One-Family for United States [A0201AUSA176NNBR]. Retrieved from Federal Reserve Bank of St. Louis (FRED), March 22, 2023, https://fred.stlouisfed.org/series/A0201AUSA176NNBR
Oster, Emily. 2019. "Unobservable Selection and Coefficient Stability: Theory and Evidence." *Journal of Business and Economic Statistics* 37 (2): 187–204.
Poterba, James M. 1992. "Taxation and Housing: Old Questions, New Answers." *American Economic Review Papers and Proceedings* 82 (2): 237–42.
Reid, Margaret G. 1962. *Housing and Income*. University of Chicago Press.
Rose, Jonathan D., and Kenneth A. Snowden. 2013. "The New Deal and the Origins of the Modern American Real Estate Loan Contract." *Explorations in Economic History* 50: 548–66.
Rosen, Harvey, and Kenneth T. Rosen. 1980. "Federal Taxes and Homeownership: Evidence from Time Series." *Journal of Political Economy* 88 (1): 59–71.
Ruggles, Steven, Catherine A. Fitch, Ronald Goeken, J. David Hacker, Matt A. Nelson, Evan Roberts, Megan Schouweiler, and Matthew Sobek. 2021. IPUMS Ancestry Full Count Data: Version 3.0 [dataset]. IPUMS. https://doi.org/10.18128/D014.V3.0.
Ruggles, Steven, Sarah Flood, Matthew Sobek, Danika Brockman, Grace Cooper, Stephanie Richards, and Megan Schouweiler. 2023. IPUMS USA: Version 13.0 [dataset]. IPUMS. https://doi.org/10.18128/D010.V13.0.
Saulnier, Raymond J., Harold G. Halcrow, and Neil H. Jacoby. 1958. *Federal Lending and Loan Insurance*. Princeton University Press.
Snowden, Kenneth. 2014. "A Historiography of Early NBER Housing and Mortgage Research." In *Housing and Mortgage Markets in Historical Perspective*, edited by P. Fishback, K. Snowden, and E. White, 15–36. University of Chicago Press and NBER.
Solon, Gary, Steven J. Haider, and Jeffrey M. Wooldridge. 2015. "What Are We Weighting For?" *Journal of Human Resources* 50 (2): 301–16.
University of Michigan, Survey Research Center, Economic Behavior Program. *Survey of Consumer Finances, 1960*. Inter-University Consortium for Political and Social Research [distributor], 2014-01-10. https://doi.org/10.3886/ICPSR07440.v2.

4

Union Army Widows and the Historical Take-Up of Social Benefits

Laura Salisbury

4.1 Introduction

Incomplete take-up of social programs is a puzzle for policymakers. In the United States, major federal income support programs have take-up rates averaging around three-quarters (Currie 2006; Ko and Moffitt 2022). In other words, roughly one-quarter of eligible Americans fail to collect benefits to which they are entitled, although this figure varies substantially by program. In theory, nonparticipation can be explained by a mixture of information, administrative, and stigma costs (Moffitt 1983), and there is a large empirical literature that seeks to tease out the relative importance of each. Understanding the extent and determinants of nonparticipation can help policymakers design more effective programs.

Scholarship on the incomplete take-up of social programs overwhelmingly focuses on the last 50 years. But social assistance in the United States has a longer history. Federal Unemployment Insurance (UI) dates from the 1930s, as does Aid to Families with Dependent Children (AFDC), a welfare program superseded by Temporary Aid to Needy Families (TANF) in the 1990s. State-level social insurance programs date to the Progressive Era and

Laura Salisbury is an associate professor of economics at York University and a research associate of the National Bureau of Economic Research.

I thank Lauren Hoehn Velasco and participants in the NBER Conference on Historical Labor Markets and Inequality for their valuable comments and suggestions. I thank Meagan Sloan, Alice Sun, and Julian Lina for excellent research assistance. I collected most of the data used in this chapter for my doctoral dissertation, which I could not have done without the support and guidance of my adviser, Robert A. Margo. For acknowledgments, sources of research support, and disclosure of the author's material financial relationships, if any, please see https://www.nber.org/books-and-chapters/economic-history-american-inequality-new-evidence-and-perspectives/union-army-widows-and-historical-take-social-benefits.

include Mothers' Pensions (Aizer et al. 2016) and Workers' Compensation (Fishback and Kantor 2000), among others. To what extent did Americans engage with social programs during these early years, and how does this compare with participation in recent programs? Are the determinants of nonparticipation similar across periods? Understanding take-up decisions from the past can provide valuable context for recent estimates of program participation.

This chapter adds an early data point to the literature on the take-up of social programs in the United States. It analyzes take-up of the Union Army (UA) pension, the first large-scale social assistance program in the United States. Introduced in 1862, this pension offered financial support to UA veterans who were wounded in the service and were unable to perform manual labor. The program also offered support to widows of UA veterans, provided their husbands served honorably and died as a direct result of their military service. Widows needed to stay unmarried to maintain eligibility for the program. In its early years, the UA pension was narrowly targeted at people injured or widowed in the service, and it was not means tested. It later grew into a broad old age and disability insurance program for northern men (Skocpol 1995). This chapter focuses on take-up of the UA pension among eligible widows in the very early years of the program.

There are similarities and differences between UA widows' pensions and modern social welfare programs. Information technology being more advanced today, it is easier for applicants to gain information about modern programs. On the other hand, the UA pension was extremely well publicized in newspapers. Moreover, it was the only program of its kind, and eligibility rules were relatively straightforward, which made it easier for applicants to determine their own eligibility. The administrative costs of applications for the UA pension were very high, including not just the assembly of documentation but physical court appearances. Collecting the UA pension was also costly, involving travel for applicants who did not live near a pension agency (see section 4.3 for details). Modern programs do not generally require applicants to make court appearances, and technological progress makes the process of assembling documentation and collecting payments significantly easier. On the other hand, modern means-tested programs require supporting documentation to be filed on a repeated basis, while documentation for a UA pension needed to be filed only once. Many modern programs, like TANF and the Supplemental Nutrition Assistance Program (SNAP), assign caseworkers to recipients, who ease some of the administrative burden of filing. Such workers were not available to UA pension applicants. On the other hand, there was an active private market for pension attorneys, who assumed part of this role (for a large fee, payable by the applicant). Finally, there is a great deal of stigma associated with collecting benefits like SNAP or TANF. While the UA pension program was politically controversial, UA widows were widely considered "deserving" of aid, at least in the north.

On the other hand, pension commissioners' reports and the contemporary popular press demonstrate a deep skepticism of applicants for widows' pensions, citing concerns about fraud and "immoral behavior" that bear some resemblance to the way in which welfare recipients are characterized today.[1]

I estimate the share of eligible Union Army widows who applied for a pension. I focus on characterizing take-up decisions by Union Army widows in the early years of the program, up to 1870. I do this with microdata on Union Army recruits (Fogel 2000) combined with data on widows' pensions and remarriages (Salisbury 2017). Because a widow's immediate eligibility depended only the circumstances of her husband's death, and not on health or financial means, it is possible to infer eligibility for both applicants and nonapplicants using this database. In addition, there was a change to the pension law as applied to widows during this period that allows for relatively clean measurement of secondary, or repeated, take-up. As of July 25, 1866, women could apply for a monthly pension increase of $2 per minor child. Because women had to indicate their children's names and birth dates in their original pension applications, I know who is eligible for this increase and who is not, so I can accurately measure the secondary take-up rate. Using a sample consisting of both applicants and eligible nonapplicants, I estimate the correlates of take-up as well as the rate.

I find that the take-up rate of the UA widows' pension was lower than the take-up rate of modern federal programs, although the gap is surprisingly small. I estimate the participation rate roughly between 35 percent and 75 percent, with a preferred estimate around 50 percent. The secondary take-up rate was much higher, likely exceeding 80 percent. As in the modern literature, the correlates of take-up are consistent with information and administrative costs affecting participation. Women who were likely to have access to greater networks of other war widows participated more often and more quickly. Older women with more children were more likely to participate than younger women without children. As age and number of children are inversely related to remarriage prospects, these women would have expected to receive the pension for more time, making it more attractive to incur the substantial administrative costs associated with applying.

4.2 Related Literature

There is a large literature on the rate and determinants of take-up of modern social programs. In general, estimating program take-up is not a trivial exercise. While administrative records may contain a comprehensive list of program participants (the numerator), it is not always easy to observe the denominator. This is especially true when eligibility rules are complicated, so eligibility is not easily inferred from survey data (Ko and Moffitt 2022).

1. See section 4.7 for details and several concrete examples.

Currie (2006) and Ko and Moffitt (2022) provide extensive surveys of this literature. The large federal social assistance programs in the United States typically have take-up rates around two-thirds to three-quarters, although there is variation over time and across programs. The Earned Income Tax Credit (EITC) has a take-up rate consistently above 80 percent. It is the most straightforward to claim, requiring only that the eligible recipient file a tax return. TANF is a low-income support program with a lower take-up rate that has changed substantially over time. The largest change occurred as a result of the 1996 welfare reforms (formally, the Personal Responsibility and Work Opportunity Reconciliation Act, or PRWORA), which established work requirements for most welfare recipients. By one estimate, these led to an almost two-thirds reduction in the take-up rate (Falk 2017).

The literature posits several theoretical determinants of incomplete take-up that build on Moffitt's (1983) model of program participation. These determinants include information, transaction costs (relative to benefits), and stigma. Separately identifying these determinants is difficult empirically, as observable characteristics of programs or individuals are often related to more than one of them. For example, Currie and Grogger (2001) show that the introduction of the Electronic Benefit Transfer (EBT) system for SNAP—which works like a debit card—increased take-up. However, it is not clear what drives this effect. The EBT may have lowered transaction costs, but it may also have lowered stigma costs if EBT cards look like debit cards to outside observers at grocery store checkouts. Moreover, there are likely strong, unobservable individual fixed effects that influence program take-up and are simultaneously related to perceived stigma, ability to navigate informationally complex programs, and expected benefits of participation relative to cost. These unobserved individual characteristics may be correlated with observables, making it even more difficult to pin down the mechanisms behind the observable correlates of take-up.

A number of studies explore the role of information in determining take-up. One source of information about programs is networks. This is difficult to pin down because of a reflection problem. People who are part of networks with many participants may be more likely to participate themselves for several reasons: a direct effect of network characteristics on the propensity to participate, correlated individual characteristics within networks, or an information-sharing effect. Aizer and Currie (2004) study network effects on the take-up of public prenatal care in California. They argue that the information-sharing effect is of limited importance, as neighborhood participation impacts repeated users as much as—if not more than—first time users. Conversely, Bertrand et al. (2000) find strong evidence for informational network effects. They use the intersection of geographic and linguistic networks to identify network effects on the probability of claiming welfare. The use of both language and geography generates variation in "network" access to social programs within neighborhoods and linguistic groups, allowing the authors to control for neighborhood and language-specific effects. This circumvents the reflection problem inherent in most studies of network effects. Duflo and Saez (2003) analyze network effects on employees' decisions to enroll in Tax Deferred Account retirement plans using experimental evidence. They show that encouraging a member of a person's network to participate has a similar effect on the probability that this person participates as does encouraging the person directly. Borjas and Hilton (1996) document a larger rate of program participation among immigrants than natives and posit that this is driven by network effects.

Informational complexity is a related deterrent of program participation. Bhargava and Manoli (2015) use experimental evidence to assess the relative importance of information, cost, and stigma in determining take-up of EITC benefits. They distributed mailings to tax filers who did not claim EITC benefits, which targeted each of the above potential drivers of nonparticipation. They conclude that informational complexity and a lack of awareness of the program on the part of potential applicants are the key drivers of low take-up. Similarly, Bhargava et al. (2017) show that low-income employees are more likely to choose less complex but suboptimal health plans than higher-income employees, which suggests that program complexity may be a driver of low take-up. Saez (2009) shows that the way in which subsidies for retirement savings are presented—as a matching contribution versus a tax credit, for example—have a significant effect on take-up, suggesting a role for both informational complexity and stigma. Madrian and Shea (2001) show that changing default rules has a significant effect on participation, which also suggests a role for informational complexity.

Administrative costs are another likely driver of low take-up. The evidence generally points to a role for administrative costs, although there are some exceptions. Bitler et al. (2003) measure correlates of take-up of the Special Supplemental Nutrition Program for Women, Infants, and Children (WIC) at the state level. They argue that poverty and unemployment do not predict greater take-up, but state-level rules that reduce transaction costs do. Blank and Ruggles (1996) study nonparticipation in the AFDC and SNAP programs using the Survey of Income and Program Participation (SIPP). They argue that expectations about future earnings, not just current earnings, reduce the probability of participating: women with short eligibility spells are less likely to participate at all. This suggests a high fixed cost of participating, which substantially discourages take-up. Currie and Grogger (2001) study the decline in participation in Food Stamps after the 1990s welfare reform using administrative and survey data on program participation. They attribute the decline in part to the growth of substitute programs, and to increasing transaction costs associated with participating, such as recertification intervals, and stigma costs. Benzarti (2017) uses taxpayers' choice to itemize deductions or claim the standard deduction to identify the time cost of filing income tax; he estimates this cost at around 1 percent of gross domestic product (GDP) in recent years.

Other studies point to a limited role for transaction costs. Ebenstein and Stange (2010) explore the effect of transaction costs on UI take-up, exploiting the introduction of remote claiming (i.e., by phone or internet). They find that remote claiming did not change the take-up rate, suggesting a limited role for transaction costs in explaining low take-up. Jones (2010) conducts an experiment in which he distributes information on the EITC program to randomly selected workplaces; this intervention is thought to lower information, administrative, and stigma costs simultaneously, so he cannot identify these effects separately from one another. He finds that the intervention increased take-up, but only by a small amount.

This chapter is also related to a literature on pre–New Deal social assistance programs in the United States. This literature has focused less participation and more on the consequences of historical transfer programs. Eli (2015) finds that Union Army pensions improved the health of sick and wounded veterans. Salisbury (2017) finds that Union Army widows receiving pensions delayed remarriage. Costa (1997, 1995) finds that Union Army pensions affected the retirement decisions and living arrangements of aging veterans. Aizer et al. (2016) study mothers' pensions, which were state-administered transfers to needy single mothers. They find evidence that these transfers had a positive causal effect on children's life expectancy and economic well-being in adulthood.

The literature on early social assistance programs also discusses the political economy of their introduction. With the exception of the Union Army Pension, pre-New Deal programs were introduced at the state level. Among the earliest programs to be widely introduced was Workers' Compensation, or publicly administered insurance for workplace injury. Fishback and Kantor (1998) argue that this program was widely adopted because it solved a real inefficiency in the existing liability regime. Eli (2015) finds that the disbursement of Union Army pensions in the 1880s and 1890s responded to the political performance of the Republican Party at the local level. Similarly, Eli and Salisbury (2016) find that state-run pensions for Confederate veterans and widows were used to shore up support for the Democratic Party.

4.3 Historical Background

The Union Army pension was the US government's first attempt at large-scale social assistance. The US had long offered pensions to wounded veterans and their widows; however, the unprecedented enlistment and casualty rate during the Civil War meant that the Union Army pension operated on a significantly larger scale. By the end of the war, the number of individuals receiving military pensions ballooned from 11,000 in 1861 to almost

Table 4.1 **Eligibility requirements for Union Army widows' pensions, General Law**

	Law:	
Rules:	July 14, 1862	July 25, 1866
Means	No means test	No means test
First husband	Served honorably in Union Army; died as direct result of military service	Served honorably in Union Army; died as direct result of military service
Marital status	Legally married to soldier husband; not remarried	Legally married to soldier husband; not remarried
Children	Not required	Not required for base; Must be legitimate children of soldier husband to quality for pension increase
Amount:	$8 per month	$8 per month + $2 per month per child under 16
Start date	Date of first husband's death	Later of date of first husband's death or July 25, 1866
End date	Death or remarriage	Base: death or remarriage; Increase: child's 16th birthday

86,000 (US Pension Bureau 1865). The Union Army pension would go on to become a general disability and old age pension for northern men, covering 28 percent of men over 65 and occupying 25 percent of the federal budget by 1910 (Skocpol 1995).

This chapter focuses on the take-up behavior of Union Army widows in the immediate aftermath of the Civil War. At this time, the eligibility rules for widows were straightforward: in order to be eligible to receive a pension, a widow needed to have been lawfully married to a man who served honorably in the Union Army and whose death was directly related to his military service. She forfeited her right to a pension if she remarried. Under the General Law of 1862, eligible widows were entitled to receive $8 per month, which was less than half the typical monthly earnings of a farm laborer in 1870 (Margo 2000). An amendment passed on July 25, 1866, entitled widows to receive an additional $2 per month for every child under the age of 16. Table 4.1 summarizes eligibility criteria for UA widows' pensions under both the General Law and the 1866 amendment.

In order to apply for a pension, a widow needed to appear before a court of record and attest to certain facts: in particular, the legality of her marriage, her husband's military service, her husband's death, and her children's names and ages. These needed to be verified with supporting documentation, such as marriage certificates, birth certificates, and death records. In the absence of original records, witness testimony (taken before a justice of the peace) could be submitted. This evidence was mailed to the pension bureau in Washington, DC, where the claim would be assessed (Salisbury 2017). Applicants whose claims were approved were issued pension certificates, which they would use to receive payment.

Each pensioner was assigned to a pension agency, which was a local office to which funds were disbursed for the payment of pensions. Payments were made quarterly. Pensioners had to present their pension certificates in person at their local pension agency, and they were paid by check on the US Treasury. There were 42 pension agencies in 1865, with no more than 3 agencies in a single state (US Pension Bureau 1866). By 1870, there were 59 pension agencies across the country, with denser coverage in some states (US Pension Bureau 1871). Agencies were located in major cities, often railroad hubs, which facilitated travel to collect pensions. Scheduled quarterly payments ("pension days") were frequently reported in newspapers, with references to "long lines" and "crowds" (e.g., *New York Times* 1869). Some pensioners opted to pay attorneys or pension brokers to collect their pensions on their behalf.[2]

It was very common for claimants to employ pension attorneys to handle their claims. These attorneys could charge a fixed fee of ten dollars per application, which was slightly more than a month's pension. This was a lucrative business. There was a handful of large, Washington, DC–based law firms that specialized in pensions, and they spent a great deal of money advertising changes to the pension law in newspapers, distributing pamphlets, and in some cases publishing entire newspapers which they populated with their own advertisements (Blanck and Song 2002). While neglectful attorneys were a common problem, of which the pension board was keenly aware (US Pension Bureau 1883), it is undeniable that attorneys were an important source of information about pension eligibility for widows, and that widows valued the administrative support they provided.

4.4 Data

This chapter uses a sample of widows drawn from the Union Army (UA) Database (Fogel 2000), with supplementary data on widows' pension outcomes and remarriages collected from original case files at the National Archives in Washington, DC (Salisbury 2017). The Union Army database contains military, demographic, and socioeconomic information on almost 40,000 recruits from a sample of 331 companies. Information comes from

2. Many newspaper articles allude to pension attorneys and brokers collecting funds on behalf of their clients, and none takes a favorable view of these brokers. A New York Times article from 1880 describes a widow who empowered her attorney to collect $1,400 of pension funds owed to her in arrears, with the help of a pension broker. The attorney and broker were both arrested on fraud charges, as they withheld all but $600 of the payment from the widow for "various charges and expenses."

multiple primary sources, including compiled military service records, pension files, and links to federal censuses. In many cases, the database also contains information on recruits' families, including wife's name, date of marriage, and the names and birth dates of their children. It is important to note that this information is not collected by survey but by examination of historical records. Thus, key pieces of information are frequently missing, and the source of such information is important for understanding what this means for the representativeness of the usable sample. Most important for this study is data on recruits' families. For recruits who lived past 1898 and were receiving a pension, this information is available from the "family circular," a mandatory form sent to all pensioners requesting a list of family members.[3] If the recruit died prior to 1898, or never filed for a pension, information about his family comes from dependents' pension applications. If the recruits' dependents never filed for a pension, this information may only be available through links to the census, in which case certain key pieces of information (e.g., marriage date) will be missing.[4]

The unit of observation in the UA database is the soldier, but the key unit of observation in this study is the widow. So, this chapter uses a dataset constructed by Salisbury (2017), which identifies widows of UA veterans who died before 1880 in the UA database, and supplements the available data on these women with additional information about widows' pension applications and subsequent remarriages from their original pension files housed at the National Archives. The widows' pension file data contain all correspondence between the widow and the pension bureau. This includes pension applications, supporting documentation (including marriage records and children's birth records), and pension decisions.

The core sample used in this chapter consists of women whose husbands died during the Civil War. I focus on two take-up decisions: the decision to apply for a pension at all and the decision to apply for the increase for minor children implemented in 1866, conditional on having made an initial pension application. The latter captures repeated engagement with the program. I use two slightly different subsamples for each. To analyze the decision to apply for an original pension, I use women identified in the 1860 census as being married to men who would go on to die during the war. To analyze the decision to apply for a pension increase, I use women who had applied for a pension but had not remarried by July 25, 1866, and who had minor children (which is observable from the original pension application).

3. The purpose of this exercise was to get ahead of pension fraud: dependents could claim pensions after an eligible veteran's death, and fraud was considered rampant. The Pension Bureau hoped to limit fraud by verifying dependents' claims against the information in the family circular.

4. Links to the census are also less likely if family information is not already contained in the database, as family information is used to construct these links. Moreover, only men who are married and living in the same household as their family during a decadal census year will have observable families through census links alone.

4.5 Estimating the Take-up Rate Among Union Army Widows

An estimate of the take-up rate of the UA widows' pension requires knowledge of the number of pension applicants and the number of eligible potential applicants. This is difficult to compute. In principle, the numerator could be computed from annual reports of the commissioner of pensions (US Pension Bureau 1865–1870), which lists the number of pensioners on the rolls, and the number of new applicants, by state, year, and applicant status (i.e., veteran or dependent). However, it does not differentiate between widows and other dependents' pensions. Some 40 percent of pension applications by dependents of soldiers who died during the war were parents of deceased soldiers, not wives or children. Moreover, aggregate pension data does not indicate which new applications are from children whose mothers had been pensioned before remarrying, so there is a degree of double counting. The denominator is also difficult. The literature contains estimates of the Union Army casualty rate (Hacker 2011; Livermore 1901), but the marital status of these dead soldiers is not known. The remarriage rate was too high—on the order of 50 percent (Salisbury 2017)—to estimate the number of Union Army widows using any of the postwar censuses.

The UA database is a more promising source of data for estimating take-up, but it also has its limitations. It is easy to count the number of widows in the database who applied for pensions. The number of eligible widows is less clear. To pin this down, I need to know how many men were killed as a result of their military service. And I need to know how many of these men were married. Neither is obvious because of the prevalence of missing data. Soldiers' death dates are available in the UA data from several sources. If a soldier died while serving, there may be a military record of his death. If the soldier survived the war and received a pension until his death, there will be a record of his death in his pension file. Finally, if the soldier left dependents, they may have filed for a pension, in which case his death would be noted in their pension file. A soldier who died after the war ended, never applied for a pension, and whose spouse never applied for a pension, will certainly have a missing death date in the UA database. Moreover, as noted earlier, a married soldier who died before 1898 and whose wife never applied for a pension will have missing information about marital status. Thus, it is possible to estimate the take-up rate among widows only under assumptions about missing data.

I construct a reasonable range of estimates of the rate of take-up of the Union Army pension among widows of men who died during the war. These are reported in table 4.2. I refer to events using the following shorthand:

APP_t = soldier's widow applies for pension by time t,
D_s = soldier dies (due to military service) by time s,
M = soldier is married.

Table 4.2 **Estimated take-up rate, Union Army widows' pensions, 1862–70**

	Low estimate	Preferred estimate	High estimate
(1)	Probability of application by 1870 if widowed during war, UA database		
$\Pr(APP_{1870}, D_{1865}, M)$	0.037	0.039	0.041
$\Pr(D_{1865})$	0.134	0.17	0.20
$\Pr(M)$	0.32	0.46	0.52
Take-up rate	0.35	0.50	0.95
(2)	Probability of application by 1870 if widowed during war and married in 1860, UA database + 1860 census links		
Take-up rate			0.76
(3)	Probability of application for increase for minor children, All pre-1866 applicants with children		
Take-up rate	0.60		0.65
(4)	Probability of application for increase for minor children, Eligible pre-1866 applicants with children		
Take-up rate	0.77		0.89

Note: Microdata from Fogel et al. (2000) and Salisbury (2017). See text for details.

The take-up rate, or the share of women widowed by year *s* who apply for a pension by year *t*, is equal to

$$\Pr(APP_t \mid D_s, M) = \frac{\Pr(APP_t, D_s, M)}{\Pr(D_s)\Pr(M)},$$

assuming marital status and death are at least roughly statistically independent.[5] Because all pension applications made on behalf of soldiers in the UA database are observed, it is relatively straightforward to estimate $\Pr(APP_t, D_s, M)$ using this database.[6] But due to the prevalence of missing information on death date and marital status, $\Pr(D_s)$ and $\Pr(M)$ are unknown.

I construct low- and high-end estimates of $\Pr(D_{1865})$ and $\Pr(M)$, which imply low- and high-end estimates of $\Pr(APP_{1870} \mid D_{1865}, M)$. I focus on war dead because wartime deaths in the UA database can be observed from sources other than pension applications, and I can rely on external estimates of wartime casualties. Assuming that war deaths are underreported, the lower-bound number of war dead in the UA database would be the number of men in the UA database with a recorded death date during the war. Thus, a low-end estimate of $PR(D_{1865})$ is 13.4 percent.

5. There is some support for this assumption, at least for $s = 1865$. Among veterans linked to the 1860 census, those who are married and unmarried are equally likely to have an observed death date between 1861 and 1865.

6. There are a few cases in which widows' application status is ambiguous, but this is sufficiently uncommon that the upper and lower bounds on this probability are essential equal.

For the high-end estimate, I inflate the conventional estimate of Union army casualties (which is 17 percent) by 20 percent, which yields $\Pr(D_{1865}) =$ 20.4 percent. The conventional estimate is from Livermore (1901). Hacker (2011) uses a census-based method to argue that Civil War deaths were undercounted. According to his preferred estimate, deaths attributable to the Civil War that occurred before 1870 are 20 percent higher than the conventional estimate of the death toll. A 20 percent upward adjustment will overstate the *wartime* deaths of *Union* soldiers for two reasons. First, many of the war-related deaths occurring before 1870 occurred after the war ended.[7] Second, undercounting of deaths was a larger problem on the Confederate side than the Union side. If the total death toll was 20 percent higher than the conventional estimate, this implies that the Union death toll ought to be inflated by less than 20 percent. As such, I consider $\Pr(D_{1865}) =$ 20.4 percent a reasonable high-end estimate. I take the conventional estimate of Union deaths as my "preferred" estimate, although the truth is probably a bit higher.

To estimate the marriage rate, I regress marital status on age and state of residence indicators in the 1860 census, then use predicted values from this regression to assign recruits in the UA database a probability of being married in a given year. The low-end estimate uses the estimated share of UA recruits who were married in 1861. This would be the probable marriage rate among UA recruits if no marriages occurred after the war began. The high-end estimate treats all wartime deaths as occurring in 1865, with normal state-year marriage rates prevailing among soldiers throughout the war. My preferred estimate assumes that normal state-year marriage rates prevailed until the median death year of wartime casualties (1864). Thus, I allow $\Pr(M)$ to range between 32 percent and 52 percent, with a preferred estimate of 46 percent.

With this range of values for $\Pr(D_{1865})$ and $\Pr(M)$, I calculate high- and low-end estimates of the take-up rate. These range from 35 percent to 95 percent, with a preferred estimate of 50 percent.

I can also use records linked to the 1860 census to calculate the take-up rate. I take all men who are married in 1860 (according to census links) and have a known wartime death date, and I compute the share whose widows filed for a pension before 1870. This is 71 percent. Among men who are household heads in 1860, this share is 76 percent.[8] If men linked to the

7. Among all widows' pension applications filed before 1870, 20 percent were on behalf of veterans who died between 1866 and 1870.

8. The 1860 census does not include a question on household relationships, so I have to make an educated guess as to the marital status of recruits linked to this census, which is based on household composition. If some soldiers are classified as "married" but really are not, I will underestimate the share of married soldiers that apply for a pension. I test my procedure for inferring marital status against the procedure used by IPUMS (Ruggles et al. 2023), and it performs very well: 97.8 percent of men in the 1860 1 percent census sample whom my algorithm would call married are also classified as married by IPUMS. Among men who are household

1860 census were representative of all married men, and if having a recorded death date was independent of having a widow file for a pension, this would be a reasonable point estimate of the take-up rate. However, neither of these things is true. Men whose wives file for a pension are overrepresented among those with a known wartime death date. And, men whose wives file for a pension are overrepresented among married men linked to the 1860 census, as spousal information is used to make these links. As such, I consider this an upper bound on the true take-up rate. Applying this upper bound to my previous estimates, it is reasonable to put the take-up rate between 35 percent and 76 percent.

How does this compare with participation rates of modern federal programs? First, note that I am capturing something slightly different from a typical take-up estimate. Most of the literature estimates the take-up rate as the share of those currently eligible who are collecting benefits at a point in time. I estimate the share of women who are eligible at at least one point who apply for benefits within a period of roughly five years. The fact that I am not using current eligibility tends to lower my estimate, relative to the modern literature. The fact that I am estimating take-up over a longer time horizon tends to raise my estimate relative to the literature. I also note that I am measuring take-up by application rather than receipt, which tends to push my estimate up. This makes a small difference, in practice, as the approval rate of pensions was extremely high—more than 90 percent of the applicants in my sample were issued pension certificates within 10 years, the overwhelming majority of whom were issued certificates within three years. And, given the high rate of secondary take-up (see below), it is unlikely that many widows were issued certificates but did not collect.

With these caveats in mind, I can make a direct comparison between the take-up rate of the UA pension and that of modern programs. Figure 4.1, panel A, plots selected estimates of the take-up rates of US federal programs between 1970 and 2020. Programs included in the figure are EITC, Medicaid, UI, SNAP, and AFDC/TANF.[9] Rates are taken from Currie (2006) and Ko and Moffitt (2022), who survey a large literature on the take-up of social programs. The figure shades the area between 35 percent and 76 percent, which constitutes a reasonable range of values for the take-up rate of the

heads, my algorithm performs better: 99.1 percent of men whom I classify as married are also classified as married by IPUMS. Thus, it appears that restricting to men who are household heads in 1860 yields more accurate assignment of marital status.

9. Social Security Disability Insurance (SSDI) is another federal program that is comparable in many ways to the UA pension. This program offers transfers to Americans who have worked in the past but are not longer able to work due to disability. There is a literature on participation in SSDI, which finds that the program grew rapidly after the mid-1980s, when screening became less stringent and lower-skilled workers' earnings declined. Autor and Duggan (2003) estimate that, in 1999, 17 percent–27 percent of nonelderly Americans who did not participate in labor force collected SSDI benefits. However, without knowing the disability status of this population, it is difficult to infer a participation rate based on this figure.

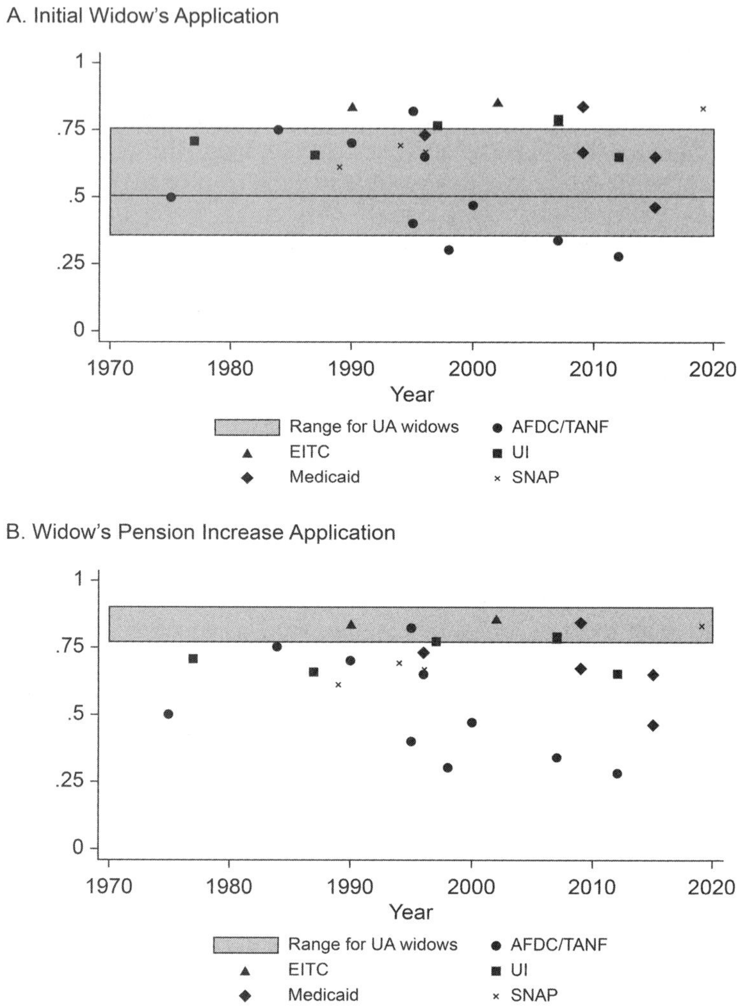

Figure 4.1 Take-up rate of modern American social programs versus Union Army widow's pension

Note: Range of values for take-up rate of UA pension based on author's calculations using data from Fogel et al. (2000) and Salisbury (2017). Take-up rates for modern programs from Currie (2004) and Ko and Moffitt (2022).

Union Army pension among the widows of war dead. Figure 4.2 summarizes the information in this figure, for ease of comparison across programs.

The EITC consistently has the highest take-up rate and AFDC/TANF the lowest. The average take-up rate for modern programs is in the ballpark of 75 percent. While the take-up rate of the UA widows' pension is certainly lower than the take-up rate of a typical modern program, it is not far off.

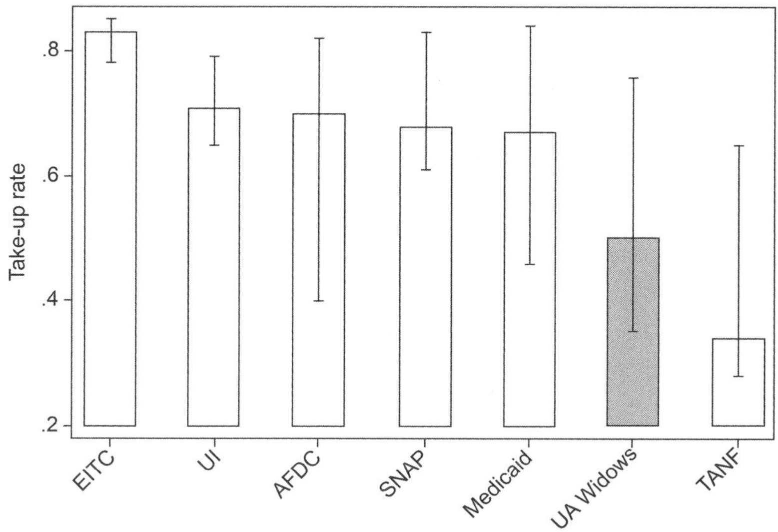

Figure 4.2 Take-up rate of modern American social programs versus Union Army widow's pension

Note: Plots median, minimum and maximum take-up estimates for US federal programs (1970 onwards) from literature, as presented in figure 4.1.

There is substantial overlap between the upper part of the reasonable take-up range of the UA widows' pension and the take-up rates of modern programs. And the take-up rate among UA widows is almost certainly higher than the TANF take-up rate following welfare reform.

In addition to the overall participation rate, I can characterize secondary participation decisions by widows who had already applied for a pension. In particular, I can calculate the share of pensioned widows who applied for additional benefits for which they were eligible. On July 25, 1866, an amendment to the pension law allowed widows to apply for an additional $2 per month for each of her children (fathered by her soldier husband) under the age of 16. This increase was not automatic. A widow had to submit an application form as well as records of her children's births. Because pre-1866 pension applications required widows to list their children's birth dates, I know whether or not applicants who filed for pensions before 1866 had qualifying children. This allows me to calculate a secondary take-up rate for eligible widows.

These application rates are also reported in table 4.2. Between 60 percent and 65 percent of widows who were married to a soldier who died during the war; had a qualifying child as of July 25, 1866; and applied for an original pension before July 25, 1866, applied for a pension increase within five years of eligibility. However, this understates the secondary take-up rate, as some

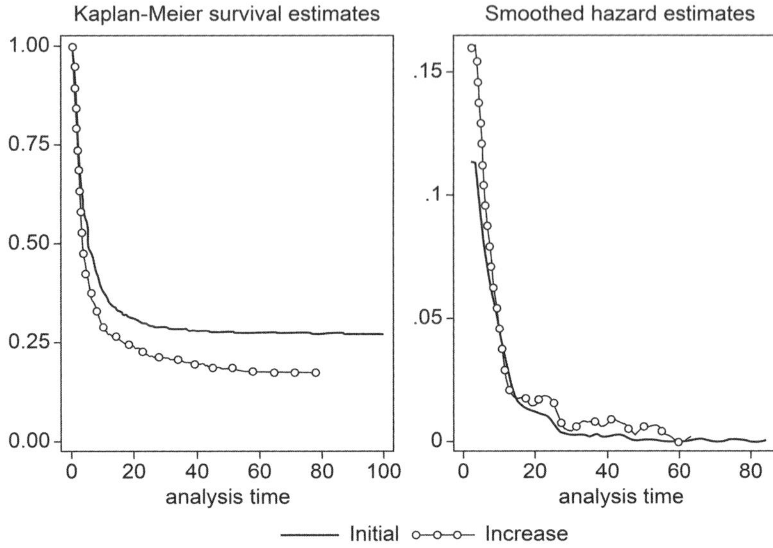

Figure 4.3 Rate of pension application: Initial and increase

Note: Microdata from Salisbury (2017) and Fogel et al. (2000). Sample of women eligible for initial pension: women who are linked to the 1860 census and are married to a Union army soldier who died during the war. Sample of women eligible for pension increase: women whose husbands dies during the war, who applied for a pension before July 25, 1866, and who have at least one child under the age of 16 as of July 25, 1866. Women enter the sample on the date they become eligible for the pension. For the initial pension application, this is the date of her husband's death or July 14, 1862, whichever is later. For the pension increase, this is July 25, 1866. The sample period ends at the end of 1872. A "failure" occurs when a widow files a pension application.

women who had been collecting pensions before 1866 had already lost their eligibility due to remarriage or death.

Whether or not a pensioned widow remarried or died before July 25, 1866, is known in some cases (from a subsequent children's pension application, or a widow's application for restoration to the pension roles after 1901) but ambiguous in others. Making different assumptions about the eligibility of these ambiguous cases allows me to establish bounds on the share of eligible widows who applied for pension increases. These are reported in the bottom row of table 4.2 and range between 77 percent and 89 percent. A comparison between this and the take-up rate of modern programs is given in panel B of figure 4.1.

The secondary take-up rate of Union Army widows' pensions is clearly much higher than the primary take-up rate. In figure 4.3, I plot empirical survival and hazard functions for pension applications of both types. This allows me to characterize the speed of application, as well as the binary outcome of participation or nonparticipation. For initial applications, I use widows linked to the 1860 census, so the nonparticipation rate is likely understated. For secondary applications, I use widows who had applied for an original pension before July 25, 1866, and who are not known to have remarried or died before then. A widow becomes at risk of applying for an original pension when her husband dies, or the General Law is passed, whichever is later. A widow becomes at risk of applying for a pension increase on July 25, 1866. A "failure" is defined as a pension application, and anyone applying later than 1872 (or not at all) is censored.

The Kaplan-Meier survival estimates clearly show the higher secondary take-up rate, even with an overstated primary take-up rate. The hazard estimates indicate clear differences in the speed of application. Widows applying for increased pensions were much more likely to apply quickly. The probability of applying within a month or so of eligibility was more than 15 percent for an increase and slightly more than 10 percent for an original application. These hazards converge quickly, with the likelihood of making an application of any type hovering around zero after 36 months. Thus, pension applications tended to happen quickly or not at all, and were faster and more common for pension increases.

4.6 Explaining Nonparticipation Among Union Army Widows

The pension take-up rate of Union Army widows is lower but comparable to take-up rates of modern federal programs. And the secondary take-up rate among Union Army widows is very high. Still, take-up was not complete in either case, and it is not obvious why. In general, we can think about nonparticipation occurring for two reasons. First, the eligible person does not know about the program, or does not understand that she is eligible. Second, the eligible person knows about the program, but makes the decision not to apply because the costs outweigh the benefits. An investigation of the correlates of take-up of the Union Army pension will shed light on the extent to which these factors are important.

To analyze the correlates of initial take-up, I use widows linked to the 1860 census who were married to soldiers known to have died during the war. Because there are often military records of wartime deaths, it is not necessary for a dependent to have filed a pension application in order for me to know that a soldier died during the war. So, from military and pension data alone, I have a list of all soldiers who died in the war and whose dependents filed pension claims and some war dead whose dependents did not. Using links to the 1860 census allows me to infer which soldiers were married in 1860, and thus left widows eligible for a pension. Widows who filed for a pension are overrepresented in this sample, so it gives a skewed picture of the rate of take-up. However, it can be used to evaluate the correlates of take-up, subject to a few caveats.

First of all, spousal information from pension applications is used to make census links. If a soldier died during the war and no dependent of his ever claimed a pension, there is no family information available to aid in linking to the census. This means that the characteristics of soldiers linked to the 1860 census might differ systematically based on whether or not their widows applied for a pension. For one thing, the linkage error rate might be higher among soldiers whose wives weren't pensioned. In addition, soldiers with no dependent pension applications on file who are linked to the 1860 census may have more unique characteristics, which make linkages possible—more unusual names, more uncommon birthplaces or places of residence, and the like. This should be kept in mind when comparing pensioned and unpensioned widows using census links.

Characteristics observable for applicants and nonapplicants include census variables (age, nativity, literacy, husband's socioeconomic characteristics, county characteristics) and variables from soldiers' compiled service records (death date, enlistment information and company-level characteristics). I present summary statistics for applicants and nonapplicants in table 4.3, including *t*-tests for equality of means across groups. In table 4.4, I present results from linear probability models in which I regress an indicator for the widow having applied for a pension by 1870 on observable characteristics. Women widowed in their 30s with at least one child in 1860 were most likely to apply for pensions. Foreign-born women were significantly less likely to apply than native-born women. Women married to household heads were substantially more likely to apply than married women living in multifamily households.

Socioeconomic status is correlated with pension application. Widows from wealthier families were less likely to apply, although this largely reflects geographic differences in application rates: the difference is not statistically significant conditional on state fixed effects. Women married to white collar workers or men who report no occupation were least likely to apply for a pension. Women married to men who served in companies with a higher death rate are more likely to apply. Women from more rural counties with a lower male-to-female ratio are more likely to apply, although the latter result does not survive the inclusion of additional controls. Women from the Northeast are overrepresented in the applicant pool, and women from the Midwest are underrepresented.

Table 4.5 reproduces the final column of table 4.4 under different sample restrictions. These are intended to reduce errors stemming from false links to the census or misassignment of marital status. In some specifications, links to the census that are coded "low quality" in the UA database are excluded. In others, only soldiers who are heads of household, or who are over 20 years old in 1860, are included. The results are qualitatively similar throughout.

To analyze the correlates of secondary take-up, I use a sample of women whose husbands died during the war, who had at least one minor child in 1866, and who applied for an original pension before July 25, 1866. To avoid limiting the sample size further, I do not require these women to have

Table 4.3 **Characteristics of war widows by application status**

Variable	Mean, nonapplicants	Mean, applicants	Difference
Age at widowhood	31.06	32.94	1.89***
No. of Children < 14, 1860	1.62	2.20	0.58***
Age oldest child < 14, 1860	6.99	7.14	0.15
Age youngest child < 14, 1860	3.04	2.87	–0.16
Spousal age gap (recruit – wife)	2.98	4.10	1.12***
Recruit HH head, 1860	0.76	0.97	0.21***
Wife literate, 1860	0.91	0.92	0.00
Wife foreign born, 1860	0.18	0.13	–0.05*
Recruit foreign born, 1860	0.16	0.16	0.00
Family personal property, 1860	0.46	0.17	–0.29***
Family real property, 1860	1.03	0.50	–0.53***
Recruit farmer, 1860	0.31	0.31	0.00
Recruit skilled white collar, 1860	0.05	0.03	–0.02
Recruit skilled blue collar, 1860	0.10	0.22	0.13***
Recruit laborer, 1860	0.24	0.22	–0.02
Recruit no occupation, 1860	0.31	0.22	–0.09***
Recruit's year of death	1863.26	1863.36	0.10
Enlisted as private	0.87	0.87	0.01
Company death rate	0.20	0.22	0.01
1,000s of people per sq. mile, 1860	1.24	0.96	–0.28
County railroad access, 1860	0.81	0.80	–0.01
County newspapers per 1000 ppl, 1860	0.10	0.10	0.00
County male–female ratio, 1860	1.06	1.05	–0.01*
New England, 1860	0.31	0.44	0.13***
Midwest, 1860	0.63	0.49	–0.14***
South, 1860	0.05	0.06	0.01

Note: Microdata from Fogel et al. (2000); county-level aggregate census data from Haines and ICPSR (2010); county-level railroad data from Atack (2017); county-level newspaper data from the Library of Congress. Sample consists of women married to UA recruits killed during the war, who were linked to the 1860 federal census, and includes 234 nonapplicants and 577 applicants. Final column indicates significance of difference between nonapplicants and applicants, using standard errors clustered by county for geographic variables and company for company-level variables: $*p < 0.10$. $**p < 0.05$. $***p < 0.01$.

been linked to the 1860 census. Thus, I am able to look at variables from the original pension application to characterize determinants of take-up. These include characteristics of the widow (age, number and age of children), her husband (death date, enlistment variables, and company-level characteristics), her county of residence at the time of initial application (based on aggregate census data from Haines and ICPSR 2010), and characteristics of her first application (time to application, decision, and use of a lawyer).

Table 4.6 presents the average characteristics of applicants and nonapplicants for pension increases. Table 4.7 contains results from regressions of

Table 4.4 **Determinants of take-up: Initial application**

	=1 if widow applied for pension before 1870					
Dependent variable	(1)	(2)	(3)	(4)	(5)	(6)
Widow age 30–39	0.046	0.096	0.108			0.109
	(0.034)	(0.041)**	(0.037)***			(0.041)***
Widow age 40+	–0.007	0.034	0.032			0.037
	(0.046)	(0.059)	(0.053)			(0.051)
No minor children	–0.117		–0.007			–0.010
	(0.050)**		(0.045)			(0.049)
2 minor children	0.054	0.086	0.048			0.050
	(0.052)	(0.054)	(0.049)			(0.050)
3+ minor children	0.094	0.178	0.040			0.040
	(0.045)**	(0.073)**	(0.043)			(0.047)
Age oldest child < 14, 1860		–0.013				
		(0.008)				
Age youngest child < 14, 1860		0.008				
		(0.010)				
Wife foreign born, 1860			–0.139			–0.103
			(0.053)***			(0.053)*
Wife literate, 1860			0.046			0.032
			(0.057)			(0.062)
Spousal age gap (recruit – wife)			0.027			0.026
			(0.017)			(0.019)
Recruit HH head, 1860			0.443			0.439
			(0.071)***			(0.069)***
Log family property			–0.004			–0.012
			(0.020)			(0.020)
Recruit farmer, 1860			–0.046			–0.055
			(0.052)			(0.048)
Recruit skilled white collar, 1860			–0.164			–0.180
			(0.099)*			(0.086)**
Recruit skilled blue collar, 1860			0.048			0.019
			(0.047)			(0.051)
Recruit no occupation, 1860			–0.178			–0.214
			(0.079)**			(0.079)***
Recruit year of death				0.021		0.009
				(0.019)		(0.019)
Enlisted as private				–0.015		–0.058
				(0.046)		(0.049)
Company death rate				0.043		0.039
				(0.019)**		(0.018)**
1,000s of people per sq. mile, 1860					–0.020	–0.038
					(0.008)**	(0.019)**
County railroad access, 1860					–0.004	–0.006
					(0.020)	(0.020)
County newspapers per capita, 1860					–0.021	–0.014
					(0.021)	(0.020)
County male–female ratio, 1860					–0.007	–0.017
					(0.030)	(0.029)
Observations	808	604	750	792	806	728
Adjusted R^2	0.056	0.018	0.145	0.027	0.024	0.152

Note: Microdata from Fogel et al. (2000); county-level aggregate census data from Haines and ICPSR (2010); county-level railroad data from Atack (2017); county-level newspaper data from the Library of Congress. Sample consists of women married to UA recruits killed during the war, who were linked to the 1860 federal census. All regressions include 1860 state of residence fixed effects. Standard errors, clustered by 1860 county of residence, in parentheses: *$p < 0.10$. **$p < 0.05$. ***$p < 0.01$.

Table 4.5 **Determinants of take-up: Initial application, robustness**

	=1 if widow applied for pension before 1870				
Dependent variable	(1)	(2)	(3)	(4)	(5)
Widow age 30–39	0.074	0.078	0.047	0.096	0.057
	(0.042)*	(0.041)*	(0.042)	(0.041)**	(0.042)
Widow age 40+	0.001	0.014	–0.020	0.021	–0.019
	(0.053)	(0.052)	(0.054)	(0.051)	(0.053)
No minor children	–0.022	–0.033	–0.041	–0.002	–0.012
	(0.049)	(0.051)	(0.051)	(0.051)	(0.052)
2 minor children	0.091	0.038	0.081	0.042	0.083
	(0.049)*	(0.052)	(0.050)	(0.051)	(0.049)*
3+ minor children	0.037	0.041	0.038	0.040	0.036
	(0.045)	(0.049)	(0.047)	(0.048)	(0.046)
Wife foreign born, 1860	–0.017	–0.127	–0.040	–0.118	–0.033
	(0.049)	(0.056)**	(0.051)	(0.053)**	(0.050)
Wife literate, 1860	0.044	0.026	0.043	0.028	0.041
	(0.060)	(0.062)	(0.061)	(0.062)	(0.061)
Spousal age gap	0.011	0.016	0.001	0.014	–0.004
(recruit – wife)	(0.019)	(0.019)	(0.020)	(0.019)	(0.020)
Recruit HH Head, 1860	0.454			0.381	0.394
	(0.079)***			(0.089)***	(0.097)***
Log family property	–0.002	–0.001	0.008	–0.016	–0.007
	(0.020)	(0.021)	(0.020)	(0.021)	(0.020)
Recruit farmer, 1860	–0.019	–0.071	–0.031	–0.065	–0.032
	(0.049)	(0.047)	(0.047)	(0.047)	(0.048)
Recruit skilled white collar,	–0.143	–0.173	–0.152	–0.199	–0.168
1860	(0.091)	(0.095)*	(0.099)	(0.087)**	(0.089)*
Recruit skilled blue collar,	0.016	0.016	0.013	0.006	0.002
1860	(0.047)	(0.051)	(0.047)	(0.051)	(0.048)
Recruit no occupation, 1860	–0.215	–0.279	–0.265	–0.189	–0.168
	(0.080)***	(0.079)***	(0.080)***	(0.090)**	(0.092)*
Recruit year of death	0.011	–0.000	0.001	0.009	0.012
	(0.017)	(0.020)	(0.018)	(0.019)	(0.017)
Enlisted as private	–0.073	–0.067	–0.057	–0.065	–0.077
	(0.046)	(0.050)	(0.044)	(0.051)	(0.047)*
Company death rate	0.035	0.041	0.036	0.036	0.033
	(0.016)**	(0.018)**	(0.017)**	(0.019)*	(0.018)*
1,000s of people per sq. mile,	–0.014	–0.036	–0.010	–0.040	–0.015
1860	(0.024)	(0.019)*	(0.023)	(0.019)**	(0.023)
County railroad access, 1860	–0.002	–0.010	–0.004	–0.008	–0.003
	(0.018)	(0.021)	(0.018)	(0.021)	(0.019)
County newspapers per	–0.003	–0.013	–0.004	–0.015	–0.004
capita, 1860	(0.020)	(0.021)	(0.020)	(0.021)	(0.020)
County male–female ratio,	–0.033	–0.026	–0.043	–0.020	–0.040
1860	(0.029)	(0.029)	(0.029)	(0.030)	(0.030)
Observations	648	671	604	699	624
Adjusted R^2	0.160	0.063	0.060	0.087	0.087
Sample restrictions:					
High-quality links	X		X		X
Recruit HH head in 1860		X	X		
Recruit > 20 in 1860				X	X

Note: Microdata from Fogel et al. (2000); county-level aggregate census data from Haines and ICPSR (2010); county-level railroad data from Atack (2017); county-level newspaper data from the Library of Congress. Sample consists of women married to UA recruits killed during the war, who were linked to the 1860 federal census. All regressions include 1860 state of residence fixed effects. Standard errors, clustered by 1860 county of residence, in parentheses: *$p < 0.10$. **$p < 0.05$. ***$p < 0.01$.

Table 4.6 **Characteristics of eligible war widows by application status: Pension increase for minor children**

Variable	Mean, nonapplicants	Mean, applicants	Difference
Age at eligibility	31.42	34.20	2.77***
# Children < 16	2.55	2.68	0.12
Age oldest child < 16, 1866	8.98	10.00	1.01*
Age youngest child < 16, 1866	5.04	5.62	0.59
Recruit's year of death	1863.59	1863.46	–0.13
Enlisted as private	0.84	0.89	0.05
Company death rate	0.19	0.20	0.01
First app. approved w/in 5 yrs	0.73	0.96	0.23***
Months to first app.	6.29	5.70	–0.59
Specialist lawyer, first app.	0.25	0.26	0.01
Local lawyer, first app.	0.66	0.63	–0.03
No lawyer, first app.	0.09	0.11	0.02
1,000s of people per sq. mile, 1860	0.20	1.78	1.57***
County railroad access, 1860	0.77	0.86	0.09*
County newspapers per 1000 ppl, 1860	0.10	0.10	0.00
County male–female ratio, 1860	1.07	1.04	–0.04***
New England, 1860	0.35	0.47	0.12
Midwest, 1860	0.63	0.47	–0.16**
South, 1860	0.02	0.03	0.01

Note: Microdata from Fogel et al. (2000) and Salisbury (2017); county-level aggregate census data from Haines and ICPSR (2010); county-level railroad data from Atack (2017); county-level newspaper data from the Library of Congress. Sample consists of women married to UA recruits killed during the war, who had applied for an original pension before July 25, 1866; had not remarried or died before July 25, 1866; and had at least one minor child on July 25, 1866. Sample includes 56 nonapplicants and 344 applicants. Final column indicates significance of difference between nonapplicants and applicants, using standard errors clustered by county for geographic variables and company for company-level variables: $*p < 0.10$. $**p < 0.05$. $***p < 0.01$.

an indicator equal to 1 if a widow applied for a pension increase within five years of becoming eligible on salient characteristics. In some cases, observables predict initial and secondary take-up in a similar fashion. As was the case with initial applications, women in their 30s were most likely to file for a pension, as were women with more children. Women from the Northeast were more likely to apply than women from the Midwest. Otherwise, geographic variables have a different effect on secondary take-up compared with primary take-up. Unlike initial applications, increase applications were more likely to come from widows living in more densely populated counties with greater railroad density.

While certain differences between applicants and nonapplicants can be seen in table 4.6, very few of these are statistically significant when included in the same regression model, and the explanatory power of these observables is very low. In most columns of table 4.7, the adjusted R^2 values are

Table 4.7 Determinants of take-up: Increase application

	Applied for increase w/in 5 yrs				
Dependent variable	(1)	(2)	(3)	(4)	(5)
Age 30–39 eligibility	0.082				0.036
	(0.049)*				(0.052)
Age 40+ eligibility	0.042				0.040
	(0.062)				(0.060)
2 minor children	0.019				0.017
	(0.056)				(0.057)
3+ minor children	0.018				–0.016
	(0.071)				(0.074)
Present value of lifetime pension	0.049				0.086
	(0.034)				(0.035)**
Veteran's year of death		–0.005			–0.006
		(0.022)			(0.022)
Enlisted as private		0.051			0.085
		(0.070)			(0.073)
Company casualty rate		0.015			0.020
		(0.022)			(0.022)
County newspapers per capita			0.016		–0.001
			(0.030)		(0.027)
County pop. density			0.008		0.007
			(0.010)		(0.011)
County railroad access			0.042		0.036
			(0.028)		(0.023)
County male–female ratio			–0.061		–0.057
			(0.043)		(0.038)
Time to first application				0.028	
				(0.035)	
First application approved				0.467	0.461
				(0.093)***	(0.101)***
Nonlocal lawyer, 1st application				–0.053	–0.069
				(0.076)	(0.076)
Local lawyer, 1st application				–0.022	–0.025
				(0.063)	(0.063)
Observations	374	374	376	379	362
Adjusted R^2	–0.002	–0.017	0.001	0.082	0.098

Note: Microdata from Fogel et al. (2000) and Salisbury (2017); county-level aggregate census data from Haines and ICPSR (2010); county-level railroad data from Atack (2017); county-level newspaper data from the Library of Congress. Sample consists of women who filed for an original pension before July 25, 1866, and had not remarried or died before that date. All regressions include state of residence fixed effects. Standard errors, clustered by county of residence at time of first pension application, in parentheses: *$p < 0.10$. **$p < 0.05$. ***$p < 0.01$.

negative, which is quite different from table 4.4. The only variable with real power to explain variation in secondary take-up is the outcome of the initial pension application. Women whose initial pension applications had not been approved within five years of applying were substantially less likely to apply for a pension increase.

Figures 4.4 through 4.9 plot survival and hazard functions for original and secondary pension applications, separated by observable characteristics. Again, these figures capture differences in the speed of application as well as the binary outcome of applying or not applying within a particular time frame.

What do these results indicate about the reasons for nonparticipation among UA widows? In particular, do they suggest that nonparticipation is primarily driven by information costs or administrative costs? It is difficult to say for certain, as many observables may plausibly be related to both. Some results are more suggestive of information costs driving nonparticipation, while others suggest a larger role for administrative costs (more on this below). As is the case for modern programs, it is likely that both information and transaction costs were drivers of nonparticipation.

First, the evidence is consistent with some nonparticipation stemming from lack of information. Widows whose husbands served in companies with higher wartime death rates were significantly more likely to apply for a pension. Table 4.4 indicates that a one standard deviation increase in a widow's husband's company's death rate increases the likelihood of applying for a pension by roughly 4 percentage points. Moreover, figure 4.4 shows that widows of soldiers from companies with higher death rates applied for original pensions much faster. This suggests that information was a channel through which the death rate affected take-up. Companies were organized locally, so a higher company death rate implies a larger local network of eligible widows. Interestingly, the company death rate matters much less for the binary outcome of secondary application. Still, widows with a larger local network of widows applied for pension increases more quickly, as can be seen in the bottom panel of figure 4.4. Also note that foreign-born widows were roughly 10 percentage points less likely to apply for a pension than native-born widows, suggesting a role for informational networks as well. On the other hand, newspaper density has no impact on the take-up rate or speed of application.

Geographic differences in take-up may also be related to information. In general, participation is highest and fastest in the Northeast. There are multiple plausible explanations for regional variation in take-up, some related to information and others related to costs. While there are regional differences in both initial and secondary take-up, there is a much larger difference in the speed of application for a pension increase. In figure 4.5, it is clear that pension increase applications are made significantly faster in the Northeast than the Midwest; this is true to a lesser extent for initial applications. Figure 4.6 shows that railroad density (within states) is associated with much faster secondary applications, but not initial applications. A similar but less pronounced pattern exists if the sample is split by population density (conditional on state fixed effects; not shown).

Why might information about pension eligibility be disseminated more

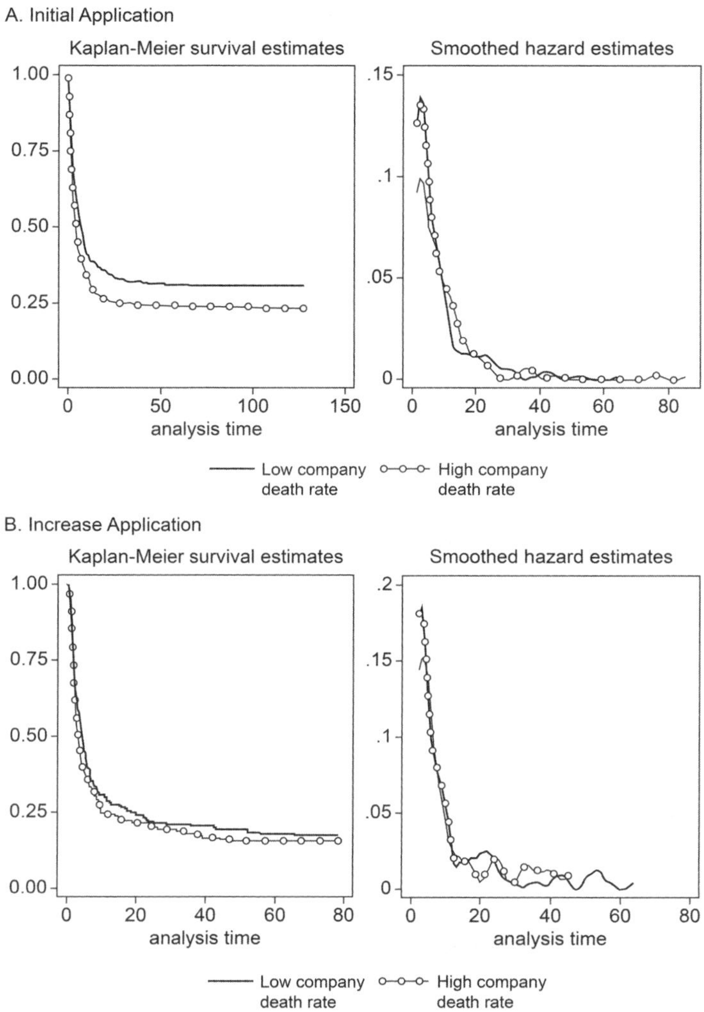

Figure 4.4 Rate of pension application by company death rate: Initial and increase

Note: Microdata from Salisbury (2017) and Fogel et al. (2000). Sample of women eligible for initial pension: women who are linked to the 1860 census and are married to a Union army soldier who died during the war. Sample of women eligible for pension increase: women whose husbands dies during the war, who applied for a pension before July 25, 1866, and who have at least one child under the age of 16 as of July 25, 1866. Women enter the sample on the date they become eligible for the pension. For the initial pension application, this is the date of her husband's death or July 14, 1862, whichever is later. For the pension increase, this is July 25, 1866. The sample period ends at the end of 1872. A "failure" occurs when a widow files a pension application. A "high" company death rate is above the median, and a "low" company death rate is below.

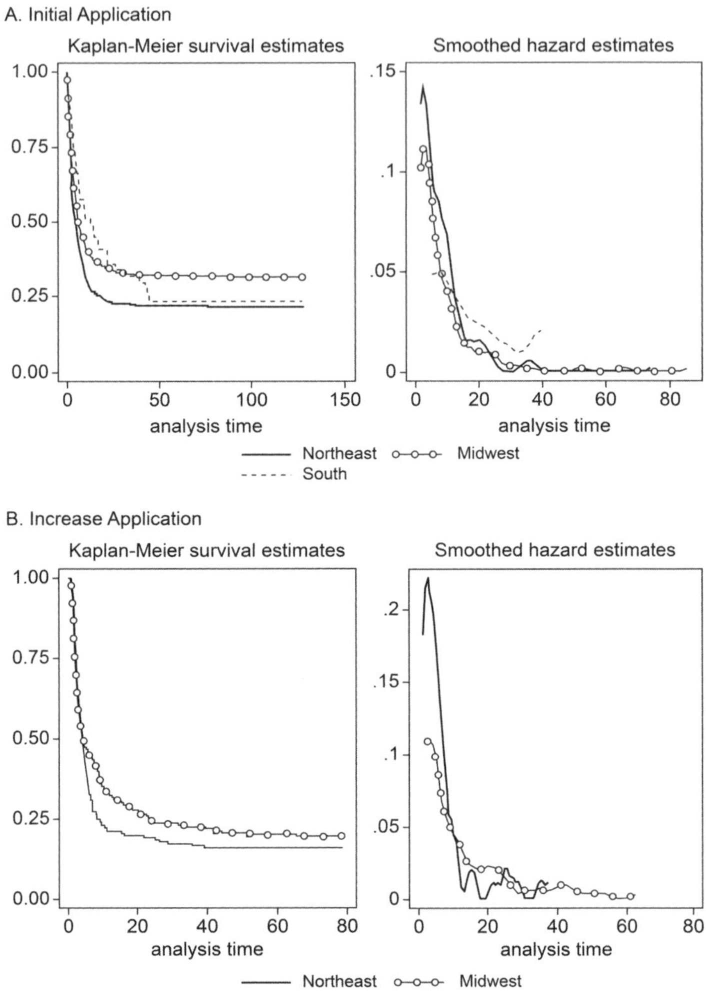

Figure 4.5 Rate of pension application by region: Initial and increase

Note: Microdata from Salisbury (2017) and Fogel et al. (2000). Sample of women eligible for initial pension: women who are linked to the 1860 census and are married to a Union army soldier who died during the war. Sample of women eligible for pension increase: women whose husbands dies during the war, who applied for a pension before July 25, 1866, and who have at least one child under the age of 16 as of July 25, 1866. Women enter the sample on the date they become eligible for the pension. For the initial pension application, this is the date of her husband's death or July 14, 1862, whichever is later. For the pension increase, this is July 25, 1866. The sample period ends at the end of 1872. A "failure" occurs when a widow files a pension application.

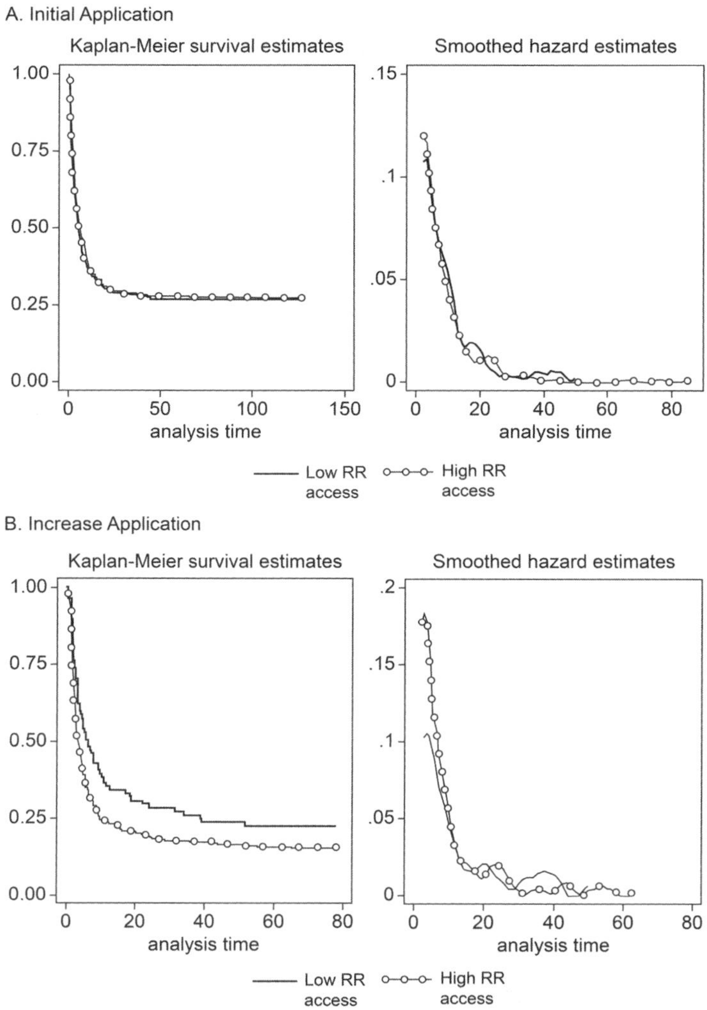

Figure 4.6 Rate of pension application by railroad access: Initial and increase

Note: Microdata from Salisbury (2017) and Fogel et al. (2000); Railroad data from Atack (2017). Sample of women eligible for initial pension: women who are linked to the 1860 census and are married to a Union army soldier who died during the war. Sample of women eligible for pension increase: women whose husbands dies during the war, who applied for a pension before July 25, 1866, and who have at least one child under the age of 16 as of July 25, 1866. Women enter the sample on the date they become eligible for the pension. For the initial pension application, this is the date of her husband's death or July 14, 1862, whichever is later. For the pension increase, this is July 25, 1866. The sample period ends at the end of 1872. A "failure" occurs when a widow files a pension application. Categories of railroad access determined by residuals from regression of county railroad density on state fixed effects.

quickly in more connected counties, and why does this seem to matter more for secondary applications? One explanation has to do with access to networks of fellow pensioners. Widows (like veterans) were paid pensions quarterly, and payments were made from pension agencies located in a handful of cities around the country. Pensions had to be collected in person, which necessitated travel if the pensioner did not live in a city with a pension agency. Widows could empower an attorney or agent to collect pensions on their behalf, which was relatively secure as pensions were paid by check rather than currency.[10] Ease of travel may have increased the likelihood that a widow collected her pension on her own behalf, which meant standing in a long line and conversing with other pensioners. This is reported in multiple newspapers.[11] For example, an 1869 article in Lancaster, Pennsylvania's *Intelligencer Journal* titled "Pension Day" describes a "real crowd in front of the different offices waiting to be served with the stamps of Uncle Sam." The article notes that "a large company of widows were there" and describes the conversation as "animated," suggesting that "the widows, with an eye to the chance to be paid early, listened to the brave deeds of warriors who had done themselves injury and the State some service."

It is also possible that widows in the northeast had access to a denser network of pension attorneys, who disseminated information about eligibility. Moreover, factors like railroad access and population density might have increased the net gains from pension increase applications, if widows who did not find the act of collecting the pension too onerous were the ones who expected to keep collecting for more time.

The evidence also suggests that some of the nonparticipation among Union Army widows was driven by women weighing costs and benefits of application and choosing not to apply. Age and number of children have a significant effect on the probability of applying. Women who were less than 30 years old when they became eligible were least likely to apply, and women who became eligible in their 30s were most likely to apply. This is true of both initial and secondary applications, although the differences for secondary applications are not significant. Differences in the speed of application by age are less pronounced, especially for secondary applications (fig. 4.7), suggesting that age differences in participation are driven by costs and benefits rather than access to information.

Children have an impact on the decision to apply for a pension, although

10. A *New York Times* article from 1869 reports on a request by pension attorneys in Pennsylvania to the Secretary of the Interior for "both their fees and the pensioners' money to be paid in currency," rather than check on the US Treasury. The Secretary of the Interior denied the request, maintaining that "the Department is in possession of proof that the pensions paid to pensioners are so often sadly reduced at the hands of middle-men that it feels bound to use every measure in its power to prevent what has become a notorious abuse."

11. Most newspaper reports on "Pension Day" are single sentences, and likely included as filler. For instance, "Yesterday was pension day; A large number of pensioners in town signing their vouche for their quarterly payments" (*Herald and Tribune* [Jonesborough, TN] 1874).

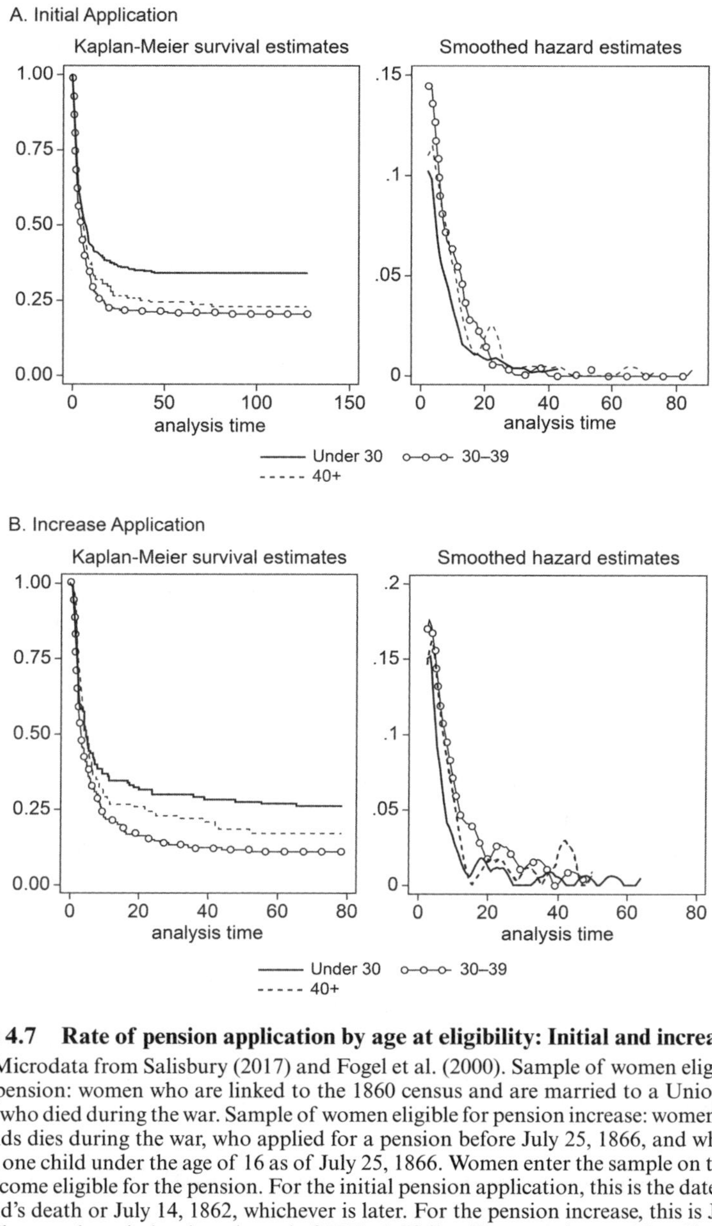

Figure 4.7 Rate of pension application by age at eligibility: Initial and increase

Note: Microdata from Salisbury (2017) and Fogel et al. (2000). Sample of women eligible for initial pension: women who are linked to the 1860 census and are married to a Union army soldier who died during the war. Sample of women eligible for pension increase: women whose husbands dies during the war, who applied for a pension before July 25, 1866, and who have at least one child under the age of 16 as of July 25, 1866. Women enter the sample on the date they become eligible for the pension. For the initial pension application, this is the date of her husband's death or July 14, 1862, whichever is later. For the pension increase, this is July 25, 1866. The sample period ends at the end of 1872. A "failure" occurs when a widow files a pension application.

this effect is not significant when all controls are added. Women who have no children in 1860 are less likely to apply for a pension, and more children are associated with a greater likelihood of applying. While women with three or more children are highly likely to apply for a pension, they were slower to make applications (see Figure 4.8). The fastest applicants were those with exactly two children. Regressions in table 4.7 include a control for the present value of the widow's lifetime pension increase at the time of eligibility.[12] Conditional on controls for number of children, this reflects variation in the age of the widow's children. Widows with a larger total pension increase at stake were more likely to apply for these increases.

Age and number of children likely affected the net benefit from applying for a pension because they affected a widow's remarriage prospects. Young widows with no children were extremely likely to remarry, whereas older widows with more children were not (Salisbury 2017). As eligibility ceased upon remarriage, this means the lifetime benefit from applying for a pension was lower for younger and childless widows. In many cases, it seems the benefits did not exceed the substantial costs associated with applying (see Section 4.3). The much higher rate of application for pension increases suggests that there were high costs associated with making an initial application, which were lower for secondary applications. This is also consistent with the fact that age and children have a less pronounced effect on secondary applications.

The negative effect of the first husband's socioeconomic status on take-up is likely due to its effect on the expected return to application. Under positive assortative mating, women who had initially married men of high economic status likely had better marriage prospects.[13]

The one factor that mattered significantly for secondary applications was the outcome of the initial pension application. This can be seen in figure 4.9. This supports the conjecture that nonparticipation was in part driven by a rational cost-benefit analysis on the part of widows. Those widows whose initial applications were not approved within five years (only some of these widows' claims were rejected; others were merely slow to process) were very unlikely to file for an increase, presumably because these women perceived a diminished benefit from filing an application and were unwilling to incur the associated costs.

4.7 Explaining the High Participation Rate Among Union Army Widows

This chapter has focused on characterizing take-up of the Union Army pension among widows early in the life of the program. The most striking

12. This is calculated by summing the annual pension increase for children over the years until they reach age 16, discounting annually at a rate of 6 percent. Such a measure is not included for original pension applications, as pension amounts were identical for all widows.

13. See Bailey and Lin (2024) in this volume for a detailed discussion of marital matching during this period.

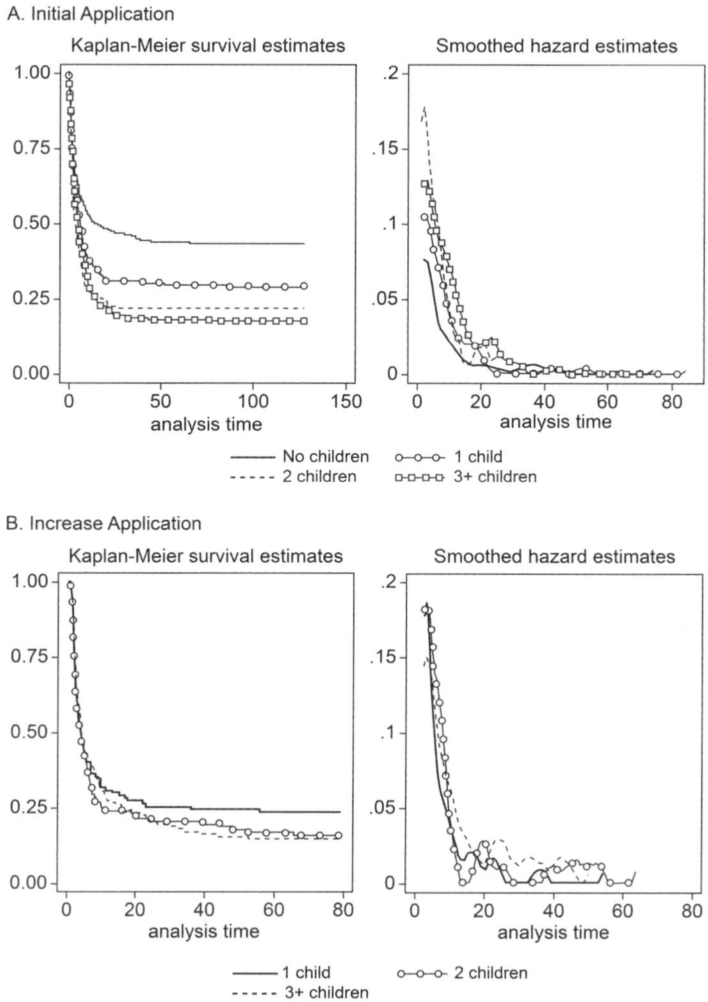

Figure 4.8 Rate of pension application by number of children: Initial and increase

Note: Microdata from Salisbury (2017) and Fogel et al. (2000). Sample of women eligible for initial pension: women who are linked to the 1860 census and are married to a Union army soldier who died during the war. Sample of women eligible for pension increase: women whose husbands dies during the war, who applied for a pension before July 25, 1866, and who have at least one child under the age of 16 as of July 25, 1866. Women enter the sample on the date they become eligible for the pension. For the initial pension application, this is the date of her husband's death or July 14, 1862, whichever is later. For the pension increase, this is July 25, 1866. The sample period ends at the end of 1872. A "failure" occurs when a widow files a pension application.

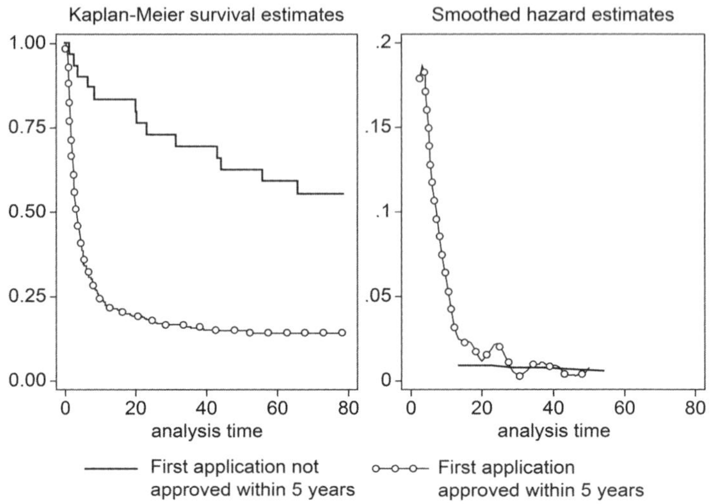

Figure 4.9 Rate of application for pension increase by outcome of first application
Note: Microdata from Salisbury (2017) and Fogel et al. (2000). Sample of women eligible for pension increase: women whose husbands dies during the war, who applied for a pension before July 25, 1866, and who have at least one child under the age of 16 as of July 25, 1866. Women enter the sample on the date they become eligible for the pension. For the pension increase, this is July 25, 1866. The sample period ends at the end of 1872. A "failure" occurs when a widow files a pension application.

result is the relatively high participation rate. Women who became widowed during the war years participated in the pension program at rate that is lower than the take-up rate of most major federal programs today, but not by much. The take-up rate of the UA widows' pension was certainly lower than that of the EITC, and likely somewhat lower than UI and SNAP. However, the take-up rate was almost certainly higher than (post–welfare reform) TANF. Conditional on eligibility, widows applied for benefit increases at a rate of roughly 80 percent, which is very comparable to the take-up rate of the EITC, a program that must be applied for annually (by filing a tax return).

It is not obvious how information costs should be ordered between the UA widows' pension and modern social programs. Information technology is certainly more developed today, which ought to make acquiring information about programs easier. Still, UA pensions were very well publicized. All amendments to the federal pension law were published verbatim in national and local newspapers. Pension attorneys had a strong financial incentive to disseminate information about pensions to the public, which was often done by newspaper. Pension attorneys advertised extensively in newspapers, and in some cases, they operated veterans' newspapers themselves (Blanck and Song 2002). That said, living in a county with greater newspaper access in no way predicts filing for a widows' pension (see tables 4.4 and 4.7). Instead, some of the evidence points to network effects, which is also an important avenue through which information about modern programs is disseminated (Bertrand et al. 2000; Borjas and Hilton 1996; Duflo and Saez 2003). Finally, with an absence of competing social programs available to Union Army widows, there was perhaps less informational complexity to navigate. This is a known source of incomplete take-up of modern programs (Bhargava and Manoli 2015).

Administrative costs are shown to have a first-order effect on participation in modern programs. How do these compare with costs associated with applying for a UA pension? Recall from Section 4.3 that applying for a widows' pension was a significant undertaking. Pension declarations (required for both original and secondary applications) had to be made before a court of record. Widows had to assemble supporting records or testimony (which could be taken before a justice of the peace rather than a court official). For initial applications, a widow had to furnish evidence of her husband's military service and the circumstances of his death, as well as proof of their marriage. For increase applications, a widow needed to provide proof of the birth dates of her and her deceased husbands' children. Collecting pensions was also costly, involving travel in many cases.

These costs are clearly higher than the costs of applying for EITC or UI benefits. Neither involves a court appearance or travel to a central office. To apply for both EITC and UI benefits, supporting documentation must be provided. However, improvements in information technology make obtaining and submitting this documentation easier than it was in the 1860s. Thus, it is striking that the take-up rate of the UA widows' pension compares so favorably to both of these programs, especially in the case of secondary take-up.[14]

Post–welfare reform TANF makes for an interesting comparison, as users of both programs consist largely of low-income single mothers. It appears that the take-up rate of the UA widows' pension is higher than the take-up rate of TANF. Applying for TANF is much more involved than applying for either EITC or UI benefits. A visit to a county welfare office is required, as is in-person consultation with a case manager. This is owing to the complexity of eligibility requirements and the consequent difficulty of verifying eligibility. A major cost of participation in TANF stems from work requirements, which were instituted as part of PRWORA in 1996. These are thought to have materially impacted participation rates, especially discouraging single mothers and the poorest individuals from applying (Falk 2017).

14. Another important factor is that a widow's pension application only had to happen once. There was no repeated provision of supporting materials required. Collecting EITC and UI benefits requires repeated engagement with administrators. As such, although the one-off costs of application are higher for widows' pensions, the total cost of collecting over a prolonged period might be less.

The role of case managers makes TANF and the UA widows' pension especially interesting to compare. TANF case managers fill two key functions. First, they offer administrative support and information to facilitate the receipt of benefits. Second, they verify eligibility. These functions can be at odds with one another. Given the complexity of the TANF application process, the supportive function of the case manager doubtless lowers the cost of applying for benefits. A literature in social work argues that case management has traditionally focused on assessing eligibility over advocacy (Bane and Ellwood 1994). This contributes to a sense among recipients that caseworkers engage in "gatekeeping" (Anderson 2001) and can increase psychic costs associated with collecting TANF benefits (Hill and Cain 2012). It is difficult to quantify the costs and benefits (as perceived by recipients) associated with the caseworker system, as this is a publicly provided service and a necessary element of the process.

Union Army widows applying for pensions did not have case managers. However, they did have pension attorneys. This more or less privatized one function of the case manager (administrative support, information, and advocacy) and separated it from the other (verification of eligibility). Pension attorneys were allowed to charge up to $10 to prosecute a pension claim, which was more than a monthly widows' pension and more than twice the monthly pension increase for a widow with two children. However, once these fixed financial costs were incurred, the administrative burden on applicants was substantially reduced.

The fact that pension attorneys were private agents subject to little oversight opened the door for abuses, both of the pension system and of the pensioners themselves. Pension commissioners' reports, as well as the popular press, are riddled with references to pension agents who falsified claims or swindled their clients.[15] As the pension program became more politically polarizing in the 1870s, pension agents became a convenient target for those arguing against expansions to the program (Blanck and Song 2002). Many were quick to draw a distinction between "deserving" veterans and widows and fraudsters or "greedy and dishonest" pension attorneys.[16]

15. One article—widely circulated in southern newspapers, but quoted here from the *Nashville Union and American* (1870)—prints a letter from a Confederate veteran to a pension attorney, allegedly refusing the attorney's offer to secure him a federal pension under a false name. The article decries pension brokers' practice of "hunting up subjects all over the country to further their operations on the Treasury." The 1883 Pension Commissioner's report makes explicit reference to attorneys who file preliminary paperwork and obtain their $10 fee, only to abandon the claim before it is complete (Salisbury 2017).

16. Another article, published in the *Vermont Journal* (1879), criticizes the passage of the Arrears Act of 1879, which granted veterans pensions in arrears, dating from the time of their injury, even if they had not immediately applied. The article emphasizes that "it would be a great consolation, and we might be content, if we could believe that the real soldiers, their widows and orphan children—the actually meritorious survivors of the army and navy were to be the chief recipients of this most prodigal distribution of funds in the Treasury; but then, when we reflect that by far the greater portion of it is to go to the impecunious army of claim

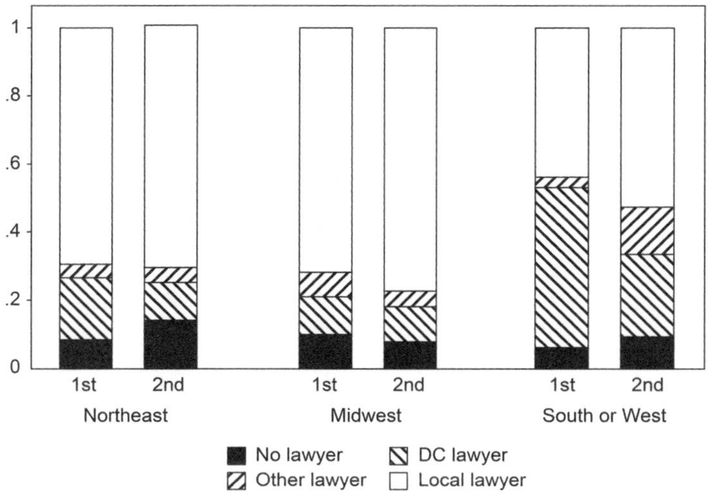

Figure 4.10 Share of widows' pension applicants using pension attorneys, by region

Note: Microdata from Salisbury (2017) and Fogel et al. (2000).

At the same time, an overwhelming majority of widows employed attorneys to prosecute their claims. Figure 4.10 plots the share of applicants using different types of attorneys, by application type and region of residence. Only about 10 percent of widows filed claims without the help of a lawyer. Most pension attorneys were from the applicant's home state. The propensity to use a lawyer from a big Washington, DC, firm varied by the widow's region of residence. Among original claimants from the northeast, almost 20 percent used a DC lawyer, whereas only about 10 percent of applicants from the Midwest used a DC lawyer. Table 4.8 contains results from a regression of different binary choices pertaining to lawyer use on observables, pooling initial and increase applications. Widows whose husbands died earlier in the war were more likely to file applications alone, as were widows living in less densely populated counties (conditional on state fixed effects). Among widows who used pension attorneys, older widows living in more densely populated counties were more likely to employ DC firms. Secondary applicants were significantly less likely to use DC lawyers than were original applicants.

The fact that 90 percent of widows were willing to pay more than a month's pension for a lawyer to handle their claims is striking. This indicates that, for most applicants, the administrative costs of applying for a pension exceeded

agents, at Washington and elsewhere, that have for a long time been marshalling their forces for this grand swoop of fortunes, achieved on the taking pretence of soldierly services, we may well dread the coming results."

Table 4.8 Determinants of widows' employment of pension attorneys

	No lawyer			DC lawyer		
Dependent variable	(1)	(2)	(3)	(4)	(5)	(6)
Age 30–39 eligibility	0.018		0.024	0.064		0.064
	(0.025)		(0.025)	(0.029)**		(0.029)**
Age 40+ eligibility	0.009		0.019	0.020		0.022
	(0.029)		(0.029)	(0.038)		(0.038)
1 minor child	0.022		0.018	–0.008		–0.003
	(0.035)		(0.035)	(0.047)		(0.046)
2 minor children	–0.005		–0.010	0.018		0.017
	(0.034)		(0.034)	(0.046)		(0.044)
3+ minor children	0.019		0.015	–0.014		–0.003
	(0.035)		(0.034)	(0.045)		(0.042)
Veteran's year of death	–0.022		–0.020	–0.004		–0.005
	(0.011)*		(0.011)*	(0.018)		(0.018)
Enlisted as private	–0.025		–0.005	0.024		0.026
	(0.035)		(0.033)	(0.041)		(0.043)
Company casualty rate	0.010		0.009	0.011		0.007
	(0.012)		(0.012)	(0.017)		(0.018)
County newspapers per capita		–0.009	–0.006		0.014	0.007
		(0.010)	(0.011)		(0.018)	(0.018)
County pop. density		–0.014	–0.015		0.035	0.036
		(0.007)**	(0.007)**		(0.011)***	(0.011)***
County railroad access		0.009	0.011		0.023	0.022
		(0.016)	(0.017)		(0.020)	(0.020)
County male–female ratio		0.009	0.012		0.048	0.049
		(0.013)	(0.013)		(0.029)*	(0.029)*
Increase Application	0.011	0.013	0.007	–0.068	–0.059	–0.063
	(0.023)	(0.021)	(0.023)	(0.029)**	(0.027)**	(0.028)**
Observations	970	973	939	873	881	848
Adjusted R^2	0.021	0.016	0.018	0.075	0.083	0.081

Note: Microdata from Fogel et al. (2000) and Salisbury (2017); county-level aggregate census data from Haines and ICPSR (2010); county-level railroad data from Atack (2017); county-level newspaper data from the Library of Congress. All regressions include state of residence fixed effects. Standard errors clustered by county in parentheses. *$p < 0.10$. **$p < 0.05$. ***$p < 0.01$.

an entire month's pay. It is hard to say by how much, as attorneys' fees were regulated. It is also notable that there was an ample supply of pension attorneys, and some of them became very wealthy.[17] There was ample market

17. Several anecdotes about pension attorneys advertising and seeking out clients have already been cited. For a later example, see Glasson (1902), who describes a large number of Washington, DC, pension attorneys decamping to San Francisco to convince returning veterans from the Spanish-American War to file for pensions, or "to pour into the ears of such soldiers as they could glowing accounts of the system of pensions provided by law, and the merits of some particular attorney who made a business of prosecuting claims" (224). The efforts attorneys spent procuring clients speaks to the profitability of this business. Major DC-based pension attorneys, such as George E. Lemon, died extremely wealthy men (Blanck and Song 2002).

Table 4.9 **Effect of pension attorneys on pension outcomes**

	(1)	(2)	(3)	(4)
Dependent variable		Never pensioned		
DC lawyer	–0.017	0.022	0.049	0.049
	(0.045)	(0.058)	(0.039)	(0.039)
Other lawyer	–0.077	–0.045	–0.006	–0.006
	(0.048)	(0.054)	(0.036)	(0.036)
Local lawyer	–0.029	–0.026	–0.018	–0.018
	(0.037)	(0.047)	(0.034)	(0.034)
Observations	658	322	1,078	702
Adjusted R^2	0.007	0.018	0.060	0.058
Dependent variable		Not pensioned w/in 10 years		
DC lawyer	0.011	–0.019	0.009	0.009
	(0.051)	(0.088)	(0.044)	(0.044)
Other lawyer	–0.037	–0.096	–0.064	–0.064
	(0.064)	(0.085)	(0.049)	(0.050)
Local lawyer	0.005	–0.121	–0.066	–0.066
	(0.042)	(0.072)*	(0.043)	(0.043)
Observations	658	322	1,078	702
Adjusted R^2	0.014	0.020	0.057	0.055
Dependent variable		Months to issuance of certificate		
DC lawyer	4.358	–5.375	1.468	1.468
	(3.587)	(3.646)	(2.865)	(2.870)
Other lawyer	1.112	–2.876	0.030	0.030
	(4.026)	(4.129)	(3.377)	(3.382)
Local lawyer	–1.757	–4.148	0.410	0.410
	(3.009)	(3.727)	(2.711)	(2.716)
Observations	593	295	977	660
Adjusted R^2	0.047	0.027	0.073	0.071
Specification	1st app., controls	2nd app., controls	Widow FEs	Widow FEs, balanced

Note: Microdata from Fogel et al. (2000) and Salisbury (2017); county-level aggregate census data from Haines and ICPSR (2010); county-level railroad data from Atack (2017); county-level newspaper data from the Library of Congress (2023). All regressions include state of residence fixed effects. Standard errors clustered by county in parentheses. $^{*}p < 0.10$. $^{**}p < 0.05$. $^{***}p < 0.01$.

provision of this service, which pension applicants clearly valued. This is not to say that this market worked perfectly. There was significant attorney turnover, which reflects the fact that pension attorneys did not always serve their clients well. Roughly 15 percent of widows fired their first pension attorney, and less than 40 percent of widows applying for pension increases used the same lawyer they had used for their first application.

Table 4.9 contains results from a regression of pension outcomes on indicators for using different categories of pension lawyer. Columns 1 and 2 include only initial or increase applications, respectively, and control for observable characteristics of the widow and her place of residence. Columns 3 and 4 pool initial and increase applications and include individual fixed effects. This effectively controls for permanent characteristics of widows that affect decisions about attorneys and pension outcomes. It is clear from these regressions that hiring attorneys did not improve the likelihood of success or speed of processing. This is consistent with Blanck and Song (2002), who find that pension attorneys did not improve pension outcomes for disabled veterans. This indicates that pension lawyers generated value by absorbing administrative costs rather than by improving pension outcomes.

While less prominent today, attorneys are still used in applications for social benefits. This is most common among applicants for Social Security Disability Insurance (SSDI). The average fee paid to an attorney representing an SSDI claimant was $2,939 in 2015, compared with an average monthly benefit of less than $1,200 (Hoynes et al. 2022). As such, attorneys' fees for SSDI claims exceed those paid to UA pension attorneys. However, the share of applicants who initiate SSDI claims with the help of an attorney is much lower, only 16 percent between 2010 and 2014. Unlike UA widows, SSDI claimants who use attorneys are highly selected, and the use of an attorney is associated with a higher probability of a claim being approved (Hoynes et al. 2022). As such, it appears that attorneys primarily add value in SSDI claims by improving outcomes, and not by shifting the administrative burden from the client, as seems to be the case with UA widows.

The high administrative costs associated with applying for the UA pension reflect a concern with overuse of the program, which in many ways mirrors the public conversation about welfare receipt today. The trade-off between accessibility and avoiding fraud is made explicit in the 1862 commissioner's report (as printed in *Raftsmen's Journal*, of Clearfield, Pennsylvania, in 1862), which notes, "Considerable difficulty has been experienced in prescribing a mode of authenticating pension claims which shall be sufficiently liberal to claimants, and at the same time protect the Government against frauds." Later pension commissioners' reports made unverifiable claims about fraud occurring in "many" or "most" pension claims, especially widows' pensions, which relied on testimony rather than surgeons' examinations.[18] There is a general suspicion of pensioners' motives visible in commissioners' reports and newspaper articles. One article floats the idea that the pension system is "practically paying a large number of women for leading immoral lives. Widows forfeit their pensions by remarriage. The result is that many of them are living in concubinage for the make of retaining their annual stipend" (*Chicago Tribune* 1875).

18. The 1872 pension commissioner's report writes that, "The evidence to sustain a widow's or dependent's case is purely *ex parte*. As a result of this, a very considerable percentage of those cases are wrongfully established" (US Pension Bureau 1872).

4.8 Conclusion

This chapter adds to the literature on the take-up of social programs by estimating the rate of participation in America's first large-scale social assistance program, the Union Army pension. The chapter focuses on take-up by Union Army widows during the early years of the program. Roughly 35 percent to 75 percent of war widows applied for a pension by 1870. Among widows who had applied for an original pension, more than 80 percent applied for pension increases once they became eligible. There is suggestive evidence that access to information—through networks rather than the press—increased take-up. And there is stronger evidence that women who perceived a larger lifetime benefit from applying were more likely to do so. This suggests that nonparticipation was driven in large part by the high administrative costs associated with application.

Overall, it seems that engagement with social programs has increased over time. Most modern programs (EITC, UI, SNAP) have take-up rates that are higher than the UA widows' pension, albeit not by much. A notable exception is TANF, which seems to have a take-up rate that is lower than the UA pension. This underscores the very high costs of participating in TANF following the 1996 welfare reforms.

References

Aizer, Anna, and Janet Currie. 2004. "Networks or Neighborhoods? Correlations in the Use of Publicly-Funded Maternity Care in California." *Journal of Public Economics* 88: 2573–85.

Aizer, Anna, Shari Eli, Joseph Ferrie, and Adriana Lleras-Muney. 2016. "The Long-Run Impact of Cash Transfers to Poor Families." *American Economic Review* 106 (4): 935–71.

Anderson, Steven G. 2001. "Welfare Recipient Views about Caseworker Performance: Lessons for Developing TANF Case Management Practices." *Families in Society* 82 (2): 165–74.

Atack, Jeremy. 2017. *Historical Transportation of Navigable Rivers, Canals, and Railroads in the United States*. Inter-University Consortium for Political and Social Research. https://doi.org/10.3886/ICPSR36353.v1.

Autor, David H., and Mark G. Duggan. 2003. "The Rise in the Disability Rolls and the Decline in Unemployment." *Quarterly Journal of Economics* 118 (1): 157–206.

Bailey, Martha J., and Peter Z. Lin. 2024. "Marital Matching and Women's Intergenerational Mobility in the Late-19th and Early-20th-Century U.S." In *The Economic History of American Inequality: New Evidence and Perspectives*, edited by Martha J. Bailey, Leah Platt Boustan, and William J. Collins. University of Chicago Press.

Bane, M. J., and D. T. Ellwood. 1994. *Welfare Realities: From Rhetoric to Reform*. Harvard University Press.

Benzarti, Youssef. 2017. "How Taxing Is Tax Filing? Using Revealed Preferences to

Estimate Compliance Costs." NBER Working Paper No. 23903. National Bureau of Economic Research.

Bertrand, Marianne, Erzo F. P. Luttmer, and Sendhil Mullainathan. 2000. "Network Effects and Welfare Cultures." *Quarterly Journal of Economics* 115 (3): 1019–55.

Bhargava, Saurabh, George Loewenstein, and Justin Sydnor. 2017. "Choose to Lose: Health Plan Choices from a Menu with Dominated Options." *Quarterly Journal of Economics* 132 (3): 1319–72.

Bhargava, Saurabh, and Dayanand Manoli. 2015. "Psychological Frictions and the Incomplete Take-Up of Social Benefits: Evidence from an IRS Field Experiment." *American Economic Review* 105 (11): 3489–3529.

Bitler, Marianne P., Janet Currie, and John Karl Scholz. 2003. "WIC Eligibility and Participation." *Journal of Human Resources* 38: 1139–79.

Blanck, Peter, and Chen Song. 2002. "Civil War Pension Attorneys and Disability Politics." *Journal of Law Reform* 35 (2): 137–217.

Blank, Rebecca M., and Patricia Ruggles. 1996. "When Do Women Use Aid to Families with Dependent Children and Food Stamps? The Dynamics of Eligibility Versus Participation." *Journal of Human Resources* 31 (1): 57–89.

Borjas, George, and Lynette Hilton. 1996. "Immigration and the Welfare State: Immigrant Participation in Means-Tested Entitlement Programs." *Quarterly Journal of Economics* 111 (2): 575–604.

Chicago Tribune. 1875. "The Pensions We Pay." October 26.

Costa, Dora. 1995. "Pensions and Retirement: Evidence from Union Army Veterans." *Quarterly Journal of Economics* 110 (2): 297–319.

Costa, Dora. 1997. "Displacing the Family: Union Army Pensions and Elderly Living Arrangements." *Journal of Political Economy* 105 (6): 1269–92.

Currie, Janet. 2006. "The Take-up of Social Benefits." In *Poverty, the Distribution of Income, and Public Policy*, edited by Alan Auerbach, David Card, and John Quigley, 80–148. Russell Sage Foundation.

Currie, Janet, and Jeffrey Grogger. 2001. "Recent Declines in Food Stamp Program Participation." *Brookings-Wharton Papers on Urban Affairs* 2001: 203–44.

Duflo, Esther, and Emmanuel Saez. 2003. "The Role of Information and Social Interactions in Retirement Plan Decisions: Evidence from a Randomized Experiment." *Quarterly Journal of Economics* 118 (3): 815–42.

Ebenstein, Avraham, and Kevin Stange. 2010. "Does Inconvenience Explain Low Take-up? Evidence from Unemployment Insurance." *Journal of Policy Analysis and Management* 29 (1): 111–36.

Eli, Shari. 2015. "Income Effects on Health: Evidence from Union Army Pensions." *Journal of Economic History* 75 (2): 448–78.

Eli, Shari, and Laura Salisbury. 2016. "Patronage Politics and the Development of the Welfare State: Confederate Pensions in the American South." *Journal of Economic History* 76 (4): 1078–1112.

Falk, Gene. 2017. "Temporary Assistance for Needy Families (TANF): Size of the Population Eligible for and Receiving Cash Assistance." Congressional Research Service Report R44724.

Fishback, Price V., and Shawn Everett Kantor. 1998. "The Adoption of Workers' Compensation in the United States, 1900–1930." *Journal of Law and Economics* 41 (2): 3.

Fishback, Price V., and Shawn Everett Kantor. 2000. *A Prelude to the Welfare State: The Origins of Workers' Compensation*. University of Chicago Press.

Fogel, Robert W. 2000. *Public Use Tape on the Aging of Veterans of the Union Army: Military, Pension, and Medical Records, 1860–1940*, Version M-5. Center for

Population Economics, University of Chicago Graduate School of Business, and Department of Economics, Brigham Young University.

Glasson, William H. 1902. "The National Pension System as Applied to the Civil War and the War with Spain." *Annals of the American Academy of Political and Social Science* 19 (March): 40–62.

Hacker, J. David. 2011. "A Census-Based Count of the Civil War Dead." *Civil War History* 57 (4): 307–48.

Haines, Michael R. and Inter-University Consortium for Political and Social Research. 2010. Historical, Demographic, Economic, and Social Data: The United States, 1790–2002 [Computer file]. ICPSR02896-v3 Inter-University Consortium for Political and Social Research. http://dx.doi.org/10.3886/ICPSR02896.

Herald and Tribune. 1874. "Pension Day." March 5.

Hill, Terrence D., and Daphne S. Cain. 2012. "Perceived Welfare Caseworker Support and Psychological Distress Among Low-Income Urban Women with Children." *Social Work* 57 (4): 353–60.

Hoynes, Hilary, Nicole Maestas, and Alexander Strand. 2022. "Legal Representation in Disability Claims." NBER Working Paper No. 29871. National Bureau of Economic Research.

Intelligencer Journal. 1869. "Pension Day." September 7.

Jones, Damon. 2010. "Information, Preferences, and Public Benefit Participation: Experimental Evidence from the Advance EITC and 401(K) Savings." *American Economic Journal: Applied Economics* 2: 147–63.

Ko, Wonsik, and Robert A. Moffitt. 2022. "Take-up of Social Benefits." IZA Discussion Paper No. 15351.

Library of Congress. 2023. "Chronicling America: U.S. Newspaper Directory, 1690-Present." https://chroniclingamerica.loc.gov/search/titles/

Livermore, Thomas Leonard. 1901. *Number and Losses in the Civil War in America, 1861–65*. Houghton Mifflin & Co.

Madrian, Brigitte C., and Dennis F. Shea. 2001. "The Power of Suggestion: Inertia in 401(k) Participation and Savings Behavior." *Quarterly Journal of Economics* 116 (4): 1149–87.

Margo, Robert A. 2000. *Wages and Labor Markets in the United States, 1820–1860*. University of Chicago Press.

Moffitt, Robert. 1983. "An Economic Model of Welfare Stigma." *American Economic Review* 73 (5): 1023–35.

Nashville Union and American. 1870. "Hunting a Pensioner." April 7.

New York Times. 1869. "Pension Brokers." September 20.

New York Times. 1880. "Widow Helfrich's Pension." February 29.

Raftsman's Journal. 1862. "Report of the Sec'y of the Interior." December 17.

Ruggles, Steven, Sarah Flood, Matthew Sobek, Danika Brockman, Grace Cooper, Stephanie Richards, and Megan Schouweiler. 2023. IPUMS USA: Version 13.0 [dataset]. IPUMS. https://doi.org/10.18128/D010.V13.0.

Saez, Emmanuel. 2009. "Details Matter: The Impact of Presentation and Information on the Take-up of Financial Incentives for Retirement Saving." *American Economic Journal: Applied Economics* 1 (1): 204–28.

Salisbury, Laura. 2017. "Women's Income and Marriage Markets in the United States: Evidence from the Civil War Pension." *Journal of Economic History* 77 (1): 1–38.

Skocpol, Theda. 1995. *Protecting Soldiers and Mothers: The Political Origins of Social Policy in the United States*. Harvard University Press.

US Pension Bureau. 1866. *Annual Report of the Commissioner of Pensions to the*

Secretary of the Interior for the Year Ending June 30, 1866. Government Printing Office.
US Pension Bureau. 1871. *Annual Report of the Commissioner of Pensions to the Secretary of the Interior for the Year Ending June 30, 1871*. Government Printing Office.
US Pension Bureau. 1872. *Annual Report of the Commissioner of Pensions to the Secretary of the Interior for the Year Ending June 30, 1872*. Government Printing Office.
US Pension Bureau. 1883. *Annual Report of the Commissioner of Pensions to the Secretary of the Interior for the Year Ending June 30, 1883*. Government Printing Office.
Vermont Journal. 1879. "A Grand Swoop." February 1.

5 Marital Matching and Women's Intergenerational Mobility in the Late 19th- and Early 20th-Century US

Martha J. Bailey and Peter Z. Lin

5.1 Introduction

Assortative matching, or marriage homogamy, measures the similarity of traits between a husband and wife. This statistic has long been of great interest to social scientists across disciplines, because it characterizes the functioning of the marriage market, including the scarcity or abundance of potential partners, the complementarity or substitutability of partners' traits in production and consumption (Becker 1973, 1974; Lam 1988; Stevenson and Wolfers 2007), and bargaining power and gender equity within marriage (Kalmijn 1991, 1994; Shorter 1977). Assortative matching also determines long-run economic outcomes, including income inequality between households (Ciscato and Weber 2020; Eika et al. 2019; Fernandez

Martha J. Bailey is a professor of economics and director of the California Center for Population Research at the University of California, Los Angeles, and a research associate of the National Bureau of Economic Research.

Peter Z. Lin is an assistant professor of economics at Western Kentucky University.

This chapter was prepared for a conference volume, *The Economic History of American Inequality*, in honor of Robert Margo. We thank Mengying Zhang, Deniz Gorgulu, Kelsey Figone, and Eric Wang for excellent research assistance. The LIFE-M project was generously supported by the National Science Foundation (SMA 1539228), the National Institute on Aging (R21 AG05691201), the University of Michigan Population Studies Center Small Grants (R24 HD041028), the Michigan Center for the Demography of Aging (MiCDA, P30 AG012846–21), the University of Michigan Associate Professor Fund, the Michigan Institute on Research and Teaching in Economics (MITRE), the Russell Sage Foundation (1911–19560), and the Washington Center for Equitable Growth. We gratefully acknowledge the use of the Population Studies Center's services and facilities at the University of Michigan (P2CHD041028) and the California Center for Population Research at UCLA (P2CHD041022). For acknowledgments, sources of research support, and disclosure of the authors' material financial relationships, if any, please see https://www.nber.org/books-and-chapters/economic-history-american-inequality-new-evidence-and-perspectives/marital-matching-and-womens-intergenerational-mobility-late-19th-and-early-20th-century-us.

and Rogerson 2001; Greenwood et al. 2014; Kremer 1997); the allocation of resources within households (Calvo et al. 2021); and the intergenerational social and economic mobility of children (Aiyagari et al. 2000; Chadwick and Solon 2002; Currie and Almond 2011; Ermisch et al. 2006).

This chapter contributes to the economic history of American inequality by describing the evolution of assortative matching in the US in the late 19th and early 20th centuries, an era characterized by rapid industrialization and economic growth, the dramatic expansion of public education, mass immigration, urbanization, the Great Depression, and war. We examine marital matching in four dimensions: age, nativity, education, and occupational standing. Our analysis uses the full-count 1850–1940 Decennial Censuses (Ruggles et al. 2021) as well as newly released data from the Longitudinal Intergenerational Family Electronic Micro-database (LIFE-M) (Bailey et al. 2022). The LIFE-M data cover the late 19th and early 20th century for individuals born in Ohio and are fundamental to our analysis of the intergenerational mobility of women. Relying on vital records that contain both birth ("maiden") and married surnames, the LIFE-M data contain high-quality, longitudinal links of more than 260,000 women from birth to adulthood. The presence of both birth and married surnames allows LIFE-M to locate both husbands and fathers, facilitating an analysis of women's social and economic mobility in very large samples of US women born between 1865 and 1920. In addition, using both sources of data allows us to compare estimates from linked samples to the census population, reweight the LIFE-M samples to resemble the population of married women, and adjust for selection into marriage by age.

Our results add new insights into the functioning of the marriage market in the 19th and early 20th centuries. Adjusting for the age composition of married women observed in the census, we find that age homogamy changed very little for women born over the 19th century. This stability contrasts with Rolf and Ferrie (2008), who found that age differences between husbands and wives increased sharply, from 2 to 5 years, for women born over the first 30 years of the 19th century. Adjusting for the age composition of married women, however, shows that the age differences between husbands and wives were fairly stable over the 19th century, rising slightly from around 4.5 to 5.2 years in the early 19th century and then returning to a 4.5-year age gap for the duration of the late 19th century. This stability in age homogamy makes the transition to smaller within-couple age gaps in the 20th century exceptional rather than a return to antebellum US marriage patterns (Atkinson and Glass 1985).

A second finding is the significant decrease in marital matching on fathers' nativity in the mid- to late 19th century. As mass immigration to the US transformed the nation, the likelihood that a woman was married to a man whose father was born in the same country as her own father declined from 0.93 to 0.75—a decrease in nativity homogamy suggesting intermarriage helped stir the US melting pot. Then, between 1890 and 1940, rates of nativity homogamy stabilized in the nation overall. But this pattern was not universal. Among Ohio-born women, nativity homogamy increased from around 0.75 to 0.82 between 1885 and 1940, signaling an increase in segregation by father's country of origin in the rapidly industrializing economies of the Midwest.

A third finding is that the association of husbands' and wives' educational attainment changed little for individuals marrying between 1900 and 1940, despite the high school movement increasing the share of Americans graduating from high school, from 10 percent in 1910 to over 50 percent by 1940 (Goldin 1998). But the results for women's intergenerational occupational mobility offer a different picture. After a period of stability in intergenerational mobility for birth cohorts born in the 30 years after the Civil War, we find that the intergenerational persistence between the occupational standing of a woman's husband and her father fell by roughly one-third for cohorts born over the next 30 years. We also find that absolute measures of intergenerational mobility increased for the same cohorts, suggesting considerably more upward mobility for women whose fathers' occupations ranked in the bottom half of the income distribution. The similarity of estimates in the LIFE-M sample to those from unlinked census samples for age and nativity lends credibility to the quality of the links and representativeness of the reweighted samples and these findings for occupational mobility. An important caveat for these findings is that they speak to patterns only in Ohio—a limitation that is being addressed with ongoing linking work to increase the number of states in the LIFE-M data.

These findings for intergenerational occupational mobility agree with but also differ from some estimates in the literature. Similar to findings using a name-based approach (Olivetti and Paserman 2015), linked Massachusetts marriage records (Eriksson et al. 2023), and retrospective surveys (Jácome et al. 2024), our analysis implies that intergenerational persistence fell for women between 1915 and 1940. However, the magnitudes of our estimates of intergenerational persistence differ. Intergenerational persistence for Ohio-born women is twice what Eriksson et al. (2023) measure in Massachusetts for similar cohorts, suggesting considerably more persistence in socioeconomic status in late 19th- and early 20th-century Ohio. This finding is robust to using correlation coefficients or rank-rank coefficients. However, our estimates of intergenerational persistence are lower than in Olivetti and Paserman (2015), who use names rather than occupations, and also lower than in Jácome et al. (2024), who measure mobility in terms of current household income and retrospective reports of father's occupation. Both levels and trends in intergenerational mobility for women in the LIFE-M Ohio data differ from the national estimates using the Census Tree (Buckles et al. 2023), leaving important puzzles for future work.

This chapter contributes a novel historical perspective to a growing body of work examining assortative matching and women's intergenerational mobility in the US in the 19th century (Althoff et al. 2023; Buckles et al. 2023; Eriksson et al. 2023; Olivetti and Paserman 2015) and the late 20th century (Aiyagari et al. 2000; Charles et al. 2013; Eika et al. 2019; Greenwood et al. 2014). It also contributes historical context for understanding changes in marital matching on nativity to modern studies focusing on the rise in interracial/interethnic marriages (Gilbertson 1996; Kalmijn 1998; Qian 1997; Schoen and Thomas 1989). Finally, it adds to recent studies using alternative approaches to studying assortative matching on socioeconomic status by considering assortative matching on fathers' occupational standing and women's own educational attainment separately (Eriksson et al. 2023; Jácome et al. 2024; Olivetti and Paserman 2015).

5.2 An Overview of Assortative Matching and Women's Intergenerational Mobility in US History

Assortative matching and women's intergenerational mobility have been difficult to study in US history, largely due to data limitations. Data linking in historical data has tended to focus on fathers and sons, because men can be linked using their full first and last names (Abramitzky et al. 2021; Collins and Wanamaker 2022; Feigenbaum 2018; Ferrie 1996; Long and Ferrie 2013; Song et al. 2020; Tan 2023; Ward 2021). Census-linking projects have been limited in their ability to follow women over time, because women change their surnames at marriage. Consequently, the availability of large, systematically linked data has expanded the possibilities for studying generational changes for men in the late 19th and early 20th centuries—but less for women.

As an example, the Early Indicators Project, led by Dora Costa, provides an important longitudinal perspective on economic outcomes for men during the middle and late 19th century (Wimmer 2003). The data consist of 39,340 Union Army (UA) soldiers, approximately 6,200 of whom were "Colored Troops." These data measure the date of death and provide rich information on disability, health, use of medical care, and pension receipt for men reaching retirement age in the late 19th century. Through links to the 1850 and 1930 censuses, the UA data also include sociodemographic and economic variables. An important limitation of the UA data is that they consist primarily of men (because women did not serve as soldiers in the Civil War) and most were born in the North.

The Minnesota Population Center's (MPC) Linked Representative Samples (LRS) merge the full-count 1880 census to the 1850–1930 census 1 percent samples (Ruggles et al. 2010). The LRS thus combine economic (e.g., occupation, literacy, labor force participation, homeownership) and demographic (e.g., age, birthplace, race, marital status, number of children) outcomes for around 500,000 people, including both men and women, across the life course. Although large in scale, important limitations of these data are that most women cannot be linked between their birth and married families (due to surname changes) and that intergenerational coverage consists of at most two generations of men (primarily father–son pairs).

More recently, MPC released the Multigenerational Longitudinal Panel (MLP), which uses supervised machine learning to link millions of individuals between every pair of adjacent censuses from 1850 to 1940 (Helgertz et al. 2020). The resulting sample sizes range from around 6 million individuals linked between the 1850 and 1860 censuses to 52 million individuals linked between the 1930 and 1940 censuses. MLP's linking strategy is implemented in two steps. First, men are linked between adjacent censuses as individuals. In this step, MLP exploits rich training data and contextual information in the linking process (e.g., place of residence, coresident individuals), in addition to names and basic demographics. This strategy increases match rates while reducing the likelihood of false matches, but the final linked sample overrepresents men who do not move and who retain the same household members. In the second step, the procedure links household members living with the men linked in the first step. This second step helps link women who are coresiding with their spouses and daughters living with their fathers. As in the LRS, census data limitations make it nearly impossible to link women who change households or their names at marriage, which means that MLP contains a nonrepresentative set of women.

Concurrent with the development of MLP, Abramitzky et al. (2020) released census links under the Census Linking Project (CLP), which also links millions of men between every available pair of censuses from 1850 to 1940. Building on the linking approaches in Abramitzky et al. (2012, 2019), CLP uses unsupervised machine learning based on name, race, and year or place of birth information in the census. (Note that the difference between supervised and unsupervised machine-learning methods is that the latter do not use training data to control error rates or optimize performance, resulting in smaller linked samples and higher error rates.) Similar to other census projects, CLP does not link women.

Recent studies have addressed these data limitations for studying women in several ways. Olivetti and Paserman (2015) take the creative approach of using children's first names to impute their childhood socioeconomic status. For example, using the 1850 census, they find that fathers of children named Edward had higher occupational rank on average than fathers of Jesse. Using this information, they compute intergenerational mobility for daughters and sons by correlating imputed occupational status of fathers in childhood and own (or husband's) occupational status in the 1850–1940 decennial censuses. They find that both father–son and father–daughter intergenerational elasticities remained stable around 0.31–0.35 for fathers and sons and 0.34–0.40 for fathers and daughters in the 19th century. The elasticities increased to around 0.49 for both father–son and father–daughter pairs observed between 1900 and 1920, then declined to 0.43 for father–son pairs and to 0.37 for father–daughter pairs between 1920 and 1940.

A more direct approach by Eriksson et al. (2023) uses a Feigenbaum's supervised machine-learning approach to link Massachusetts marriage certificates to the 1850, 1860, 1870, 1880, 1900, 1910, and 1920 censuses to examine the socioeconomic mobility of women in terms of the occupational standing of their husbands and fathers. They linked 38,760 couples (3 percent of all marriage records) to both husbands' and wives' adult and childhood census records at an error rate between 9 percent and 14 percent in the first stage (linking marriage records to postmarriage censuses) and between 6 percent and 10 percent in the second stage (linking postmarriage to premarriage censuses), depending on the marriage cohort.[1] They find intergenerational mobility for women, based on either the occupational income scores or occupational wealth scores of the father and husband, is higher than for men for the 1850–1870 marriage cohorts.[2] By 1880–1900 marriage cohorts, men's mobility increased, but the women's did not, leading rates of intergenerational mobility to converge between the two cohorts.

Buckles et al. (2023) combine census information with a rich and unique set of records on FamilySearch.org, one of the largest, user-created genealogical platforms, to create the "Census Tree." FamilySearch.org information is largely generated by its users, who search the website's trove of information (e.g., vital records, newspapers, cemetery documents, census records) to link their own family's records. The Census Tree combines these user links (which they estimate to be correct around 95 percent of the time) with machine links (which they estimate to be correct around 86 percent–89 percent of the time) to produce a large intergenerational database containing both men and women (Price et al. 2021). Because the final Census Tree differs from the population (in particular, they are less mobile from their birth state; Price et al. 2021, table 7), Buckles et al. (2023) estimate inverse-propensity scores to reweight the data to match the census population following the procedure in Bailey et al. (2020a, 2020b). Their intergenerational mobility estimates for men and women use a variety of occupation scores and an instrumental-variables strategy to account for measurement error in occupational status (Solon 1992; Ward 2021). Their results show that intergenerational persistence for men and women is almost identical, falling from around 0.85 to 0.64 between the cohorts of 1840 and 1890 and remaining roughly constant through the cohort of 1910.

More recently, Jácome et al. (2024) pool multiple retrospective surveys from the second half of the 20th century to characterize the long-run evolution of intergenerational income mobility. Although these surveys are not

1. The linkage process and false positive rates are reported in Table A3.

2. Eriksson et al. (2023) calculate occupational wealth score based on the value of real and all property reported in the 1870 decennial census 1 percent sample.

drawn from the early 20th century, they contain information on cohorts that were born between 1900 and 1920, which overlaps with the youngest cohorts in our analysis sample. An important feature of these survey data is that they contain a fairly representative set of women as adults, who report retrospectively on their fathers' occupations. For men and women born between the 1910s and 1940s, they find that intergenerational income persistence fell, and relative intergenerational mobility rose.

Finally, Bailey et al. (2022) use supervised machine learning and rich features in the Social Security Application Records (SS-5) to link over 1.7 million men and women born in the US between 1910 and 1919 and their parents to the 1940 census at a 3-percent error rate. The SS-5 records contain detailed information on applicants (full birth and married names, sex, race, exact date of birth, state, or country of birth) as well as the full names of both parents. These features allow the analysis to identify parent–child relationships and create nationally representative samples containing all states. The limitation of these records is that they contain very few records before the birth cohorts of 1900, which limits their historical perspective. Importantly for this paper, Bailey et al. (2022) find a high degree of intergenerational persistence in education for both women and men, born from 1910 to 1989.

The estimates of rising occupational mobility and stable rates of educational mobility in Jácome et al. (2024) and Bailey et al. (2022) serve as important points of reference for our estimates of women's occupational and educational mobility.

5.3 New Data to Measure Assortative Matching and Women's Intergenerational Mobility

This chapter uses the 1850–1940 decennial censuses as well as the Longitudinal Intergenerational Family Electronic Micro-database (LIFE-M) to construct new estimates of marital matching in the late 19th and early 20th centuries. This section describes the 1850–1940 decennial censuses and LIFE-M data; our analysis samples for age, nativity, education, and occupational homogamy; and our methods to reweight the linked data.

5.3.1 The Full-Count 1850–1940 Decennial Censuses

For our analysis of age homogamy, we use the 1850–1940 decennial censuses from the Minnesota Population Center's (MPC) Integrated Public Use Microdata Series (IPUMS; Ruggles et al. 2021). We restrict all analytic samples to women who (1) were born in the US, (2) were of marriageable age (20–60) at the time of enumeration, and (3) were coresiding with their husbands. Because we focus on marriage in the US, we exclude from our analysis foreign-born women—many of whom may have married before immigrating to the US. This choice also increases comparability of the census with the LIFE-M data, because foreign-born individuals are not included in the LIFE-M sampling frame of US birth certificates. In addition, many foreign-born women married in their country of origin before immigrating and these marriage outcomes may reflect the dynamics of marriage markets outside the US. Note that although all daughters are US-born, many have fathers who are immigrants.

For our analysis of marital matching on nativity, we use the full-count 1880–1930 censuses, in which individuals reported fathers' birthplaces to the census enumerator. This allows us to consider changes in nativity homogamy for a census population without the need to link individuals.[3]

For our analysis of marital matching on education, we only use the 1940 census, which was the first census in which individuals reported their educational attainment. This analysis is restricted to husbands and wives residing together at the time of enumeration.

5.3.2 The Longitudinal, Intergenerational Family Electronic Micro-Database (LIFE-M)

For each of these analyses, we supplement the census data with the newly available LIFE-M database, which links millions of birth records to other vital records (death and marriage records) and the historical censuses (1880, 1900, 1910, 1920, and 1940 censuses), with the goal of minimizing Type I linking errors while maximizing link rates.[4] The project's supervised learning models target Type I error rates below 3 percent, which are further reduced in thorough cross-checks across multiple record links. The LIFE-M data is particularly useful for examining women's intergenerational outcomes, because vital records contain rich information on women's birth (or "maiden") names, their parents' names, and their spouses' names and allow women to be tracked from their birth to marriage families (Bailey et al. 2022). The large sample of linked women allows us to study the evolution of marriage outcomes for women across birth cohorts. We restrict our analysis to the LIFE-M women who were (1) born in Ohio between 1865 and 1920 (a narrower time frame than our restriction on the census data due to data

3. This question is not available prior to 1880. In the 1940 census, only a sample-line person was asked for their father's birthplace. This means that a woman who is the sample-line respondent will report her own father's birthplace. However, her spouse, who is not a sample-line respondent, will not. Therefore, we cannot observe both father and father-in-law's birthplace for women who do not coreside with their fathers-in-law, which is a selected sample. For instance, in the 1940 census, among 1,255,870 women satisfying our data restrictions and being the sample-line respondent, only 24,927 women (2 percent) coresided with their fathers-in-law.

4. Type I linking errors are cases in which an individual is linked to a different person. LIFE-M does not yet link birth records to the 1890 or the 1930 census. The full-count 1890 census is not available, and the 1930 census is planned for future work. Bailey et al. (2022b) present detailed information on data coverage and linking procedures for interested readers. This analysis excludes LIFE-M's North Carolina links, because of the limited sample sizes for our birth cohorts of interest.

availability), (2) of marriageable age (20–60) when observed in the censuses, and (3) coresiding with their husbands in the linked censuses. The decennial census data provide the target population for our reweighting of the linked samples (Bailey et al. 2020a, 2020b). Our methodology for this reweighting is discussed in later sections.

5.3.3 LIFE-M Sample Sizes for Different Dimensions of Assortative Matching

Table 5.1 reports the number of women in the LIFE-M analytic samples for different measures of assortative matching, as well as the percentage of analogous population covered by the LIFE-M samples. The LIFE-M samples cover between 21 percent (or 79,122 women in the 1900 census) and 30 percent (or 391,643 women in the 1940 census) of the female population that satisfies our sample restrictions. If a woman is linked to more than one census, we include these links as separate observations in our dataset. This data structure allows us to observe women from the same birth cohort at different ages across censuses and, therefore, model marriage patterns across ages.[5]

Panel B shows descriptive statistics for the sample for age homogamy, which is the least restrictive because it requires only the age of a woman and her husband (no information about her father is needed). The sample for nativity homogamy in panel C requires the birthplaces of both a woman's father and her father-in-law. We observe the father's birthplace either from the couple's direct reports (for couples linked to the 1900, 1910, and 1920 censuses) or through a father's own links to any census (where he reported his own birthplace).[6] Panel D shows couples linked to the 1940 census to examine assortative matching by education.

The sample to estimate intergenerational mobility by occupation requires the most information, including both the occupations of a woman's father and her husband.[7] Whereas a husband's occupation is reported directly in the census in which he coresides with his wife, we must additionally link women to their fathers to obtain fathers' occupations. As shown in table 5.1, these additional data restrictions reduce sample sizes: the age sample contains 919,025 observations (panel B, column 5), while the intergenerational mobility sample contains 263,258 observations (panel E, column 5).

5. Note that women born after 1900 are only observed in the 1940 census, because they were younger than 20 in 1920.

6. An alternative measure of nativity homogamy compares the birthplaces of a woman's father and her husband. In that case, the analysis requires additional information on the father's birthplace, as the husband's birthplace is always reported in the censuses. See Appendix C, http://www.nber.org/data-appendix/c14841/appendix.pdf.

7. As an alternative measure of occupational homogamy, we also compare the occupations of a woman's father and father-in-law in Appendix D (http://www.nber.org/data-appendix/c14841/appendix.pdf). In this case, the data require additional information on the father-in-law's occupation, which makes the analytic sample even more restrictive.

Table 5.1 Summary of LIFE-M linked data and analysis samples

	1850 census (1)	1860 census (2)	1870 census (3)	1880 census (4)	1900 census (5)	1910 census (6)	1920 census (7)	1930 census (8)	1940 census (9)	All censuses (10)
A. Ever-married woman born in the US and ages 20–60 in the census										
All	2,402,578	3,074,331	4,372,836	7,116,727	11,263,010	14,301,494	17,509,586	22,037,814	26,552,781	108,631,120
Born in Ohio, 1865–1920					371,560	671,904	977,037		1,301,988	3,322,489
LIFE-M links					79,122	179,210	293,196		391,643	943,171
% population linked					***21.3%***	***26.7%***	***30.0%***		***30.1%***	***28.4%***
B. Age sample: Panel A and coresident with husband										
All	2,402,578	3,074,331	4,372,798	5,992,634	9,502,522	12,132,365	14,902,751	18,616,633	22,275,760	93,272,372
Born in Ohio, 1865–1920					342,633	609,060	862,236		1,123,879	2,937,808
LIFE-M links					78,078	176,882	290,337		373,728	919,025
% population linked					***22.8%***	***29.0%***	***33.7%***		***33.3%***	***31.3%***
C. Nativity sample: Panel B and nonmissing birthplace of father and father-in-law										
All				5,992,634	9,502,522	12,132,365	14,902,749	18,616,633		61,146,903
Born in Ohio, 1865–1920					342,633	609,060	862,236			1,813,929
LIFE-M links					78,091	176,885	290,331		164,969	710,276
% population linked					***22.8%***	***29.0%***	***33.7%***			
D. Education sample: Panel B and nonmissing education of couple										
All									21,807,116	
Born in Ohio, 1865–1920									1,110,811	
LIFE-M links									368,720	
% population linked									***33.2%***	
E. Occupational intergenerational mobility: Panel B and nonmissing occupations of father and husband										
LIFE-M links					9,669	28,223	68,524		156,842	263,258

Note: The table reports the number of women that satisfy various criteria for different samples. We first report the US-born female population and then the Ohio-born female population satisfying the sample conditions. Then we report the number of women in the LIFE-M who are linked to each census and satisfy the same conditions. Finally, we calculate the percentage of the female population linked through LIFE-M (bold and italic). In panel C, the population in the 1940 census is missing because father's birthplace is only reported for sample-line respondents but not all individuals. Panel E excludes the census population and the link rate because it is unknown how many fathers and husbands have nonmissing information outside the LIFE-M sample. The occupation of the father is only available in the LIFE-M sample, which contains the occupation of the father from his own link to any census between 1880 and 1940.

5.3.4 Representativeness of Linked Samples

One major concern with historical linked samples relates to their representativeness (Bailey et al. 2020a, 2020b), especially because nonrepresentative samples may lead to misleading inferences about population-level intergenerational mobility (Bailey et al. 2020a, 2020b; Jácome et al. 2024). To improve the representativeness of our samples, we create custom weights for each linked sample in table 5.1 using inverse propensity scores for each birth cohort and census year (Bailey et al. 2020a, 2020b; DiNardo et al. 1996; Heckman et al. 1998). Appendix A (http://www.nber.org/data-appendix/c14841/appendix.pdf) describes this procedure in detail.

Table 5.2 presents descriptive statistics for the 1900 to 1940 censuses (panel A, column 1; panel B, columns 1, 6) as well as the unweighted and inverse-propensity-score weighted samples of the LIFE-M data (panel A, columns 2, 4, 6, 8; panel B, columns 2, 4, 7, 9). Differences between the target census population and the weighted LIFE-M samples are in panel A (columns 5 and 9) and panel B (columns 5 and 10), with standard errors listed beneath in parentheses. The unweighted samples are noticeably different from the censuses in almost every characteristic, including individuals' birth years (due to the LIFE-M sampling frame) as well as other characteristics such as husband's occupational income score, coresidence with parents, out-of-birth-state migration, and urban residence, among others. In contrast, the weighted samples are more balanced in terms of these characteristics. Although some of the reweighted means for the LIFE-M data are statistically different from the census, this is due to very large sample sizes: the magnitudes of these differences are very small, especially relative to the unweighted sample differences. Similarity in observed characteristics does not guarantee balance in unobserved characteristics, but the comparability in observed characteristics is reassuring. As an additional point of comparison, we later show that both the magnitudes and trends in our weighted LIFE-M linked samples closely track the results in the census across cohorts when available, whereas the unweighted samples do not (figs. 5A.1–5A.4, http://www.nber.org/data-appendix/c14841/appendix.pdf).

5.4 Statistical Methodology

We characterize historical trends in assortative matching in four dimensions: age, nativity, education, and intergenerational occupational mobility. Ideal data for our analysis would include marital outcomes with educational and occupational histories for all individuals in the US. In practice, we observe only couples who are married and coresiding at a point in time, which means that observed married couples are often different from the population of married couples from the same birth cohort. Figure 5.1 shows this changing selection of the observed couples by age, which presents a key challenge for the analysis. Panel A depicts the average age difference

Table 5.2 **Sample means in the Ohio-born population and LIFE-M data**

	Panel A. Age and Nativity Sample								
	Ohio-born sample table 5.1, panel B	Age sample				Nativity sample			
	1900–40 censuses (1)	LIFE-M unweighted (2)	Diff. (2)–(1) (3)	LIFE-M weighted (4)	Diff. (4)–(1) (5)	LIFE-M unweighted (6)	Diff. (6)–(1) (7)	LIFE-M weighted (8)	Diff. (8)–(1) (9)
Woman's birth year	1888	1889	1.157***	1888	0.00	1885	–3.019***	1888	0.00
			(0.016)		(0.030)		(0.0154)		(0.048)
Woman's age	35.52	35.63	0.107***	35.52	0.00	35.25	–0.270***	35.52	0.00
			(0.012)		(0.018)		(0.013)		(0.023)
Husband's age	39.53	39.37	–0.160***	39.48	–0.052**	39.07	–0.468***	1884	0.089***
			(0.013)		(0.020)		(0.014)		(0.025)
Urban residence	0.576	0.513	–0.062***	0.576	0.0004	0.481	–0.094***	0.575	–0.0004
			(0.0006)		(0.001)		(0.0007)		(0.0011)
Farm residence	0.218	0.272	0.054***	0.218	0.0001	0.300	0.082***	0.219	0.0007
			(0.0005)		(0.001)		(0.0006)		(0.0008)
Migration out of birth state	0.242	0.058	–0.184***	0.241	–0.001	0.052	–0.190***	0.238	–0.004**
			(0.0003)		(0.001)		(0.0004)		(0.0015)
Coresidence with father	0.031	0.027	–0.004***	0.031	–0.0004	0.026	–0.005***	0.030	–0.0008*
			(0.0002)		(0.0003)		(0.0002)		(0.0004)
Coresidence with child under 5	0.352	0.459	0.107***	0.352	0.0004	0.509	0.157***	0.353	0.001
			(0.0006)		(0.0008)		(0.0007)		(0.001)
Foreign-born husband	0.058	0.047	–0.011***	0.057	–0.0008	0.045	–0.013***	0.055	–0.003***
			(0.0003)		(0.0006)		(0.0003)		(0.0008)
Husband's occupational income score	24.81	24.31	–0.500***	24.81	0.007	23.62	-1.184***	24.82	0.013
			(0.014)		(0.023)		(0.016)		(0.028)

Note: This table presents means for the population of interest (columns 1, 10, 15), the unweighted LIFE-M samples (columns 2, 6, 11, and 16), the inverse propensity-score reweighted LIFE-M samples (columns 4, 8, 13, and 18). The mean differences between the unweighted linked samples and the target population are reported in columns 3, 7, 12, and 17. The differences between the reweighted linked samples and the target population are reported in columns 5, 9, 14, and 19. See text for more details. ***$p < .01$. **$p < .05$. *$p < .10$. Husbands' occupational income scores are based on the median total income (in hundreds of 1950 dollars) of all persons with that particular occupation in 1950. The occupational scores are provided by IPUMS (Ruggles et al. 2021).

Source: 1880–1940 Full-Count Census Data (Ruggles et al. 2021) and LIFE-M samples (Bailey et al. 2022).

Table 5.2 **(cont.)**

	Panel B. Education and Occupation Sample									
	Ohio-born Sample table 5.1, panel D	Education Sample				Ohio-born Sample table 5.1, Panel E	Occupation Sample			
	1940 census (10)	LIFE-M unweighted (11)	Diff. (11)–(10) (12)	LIFE-M weighted (13)	Diff. (13)–(10) (14)	1900–40 censuses (15)	LIFE-M unweighted (16)	Diff. (16)–(15) (17)	LIFE-M weighted (18)	Diff. (18)–(15) (19)
Woman's birth year	1897	1897	–0.169***	1897	0.000	1888	1896	7.927***	1888	0.000
			(.0173)		(0.023)			(0.027)		(0.111)
Woman's age	43.17	43.34	0.169***	43.17	0.000	35.37	34.03	–1.342***	35.37	0.000
			(0.0173)		(0.023)			(0.019)		(0.060)
Husband's age	46.53	46.66	0.132***	46.51	0.02	39.28	37.52	–1.765***	39.12	–0.160**
			(0.0193)		(0.025)			(0.020)		(0.064)
Urban residence	0.6348	0.584	–0.051***	0.6350	0.0002	0.572	0.515	–0.057***	0.577	0.005
			(0.0010)		(0.001)			(0.001)		(0.003)
Farm residence	0.1778	0.222	0.044***	0.1780	0.0002	0.225	0.269	0.044***	0.224	–0.001
			(0.0009)		(0.0009)			(0.001)		(0.003)
Migration out of birth state	0.2246	0.080	–0.145***	0.2247	0.0001	0.238	0.055	–0.183***	0.231	–0.007
			(0.0007)		(0.0013)			(0.0005)		(0.005)
Coresidence with father	0.0251	0.023	–0.002***	0.0250	–0.0002	0.031	0.067	0.036***	0.032	0.001
			(0.0003)		(0.0004)			(0.0005)		(0.001)
Coresidence with child under 5	0.1563	0.163	0.007***	0.1562	–0.0001	0.356	0.456	0.100***	0.351	–0.005*
			(0.0008)		(0.0009)			(0.001)		(0.003)
Foreign-born husband	0.0546	0.046	–0.009***	0.0542	–0.0004	0.057	0.034	–0.024***	0.054	–0.003
			(0.0004)		(0.0006)			(0.0004)		(0.002)
Husband's occupational income score	26.65	26.21	–0.442***	26.67	0.015	26.11	25.52	–0.586***	26.08	–0.023
			(.0246)		(0.029)			(0.022)		(0.076)

Note: See notes to table 5.2.

Source: 1880–1940 Full-Count Census Data (Ruggles et al. 2021) and LIFE-M samples (Bailey et al. 2022).

between husbands and wives by the women's birth cohort in the 1850 to 1940 censuses. Within each census year, the average age difference within a couple is largest when the cohort is younger and smaller when the cohort is older. For example, married women born in 1880 who were age 20 in the 1900 census (empty square markers) were more than six years younger than their husbands on average, whereas the same cohort of women age 60 in the 1940 census (cross markers) were only about three years younger than their husbands. This pattern reflects the fact that women who marry at younger ages disproportionately marry older men. It also reflects survival bias in marriages: women who are age 60 are much less likely to be married to a partner who is much older than them, because his mortality risk increases with age. Figure 5A.1 (http://www.nber.org/data-appendix/c14841/appendix.pdf) presents age selection in terms of nativity homogamy. Failing to adjust for this selection could severely bias estimates of age homogamy and, potentially, other measures of marital sorting.

To adjust for selection into marriage by age, we estimate the following linear regression model by ordinary least squares (OLS):

$$Y_{it} = f_k + q(age_{it}) + \varepsilon_{it}, \quad (1)$$

where the dependent variable, Y_{it}, is the marriage outcome of interest, either the husband–wife age difference or a binary variable for same nativity of father and father-in-law for woman i coresiding with her husband in the census year t.[8] We code "same nativity" if a woman's father and father-in-law were born in the same grouping of countries. Considering the border changes in many nations in the late 19th and early 20th centuries, we combine countries that are close to each other geographically and culturally that changed borders into the same country group. While this measure will overstate the share of father-father-in-law nativity homogamy in terms of individual countries, we are more confident that changes in this measure capture real differences in country and culture of origin rather than changes in national borders.[9] We group women into five-year cohort bins, f_k, to reduce

8. We also consider alternative measures, such as the absolute difference in age between husbands and wives and a binary measure of whether a woman is over three years younger than her husband. These results are reported in Appendix B (http://www.nber.org/data-appendix/c14841/appendix.pdf) and change the story of our main analysis little.

9. Appendix C (http://www.nber.org/data-appendix/c14841/appendix.pdf) describes these detailed country groups. We also consider an alternative measure of same-nativity marriage: whether the woman's father and husband had the same birth country group. Although closely related to the baseline measure, the two definitions capture marital sorting in different ways. For instance, if a US-born daughter of a German immigrant married a US-born son of another German immigrant, the marriage is a same-nativity marriage according to our baseline definition. However, it is regarded as a cross-nativity marriage using the second definition because the woman's father was born in Germany and her husband was born in the US. The baseline definition is thereby less affected by immigration shocks and better reflects the intergenerational persistence of nativity preference for partners. These alternative measures yield similar results and are presented in Appendix C (http://www.nber.org/data-appendix/c14841/appendix.pdf).

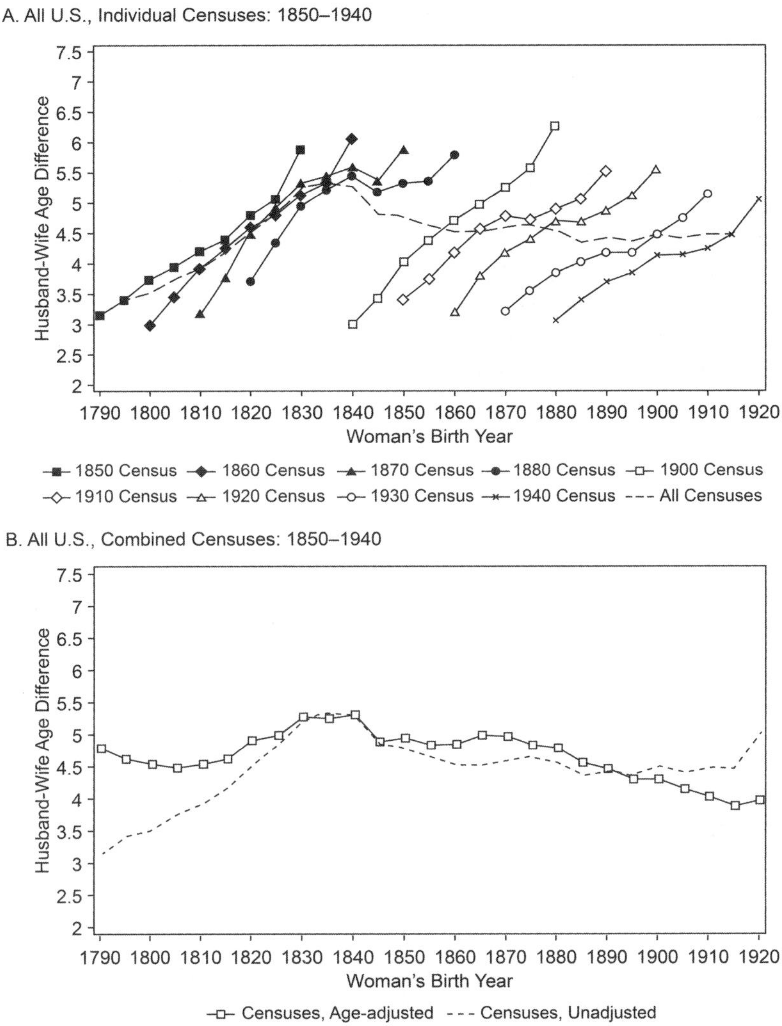

Figure 5.1 Husband–wife age differences, by wife's birth cohort

Note: The figures depict the mean husband-wife age difference (husband's minus wife's age) by wife's birth year. Due to the age heaping in the census and sample sizes in LIFE-M, we group women into five-year birth cohorts and plot the estimates for the midpoint of each five-year birth-year group. Panel A presents the mean age differences by census for the sample in panel A of table 5.1 and also the birth cohort (dashed line). Panel B presents the cohort-specific mean age differences, unadjusted and age-adjusted as described in the text.

Source: 1850–1940 Full-Count Census Data (Ruggles et al. 2021).

noise, and $q(age_{it})$ is a quartic function of the cohort's age in census year t. After estimating this model using the full-count 1850–1940 US decennial censuses (omitting the unavailable 1890 census), we predict outcomes for each birth cohort at a common age—35—thereby adjusting the data for selection into or out of married coresidence at different cohort ages in the census. Standard errors are clustered for dependence at the birth-cohort year level (Moulton 1986).

These census estimates can be compared to those from the LIFE-M sample, which are weighted to reflect observed characteristics in the census using inverse-propensity-score weights (Bailey et al. 2020a, 2020b). Our ability to compare estimates across these samples allows us to assess the quality of the LIFE-M sample as well as assess the external validity of Ohio relative to a nationally representative, unlinked source. Because the censuses are available, the LIFE-M sample is not necessary to examine age or nativity homogamy. However, the comparison of the LIFE-M estimates to census estimates is useful for analyses in which the census cannot be used, for example, for the intergenerational occupational mobility analyses.

Our analysis of marital matching on education builds on a large literature on intergenerational mobility (Black and Devereux 2011; Chetty et al. 2014a, 2014b, 2017; Deutscher and Mazumder 2023). We measure the educational attainment of wives and their husbands in the 1940 census, the first census to report this outcome.[10] Because we observe education in only one census, we cannot adjust by age as we do in the previous analysis. For this reason, the analysis uses women ages 30 to 60 to minimize the effects of selection into marriage by age. Following Greenwood et al. (2014, 2016) and Eika et al. (2019), we examine assortative matching using OLS to estimate the following linear model,

$$Educ_i^W = \sum_j \gamma_j D_j \times Educ_i + f_j + \varepsilon_i, \tag{2}$$

where $Educ_i^W$ is the educational attainment for wife i; $Educ_i$ is her husband's educational attainment; D_j is a dummy variable for women born in year j; and f_j captures individual birth-year fixed effects. The cohort-specific homogamy coefficient γ_j is a measure of educational homogamy for women of birth cohort j. To account for changes in the marginal distributions of education across time, we also present intergenerational educational correlation estimates, in which $Educ^W$ and $Educ$ in equation 3 are normalized to have a mean of zero and a standard deviation of 1 within cohort groups. Because there are so many ties (identical values) for educational attainment, we do not use the rank-rank approach that is often used for income (Chetty et al. 2014a, 2014b). Standard errors are clustered for dependence at the birth-cohort year level (Moulton 1986).

10. Censuses before 1940 ask about literacy but not detailed educational attainment.

A final analysis uses only the LIFE-M sample to compute intergenerational occupational persistence between a woman's father and her husband using the occupational score of their occupation. For the occupational score, we use those calculated by IPUMS (Ruggles et al. 2021). These represent the median total income (in hundreds of 1950 dollars) of all persons with that particular occupation in 1950.[11] We choose to associate a husband's occupation score rather than women's own, because few women participated in the labor market in this period. This measure has several other advantages as well. First, occupations are readily reported in all historical censuses, which allows us to consider a long period of time. Second, occupation captures a more permanent component of socioeconomic status than income, because it does not experience transitory shocks and is less subject to measurement error. In addition, occupational scores are used in other studies of intergenerational mobility (Eriksson et al. 2023; Olivetti and Paserman 2015), which facilitates straightforward comparisons to important findings in the literature.

We estimate the following specification of intergenerational persistence by OLS,

$$\text{(3)} \qquad \log(OccScore)_{it} = \sum_{k} \gamma_k D_k \times \log(ParentOccScore)_i + \log(ParentOccScore)_i \times q(age_{it}) + f_k + \varepsilon_i,$$

where $\log(OccScore)_{it}$ captures the occupational standing of the husband of woman i, in the observed census year t, and $\log(ParentOccScore)_i$ captures the occupational standing of the woman's father. We group women into cohort bins such that D_k is a dummy variable for women born in cohort $k (k = 1865–1867, 1868–1872, 1873–1877, \ldots, 1912–1917, 1918–1920)$ and f_k is a set of individual cohort fixed effects.[12] A quartic function of the woman's age in the census, $q(age_{it})$, helps capture lifecycle bias and age-based selection into marriage.

The coefficient of interest, γ, is the intergenerational elasticity (IGE)—an estimate of intergenerational persistence that measures how fathers' occupational standing is associated with the occupational standing of their daughters' husbands. A higher value of γ corresponds to higher persistence in

11. The use of occupational income score facilitates comparisons with some studies related to our question of interest, particularly with Olivetti and Paserman (2015) who use the same occupational income score. However, this is a departure from other work such as Collins and Wanamaker (2022), who generate occupational scores based on 1940 wage income information by 3-digit occupation, with some adjustments for self-employed workers and farm workers; these scores are computed separately by race and census division of residence. Song et al. (2020) use a status measure that is based on literacy/education and occupation. Ward (2021) adjusts for racial and regional inequality in his "adjusted Song score" which is based on literacy/education by occupation, race, and region.

12. We chose to center these bins on multiples of five for all but the first and last bins to account for age heaping.

socioeconomic status across generations, or alternatively lower social mobility. Importantly, γ is both affected by the parent–child correlation but also the relative variance in their outcomes (Eika et al. 2019; Gihleb and Lang 2020). To adjust for the fact that the distribution of occupational scores evolves over time, we also present intergenerational correlation estimates, in which log*Occscore* and log*ParentOccScore* in equation 2 are normalized to have a mean of zero and a standard deviation of 1 within cohort groups.

We supplement these log-log estimates using a rank-rank approach (Chetty et al. 2014a, 2014b). For these analyses, we rank father's occupational score relative to all the fathers of the US-born women in cohort *j* from the most recent census when children were under age 10. For instance, we use the national distribution of fathers' occupational income scores in the 1910 census for women born between 1901 and 1910, when most girls were coresiding with their fathers. We rank husbands by occupational score for a woman in birth cohort *j* observed in census year *t*. We then estimate equation 2, replacing log*Occscore* with occupational rankings. A higher rank-rank coefficient suggests stronger marital sorting on occupation and lower intergenerational mobility for women. All regressions are weighted by the inverse propensity-score weights, and standard errors are clustered at the birth-cohort level (Moulton 1986).

Both the rank-rank coefficients and intergenerational elasticities measure relative mobility, without much information on upward or downward mobility. Following Chetty et al. (2017), our third measure is absolute mobility: (1) the mean husband's occupational rank for a woman born to a father ranked below the median in the fathers' occupational score distribution and (2) the mean husband's occupational rank for a woman born to a father ranked above the median. The former measures absolute upward mobility, whereas the latter measures absolute downward mobility. See Deutscher and Mazumder (2023) for an in-depth comparison of these measures.

5.5 Results: Marital Matching in the Late 19th and Early 20th Centuries

We begin with an analysis of age homogamy. Panel B of figure 5.1 compares the age-adjusted and unadjusted (raw) series of husband-wife age differences for cohorts born from 1790 to 1920 and married from around 1810 to 1940. The unadjusted series is based on the simple averages by cohort in the combined censuses. The age adjustment significantly changes the antebellum national trends, correcting the sharp upward rise in husband-wife age differences for the fact that women born earlier in the century are older when they are observed in the 1850 census. The unadjusted series increases from 3.2 years to 5.3 years between the 1790 and 1840 cohorts, whereas the age-adjusted series only increases from 4.7 years to 5.2 years for the same cohorts. After peaking for cohorts born from 1830 to 1840 at 5.2, husband–wife age differences decrease to around 5 years for the 1880 birth cohort—women getting married around the turn of the century. In short, age homogamy in marriage changed more modestly over the 19th century than previously believed—much less than implied by the series unadjusted for age selection (Rolf and Ferrie 2008).[13] The big picture is that relative stability in age homogamy during the 19th century makes the transition to smaller within-couple age gaps beginning in the 20th century appear more exceptional rather than a return to antebellum US marriage patterns.

We also compare changes in age homogamy for the weighted LIFE-M sample to two reference groups: (1) the age-adjusted population for Ohio-born women for the same cohorts from the census and (2) the age-adjusted population for all US-born women. Panel A of figure 5.2 plots these results for women born between 1865 and 1920 and married between roughly 1885 and 1940. Importantly, both the levels and trends in the LIFE-M data track those for the population of Ohio-born women in the census. This finding underscores the ability of high-quality links and inverse-propensity score reweighting to recover population parameters even when linked samples are not representative. It also increases our confidence in the results for occupational sorting that are based only on linked samples when census estimates are unavailable.

Another key finding is that, while trends in age homogamy among Ohio-born women appear similar to changes in the US after 1880, the average husband–wife age difference was around half a year smaller in Ohio—a difference likely due to Ohio's industrialization and economic development relative to the nation. Indeed, panel B of figure 5.2 makes clear the pattern in age differences by level of economic development, with the most developed census region (Northeast) having smaller husband-wife age differences than the least developed census region (South). The Ohio sample from LIFE-M exhibits a smaller age gap on average but follows patterns identical to the Midwest.

We next extend our analysis of marital homogamy to nativity. Figure 5.3 plots the age-adjusted estimates of the likelihood of same-nativity marriages based on birth country groups of a woman's father and father-in-law. The age-adjusted trend shows a continuous decline in same-nativity marriages between the 1820 and 1890 cohorts, roughly married between 1840 and 1930. The probability of a woman marrying a husband from the same nativity group decreased, from 92 percent for the 1820 cohort to around 75 percent for the 1890 cohort. After that, the age-adjusted probability of a same-nativity marriage remained fairly stable between the 1890 and 1910 cohorts (marriages roughly occurring between 1910 and 1940), whereas the unadjusted trend shows significantly increasing same-nativity

13. Appendix Figure B.1, Panels A and B, (http://www.nber.org/data-appendix/c14841/appendix.pdf) shows a similar trend in the absolute age difference and the probability of marrying a husband at least three years older.

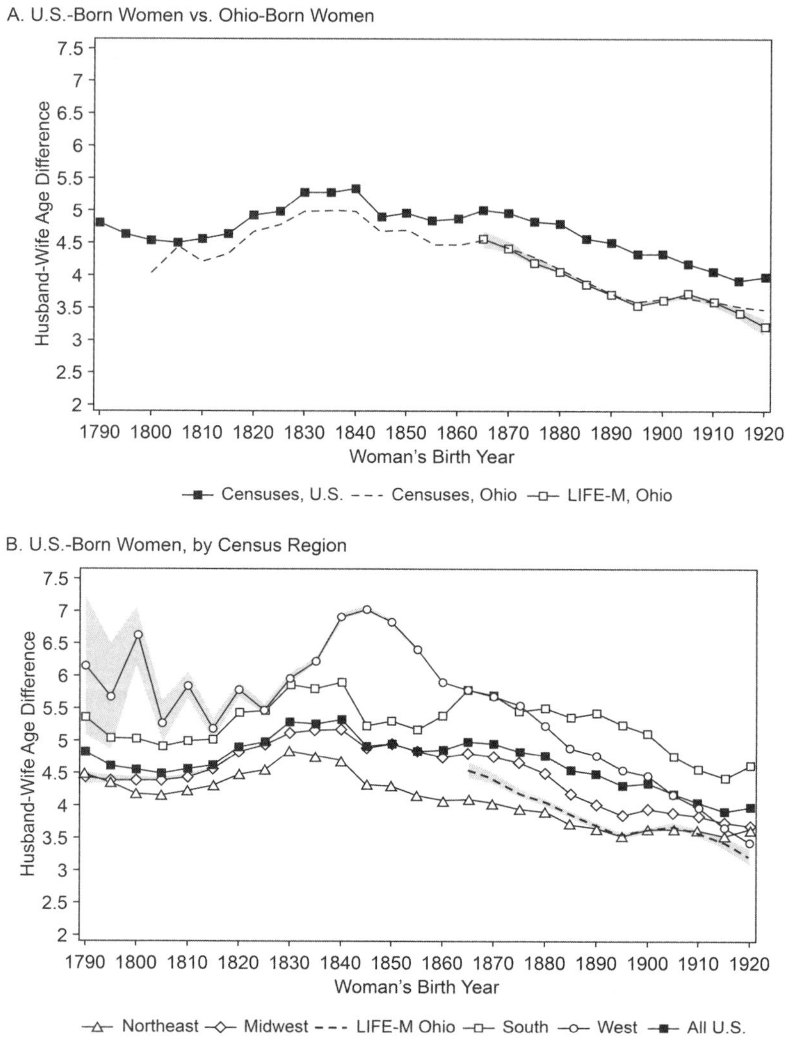

Figure 5.2 Husband–wife age differences, by wife's birth cohort

Note: The figures depict the mean husband-wife age difference by wife's year of birth. Panel A presents the age-adjusted cohort-specific mean age differences for US-born women in the censuses, Ohio-born women in the censuses, and weighted LIFE-M sample of Ohio-born women. The LIFE-M data are weighted using inverse propensity scores as described in the text. Panel B presents the age-adjusted cohort-specific mean age differences for US-born women by their census region of residence along with the Ohio-born women in LIFE-M data. Due to age heaping in the census, we group women into five-year birth cohorts and plot the estimates for the midpoint of each five-year birth-year group. The 95-percent confidence intervals are shown as the shaded area.

Source: 1850–1940 Full-Count Census Data (Ruggles et al. 2021) and LIFE-M samples (Bailey et al. 2022).

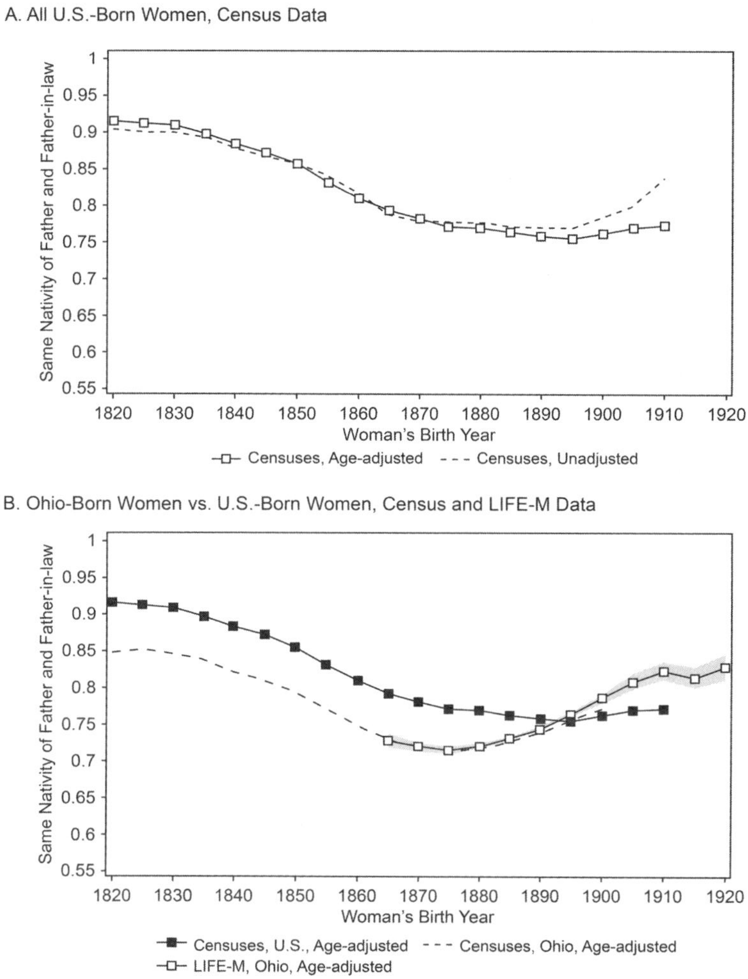

Figure 5.3 Nativity homogamy by father and father-in-law's country group of origin, by wife's birth cohort

Note: The figures show nativity homogamy, defined as a woman's father and her father-in-law being born in the same group of countries. Panel A plots the age-adjusted nativity homogamy by the woman's birth year. (See corresponding series by census and not adjusted by age in Appendix Figure C.1.) Panel B plots the age-adjusted nativity homogamy by the woman's birth year for all US-born women and Ohio-born women in the weighted LIFE-M and census data. The LIFE-M data are weighted using inverse propensity score weights as described in the text. Panel C plots age-adjusted nativity homogamy in census samples by women's census region of residence. Due to age heaping in the census, we group women into five-year birth cohorts and plot the estimates at the midpoint of the group. The 95-percent confidence intervals are shown as the shaded area.

Source: 1880–1930 census data (Ruggles et al. 2021) and LIFE-M samples (Bailey et al. 2022).

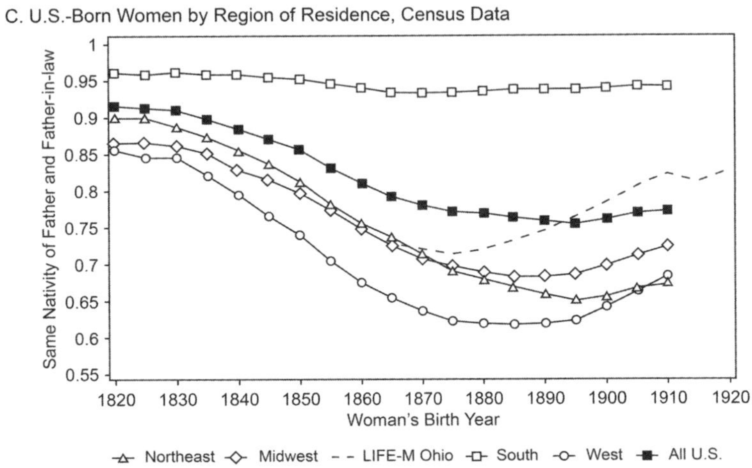

Figure 5.3 (cont.)

marriages for this period. The differences between the unadjusted trend and the age-adjusted trend can also be explained by selection into marriage for more recent cohorts. As Appendix Figure C.1 (http://www.nber.org/data-appendix/c14841/appendix.pdf) shows, women marrying at younger ages (which are the ones we observe for these younger cohorts) tended to marry husbands in the same nativity group, and the age adjustment helps adjust for this tendency.[14]

Panel B of figure 5.3 presents the probability of a same-nativity marriage for Ohio-born women in both the LIFE-M sample and analogous census population data. Similar to the estimates for husband-wife age differences, the age-adjusted LIFE-M estimates and census estimates for Ohio-born women are almost identical—so much so that the dashed line for the census is barely visible in the figure once the LIFE-M data appear for women born after 1865. This similarity again lends credibility to the linked LIFE-M sample's findings and underscores the power of using inverse-propensity reweighting to achieve balance. A second finding, however, is the divergence in the trend for Ohio-born women from US-born women. Among Ohio-born women, nativity homogamy increased from around 0.75 to 0.82 between 1885 and 1940 (cohorts born between 1865 and 1910), signaling an increase in marital sorting by father's country group of origin in the rapidly industrializing economies of the Midwest. Examining regional trends for all

14. Appendix Figure C.2 (http://www.nber.org/data-appendix/c14841/appendix.pdf) shows a similar national trend when defining same-nativity marriages as a woman's father and husband being born in the same group of countries. Similar to the series in Figure 5.3A, we find a significant decline in same-nativity marriage between the 1820 and 1870 cohort, and after that, the probability of a same-nativity marriage remained steady between 1870 and 1910.

US-born women in panel C of figure 5.3 shows only slight increases in nativity homogamy in the broader Midwest census region and West in the early 20th century (cohorts marrying between 1910 and 1930), suggesting that the patterns in Ohio were more the exception than the norm in this period.

Next, we consider changes in marital matching on education, as measured by the association of husbands' and wives' education in the 1940 census using equation 2. Although these trends are not well estimated for cohorts born before 1880, these comparisons are available for all US-born individuals as well as for Ohio-born individuals in the 1940 census and LIFE-M samples.[15] Figure 5.4 shows the cohort-specific slope coefficients (panel A) and correlations (panel B) using equation 2. Notably, the reweighted LIFE-M data again track the census estimates for Ohio-born individuals very closely, which again lends credibility to results using the LIFE-M sample when it cannot be benchmarked in the intergenerational analyses. The results show that the association of husbands' and wives' slope coefficients remained stable for 30 years, for women born between 1880 and 1910 (married between 1900 and 1930), decreasing very slightly for the youngest cohorts (born between 1905 and 1910). Similarly, correlation coefficients increased by only a few points over the period, suggesting very slight increases in assortative matching on education after accounting for the decreasing variance in women's educational attainment relative to men's across cohorts.

In addition, differences between the estimates for the entire US versus Ohio-born residents suggest that Ohio had less assortative matching on education, which is important to keep in mind when considering the external validity of the estimates from the LIFE-M sample. Figure 5.5 shows the correlation coefficients by census region, which indicates that women in the Northeast, Midwest, and West were less assortatively matched on education than women in the South, which raises the estimates for the nation. Like the national trends, however, the regional trends are very stable over time.

In contrast, figure 5.6 shows that women's intergenerational mobility, as measured by fathers' and husbands' occupational standing, was stable in the 19th century and increased meaningfully in the early 20th century. Importantly, these comparisons are not available for all US-born women, so figure 5.6 only uses the LIFE-M sample for women born in Ohio from 1865 to 1920. Panel A plots the cohort-specific rank-rank coefficients, the intergenerational elasticities (IGE, or log-log coefficients), and correlations based on the regressions specified in equation 3. For the 1865 to 1890 cohorts (marriages from 1890 to 1910), we find little change in either the rank-rank or IGE estimates. Assortative matching in terms of husbands' and fathers' occupational standing was fairly stable in the 19th century.

However, intergenerational persistence declined, and mobility increased,

15. The 1940 census is the first to ask this question and the education-mortality gradient makes older cohorts more selected and less representative.

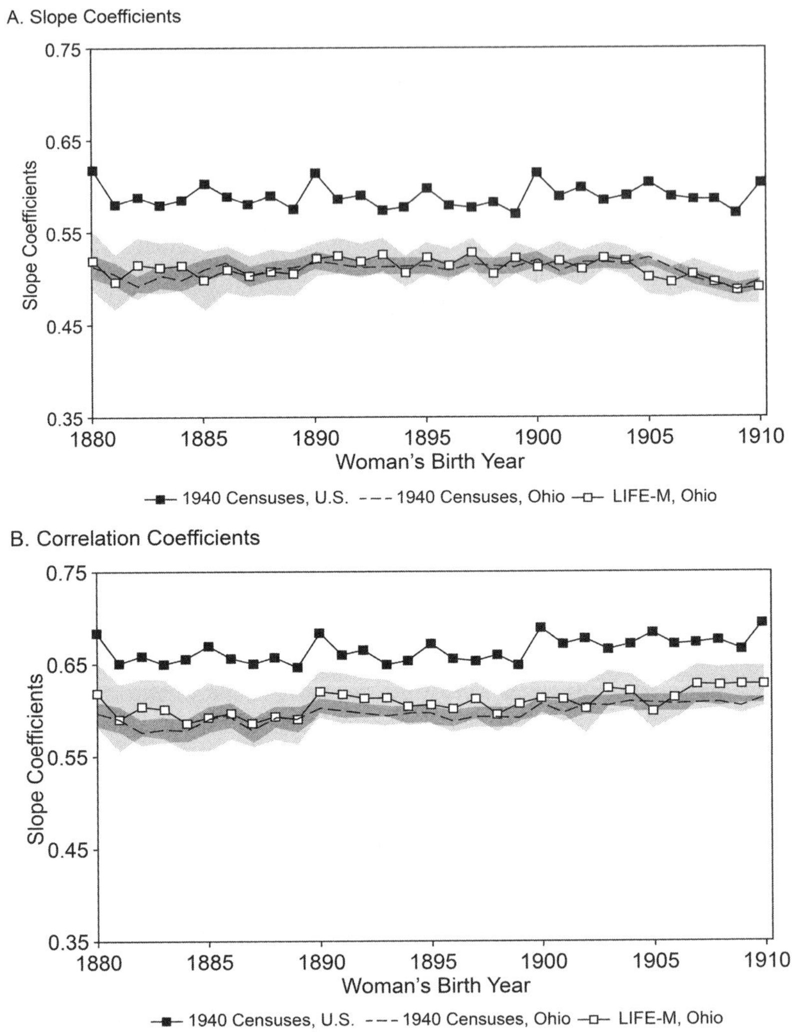

Figure 5.4 Assortative matching by educational attainment, by wife's birth cohort

Note: Panel A depicts education homogamy as captured by regressing a wife's educational attainment on her husband's educational attainment. Educational attainment measures the highest grade completed as reported in the 1940 census. Panel B presents the correlation coefficients. The LIFE-M data are weighted using inverse propensity score weights as described in the text, and 95-percent confidence intervals are shown as the shaded area.

Source: 1880–1940 Full-Count Census Data (Ruggles et al. 2021) and LIFE-M samples (Bailey et al. 2022).

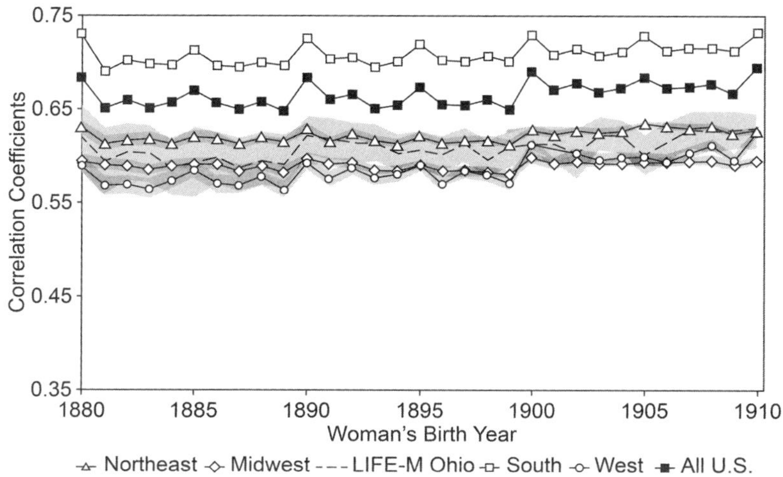

Figure 5.5 Assortative matching by educational attainment, by wife's birth cohort and census region

Note: The series plots the correlation coefficients in educational attainment between husband and wife by wife's birth cohort using the 1940 census. For region-specific coefficients, we group women into five-year cohorts centering on years ending with 5 or 10. For the earliest cohorts, we group the 1880–1882 cohorts and plot them as the 1880 cohort. For the latest cohorts, we group the 1908–1910 cohort and plot their estimates as the 1910 cohort. The shaded area shows the 95-percent confidence intervals. See also notes to figure 5.6.

Source: 1880–1940 Full-Count Census Data (Ruggles et al. 2021).

rapidly for the cohorts born between 1890 and 1920, marriages taking place between 1910 and 1940. Both the IGE and rank-rank coefficients decreased, from 0.32 for the 1890 cohort to 0.15 for the 1920 cohort, which correspond to marriages occurring between 1910 and 1940. Changes in absolute mobility follow similar patterns (panel B). For all cohorts, the average occupational rank of husbands was significantly higher for daughters of above-median occupational rank fathers than for daughters of below-median occupational rank fathers. This is strong evidence for assortative marital matching by socioeconomic status. These patterns remained fairly stable for cohorts born between 1865 and 1890 (marriages from 1885 to 1910), but both upward and downward mobility increased sharply for cohorts born between 1890 and 1920 (marriages from 1910 to 1940).

Although we cannot compute estimates for other census regions, Figure 5.7 compares our estimates to those from other studies. Our estimates of Ohio-born women are slightly lower in level but compare favorably to Olivetti and Paserman (2015), especially for their Midwest sample. The fact that names are stickier than occupations, which can be upgraded over one's lifetime, may explain why occupational homogamy appears lower and economic mobility appears higher using occupational measures. Differences from levels in

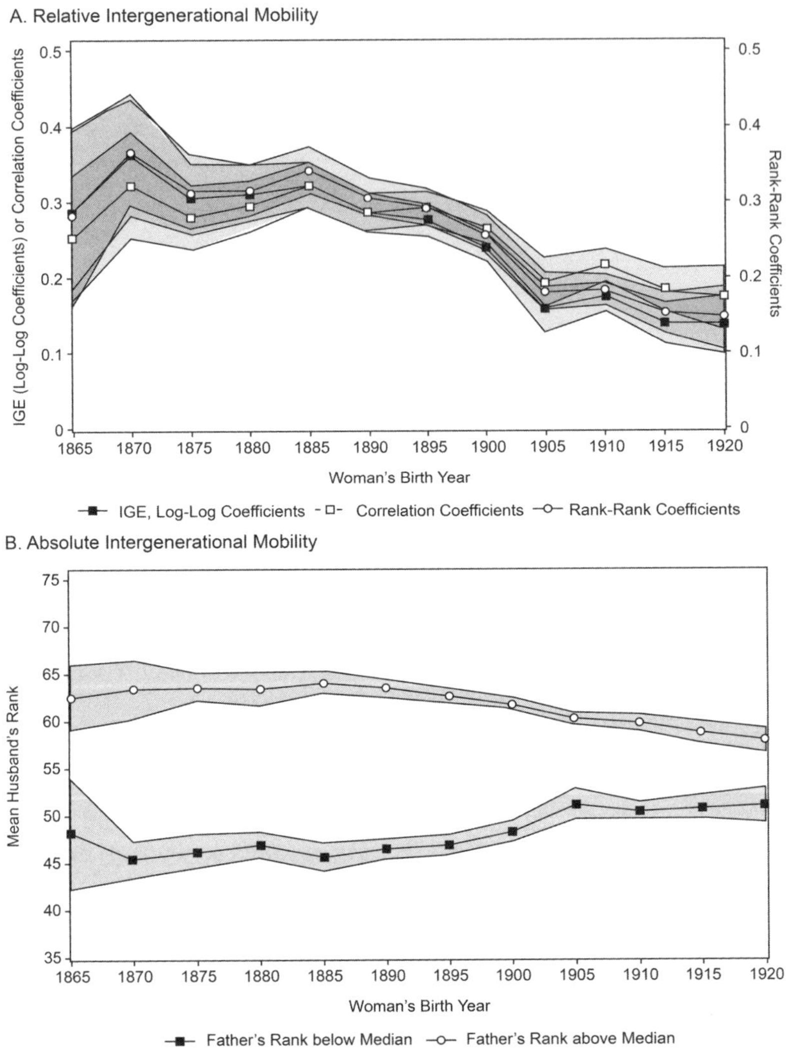

Figure 5.6 Intergenerational mobility by husband's and father's occupation score, by wife's birth cohort

Note: The figures depict changes in occupational homogamy by wife's year of birth according to the relationship between her father's and husband's occupational income scores, which are based on the median income by occupation in the 1950 Census. Panel A characterizes relative mobility in terms of log-log and rank-rank coefficients derived from regressing the log/rank of husband's occupational score on the log/rank of father's occupational score. Panel B plots absolute upward and downward mobility by plotting the husband's occupational rank for women whose fathers fall below or above the national median. We group women into five-year birth cohorts and plot the estimates for the midpoint of each five-year birth-year group. The LIFE-M data are weighted using inverse propensity score weights as described in the text. The 95-percent confidence intervals are shown as the shaded area.

Source: LIFE-M samples (Bailey et al. 2022).

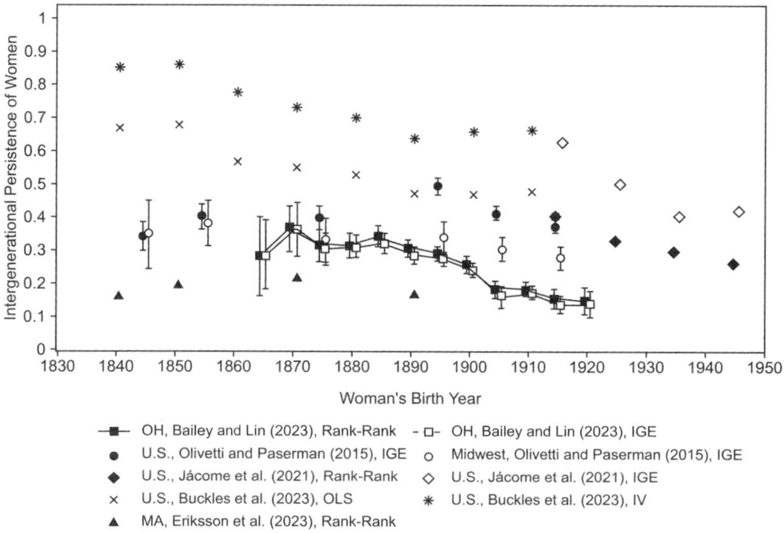

Figure 5.7 Estimates from different studies of intergenerational mobility, by wife's birth cohort

Note: The figure depicts estimates of intergenerational persistence of women in this paper (the squares), as well as the other three related works. The asterisks and cross marks refer to the estimates by Buckles et. al. (2023). The circles refer to the estimates by Olivetti and Paserman (2015). Their estimates are based on a child's first name and pseudo-linking between a father's occupational income score and a husband's occupational income scores, as defined by median total income (in hundreds of 1950 dollars) of all persons with that particular occupation in 1950 (Ruggles et al. 2021). Their estimates are calculated by census years, and we realign them on the woman's birth cohort by subtracting 25 from the census years. The diamonds refer to the estimates by Jácome et al. (2024), which uses surveys reporting fathers' occupations to create occupational-income scores and daughters' family incomes. Their estimates are calculated by the woman's birth cohort and are plotted accordingly. The triangles are estimates from Eriksson et. al. (2023), which are based on links between Massachusetts marriage certificates from 1850 to 1915 to the 1850, 1860, 1870, 1880, 1900, 1910, and 1920 censuses. We plot their estimates based on 1950 occupational income scores for best comparison with our estimates. They do not report confidence intervals so these are not reported here. We translate their estimates for the marriage cohorts 1850–1870, 1860–1880, 1880–1900, and 1900–1920 to the birth cohorts of the 1840s, 1850s, 1870s, and 1890s.

Source: LIFE-M samples (Bailey et al. 2022).

Jácome et al. (2024) likely reflect the fact that retrospective reports of fathers' occupations may reflect his most persistent occupation rather than his work at only one point in time, as measured in the census.[16] Said another way, our measures of occupation from the census may mismeasure socioeconomic standing for much of childhood relative to retrospective reports due to transitory factors or life cycle biases (Mazumder 2005; Solon 1992).

16. See Ward (2021) for an in-depth discussion of this source of measurement error in occupations in historical census data and Haider and Solon (2006) for a discussion of lifecycle bias more generally.

It is harder to interpret the differences in levels from Eriksson et al. (2023). Like Eriksson et al. (2023), this chapter also uses occupational measures but has lower match rates (7 percent to 9 percent) and higher linking error rates (9 percent to 13 percent) than in the LIFE-M data. The former could make their data less representative and the latter could attenuate intergenerational elasticities. In addition, intergenerational occupational mobility may differ between Massachusetts and Ohio, as suggested by stratifications by region for our age, nativity, and education results.

The largest differences in levels and trends emerge between our estimates and those of Buckles et al. (2023), who use the Census Tree data, a different occupational-income score definition, and an instrumental variables approach to account for measurement error in occupational status. These differences in estimates remain open questions for future research to resolve.

To complement these findings, we also examine marital sorting by occupational standing of a woman's father and father-in-law, instead of the husband. The level of marital sorting by parents' socioeconomic outcomes can reflect the relative strength of ascribed and acquired traits in the marriage market (Charles et al. 2013). We measure the sorting by fathers' occupations by estimating equation 3, but we replace the husband's occupational standing with that of his own father. Appendix Figure D.1 (http://www.nber.org/data-appendix/c14841/appendix.pdf) plots the results. We find a similar trend between the 1870 and 1890 cohorts, and the rank-rank coefficients decreased significantly from 0.35 for the 1890 cohort to around 0.25 for the 1910 cohort. The decline is smaller than that of rank-rank coefficients between father and husband (fig. 5.6, panel A), suggesting that the increase in intergenerational mobility of women was caused by both decreasing marital sorting on parents' socioeconomic status and increasing intergenerational mobility of husbands.

Overall, the trends in figure 5.7 reinforce the conclusion that occupational homogamy changed little in the late 19th century for marriages starting between 1880 and 1900 (cohorts born between 1860 and 1880). However, for women born in the early 20th century intergenerational persistence decreased and economic mobility increased.

5.6 Conclusion

This chapter contributes to the economic history of American inequality by characterizing the evolution of marital matching during the late 19th and early 20th century, the eras of mass immigration, rapid industrialization and economic growth, urbanization, the Great Depression, and war. We find that age homogamy changed very little during the 19th century, which makes the rapid transition to smaller within-couple age gaps in the 20th century appear exceptional rather than a return to antebellum US marriage patterns. As mass immigration to the US transformed the nation, the likelihood that a woman was married to a man whose father was born in the same group of countries as her father declined rapidly—a decrease in nativity homogamy, suggesting intermarriage helped stir the US melting pot. From 1900 to 1940, women's intergenerational mobility in terms of her husband's occupational standing relative to her father's increased, whereas the association of husbands' and wives' educational attainment changed little. As the high school movement transformed America's public school landscape, we conclude that women's own educational attainment remained a powerful force in shaping their socioeconomic status in adulthood. Understanding how these trends shaped—and were themselves shaped—by the demographic transition, rapid industrialization, and the transformation of women's paid work remains for future research.

References

Abramitzky, R., L. P. Boustan, and K. Eriksson. 2012. "Europe's Tired, Poor, Huddled Masses: Self-Selection and Economic Outcomes in the Age of Mass Migration." *American Economic Review* 102 (5): 1832–56.

Abramitzky, R., L. Boustan, K. Eriksson, S. Pérez, and M. Rashid. 2020. Census Linking Project: Version 2.0 [dataset]. https://censuslinkingproject.org.

Abramitzky, R., L. Boustan, E. Jácome, and S. Pérez. 2021. "Intergenerational Mobility of Immigrants in the United States over Two Centuries." *American Economic Review* 111 (2): 580–608.

Abramitzky, R., R. Mill, and S. Pérez. 2019. "Linking Individuals Across Historical Sources: A Fully Automated Approach." NBER Working Paper No. 24324. National Bureau of Economic Research.

Aiyagari, S. R., J. Greenwood, and N. Guner. 2000. "On the State of the Union." *Journal of Political Economy* 108 (2): 213–44.

Althoff, Lukas, Harriet Brookes Gray, and Hugo Reichardt. 2023. "The Missing Link: Women and Intergenerational Mobility." https://hugoreichardt.github.io/pdf/igm_women.pdf.

Atkinson, M. P., and B. L. Glass. 1985. "Marital Age Heterogamy and Homogamy, 1900 to 1980." *Journal of Marriage and the Family* 47: 685–91.

Bailey, M. J., Connor Cole, Morgan Henderson, and Catherine Massey. 2020a. "How Well Do Automated Methods Linking Perform? Evidence from the LIFE-M Project." *Journal of Economic Literature* 58 (4): 997–1044.

Bailey, M., C. Cole, and C. Massey. 2020b. "Simple Strategies for Improving Inference with Linked Data: A Case Study of the 1850–1930 IPUMS Linked Representative Historical Samples." *Historical Methods: A Journal of Quantitative and Interdisciplinary History* 53 (2): 80–93.

Bailey, M., P. Z. Lin, A. R. S. Mohammed, P. Mohnen, J. Murray, M. Zhang, and A. Prettyman. 2022. *LIFE-M: The Longitudinal Intergenerational Family Electronic Micro-Database*. Inter-University Consortium for Political and Social Research. https://doi.org/10.3886/E155186.

Bailey, Martha J., A. R. Shariq Mohammed, and Paul Mohnen. 2023. "US Educational Mobility in the Early Twentieth Century." UCLA Working Paper, November.

Bailey, M., P. Z. Lin, A. R. S. Mohammed, P. Mohnen, J. Murray, M. Zhang, and A. Prettyman. 2023. "The Creation of LIFE-M: The Longitudinal, Intergenerational Family Electronic Micro-Database Project." *Historical Methods: A Journal of Quantitative and Interdisciplinary History* 56 (3): 138–59.
Becker, G. S. 1973. "A Theory of Marriage: Part I." *Journal of Political Economy* 81 (4): 813–46.
Becker, G. S. 1974. "A Theory of Marriage: Part II." *Journal of Political Economy* 82 (2): S11–S26.
Black, S. E., and P. J. Devereux. 2011. "Recent Developments in Intergenerational Mobility." *Handbook of Labor Economics* 4b: 1487–1541.
Buckles, Kasey, Joseph Price, Zachary Ward, and Haley E. B. Wilbert. 2023. "Family Trees and Falling Apples: Historical Intergenerational Mobility Estimates for Women and Men." NBER Working Paper No. 31918. National Bureau of Economic Research.
Calvo, P., I. Lindenlaub, A. and Reynoso. 2021. "Marriage Market and Labor Market Sorting." NBER Working Paper No. 28883. National Bureau of Economic Research.
Chadwick, L., and G. Solon. 2002. "Intergenerational Income Mobility Among Daughters." *American Economic Review* 92 (1): 335–44.
Charles, K. K., E. Hurst, and A. Killewald. 2013. "Marital Sorting and Parental Wealth." *Demography* 50 (1): 51–70.
Chetty, R., D. Grusky, M. Hell, N. Hendren, R. Manduca, and J. Narang. 2017. "The Fading American Dream: Trends in Absolute Income Mobility since 1940." *Science* 356 (6336): 398–406.
Chetty, R., N. Hendren, P. Kline, and E. Saez. 2014a. "Where Is the Land of Opportunity? The Geography of Intergenerational Mobility in the United States." *Quarterly Journal of Economics* 129 (4): 1553–1623.
Chetty, R., N. Hendren, P. Kline, E. Saez, and N. Turner. 2014b. "Is the United States Still a Land of Opportunity? Recent Trends in Intergenerational Mobility." *American Economic Review: Papers & Proceedings* 104 (5): 141–47.
Ciscato, E., and S. Weber. 2020. "The Role of Evolving Marital Preferences in Growing Income Inequality." *Journal of Population Economics* 33 (1): 307–47.
Collins, W. J., and M. H. Wanamaker. 2022. "African American Intergenerational Economic Mobility Since 1880." *American Economic Journal: Applied Economics* 14 (3): 84–117.
Currie, J., and D. Almond. 2011. "Human Capital Development Before Age Five." In *Handbook of Labor Economics*, 4:1315–1486. Elsevier.
Deutscher, Nathan, and Bhashkar Mazumder. 2023. "Measuring Intergenerational Income Mobility: A Synthesis of Approaches." *Journal of Economic Literature* 61 (3): 988–1036.
DiNardo, J., N. Fortin, and T. Lemieux. 1996. "Labor Market Institutions and the Distribution of Wages, 1973–1992: A Semi-Parametric Approach." *Econometrica* 64 (5): 1001–44.
Eika, L., M. Mogstad, and B. Zafar. 2019. "Educational Assortative Mating and Household Income Inequality." *Journal of Political Economy* 127 (6): 41.
Eriksson, K., G. T. Niemesh, M. Rashid, and J. Craig. 2023. "Marriage and the Intergenerational Mobility of Women: Evidence from Marriage Certificates 1850–1910." Working Paper. https://niemesgt.github.io/files/WomenMobilityMarriage.pdf.
Ermisch, J., M. Francesconi, and T. Siedler. 2006. "Intergenerational Mobility and Marital Sorting." *Economic Journal* 116 (513): 659–79.

Feigenbaum, J. J. 2018. "Multiple Measures of Historical Intergenerational Mobility: Iowa 1915 to 1940." *Economic Journal* 128 (612): F446–F481.
Fernández, R., and R. Rogerson. 2001. "Sorting and Long-Run Inequality." *Quarterly Journal of Economics* 116 (4): 1305–41. http://www.jstor.org/stable/2696460.
Ferrie, J. P. 1996. "A New Sample of Males Linked from the Public Use Microdata Sample of the 1850 U.S. Federal Census of Population to the 1860 U.S. Federal Census Manuscript Schedules." *Historical Methods: A Journal of Quantitative and Interdisciplinary History* 29 (4): 141–56.
Gihleb, Rania, and Kevin Lang. 2020. "Educational Homogamy and Assortative Mating Have Not Increased." *Research in Labor Economics* 48: 1 - 1 (26).
Gilbertson, G. A. 1996. "Hispanic Intermarriage in New York City: New Evidence from 1991." *International Migration Review* 16:445–59.
Goldin, C. 1998. "America's Graduation from High School: The Evolution and Spread of Secondary Schooling in the Twentieth Century." *Journal of Economic History* 58 (2): 345–74.
Greenwood, J., N. Guner, G. Kocharkov, and C. Santos. 2014. "Marry Your Like: Assortative Mating and Income Inequality." *American Economic Review* 104 (5): 348–53.
Greenwood, J., N. Guner, G. Kocharkov, and C. Santos. 2016. Technology and the changing family: A unified model of marriage, divorce, educational attainment, and married female labor-force participation. *American Economic Journal: Macroeconomics* 8 (1): 1–41.
Haider, S., and G. Solon. 2006. "Life-Cycle Variation in the Association Between Current and Lifetime Earnings." *American Economic Review* 96 (4): 1308–20.
Heckman, James J., Hidehiko Ichimura, Jeff Smith, and Petra Todd. 1998. "Characterizing Selection Bias Using Experimental Data." *Econometrica* 66 (5): 1017–98.
Helgertz, J., S. Reggles, J. Warren, C. Fitch, R. Goeken, J. D. Hacker, M. A. Nelson, J. Price, E. Roberts, and M. Sobek. 2020. *IPUMS Multigenerational Longitudinal Panel: Version 1.0* [dataset]. IPUMS.
Jácome, E., I. Kuziemko, and S. Naidu. 2024. "Mobility for All: Representative Intergenerational Mobility Estimates over the 20th Century." *Journal of Political Economy* 132 (12).
Kalmijn, M. 1991. "Shifting Boundaries: Trends in Religious and Educational Homogamy." *American Sociological Review* 56 (6): 786.
Kalmijn, M. 1994. "Assortative Mating by Cultural and Economic Occupational Status." *American Journal of Sociology* 100 (2): 422–52.
Kalmijn, M. 1998. "Intermarriage and Homogamy: Causes, Patterns, Trends." *Annual Review of Sociology* 24 (1): 395–421.
Kremer, M. 1997. "How Much Does Sorting Increase Inequality?" *Quarterly Journal of Economics* 112 (1): 26.
Lam, D. 1988. "Marriage Markets and Assortative Mating with Household Public Goods: Theoretical Results and Empirical Implications." *Journal of Human Resources* 23 (4): 462.
Long, J., and J. Ferrie. 2013. "Intergenerational Occupational Mobility in Great Britain and the United States Since 1850." *American Economic Review* 103 (4): 1109–37.
Moulton, B. R. 1986. "Random Group Effects and the Precision of Regression Estimates." *Journal of Econometrics* 32 (3): 385–97.
Olivetti, C., and M. D. Paserman. 2015. "In the Name of the Son (and the Daughter): Intergenerational Mobility in the United States, 1850–1940." *American Economic Review* 105 (8): 2695–2724.

Price, Joseph, Kasey Buckles, Jacob Van Leeuwen, and Isaac Riley. 2021. "Combining Family History and Machine Learning to Link Historical Records." *Explorations in Economic History* 80: 1–28.

Qian, Z. 1997. "Breaking the Racial Barriers: Variations in Interracial Marriage Between 1980 and 1990." *Demography* 34 (2): 263–76.

Rolf, K., and J. Ferrie. 2008. "The May–December Relationship Since 1850: Age Homogamy in the U.S." Working paper.

Ruggles, S., C. A. Fitch, R. Goeken, J. D. Hacker, M. A. Nelson, E. Roberts, S. Megan, and M. Sobek. 2021. *IPUMS Ancestry Full Count Data: Version 3.0* [dataset]. IPUMS.

Schoen, R., and B. Thomas. 1989. "Intergroup Marriage in Hawaii, 1969–1971 and 1979–1981." *Sociological Perspectives* 32 (3): 365–82.

Shorter, E. 1977. *The Making of the Modern Family*. Basic Books.

Solon, Gary. 1992. "Intergenerational Income Mobility in the United States." *American Economic Review* 82 (3): 393–408.

Song, X., C. G. Massey, K. A. Rolf, J. P. Ferrie, J. L. Rothbaum, and Y. Xie. 2020. "Long-Term Decline in Intergenerational Mobility in the United States since the 1850s." *Proceedings of the National Academy of Sciences* 117 (1): 251–58.

Stevenson, Betsey, and Justin Wolfers. 2007. "Marriage and Divorce: Changes and Their Driving Forces." *Journal of Economic Perspectives* 21 (2): 27–52.

Tan, H. R. 2023. "A Different Land of Opportunity: The Geography of Intergenerational Mobility in the Early Twentieth-Century United States." *Journal of Labor Economics* 41 (1): 77–102.

Ward, Z. 2021. "Intergenerational Mobility in American History: Accounting for Race and Measurement Error." NBER Working Paper No. 29256. National Bureau of Economic Research.

Wimmer, L. T. 2003. "Reflections on the Early Indicators Project: A Partial History." In *Health and Labor Force Participation over the Life Cycle: Evidence from the Past*, edited by Dora L. Costa, 1–11. University of Chicago Press.

III

Consequences of Inequality

6

The Political Fallout of Machine Tool Automation in the Mid-20th-Century United States

Leah Platt Boustan, Jiwon Choi, and David Clingingsmith

6.1 Introduction

The late 1960s and early 1970s marked the beginning of two profound shifts to the political landscape in the United States. First, Americans began to express lower levels of confidence in a wide range of institutions, including political institutions like Congress and the presidency, as well as elite organizations like major companies, the press, medicine, and education (Twenge et al. 2014). Second, many white Southerners switched from the Democratic Party to the Republican Party in a process of partisan realignment (Kuziemko et al. 2023; Kuziemko and Washington 2018).

Scholars have emphasized cultural explanations for these shifts in political attitudes and affiliation including: disaffection with the civil rights and feminist movements, conflict between those who fought in Vietnam and those who protested the war, mistrust in government after misdeeds in Vietnam were uncovered, and the 1974 resignation of President Richard Nixon following the Watergate break-in (Kuziemko and Washington 2018; Lipset and Schneider 1983; Maxwell and Shields 2019; Perlstein 2001; Pharr et al. 2000).

We offer a complementary explanation for these social trends that focuses on the role of technological change. Specifically, between 1970 and 1990,

Leah Platt Boustan is a professor of economics and director of the Industrial Relations Section at Princeton University, and a research associate and codirector of the Development of the American Economy Program at the National Bureau of Economic Research.

Jiwon Choi is an assistant professor of economics at Brandeis University.

David Clingingsmith is an associate professor of economics at Case Western Reserve University.

For acknowledgments, sources of research support, and disclosure of the authors' material financial relationships, if any, please see https://www.nber.org/books-and-chapters/economic-history-american-inequality-new-evidence-and-perspectives/political-fallout-machine-tool-automation-mid-20th-century-united-states.

an automation shock eliminated many production jobs in the key sector of metal manufacturing. A technology called computer numerical control (CNC) automated a significant part of the machining tasks needed for the creation of metal parts for manufactured goods. CNC uses motors, sensors, and computers to codify and automate the precise movements formerly performed by skilled workers. We focus on the CNC shock not because it is the only source of economic dislocation during this period but because it is one that we can identify clearly in the data.

This work builds on our investigation of how the diffusion of CNC machine tools changed employment patterns both at the industry and local labor market levels (Boustan et al. 2022). We constructed a new measure of exposure to CNC technology that combines baseline variation at the industry level in installed machine tools by type—such as lathes, mechanical presses, grinding machines and so on—with differential shifts by tools from hand-based to computerized tools. We found that affected industries shed workers, particularly on the production floor and among workers with a high school degree or less. The negative effect of CNC automation was stronger in the non-unionized sector. The diffusion of CNC technology influenced the broader labor market outside adopting industries through worker flows.

In this chapter, we find that CNC automation was a factor in both the rising distrust in American social institutions and in the shift in partisan affiliation of workers in the affected industries. Starting with a sample of respondents to the General Social Survey (GSS), we show that workers who were more exposed to CNC automation report less confidence in American institutions as measured by a 12-institution index. The relationship is about twice as strong for workers in the South, where unionization rates were lower. A 10-percentage-point change in CNC exposure, approximately the difference between the most and least exposed metal manufacturing industries in 1990, is associated with a 3-percentage-point decline in confidence in the non-South and a 6-percentage-point decline in the South (relative to a base of around 80 percent confidence in the 1970s). We calculate that the CNC shock, which directly affected an industry employing only 12 percent of the workforce, alone accounted for about 3 percent of the decline in confidence. While a small percentage overall, CNC was only one of several similar economic shocks experienced by American workers in the 1970s and 1980s. The overall effect of economic dislocation due to technical change may have been far larger. CNC exposure also changes the stated political preferences of affected workers, reducing their identification with the Democratic Party.

We further examine the effect of the advent of CNC technology on voting behavior in local labor markets that were more or less exposed to CNC automation. We produce a local measure of exposure to CNC technology by weighting our industry-level CNC exposure measure by the initial industrial composition of the labor markets. In the South, CNC exposure induced substantial voter substitution toward third-party candidates (particularly

Ross Perot in the 1992 election) and a decline in voter turnout. These effects appear consistent with the stronger decline in institutional trust in the South and with the partisan realignment taking place in the region in this period. These results complement our worker-level findings by capturing the effect of CNC on all voters rather than only on workers still employed in affected industries (a limitation of how we identify exposure in the GSS data) and by measuring changes in voting behavior rather than stated political preference.

6.1.1 Contributions to the Literature

Our chapter contributes to both a contemporary literature assessing the relationship between economic shocks, social dislocation, and political change, as well as a longer historical literature identifying the winners and losers from automation through the 19th and 20th centuries.

Robert Margo's many seminal contributions to our understanding of American economic history inspire our work in this volume. In many careful studies, Margo documented and analyzed the impact of technical change on firms and workers in the 19th century. Since 1850, key technological innovations contributing to factory automation have included: the rise of steam power, the creation of interchangeable metal parts, the adoption of powered machine tools, factory electrification, and the development of the assembly line. Margo and various coauthors have shown that the use of powered machine tools displaced skilled artisanal workers with lower-skilled operatives, who each completed one of many tasks in the production of a final product. The resulting division of labor and capital intensity associated with this shift resulted in heightened labor productivity, but at the cost of job loss for a set of skilled artisans (Atack et al. 2004, 2008, 2019, 2022; Katz and Margo 2014; see also and Atack, Margo, and Rhode's chapter in this volume).

The job dislocation associated with automation engendered protest, social disaffection, and conflict since the beginning of the Industrial Revolution. Perhaps most famously, textile workers in 18th- and 19th-century England destroyed spinning and weaving equipment that reduced their bargaining power and threatened their livelihoods (Hobsbawm 1952). The introduction of threshing machines in Britain, which displaced agricultural labor, led to rioting, and induced political change (Aidt and Franck 2015; Caprettini and Voth 2020). In the United States, automation was a factor in the frequent, widespread, and disruptive strikes in the US auto industry in the late 1940s (Clark 2018). At this time, automakers were deploying transfer machines, then the most advanced automation technology (Hounshell 2000). A compromise reached in 1950, the so-called Treaty of Detroit, held that unions would bargain over wages and working conditions while firms would determine the organization of production (Milkman 1997).

In recent years, scholars have documented the social and political consequences of job loss following the diffusion of industrial robots, as well as due to shocks like the Great Recession and rising import competition from Japan and later from China. Workers facing job loss due to plant closures experience declining mental health and are more likely to commit crime (Amorim et al. 2023; Britto et al. 2022; Kuhn et al. 2009; Rege et al. 2019; Strully 2009). Case and Deaton (2020) argue that faltering economic opportunities for lower-skilled workers have been an important cause of rising rates of "deaths of despair," including deaths from suicides or drug overdoses, although the strength of this relationship has been questioned (Dow et al. 2020; Ruhm 2018). Employees who face dislocation with the spread of industrial robots or competition with China increasingly support right-wing parties, which tend to promote the distrust of social institutions (Anelli et al. 2021; Autor et al. 2020; Caselli et al. 2021; Frey et al. 2018; Gallego and Kurer 2022). Survey evidence documents that workers with higher expectations of automation-driven unemployment exhibit more populist views (Golin and Rauh 2023).[1]

We bridge these two strands of literature on the social dislocations of automation—the historical and the contemporary—by considering the diffusion of CNC machine tools in the 1970s and 1980s, a period that coincided with a weakening of trust in institutions.

Our work also contributes to a broader literature on the causes of decline in social trust and confidence in institutions in the latter part of the 20th century. Here, our chapter is most closely related to studies that identify individual economic fortunes as a cause of declining trust in institutions (Brandt et al. 2015; Kim et al. 2022; Mewes et al. 2021). Newton and Norris (2000) examined confidence in institutions across advanced countries and argued that government failures in both economic and foreign policy, rather than social-psychological or cultural factors, can explain declines in confidence. Others have argued that episodes such as the Vietnam War and the Watergate scandal contributed to broad declines in trust in government (Lipset and Schneider 1983; Pharr et al. 2000; Schulman 2001).

6.2 Historical background

6.2.1 Erosion of Confidence in Institutions

Trust in the federal government and other important institutions of American life has been in decline since the mid-1960s. Figure 6.1 documents this pattern with data from the National Election Study. In the late 1950s and early 1960s, nearly 75 percent of Americans trusted the government to do the right thing "just about always" or "most of the time" (Pew Research Center 2023). This trust was broadly shared by members of the Republican and Democratic Parties. Trust declined precipitously from the mid-1960s

1. See Guriev and Papaioannou (2022) for a review of the political economy of populism.

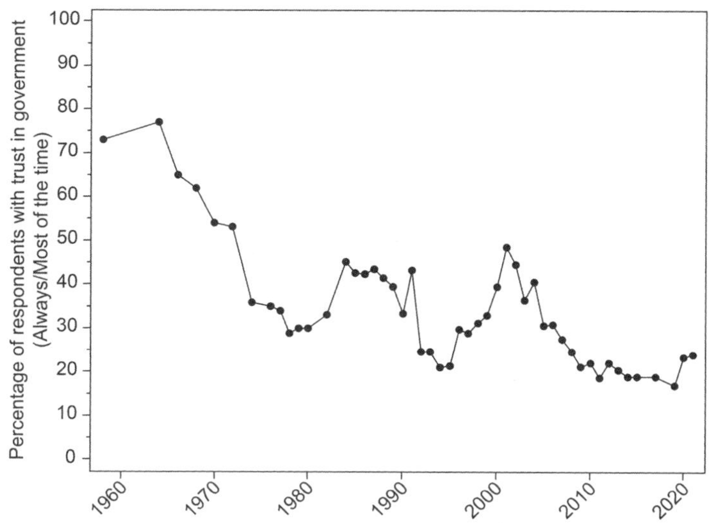

Figure 6.1 Trust in government over time

Note: The figure shows percentage of respondents who have trust in government about always or most of the time. The data is from Pew Research, with original sources including the Pew Research Center, National Election Studies, Gallup, ABC/Washington Post, CBS/New York Times, and CNN Polls. Question wording is consistent over time.

to 1980, bottoming out at around 20 percent. Despite rebounds in the early 1980s (the first Reagan administration) and mid-late 1990s (the Clinton administration), trust in the federal government never approached its earlier peak, and since 2007 has hovered around 25 percent.

Figure 6.2 presents broader patterns of confidence in a set of 12 major institutions using the data from the General Social Survey that we analyze in this paper. Since 1973, the GSS has asked respondents about confidence in major institutions, including economic organizations like major companies and organized labor; political institutions like the executive branch, Congress, the Supreme Court, and the military; and other social institutions like the press, television, organized religion, education, medicine, and science. In the early 1970s, the average American had some or a great deal of confidence in 83 percent of these institutions (10 out of 12). Confidence fell gradually in the 1970s and 1980s, and then more rapidly. By 2014, confidence had fallen to 73 percent (8.75 out of 12). Figure 6A.1 presents separate time trends for each of the 12 major institutions. By the end of the series, some institutions retained some/great confidence of close to 95 percent of respondents (science and the miliary), while other institutions commanded some/great confidence from only 55 percent of the sample (Congress, the press, and the executive branch).

Why did trust in government and major institutions decline from the mid-

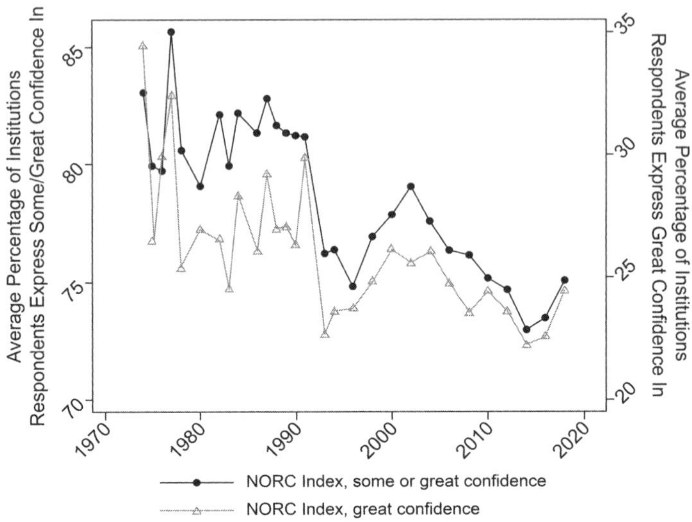

Figure 6.2 Confidence in institutions over time

Note: The figure plots the average percentage of institutions respondents express confidence in over time, using the NORC index from the General Social Survey (GSS). The NORC Index is constructed using 12 underlying measures of confidence in: major companies, labor, press, TV, religion, education, medicine, science, the Executive Branch, Congress, the Supreme Court, and the military. The some or great confidence series plots the mean percentage of institutions a respondent has some or great confidence in, in a given year. The great confidence series plots the same, but for a higher degree of confidence.

1960s onward? We divide this question into two parts. First, why did Americans once have such high confidence in government and other institutions circa 1950? Second, what forces led to the decline in confidence?

Americans' high levels of confidence in government and major institutions reflects a confluence of events in the mid-20th century. In the late 1940s, the US was emerging from an exceptional period of transformation of the role of the federal government in American life. The New Deal and World War II expanded the role played by government in ensuring individual welfare and in managing economic activity (Fishback 2017; Levy 2021; Lindert 2004). The United States won the war against Japan and contributed to the defeat of Germany. The postwar economy boomed (Field 2003; Gordon 2017). The combination of strong economic growth and government support for homeownership and collective bargaining ushered in a sustained era of middle-class comfort and broadly shared prosperity (Fetter 2013; Goldin and Margo 1992). Into the 1950s, there was a broad bipartisan liberal consensus in American politics that embraced the expanded role of the federal government in American life. Through the early 1960s, the liberal consensus expanded to include support for full civil rights for black Americans, particularly focused on ending the Jim Crow laws that restricted black economic opportunity and political participation in the South (Perlstein 2001).

The initial fissures in this bipartisan liberal consensus came from the political right. An antigovernment ideology began to take shape in the latter 1950s, focused on animosity toward the New Deal, fear of communist infiltration of government, and the emerging civil rights reforms. Political entrepreneurs such as Clarence Manion forged partnerships between conservative southern Democrats and anti–New Deal Republicans under the umbrella of resistance to the expansion of federal power. This movement coalesced around the Arizona senator Barry Goldwater, who ran an insurgent campaign for the Republican nomination in the 1964 presidential election. Although Goldwater lost, the movement was energized by the substantial support he garnered both in the old South and the emergent Sunbelt.

The political left in the United States was also transformed by the consolidation of the Cold War in the 1950s. The discrediting of orthodox Marxism following the spread of reports of Soviet repression, both internally and in Eastern Europe, and the rise of a radical youth culture in the 1960s shifted the left toward domestic social issues (Gitlin 1996). Resistance to the Vietnam-era draft and support for new movements such as feminism, gay liberation, and environmentalism created a strong antiestablishment ethos on the left.

Against this backdrop of weakening consensus, trust in mainstream institutions collapsed in the late 1960s and early 1970s, following a set of specific events and a general weakening of economic conditions. The year 1968 was a turning point moment, marked by a "dreary catalogue of depressing events" that undermined national consensus further (Schulman 2001, xii). Student and labor protest movements erupted in the US and across the world. The Tet Offensive cast the grinding failure of the Vietnam War into sharp relief, although it took a further seven years for the United States to exit the conflict. Soviet forces invaded Czechoslovakia, crushing the hopes of the Prague Spring. American cities burned with race riots and both businesses and many white families left for the suburbs. Upheaval and widespread political violence continued into the early 1970s with the FBI reporting 2,500 bombings in the United States in 1971 and 1972 (Burrough 2015). In 1974, President Nixon resigned after it was discovered he authorized and then covered up a break-in at the Democratic National Committee's headquarters. The Vietnam War officially came to an end in 1975 with the capture of Saigon by the North Vietnamese.

The pall continued to spread over national politics through the late 1970s, accelerated by weak economic conditions. The OPEC oil embargo of 1973 ushered in a decade of energy crisis and, along with loose monetary policy in the early 1970s, sparked double-digit inflation. The New Majority coalition of working-class and white ethnic voters that came together to elect Nixon was initially willing to back President Carter, but his policies were not able to break the hold of the stifling combination of high unemployment and high inflation. In July 1979, President Carter surprised the electorate by telling the truth: America was facing a crisis of confidence. "The erosion of our confidence in the future," President Carter (1979) warned, "is threatening to destroy the social and the political fabric of America." But telling the truth did not fix the problem.

Eventually, President Carter's nominee to the Federal Reserve, Paul Volcker, was able to halt the spiraling inflation, but not without a major recession that *Time* magazine declared on its cover was "Gathering Gloom for Workers" (Alexander 1981). Ronald Reagan capitalized on the dour national mood by combining attacks on the federal government with a sunny optimism about the private sector, memorably declaring in his 1981 inaugural address that "In this present crisis, government is not the solution to our problem, government is the problem" (Perlstein 2021).

6.2.2 Political realignment

Rising antiestablishment sentiment was particularly directed at the Democratic Party, which had held the House of Representatives in all but four years between 1932 and 1980. The shift away from the establishment Democrats had a marked pattern, first by region and later by education group.

The allegiances of Southern voters turned against the Democratic party first. At mid-century, 80 percent of white voters in the "Solid South" identified as Democrats in the Gallup data (Kuziemko and Washington 2018, fig. 1). This share fell continuously over the next sixty years, converging with the non-Southern average (40 percent) by 1985 and then dipping below the non-South by 2005 (low 20 percent). Kuziemko and Washington (2018) argue that, in the 1960s, and particularly after Kennedy's civil rights speech in 1963, the southern shift away from the Democrats was driven by racial conservatism and opposition to civil rights. Figure 6.3, panel A, replicates this regional pattern using partisan self-identification in the GSS from 1972 onward. The broad patterns are similar, even if the levels differ in some years. We find that white respondents shifted away from the Democratic party in both the South and non-South between 1970 and 1990. After 1990, the Democratic share stabilized at around 45 percent in the non-South but continued to fall in the South, reaching the low 30 percent in the 2010s.

Voting patterns by education group began to shift in the 1980s. Before 1975, less educated and working-class voters were more likely to vote for the Democratic Party. This relationship began weakening in the 1980s as the Democratic Party platform shifted away from direct support for labor toward the idea of redistribution through the tax system. Kuziemko et al. (2023) show that, by 2005, the partisan divide by education had entirely flipped, with more educated voters now more likely to vote for the Demo-

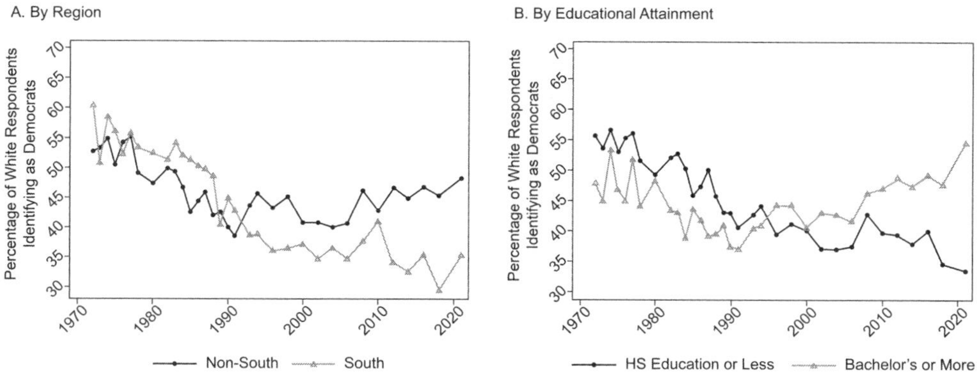

Figure 6.3 Partisan identification by region and educational attainment
Note: The figures show the partisan identification by region and educational attainment. The partisan identification is constructed from the General Social Survey (GSS). We use a sample of white respondents to compute the share of the respondents who identify as Democrats over time. We create the series by Southern states and non-South states in panel A, and by educational attainment in panel B.

cratic party. We replicate this pattern in figure 6.3, panel B. We find a fall in Democratic affiliation between 1970 and 1990, for respondents both with a bachelor's degree or higher and with a high school degree or less. In the mid-1990s, around 42 percent of both education groups identified as Democrats. Subsequently, more educated respondents increasingly identified as Democrats, reaching a high of 55 percent in 2020, while respondents with high school or less fall to around 35 percent.

6.2.3 CNC Technology, Job Loss, and the Transformation of Attitudes

This chapter links the transformation of confidence and political affiliation to the diffusion of CNC technology. CNC technology automated machine tools that had relied on human operatives to select and perform the tool's physical movements, instead using computer programs and sensors to direct the machine. The first numerically controlled machine tool was invented in the United States in the early 1950s at the MIT Servomechanisms Lab, building on the advances in computing and servomechanisms that emerged during World War II, but CNC tools were not developed for wide commercial applications until the late 1960s. In our previous work tracing the effect of CNC technology on the labor market, we found that the diffusion of CNC-enabled tools led to the elimination of jobs on the factory floor, particularly affecting workers with a high school education or less.

The disruption of metal manufacturing jobs due to CNC automation may have accelerated the decline in institutional confidence for several reasons. First, job loss has long-term negative effects on income in general, which can lead workers to believe that the economy doesn't work for them and that policy makers do not have their best interests at heart. Second, other production workers may realize that employment is not secure in an environment of technical change. CNC diffusion began in an era when long careers with one firm were expected and when high school graduates believed it was possible to have a middle-class life from industrial labor.

Job loss and factory reorganization may produce resentment and dissatisfaction with the status quo. The shift of less educated voters toward the Republican Party coincided with a shift in beliefs about which party would best maintain prosperity. During the 1960s, the Democrats held a strong edge on economic issues, but, beginning in the mid-1970s, the Republicans began gaining ground and held an edge on this question for the 1980s and much of the 1990s (Gallup News Service 2023).

6.3 Data

6.3.1 Political and Social Outcomes

We consider the effect of computer numerical control technology on three measures of social and political change: confidence in major institutions, self-reported partisan affiliation and vote shares for the Republican Party and for third parties.

Confidence, political self-identification, and union membership: The General Social Survey (GSS) contains individual-level questions on attitudes and opinions. Most important for our purposes are questions about confidence in social institutions, partisan affiliation, and union membership.

The GSS elicited reports on levels of confidence in 12 major economic, political, and social institutions using the following question: "I am going to name some institutions in this country. As far as the people running these institutions are concerned, would you say you have a great deal of confidence, only some confidence, or hardly any confidence at all in them?" The question is asked annually from 1972 to 1991 and biannually thereafter.

For each respondent, we create measures of confidence for each of the 12 major institutions and a composite measure of confidence in all 12 institutions. We consider two definitions of having confidence in an institution: either reporting at least "some confidence" in the institution or reporting "great confidence" in the institution. Following the National Opinion Research Center (NORC), our composite measure of individual confidence is a simple average of reported confidence across all 12 institutions.

We measure partisan affiliation using a question on political self-identification, which asks respondents to characterize themselves as Republican, Democrat, or Independent. We construct indicator variables for identification as a Democrat and for membership in a union.

Exposure to CNC technology is captured at the individual level based on an individual's industry of employment and survey year. We further split the sample by region (South and non-South) using GSS information on region of residence because unionization levels varied by region and unionization mediated the effect of CNC exposure on worker outcomes. Our GSS sample includes only workers employed in one of the seven subindustries of metal manufacturing classified in Boustan et al. (2022) as experiencing CNC-based automation in this period.

Voting outcomes: We supplement our results on individual-level partisan affiliation with local area results on votes cast by political party. We construct commuting-zone (CZ) level vote counts by party using the county-level voting data from ICPSR (1964–1996), the MIT Election Lab (2000), and David Leip's (2021) data archive. We map these county-level outcomes to 1990 CZ geographies using the crosswalk by Eckert et al. (2020). For each election, we measure the share of votes cast for Republican candidates, the share of votes cast for third parties (neither Republicans nor Democrats), and the share of eligible voters who cast a vote in the election.[2]

We measure exposure to CNC technology at the CZ level by weighting exposure to the CNC shock at the industry level by initial employment by industry in the CZ from the 1970 Census. This CZ-level measure of exposure will capture all workers affected by CNC automation, regardless of their current employment status.

Given the idiosyncrasies of each presidential election cycle, we group three elections before CNC diffusion (1964, 1968, and 1972) and three elections after CNC had penetrated US manufacturing (1992, 1996, and 2000). In the first period, the largest third-party candidate was George Wallace, a conservative states' rights, segregationist candidate who garnered 13.5 percent of the vote in 1968, and in the second period the largest independent candidate was Ross Perot, an anti-free-trade businessman who received 18.9 percent of ballots cast in 1992. We calculate the "long difference" for each voting outcome at the CZ level to measure political changes from the periods before and after intensive CNC diffusion.

6.3.2 Exposure to CNC Automation

We adopt industry-by-year level measures of exposure to CNC technology that were developed by Boustan et al. (2022). This measure relies on two sources of variation: the initial share of each machine tool in an industry's tool base in 1958, before the diffusion of CNC technology, and the shift in the market for each tool type from hand-based tools to computerized

2. We drop data from Alabama and Minnesota because of missing information for some political parties in some years. We also exclude 32 CZs (4.4 percent of observations) for which our population estimates at the CZ level diverge from the true population counts by more than 10 percent. In particular, we merge in county-level Census population counts to the voting data for the initial year in each decade (e.g., 1960 population counts for the 1964 election). We then crosswalk this county level file to the CZ level, collapse at the CZ level, and compare our population estimates with CZ-level population counts. We exclude the few cases in which these two population counts diverge by more than 10 percent.

tools.[3] Tool-level shifts to CNC technology are observed from trade data counting the number and value of tools exported by type and by CNC-status for the three major machine tool exporters (Japan, Germany, and Italy).[4]

Combining these two sources of variation, this measure of CNC exposure reflects the cumulative share of CNC tools in the global market by tool type, weighted by baseline tool use in a given industry. In particular, CNC exposure for industry j in year t can be calculated as follows:

$$(1) \qquad Exposure\_CNC_{j,t} = \sum_k \left(\frac{VT_{k,j,1958}}{\sum_k VT_{k,j,1958}} Share\_CNC_{k,t} \right),$$

where

$$\frac{VT_{k,j,1958}}{\sum_k VT_{k,j,1958}}$$

is the value share of tool k among the tool inventory for industry j in 1958, and $Share\_CNC_{k,t}$ is the cumulative share of CNC tools among machine tool k.

The measure is populated for seven (aggregated) subindustries of metal manufacturing that were exposed in some way to CNC automation. All metal industries had very low exposure to CNC in the early 1970s. By 1990, industries like aircraft increased exposure to CNC tools dramatically, while industries like motor vehicles were less affected.

Industry-by-year variation in CNC exposure can then be assigned to commuting zones according to the baseline share of commuting-zone employment in each industry in 1970, prior to the CNC diffusion. CNC exposure in commuting zone m in year t is calculated as

$$(2) \qquad Exposure\_CNC_{m,t} = \sum_j \left(\frac{EMP_{m,j,1970}}{EMP_{m,1970}} Exposure\_CNC_{j,t} \right),$$

where

$$\frac{EMP_{m,j,1970}}{EMP_{m,1970}}$$

is the share of workers in commuting zone m employed in industry j in 1970.[5] Here, $Exposure\_CNC_{j,t}$ is defined as above at the industry-by-year level and is defined to be zero for any non-metal manufacturing industry.

3. Industry-level tool use in 1958 is from the 1958 *American Machinist Inventory of Metal-working Equipment* (AMIME). The AMIME records the value of tool inventories for metal-working subindustries.

4. The export values of each machine tool by major exporter are collected from the *Economic Handbooks of Machine Tool Industry*, from 1971 to 2009.

5. The baseline share of employment by industry and commuting zone is computed from the 1970 census.

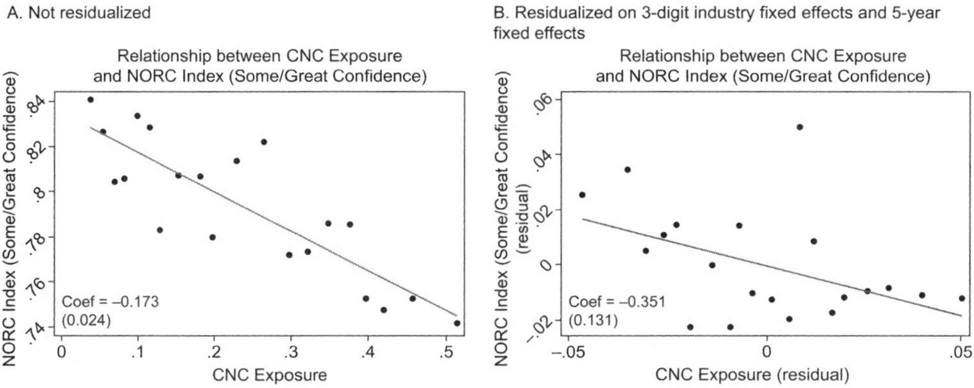

Figure 6.4 Confidence in institutions and CNC exposure
Note: The figures show the binscatters of CNC exposure measure and the NORC index described in Figure 6.2. CNC exposure measure is developed by Boustan, Choi, and Clingingsmith (2023). Panel B scatters the residualized NORC index which removes five-year and three-digit industry fixed effects against the CNC exposure measure.

6.4 CNC Exposure and Trends in Social Outcomes

6.4.1 Confidence in Institutions and Partisan Self-identification

We start by investigating whether workers in industries with growing exposure to CNC technology report lessened confidence in major institutions. In earlier work, we find that CNC exposure is associated with declines in employment, particularly for workers on the production floor and for workers in the non-union sector (Boustan et al. 2022). This job loss and industrial change may weaken faith in various social institutions.

Our main individual-level outcomes $y_{i,j,t}$ include average confidence in 12 major institutions and self-reported partisan affiliation. Our preferred specification regresses individual-level measure of confidence and affiliation on a measure of CNC exposure based on an individual's industry of employment in year t, controlling for fixed effects for three-digit industry (α_j) and five-year bin (γ_t):[6]

$$y_{i,j,t} = \alpha_j + \gamma_t + \beta Exposure\_CNC_{j,t} + X'\Gamma + \varepsilon_{i,j,t}. \quad (3)$$

Before turning to our regression analysis, figure 6.4 depicts correlations between CNC exposure at the industry-year level and the average share of workers reporting "some or great" confidence according to the composite index. Panel a plots the raw correlation and panel b controls for industry and year-bin fixed effects. In both cases, we find that workers in industries more

6. Five-year bins are defined as 1972–1976, 1977–1981, and so forth.

Table 6.1 **The effect of CNC exposure on confidence and group membership**

	12-Institution NORC Index		Group membership	
	Some/great confidence (1)	Great confidence (2)	Identify as Democrat (3)	Union membership (4)
Full Sample	−0.363**	−0.286	−1.120***	−0.519
	(0.137)	(0.174)	(0.327)	(0.327)
Observations	2,986	2,986	4,083	3,230
Non-South	−0.316*	−0.071	−1.135**	−0.295
	(0.155)	(0.202)	(0.375)	(0.372)
Observations	2,286	2,286	3,097	2,448
South	−0.605**	−0.908***	−1.324*	−1.494**
	(0.304)	(0.334)	(0.687)	(0.687)
Observations	700	700	986	782

Note: Standard errors in parentheses. Number of observations follows. *$p < .1$. **$p < .05$. ***$p < .01$. The specification includes five-year fixed effects and three-digit industry fixed effects and demographic controls (age, age squared, nonwhite indicator, indicators for educational attainment, and sex). Observations are at the person level. Columns 1 and 2 use the 12-Institution NORC Index as the outcome variables. In the General Social Survey (GSS), levels of confidence are "hardly any," "only some," or "a great deal." In column 1, respondents who reply "only some" or "a great deal" are coded as having confidence in a given institution. In column 2, only respondents who reply "a great deal" receive the same classification. Columns 3 and 4 use identification as Democrats and union membership as the outcome variables.

exposed to CNC technology express lower confidence in major institutions. Even after controlling for industry and year-bin fixed effects in panel b, we continue to find a strong negative relationship between CNC exposure and confidence in institutions ($\beta = -0.35$). Controlling for year-bin effects is important because CNC exposure is generally rising over time, while confidence was falling over this period, which could lead to a spurious relationship.

In table 6.1, we estimate the effect of CNC exposure on workers' average confidence in major institutions, partisan affiliation, and union membership. We present our preferred specification, which controls for industry fixed effects, year-bin fixed effects, and individual demographic controls.[7] We weight each person-year observation by the representative weight provided in the GSS. We report results for the full sample, as well as two regional subsamples (non-South and South).

Exposure to CNC technology is associated with a decline in confidence in major institutions, defined either as having "some or great confidence"

7. Demographic controls include age, age squared, indicators for being female and for being nonwhite and indicators for educational attainment.

(column 1) or "great confidence" (column 2). The relationship between CNC exposure and confidence is stronger in the South than outside of the South. A 10-percentage-point increase in CNC exposure, approximately the difference between least and most exposed industries at the peak of our sample period, is associated with a 3.6-percentage-point decline in some or great confidence nationwide and an even stronger decline in this measure in the South (6.1 percentage points).

Overall, the average confidence level fell by 10 percentage points over this time period (fig. 6.2). To put the magnitude of the CNC shock into perspective, consider that 9 percent of the adult population (12.2 percent of the workforce) was employed in metal manufacturing in 1970. We thus multiply the coefficients by 0.09, suggesting that CNC automation itself can explain 0.32 percentage points of this national trend, or around 3 percent of the total decline in confidence. Explaining 3 percent of the total national decline due to an economic shock hitting one industry alone suggests that the overall effect of economic dislocation due to technical change and the resulting displacement could be far larger.

Alongside the declining confidence in mainstream institutions, we also find a shift away from self-identification with the Democratic Party, which was the party in power for most of this period. Coefficients in column 3 suggest that a 10-percentage-point increase in CNC exposure is associated with an 11- to 13-percentage-point decline in the likelihood that a respondent identifies as a Democrat in both regions. Identification with the Democratic party fell by around 20 points during this period (fig. 6.3). Multiplying the coefficients by 0.09 to account for the share of metal manufacturing in the workforce implies that the CNC shock can explain 1.1 percentage points (6 percent) of this decline.

Exposure to CNC automation appears to have a stronger effect on confidence in the South. To understand this regional pattern, column 4 considers the effect of CNC exposure on union membership. In earlier work, we find that the effect of CNC technology on job loss was stronger in the non-union sector. Not only did the South have lower levels of unionization at baseline (15 percent versus 35 percent of the non-Southern workforce; see fig. 6A.2, but we also find that exposure to CNC technology lowers union density further in the South. A 10-percentage-point increase in exposure to CNC corresponds to a 15-percentage-point decline in union affiliation in metal working in the South, or a 3-percentage-point decline in overall union affiliation (given that metal working represented around 20 percent of the union workforce at the time) but has essentially no effect on union membership in the rest of the country.

Thus far, we have examined the combined effect of CNC exposure on confidence in all major institutions. However, we might expect that workers fearing displacement may blame economic institutions like major corporations

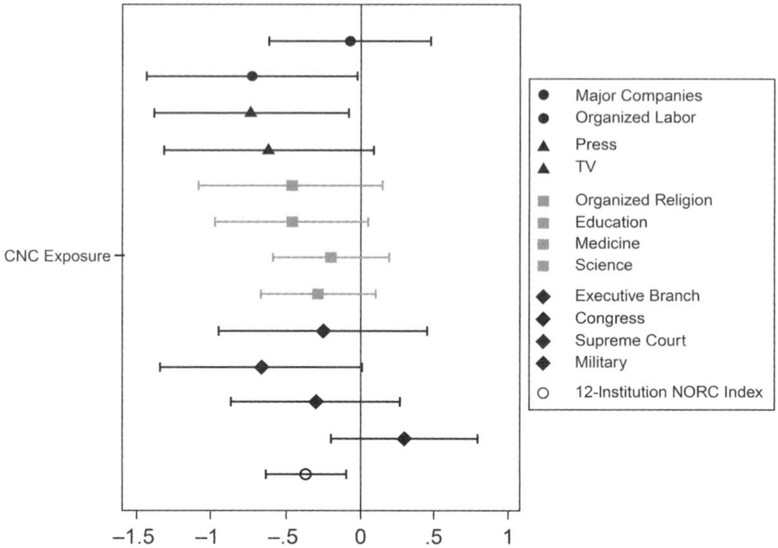

Figure 6.5 Effect of CNC Exposure on Some or Great Confidence in Institutions

Note: The figure plots the coefficients on CNC exposure, the effect of CNC exposure on confidence in each of the 12 social institutions. This figure shows results from the preferred specification, which includes five-year fixed effects and three-digit industry fixed effects. This specification includes demographic controls (age, age squared, nonwhite indicator, indicators for educational attainment, and sex). Observations are at the person level.

or organized labor, or political institutions like Congress or the president, but may not lose confidence in other institutions like scientific establishment or organized religion.

Figure 6.5 plots the coefficient on CNC exposure for confidence in all 12 institutions separately using the broader definition of confidence ("some or great confidence"). We break the institutions into rough categories (economic, media, cultural, political), but we do not observe a clear relationship between the type of institution and the effect of CNC exposure. Instead, we identify a negative point estimate for 11 of 12 institutions (the military is the exception), with a statistically significant decline ($p < 0.1$) in confidence in organized labor, the press, and Congress. Automation-based economic change appears to weaken confidence in mainstream institutions across the board. Figure 6A.3 replicates this pattern for the narrow definition of confidence ("great confidence"). Again, we observe negative point estimates for most institutions.

6.4.2 Voting Patterns

We now turn to studying the effect of CNC exposure on voting behavior in presidential elections at the commuting zone level. Our main outcomes

Δy_m are the changes in the share of Republican votes, the share of third-party votes (non-Republican, non-Democrat), and the share of eligible voter participation in commuting zone *m*. The changes are constructed as long differences between elections conducted before and after the widespread diffusion of CNC technology. Given the idiosyncrasies of individual elections, we group three elections to represent each time period, averaging vote shares and voter turnout for the elections of 1992, 1996, and 2000 (after CNC) relative to these values for the elections of 1964, 1968, and 1972 (before CNC).

In particular, we estimate the following long-difference regression relating changes in vote shares and voter turnout to changes in exposure to CNC at the commuting zone (CZ) level:

$$(4) \qquad y_m = \alpha_d + \beta \Delta Exposure\_CNC_m + X'\Gamma + \varepsilon_m.$$

We measure exposure to automation at the CZ level by weighting our CNC exposure measure for each industry and period (1970, 2000) by the initial share of industry employment in a given CZ, according to equation 2. Our preferred specification controls for Census division fixed effects (α_d), base-period (1970) labor market demographic characteristics, and one-digit industry shares (in the vector X). Outside of the South, CZs with high exposure (90th percentile) to CNC automation include Elmira, NY, a Rust Belt factory town once home to large plants for General Electric and Westinghouse, and low exposure (10th percentile) include Sioux Falls, SD, which was primarily engaged in food processing. In the South, low exposure CZs are often central places in agricultural areas (e.g., Monroe, LA) whereas high exposure CZs are manufacturing areas like Louisville, KY.

Our main regression analysis is presented in table 6.2. Panels a–c show results for the share of Republican votes, share third-party votes, and eligible voter participation, respectively. We report results separately for the non-South and for the South. For each region, we first report a basic regression with only CNC exposure on the right-hand side, and then we report a regression with our set of additional controls.

In the South, which was going through a partisan realignment at the time, we document two types of shifts away from the dominant Democratic Party. First, voters shifted toward third-party candidates, particularly Ross Perot, who was on the ballot in 1992 and won close to 20 percent of the electorate with a campaign focused on manufacturing decline (column 4, panel b). Second, eligible voters were less likely to cast ballots in elections (column 4, panel c). By contrast, outside the South and once we include controls, particularly for one-digit industry, CNC exposure is much less strongly associated with changes in voting behavior despite the negative effect on party identification reported earlier (column 2).

To interpret the magnitude of the political effects of CNC exposure, consider a 1-standard-deviation increase in CNC exposure at the commuting

Table 6.2 The effect of CNC exposure on voting outcomes

	Non-South		South	
	(1)	(2)	(3)	(4)
Panel A: Share Republican votes				
Change in CNC exposure	−0.367**	−0.234	−0.289	−0.358
	(0.116)	(0.281)	(0.361)	(0.366)
Observations	408	408	275	275
Mean 30-year change in dependent variable	−0.0369	−0.0369	−0.0369	−0.0369
Panel B: Share non-Republican, non-Democrat votes				
Change in CNC exposure	−0.275***	−0.037	0.233	0.775**
	(0.054)	(0.116)	(0.437)	(0.269)
Observations	371	371	244	244
Mean 30-year change in dependent variable	0.0564	0.0564	0.0564	0.0564
Panel C: Share of eligible voter participation				
Change in CNC exposure	−0.118	−0.193	0.171	−0.786**
	(0.143)	(0.300)	(0.445)	(0.332)
Observations	408	408	282	282
Mean 30-year change in dependent variable	−0.0191	−0.0191	−0.0191	−0.0191
Controls				
Census divisions		X		X
Demographics		X		X
Industry shares		X		X

Note: Standard errors in parentheses. $*p < .1$. $**p < .05$. $***p < .01$. Analysis is at the commuting zone (CZ) level with collapsed county-level voting data from ICPSR 13 (1964–1988), Dave Leip's Atlas of U.S. Elections (1992, 1996) and the MIT Election Lab (2000). Outcomes are from Presidential elections in the United States and are calculated by taking the long difference of the average dependent variable share in 1992, 1996, and 2000 versus the average in 1964, 1968, and 1972, for a given CZ. Columns 1–2 are CZs in non-South, while columns (3–4) are CZs in the South. Column 1 includes no controls. Column 2 includes controls for Census Division, demographic controls (age, age squared, nonwhite indicator, indicators for educational attainment, and sex), and controls for 1-digit industry shares. All controls utilize 1970 data unless otherwise noted. Columns 3 and 4 repeat this structure, but for CZs in the south. The final two table rows in each panel show the number of observations and the mean change in the dependent variable. Some CZs are missing voting data, which explains fewer than 722 CZs represented in the table. We exclude 32 commuting zones whose population estimates diverge from the census population counts by more than 10 percent.

zone level in the South (1.4 percentage points). This heightened exposure is associated with a 1.1-point increase in the share of third-party votes (= 0.775 × 1.4). Votes for non-Democrats rose from 20 percent to 75 percent of the Southern electorate since 1940 (55 points). Exposure to an additional standard deviation of factory automation—just one of a series of relevant economic shocks—can explain 2 percent of this total (= 1.1/55). A one standard deviation increase in CNC exposure is also associated with a 1.1-point decline in the share of eligible voters turning out for the election (= –0.786 × 1.4). To put this value in context, consider that a 1.1-point decline in voter turnout is 6 percent the size of a typical gap in voter participation between presidential election and midterm election years (58 percent vs. 40 percent turnout; DeSilver 2023).

Taken together, we find notable differences in the political response to automation by region. The CNC automation shock hit the South during an era of political realignment. The Democratic Party was on the decline, driven by voters angry about civil rights reforms, cultural change, and economic dislocation. Outside of the South, the Democratic Party was still a viable option for working-class voters, particularly those in union positions. Southern voters responded to the CNC shock both by shifting toward third-party candidates and by disengaging from the electoral process entirely.

6.5 Conclusion

Americans both lost confidence in many central social institutions during the late 20th century and engaged in a related political realignment that saw many traditionally Democratic voting blocs shift their allegiance to the Republican Party. Traditional accounts of these processes emphasize the role of social and political events, such as the civil rights movement, the Vietnam War, and the Watergate scandal.

The 1970s and 1980s also saw major transformations in the working lives of Americans, including factory automation, deindustrialization, offshoring, trade shocks, and the rising importance of computers in the workplace. In this chapter, we have studied one important aspect of factory automation, the diffusion of CNC machine tools, as driver of loss of confidence and political realignment. We found that CNC diffusion is associated with reduced confidence in institutions for workers in affected industries, especially in the South where union membership was lower, and that it contributed to both partisan realignment and to voter disengagement. Although the diffusion of CNC alone—a shock to one sector, the metalworking industry—explains a small part of the transformation of American politics in this era, we view CNC as emblematic of a wider set of automation forces that collectively had a transformative effect on work and workers.

The past decade has seen a surge in populism and in widespread skepticism of American institutions. With a few exceptions, both journalists and scholars are again more focused on cultural explanations, such as racial resentment and an increasing divergence in values between urban and rural voters, and less on economic factors. Our work emphasizes that economic transformation is an enduring cause of political dissatisfaction and should be higher on the agenda for those seeking to understand the current rise in populism.

Appendix

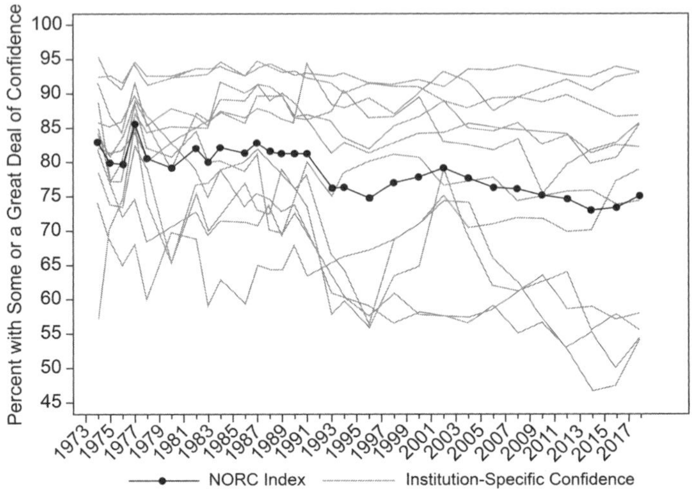

Figure 6A.1 Index of confidence over time

Note: The figure plots the average percentage of institutions that respondents express confidence in over time, using the NORC index from the General Social Survey (GSS). The NORC Index is constructed using 12 underlying measures of confidence in: major companies, labor, press, TV, religion, education, medicine, science, the Executive Branch, Congress, the Supreme Court, and the military. The faded lines represent confidence in these institution-specific measures.

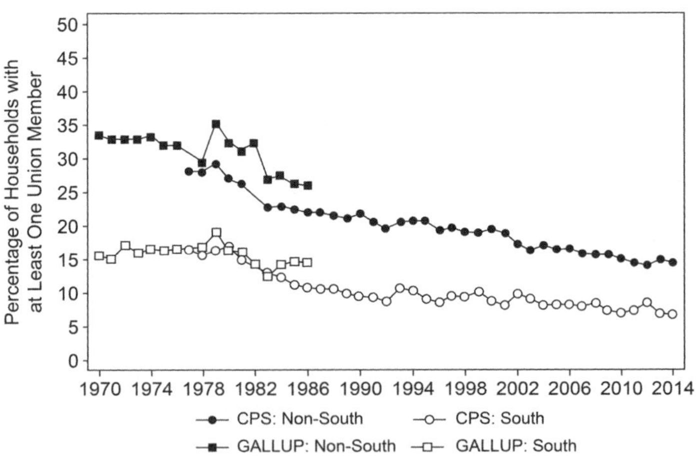

Figure 6A.2 Union membership over time

Note: This time series uses data from GALLUP (1970–1986) and the CPS (1977–2014).

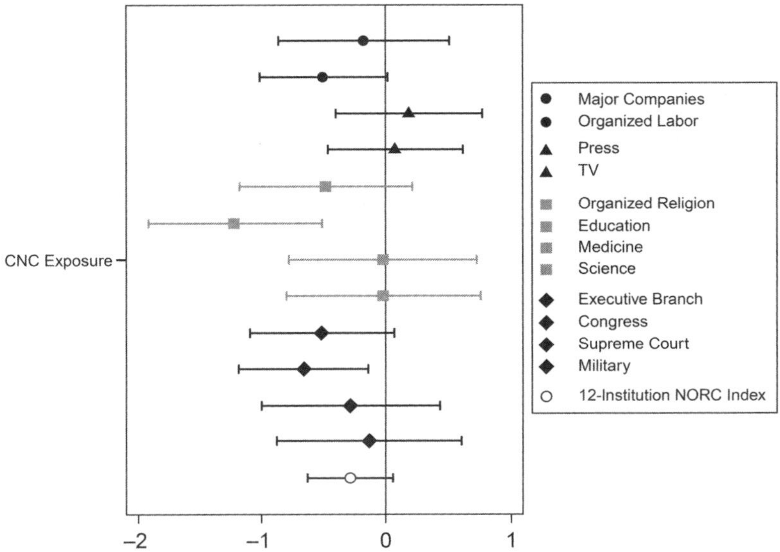

Figure 6A.3 Effect of CNC exposure on great confidence in institutions

Note: The figure plots the coefficients on CNC exposure for confidence in each of the 12 social institutions. This figure shows results from the preferred specification, which includes five-year fixed effects and three-digit industry fixed effects and demographic controls (age, age squared, nonwhite indicator, indicators for educational attainment, and sex). Observations are at the person level.

References

Aidt, T. S., and R. Franck. 2015. "Democratization Under the Threat of Revolution: Evidence from the Great Reform Act of 1832." *Econometrica* 83 (2): 505–47.

Alexander, C. 1981. "Gathering Gloom for Workers." *Time*, December 14. https://content.time.com/time/subscriber/article/0,33009,925110,00.html.

Amorim, G., D. G. C. Britto, A. de A. Fonseca, and B. Sampaio. 2023. "Job Loss, Unemployment Insurance and Health: Evidence from Brazil." BAFFI CAREFIN Centre Research Paper No. 192. https://dx.doi.org/10.2139/ssrn.4325173

Anelli, M., I. Colantone, and P. Stanig. 2021. "Individual Vulnerability to Industrial Robot Adoption Increases Support for the Radical Right." *Proceedings of the National Academy of Sciences* 118 (47): 1–8.

Atack, J., F. Bateman, and R. A. Margo. 2004. "Skill Intensity and Rising Wage Dispersion in Nineteenth-Century American Manufacturing." *Journal of Economic History* 64 (1): 172–92.

Atack, J., F. Bateman, and R. A. Margo. 2008. "Steam Power, Establishment Size, and Labor Productivity Growth in Nineteenth-Century American Manufacturing." *Explorations in Economic History* 45 (2): 185–98.

Atack, J., R. A. Margo, and P. W. Rhode. 2019. "'Automation' of Manufacturing in the Late Nineteenth Century: The Hand and Machine Labor Study." *Journal of Economic Perspectives* 33 (2): 51–70.

Atack, J., R. A. Margo, and P. W. Rhode. 2022. "'Mechanization Takes Command?': Powered Machinery and Production Times in Late Nineteenth-Century American Manufacturing." *Journal of Economic History* 82 (3): 663–89.
Autor, D., D. Dorn, G. Hanson, and K. Majlesi. 2020. "Importing Political Polarization? The Electoral Consequences of Rising Trade Exposure." *American Economic Review* 110 (10): 3139–83.
Boustan, L. P., J. Choi, and D. Clingingsmith. 2022. "Automation After the Assembly Line: Computerized Machine Tools, Employment and Productivity in the United States." NBER Working Paper No. 30400. National Bureau of Economic Research.
Brandt, M. J., G. Wetherell, and P. J. Henry. 2015. "Changes in Income Predict Change in Social Trust: A Longitudinal Analysis." *Political Psychology* 36 (6): 761–68.
Burrough, B. 2015. *Days of Rage: America's Radical Underground, the FBI, and the Forgotten Age of Revolutionary Violence*. Penguin Books.
Britto, D. G. C., P. Pinotti, and B. Sampaio. 2022. "The Effect of Job Loss and Unemployment Insurance on Crime in Brazil." *Econometrica* 90 (4): 1393–1423.
Caprettini, B., and H. J. Voth. 2020. "Rage against the Machines: Labor-Saving Technology and Unrest in Industrializing England." *American Economic Review: Insights* 2 (3): 305–20.
Carter, J. 1979. "Crisis of Confidence." Transcript of televised speech of July 15, 1979. PBS. https://www.pbs.org/wgbh/americanexperience/features/carter-crisis/.
Case, A., and A. Deaton. 2020. *Deaths of Despair and the Future of Capitalism*. Princeton University Press.
Caselli, M., A. Fracasso, and S. Traverso. 2021. "Globalization, Robotization, and Electoral Outcomes: Evidence from Spatial Regressions for Italy." *Journal of Regional Science* 61 (1): 86–111.
Clark, Daniel J. 2018. *Disruption in Detroit: Autoworkers and the Elusive Postwar Boom*. University of Illinois Press.
DeSilver, D. 2023. "Turnout in 2022 House Midterms Declined from 2018 High, Final Official Returns Show." Pew Research Center, March 10. https://www.pewresearch.org/short-reads/2023/03/10/turnout-in-2022-house-midterms-declined-from-2018-high-final-official-returns-show/.
Dow, W. H., A. Godøy, C. Lowenstein, and M. Reich. 2020. "Can Labor Market Policies Reduce Deaths of Despair?" *Journal of Health Economics* 74: art. 102372.
Eckert, Fabian, Andrés Gvirtz, Jack Liang, and Michael Peters. 2020. "A Method to Construct Geographical Crosswalks with an Application to US Counties Since 1790." NBER Working Paper No. 26770.
Fetter, D. K. 2013. "How Do Mortgage Subsidies Affect Home Ownership? Evidence from the Mid-Century GI Bills." *American Economic Journal: Economic Policy* 5 (2): 111–47.
Field, A. 2003. "The Most Technologically Progressive Decade of the Century." *American Economic Review* 93 (4): 1399–1413.
Fishback, P. 2017. "How Successful Was the New Deal? The Microeconomic Impact of New Deal Spending and Lending Policies in the 1930s." *Journal of Economic Literature* 55 (4): 1435–85.
Frey, C. B., T. Berger, and L. Chen. 2018. "Political Machinery: Did Robots Swing the 2016 US Presidential Election?" *Oxford Review of Economic Policy* 34 (3): 418–42.
Gallego, A., and T. Kurer. 2022. "Automation, Digitalization, and Artificial Intelligence in the Workplace: Implications for Political Behavior." *Annual Review of Political Science* 25: 463–84.

Gallup News Service. 2023. *Gallup Poll Social Series: Governance*. https://news.gallup.com/file/poll/512057/20231003PartyRatings.pdf.
Gitlin, Todd. 1996. *The Twilight of Common Dreams: Why America Is Wracked by Culture Wars*. Henry Holt.
Goldin, C., and R. Margo. 1992. "The Great Compression: The Wage Structure in the United States at Mid-Century." *Quarterly Journal of Economics* 107 (1): 1–34.
Golin, M., and C. Rauh. 2023. "The Impact of Fear of Automation." CEPR Press Discussion Paper No. 17816.
Gordon, R. 2017. *The Rise and Fall of American Growth: The U.S. Standard of Living Since the Civil War*. Princeton University Press.
Guriev, S., and E. Papaioannou. 2022. "The Political Economy of Populism." *Journal of Economic Literature* 60 (3): 753–832.
Hobsbawm, E. J. 1952. "The Machine Breakers." *Past & Present* 1: 57–70.
Hounshell, D. A. 2000. "Automation, Transfer Machinery, and Mass Production in the U.S. Automobile Industry in the Post–World War II Era." *Enterprise and Society* 1 (1): 100–138.
Katz, L. F., and R. A. Margo. 2014. "Technical Change and the Relative Demand for Skilled Labor: The United States in Historical Perspective." In *Human Capital in History: The American Record*, edited by Leah Platt Boustan, Carola Frydman, and Robert A. Margo, 15–57. University of Chicago Press.
Kim, Y., N. Sommet, J. Na, and D. Spini. 2022. "Social Class—Not Income Inequality—Predicts Social and Institutional Trust." *Social Psychological and Personality Science* 13 (1): 186–98.
Kuhn, A., R. Lalive, and J. Zweimüller. 2009. "The Public Health Costs of Job Loss." *Journal of Health Economics* 28 (6): 1099–1115. https://doi.org/10.1016/j.jhealeco.2009.09.004.
Kuziemko, I., N. L. Marx, and S. Naidu. 2023. "Compensate the Losers? Economic Policy and Partisan Realignment in the US." NBER Working Paper No. 31794. National Bureau of Economic Research. https://www.nber.org/papers/w31794.
Kuziemko, I., and E. Washington. 2018. "Why Did the Democrats Lose the South? Bringing New Data to an Old Debate." *American Economic Review* 108 (10): 2830–37.
Leip, David. 2021. *Dave Leip's Atlas of U.S. Presidential Elections*. http://uselectionatlas.org.
Levy, J. 2021. *Ages of American Capitalism: A History of the United States*. Random House.
Lindert, P. 2004. *Growing Public*. Vol. 1, *Social Spending and Economic Growth Since the Eighteenth Century*. Cambridge University Press.
Lipset, S., and W. Schneider. 1983. "The Decline of Confidence in American Institutions." *Political Science Quarterly* 98 (3): 379–402.
Maxwell, A., and T. Shields. 2019. *The Long Southern Strategy: How Chasing White Voters in the South Changed American Politics*. Oxford University Press.
Mewes, J., M. Fairbrother, G. N. Giordano, C. Wu, and R. Wilkes. 2021. "Experiences Matter: A Longitudinal Study of Individual-Level Sources of Declining Social Trust in the United States." *Social Science Research* 95: art. 102537.
Milkman, R. 1997. *Farewell to the Factory: Auto Workers in the Late Twentieth Century*. University of California Press.
Newton, K., and P. Norris. 2000. "Confidence in Public Institutions: Faith, Culture or Performance?" In *Disaffected Democracies: What's Troubling the Trilateral Countries?* edited by S. J. Pharr and R. D. Putnam, 52–73. Princeton University Press.

Perlstein, Rick. 2001. *Before the Storm: Barry Goldwater and the Unmaking of the American Consensus*. Bold Type Books.
Perlstein, Rick. 2021. *Reaganland: America's Right Turn 1976–1980*. Simon and Schuster.
Pew Research Center. 2023. "Public Trust in Government: 1958–2023." Pew Research Center—U.S. Politics & Policy, June 24. https://www.pewresearch.org/politics/2023/09/19/public-trust-in-government-1958–2023/.
Pharr, S., R. Dalton, and R. Putnam. 2000. "Trouble in the Advanced Democracies? A Quarter-Century of Declining Confidence." *Journal of Democracy* 11 (2): 5–25.
Rege, M., T. Skardhamar, K. Telle, and M. Votruba. 2019. "Job Displacement and Crime: Evidence from Norwegian Register Data." *Labour Economics* 61: art. 101761.
Ruhm, C. J. 2018. "Corrected US Opioid-Involved Drug Poisoning Deaths and Mortality Rates, 1999–2015." *Addiction* 113: 1339–44.
Schulman, B. J. 2001. *The Seventies: The Great Shift in American Culture, Society, and Politics*. Simon and Schuster.
Strully, K. W. 2009. "Job Loss and Health in the U.S. Labor Market." *Demography* 46 (2): 221–46.
Twenge, J. M., W. K. Campbell, and N. T. Carter. 2014. "Declines in Trust in Others and Confidence in Institutions Among American Adults and Late Adolescents, 1972–2012." *Psychological Science* 25 (10): 1914–23.

IV

Coda

7 The Incubator of Human Capital
The NBER and the Rise of the Human Capital Paradigm

Claudia Goldin and Lawrence F. Katz

The field of human capital was not invented by National Bureau of Economic Research (NBER) staff members and researchers, but it was nurtured and expanded at the NBER. We explore how the NBER was an incubator of human capital research and the ways human capital theory brought the NBER into the modern era of economics.

7.1 What Is Human Capital Theory?

Human capital theory is the notion that an investment in human beings today has a payoff in the future. The investment can be in education, training, health, job search, migration, or anything that impacts income or productivity in the future. One implication of human capital theory is that

Claudia Goldin is the Henry Lee Professor of Economics and the Lee and Ezpeleta Professor of Arts and Sciences at Harvard University, and a research associate of the National Bureau of Economic Research.

Lawrence F. Katz is the Elisabeth Allison Professor of Economics at Harvard University and a research associate of the National Bureau of Economic Research.

Presented at the NBER Conference on "Historical Labor Markets and Inequality," April 1, 2023. A previous version of this chapter was presented at the session "NBER and the Evolution of Economic Research, 1920–2020," 2020 AEA Meetings in San Diego, CA. We thank our discussants: Kevin Lang at the 2023 event and James Heckman at the 2020 meetings. Stanley Engerman provided constructive comments. Jennifer Walsh located Library of Congress codes for the NBER volumes; Alice Wu and Christina Zhao helped with the final data compilations. We dedicate the paper to Martin Feldstein, whose vision brought the NBER into the modern age and made 1050 Massachusetts Avenue the meeting place for economists and an incubator of human capital. For acknowledgments, sources of research support, and disclosure of the authors' material financial relationships, if any, please see https://www.nber.org/books-and-chapters/economic-history-american-inequality-new-evidence-and-perspectives/incubator-human-capital-nber-and-rise-human-capital-paradigm.

individuals have a capitalized value (based on their expected future earnings) that can be augmented through investments, as well as reduced by depreciation, illness, injury, or job loss. The theory expands the static notion of the value of skills and places it in a dynamic framework.

When aggregated across all individuals, human capital is the economy's stock of intangibles embedded in individuals.[1] Human capital is the wealth of a nation separate from the stock of land and physical capital. Human capital theory became ascendant when the economic growth of many richer nations became increasingly difficult to fully attribute to the growth of the physical capital stock and the size of the labor force.

The concept of human capital is the neuronal fiber that connects the two halves of the economist's brain—the micro and macro. The micro advances of human capital concern the dimension of time, its value, and the allocation of time use over the life cycle. Human capital gives individuals the ability to transform time today into more productive time tomorrow. Getting more goods tomorrow involves borrowing from one's own time today and possibly also from the capital market.[2]

Even though human capital theory has become a staple of micro theory, it was called into being through the macro part of the economist's brain. The impetus was to understand the residual in growth accounting and the fact that increases in physical capital were slowing even though output was greatly increasing during the 20th century. The fact that economic growth was so much higher than could be explained by increases in conventional inputs was apparent to many economists long before Robert Solow gave it mathematical precision. Deming's (2022) recent review of research on human capital since Becker (1962) concludes that observed measures of human capital explain at least one-third of the variation in labor market earnings within countries and differences in human capital stocks may explain at least half of the variation in income per capita between counties.

7.2 Spread of Human Capital Ideas

The human capital construct is deep in the bones of economics and finds mention by many of the classical economists, even if they did not use the precise phrase. In his fourth definition of capital in *The Wealth of Nations*, Adam Smith noted: "The acquisition of . . . talents during . . . education, study, or apprenticeship, costs a real expense, which is *capital in* [a] *person*. Those talents [are] part of his fortune [and] likewise that of society" (empha-

1. Intangible capital items (including software and computerized databases, research and development, and brand equity and firm-specific resources) are increasingly recognized as a source of national wealth and economic growth (Corrado et al. 2009, 2022). See Abraham and Mallatt (2022) on the measurement of the aggregate human capital stock.

2. See Ghez and Becker (1975).

sis added).[3] Marshall noted that "the most valuable of all capital is that invested in human beings," and he termed the concept "personal capital."[4] Irving Fisher used the precise phrase "human capital."[5]

The phrase "human capital" was increasingly used in British publications during World War I to describe and often estimate the war's toll on Europe. In the US, the term experienced greater usage during the Great Depression, when it is encountered in discussions of unemployment and social insurance.

Yet, even with these added cites, the phrase "human capital" was seldom found in any print materials in both countries before the 1950s. That is clear from the Google Ngram of figure 7.1, which gives the ratio of all books and other printed material in the Google Books English US corpus using the phrase "human capital" to those that mention the word "economics."[6] We will take this ratio to mean the percentage of all books concerning economics that reference "human capital."

In 1950, only about 0.1 percent of all books concerning economics referenced "human capital." Astoundingly, when the series ends in 2019, around 18 percent did. The human capital series increases almost continuously from around 1958. The peak around 2005 is robust to the use of various corpora (e.g., British English). The sharp rise in the 1990s may be indicative of a realization that rising inequality was due, in part, to the increased returns to human capital. The subsequent decrease is less easily explained. It should also be noted that an Ngram of the term "education," although many times the magnitude of "human capital," does not reveal as large an increase in the late 1950s. The term "business cycle," of great importance in the early history of the NBER, was far more popular in economics until around 1970 when, according to the Google Books search displayed in figure 7.1, the term "human capital" surpassed "business cycle" in importance. Today three times the fraction of economics books use human capital relative to business cycle.

It should come as no surprise that the concept of human capital was

3. See the discussion in Spengler (1977). The quotation is from Smith (1776), bk. 2, chap. 1.

4. Marshall added: "And of that capital the most precious part is the result of the care and influence of the mother, so long as she retains her tender and unselfish instincts and has not been hardened by the strain the stress of unfeminine work" (Marshall 1890, bk. 6, chap. 4, sec. 3). In fact, Marshall even proposed limitations on the working hours of laborers to enable parents, especially mothers, to have more time to spend with their children (see Marshall 1890, bk. 6, chap. 13, sec. 15). Although the first part of the Marshall quotation is often used (it is given at the start of Becker's *Human Capital*), the rest of the sentence is not.

5. Fisher (1897). This discussion and the references draw on Kiker (1966).

6. The graph gives the ratio of books and other printed material in the corpus that use the phrase "human capital" to those that use the word "economics." One cannot search for all material that uses the word "economics" and that also contained the phrase "human capital." But no books that were randomly searched that used the phrase "human capital" did not have the word "economics" in the pages available on Google. The addition of other terms, such as "personal capital," has little impact on the series.

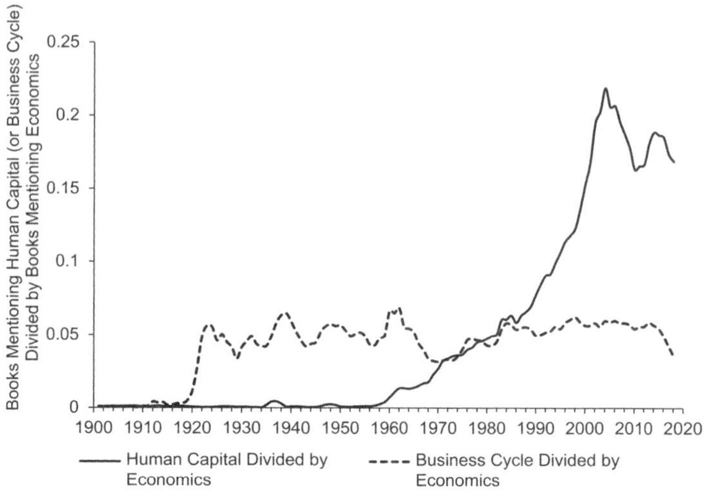

Figure 7.1 "Human capital" and "business cycle" Google Ngrams of US books, 1900 to 2019

Source: Google Ngram using the American English 2019 corpus with no smoothing and case insensitive.

Note: The graph gives the number of books mentioning "human capital" ("business cycle") divided by those mentioning "economics." Because almost all books that mention either human capital or business cycle also mention economics these graphs give the approximate fraction of all books that mention economics that also mention either human capital or business cycle. Three-year centered moving averages are shown.

known and discussed throughout the history of our profession. The question is why the phrase did not become a serious part of the economists' jargon until the late 1950s and why it took so long for the phrase to be widely used.[7]

We use the term today as if it were always part of our lingua franca. But it wasn't. Not that long ago, even economists scoffed at the notion of "human capital." As Theodore Schultz (1961) noted in his American Economic Association presidential address in 1961, many thought that free people were not to be equated with property and marketable assets. To them, that implied chattel slavery.

In *Human Capital* (published first in 1964 and preceded by his 1962 *Jour-*

7. There is also a question whether the term took on new meaning especially by those at the NBER. The phrase had been used in a variety of ways before the 1950s. One was to estimate the losses of a nation during war; another was to measure the losses to certain individuals in periods of rapid technological change. But there was little or no discussion of the act of investment to produce human capital. It was rare to encounter statements whether human capital was specific to an occupation and to a firm, or whether it was more generally demanded. In fact, virtually all the additions to the concept made by Becker, Mincer, Schultz, and others in the 1950s and early 1960s were novel innovations.

nal of Political Economy article "Investment in Human Capital"), Gary Becker admitted that he hesitated to use the term "human capital" as the title of the book and employed a long subtitle—*A Theoretical and Empirical Analysis, with Special Reference to Education*—to guard against criticism (Becker 1964). Becker noted that "passions are easily aroused on this subject," and he offered several reasons why.

Many in the early 1960s viewed education as serving a multitude of purposes that went beyond increasing future income. Education has cultural aims, it uplifts, and it gives meaning to life. The idea that education was undertaken primarily to increase income was seen by many as base and disreputable.

Becker also mentioned another factor, one that went in the opposite direction. The derision of the term human capital was not just that education was largely for economic gain. It was that economists had not proven that the relationship between economic gain and education was causal since the correlation of education with ability or parental income could produce major biases. Therefore, some were revulsed at the notion that education was mainly for economic gain and others questioned that the gain was caused by education.

Yet, by the third edition of *Human Capital*, published in 1993, Becker marveled that the phrase and concept had gained traction in economics, and across a variety of academic fields and by the general public. The Google Ngram of figure 7.1 gives credence to that statement. Between the publication of the first and the third editions of *Human Capital*, the use of the phrase in books that mentioned economics had increased more than seven times and was found in 9 percent of books mentioning economics. The phrase had lost its offensiveness and had caught on.

But it is not clear what enabled the phrase to lose its negative press. Perhaps it was the greater acceptance of the economic model for providing insights into many areas of "nonmarket" behaviors including marriage and cohabitation, fertility, child-rearing, crime, and education (Becker 1976). Perhaps it was stronger causal evidence that education actually boosted earnings (even as it elevated the soul).[8] Perhaps, in addition, economists and economics became more respectable (actually, banish the thought).

"Human capital" as a concept was, according to this logic, called into being by various changes in the economy. As Schultz noted, the "unexplained rise in the economic value of man" (1972, 1) needed an explanation. Furthermore, the greatly increased use of the term in the 1990s was necessitated by vastly increased income and wage inequality in the US and elsewhere, coinciding with rising economic gaps by educational attainment. Human capital had become more fashionable because it was needed to help

8. See the summary in Card (2001).

explain various aspects of the economy in the modern era, such as labor productivity changes.[9]

7.3 The Early Human Capital Incubators of the NBER

7.3.1 Early Macro Incubators

The NBER played an outsized role in many facets of the rise of the concept of human capital and in its measurement. In large part this was because of the critical importance of empiricism at the NBER ever since its founding.

As Becker noted in his preface to the first edition of *Human Capital* in 1964: "The origins of this study can be traced . . . to the finding that a substantial growth in income in the United States remains after the growth in physical capital and labor has been accounted for." That is, the subject was motivated by a need to understand the "residual" in economic growth estimates.

NBER researchers were among the first to notice that changes in physical input measures could not explain changes in aggregate output (see Griliches 1995 on the discovery of the residual). Many at the NBER, including Stigler (1947) and Abramovitz (1956), breathed empirical life into these theoretical notions.[10] Kendrick's (1961) important work on productivity trends discussed the notion of human capital, which he termed "investment in persons," and in chapter 4, "Productivity and Economic Growth," he considered the potential importance of education and health to productivity. But, because his book was on productivity trends in separate industries and data on the education and health of workers by industry over time did not exist, Kendrick could not incorporate these inputs into his analyses. The job of adding the role of education to aggregate productivity measures was left to others, such as Edward Denison (1962).

In his work on the capital stock, Kuznets bemoaned that "the concept of capital formation . . . was too narrow" and that conventional ways of measuring capital understated it. "For many purposes—particularly the study of economic growth over long periods and among widely different societies—the concept of capital and capital formation should be broadened to include investment in the health, education, and training of the population itself, that is, *investment in human beings*" (1961, 390, emphasis added).

The study of human capital gave NBER research on productivity and

9. Holden and Biddle (2017) discuss the impact that the human capital concept had on education policy in the US beginning in the early 1960s. Engerman (1971) is an early economic history paper that discusses the role played by human capital formation to economic growth.

10. Griliches notes that Copeland (1937) provided the earliest attempt to express an index of outputs divided by inputs. Stigler has written that his own empirical work on the subject was probably the first ever.

growth a means to comprehend the mystery of the residual. It connected the world of macroeconomics and financial capital with that on investments in people.

7.3.2 Early Micro Incubators

Becker's preface to *Human Capital* included a second motivation for the study human capital: "the importance of education in the promotion of economic development." Oddly, few NBER studies before 1962 mention education at all. The neglect seems odd since educational advances in the US were already enormous, both in absolute terms and relative to educational improvements in other nations (Goldin and Katz 2008). The US had been a leader in the education of its people. How could NBER researchers have neglected such an important part of the US economy?

One reason concerns measurement. Until the publication of the 1940 US population census, there were no national data available that could reveal the relationship between earnings and education. But there were a host of other data that could have been mined on the increase of educational inputs and their role in enhancing skill. See, for example, the many series in Goldin and Katz (2008) from the US Office (Bureau) of Education that chart the expansion of education, as well as those that use occupational wage data and the 1915 Iowa state census containing microdata on earnings by education level.

Another possibility for the absence of an NBER study of education is that NBER research was steered toward the issues that had occupied the minds of its leaders Wesley Clair Mitchell, Arthur Burns, and Solomon Fabricant. Until the late 1950s, these did not include areas such as education, health, training, and other aspects of the labor market, although several important publications early in NBER history concerned international migration and labor unions.[11]

There was one important exception, and that study used data that were part of a survey by the US Department of Commerce that eventually spanned the years 1929 to 1936. The data had been collected to inform national income statistics and provide better estimates of the incomes of those in private professional practice. The project that used these data became the most controversial published book in the history of the NBER.

The initial author was Simon Kuznets, whose interest in the data concerned national income statistics. But Kuznets was preoccupied with his other studies at the NBER and hired a research assistant to help with the study. That researcher was Milton Friedman, who would become among the most important economists of the 20th century.

Friedman had already earned an MA at the University of Chicago and

11. Blank and Stigler (1957) on the demand and supply of scientific personnel was somewhat of an aberration. It was not apparently motivated by productivity concerns and was funded by the National Science Foundation.

then worked in Washington, DC, on New Deal projects.[12] He became a staff economist at the NBER in 1937. The study with Kuznets, *Income from Independent Professional Practice* (1945), became Friedman's PhD dissertation at Columbia University, which he earned around 1940. But the NBER volume was delayed for four years in large part due to a dissent by one of the NBER directors, although also because of the exigencies of the war.[13]

The research was important in a host of ways. It introduced the concepts of permanent and transitory income and it grappled with many of the issues at the heart of human capital theory, including investment under uncertainty, the financing of strangers, "equalizing differentials," "noncompeting groups," and the reasons for variability in individual professional incomes as well as differences in earnings across professions.[14] Many of Friedman's key lifetime insights were nascent in this early work including income contingent loans to finance occupational training and the theory of the consumption function.

The volume had a seminal impact on another great mind of human capital research—Jacob Mincer. That influence came up in an interview one of us (Goldin) did with Mincer in 2002.[15] The story, of how Mincer in 1957 saw the "human capital" light and its impact on his life, was told by Mincer as follows:

> *Mincer*: [The Friedman and Kuznets] work had a very big impact on me . . . [As a graduate student] at Columbia my interest was in wage determination . . . I was approaching it like a Bureau person by looking at various comparisons—by industry, occupation, age, sex, race. I had chapters along those lines. A fellow student of mine . . . suggested looking up [*Income from Independent Professional Practice*]. When I read this book it took me back to Adam Smith and then I realized that all the comparisons I was making had as a basic principle education and age. If you pushed the comparisons, each one of them had underlying differences in human capital.

12. Milton Friedman appears as a member of the NBER research staff with the 1937 Report of the Executive Director.

13. All NBER publications had to undergo NBER Board review, and one member of the Board (C. Reinhold Noyes) disagreed with the Friedman and Kuznets conclusion, particularly the discussion in chapter 4, that supply restrictions for doctors (due to the American Medical Association) increased the earnings of physicians above those of dentists, who faced fewer entry restrictions. See also a letter from Mitchell to Burns, from the Duke University archives, that shows Mitchell's agreement with Noyes and his lack of confidence in Friedman. The letter is cited in Edward Nelson's book on Milton Friedman (Nelson 2020).

14. "A young man must not only have the ability to practice a profession and must not only want to enter it; he must also be able to finance his training and be cognizant of opportunities; and both entry into the profession and his success in it will be greatly facilitated if he has the proper background and connections. . . . Unlike high returns on capital invested in machinery, high returns on capital invested in professional training need not lead to an increase in investment. Capital invested in human beings is not separable from the individual and cannot be bought and sold on the open market" (Friedman and Kuznets 1945, 391).

15. See NBER Historical Archives, Oral Histories of the NBER, https://data.nber.org/nberhistory/jacobmincer/Mincer_interview.pdf.

Goldin: Would you have used that term, "human capital" at that point?

Mincer: Yes, I used it immediately . . . This was like a revelation. That same afternoon . . . I had this principle established, written out and shown with empirical data. My sponsor, [Harold] Barger, immediately said "this is great" and sent a copy to Ted Schultz. I didn't know there was a whole industry brewing in Chicago involving economic growth and human capital . . . It took me [just] a few days to turn around all the material I had into an organized analysis of wage differentials. I then got the offer from Ted Schultz to come to Chicago for a post-doctoral fellowship . . . [It was] 1957 . . . I immediately went to Chicago.[16]

7.4 The Flowering of Human Capital at the New York City NBER

The NBER was enabled to explore education and human capital in large measure because of several grants from the Carnegie Corporation. A Carnegie grant was first mentioned in the 1958 NBER annual report as funding Becker's research on the returns to education. Becker later credited the grant and other NBER support with why he took a job at Columbia and the NBER rather than a higher-paying one at Chicago, after completing his PhD at Chicago: "For twelve years I divided my time between teaching at Columbia and doing research at the Bureau. My book on human capital was the outgrowth of my first research project for the Bureau."[17]

A Carnegie grant also funded an event, sponsored by the Universities-NBER Committee for Economic Research and held in 1961, called "The Exploratory Conference on Capital Invested in Human Beings." The planning committee included, among others, George Shultz (chair), Theodore Schultz, Robert Solow, and Gary Becker.

The resulting volume, published as a special supplement in the *Journal of Political Economy*, foretold the outpouring of research on human capital that was to come. As Selma Mushkin, one of the participants, surmised: "A theory of human capital is in the process of formulation" (1962, 129).

Looking back, the conference contained the "Who's Who" of human capital. The volume opens with Schultz's overview of the subject and continues with a star-studded cast: Becker on human capital, Mincer on on-the-job training, Sjaastad on migration, Stigler on modern search theory, Weisbrod on education, Denison on economic growth and augmented labor, and Mushkin on health—the human capital Oscars and Emmys rolled together![18]

16. Mincer's doctoral dissertation, "A Study of Personal Income Distribution," was summarized in Mincer (1958) and grew into his critically important book *Schooling, Experience, and Earnings* (1974).

17. Becker mentions this in his Nobel statement: https://www.nobelprize.org/prizes/economic-sciences/1992/becker/facts/.

18. Schultz (1962), "Reflections on Investment in Man," opens the volume. The others in the volume are in order: Becker (1962), Mincer (1962), Sjaastad (1962), Stigler (1962), Weisbrod (1962), Denison (1962), and Mushkin (1962).

By 1970, research on human capital had become sufficiently important that John Meyer, then the president of the NBER, asked Schultz to head one of the Fiftieth Anniversary colloquia. Its purpose was to assess the human capital efforts of the NBER and to evaluate the future. The Human Resources Colloquium was held in 1971 and was published in Schultz (1972).

Another NBER conference on human capital was organized by Schultz (1974) and published as a special issue of the *Journal of Political Economy*. The volume was titled "Marriage, Family, Human Capital, and Fertility" and added a host of new subjects that were informed by human capital and featured newly minted researchers, including James Heckman, Arlene Leibowitz, and Sol Polachek.

Prior to the 1962 volume, just a handful of NBER pieces directly related to human capital subjects and notions. We just mentioned the Friedman and Kuznets volume. Research on fertility was begun by Easterlin (1962) in a short piece that presaged his important work on the baby boom and his theory of fertility cycles. Easterlin (1968) is a major work tying together the business cycle side of the NBER with the emerging one relating to fertility, family, and human capital more generally.

Becker presented an early version of his work on fertility at a Universities-NBER conference and published as an NBER volume (Becker 1960). According to Becker, his paper was savaged by all except Kuznets, who also gave a paper at the conference.[19] Becker was grappling with an explanation for long-run changes in fertility. He had not yet worked out the model in his piece with H. Gregg Lewis (Becker and Lewis 1973) on the "quality-quantity" trade-off, and a comparison of the two papers shows how human capital theory altered Becker's thinking on the subject.

We would be remiss if we did not mention the work by NBER researchers on slavery. The now-famous paper by Alfred Conrad and John Meyer, published in the *Journal of Political Economy* in 1958, was originally presented at a Universities-National Bureau Committee on Economic Research conference.[20] Although Conrad and Meyer did not use the phrase "human capital," they did use the term "slave capital."

After the early 1960s, NBER work in various fields began to blossom under the direction and guidance of senior NBER staff members Becker, Victor Fuchs, F. Thomas Juster, and Mincer. In 1967 a program on health

19. See NBER Historical Archives, Oral Histories of the NBER, https://data.nber.org/nber history/oralhistories2.html. Becker did not ingratiate himself with the demographers and sociologists by beginning his paper remarking on "the inability of demographers to predict western birth rates accurately in the postwar period."

20. The event was held in 1957 at Williams College. The resulting volume (known as "volume 24") contains classics in economic history, but not the piece by Conrad and Meyer, possibly because they preferred publication in the *Journal of Political Economy*. Another paper on slavery, by Robert Evans, was published in *Aspects of Labor Economics* (Universities-National Bureau Committee for Economic Research 1962).

under the direction of Fuchs was announced with research contributions by Michael Grossman.

By 1970—the NBER's fiftieth anniversary—the list of human capital researchers who spent extensive or limited periods at the NBER expanded to include V. K. Chetty, Barry Chiswick, Carmel Chiswick, Isaac Erlich, Albert Fishlow, Gil Ghez, Reuben Gronau, Sherwin Rosen, Jim Smith, Lewis Solmon, and Robert Willis. Some were short-term research fellows in residence from other institutions; others were graduate students at Columbia. Still others were Columbia and Baruch graduate students and faculty, whom we shall not separately enumerate, who spent part of their days at the NBER, just as graduate students and faculty in the Cambridge and Boston area did so more recently.

Jacob Mincer's influential 1974 NBER book *Schooling, Experience, and Earnings* deserves special mention for pioneering the human capital earnings function. Mincer posited and documented a positive linear relationship between log earnings and years of schooling and a positive but concave (quadratic) relationship between log earnings and years of (potential) labor market experience. Mincer interpreted the positive labor market returns to schooling and to experience as reflecting returns to general human capital investments with the concave experience-earnings profile arising from initially high and then declining on-the-job training investments over the course of a career.[21]

Mincer and Polachek (1974) extended the human capital earnings function approach by examining the role of women's labor market discontinuity. Breaks in women's employment altered their optimal choice of occupations and that served to explain some part of the gender earnings gap.

The work of Gil Ghez and Gary Becker on the allocation of time also merits special notice. Their coauthored book, *The Allocation of Time and Goods over the Life Cycle*, was foundational and became the bedrock for many of the human capital theory developments that followed, as well as for Becker's work on the family.[22]

7.5 Transforming the NBER

7.5.1 Book Publications and "Human Capital"

We previously noted the apparent paucity of research at the NBER on human capital until the early 1960s. But that may be misleading since the use of a catchword or phrase may indicate that a basic element had been discovered, not that the subject was entirely unknown. Biologists, for example,

21. See Bhuller et al. (2017) for a reassessment and test of the underlying assumptions behind the Mincerian human capital earnings function.

22. Ghez and Becker (1975) and Becker (1981). See also Heckman (2015).

knew that various traits were inherited, but the use of the term "genetics" gained traction only after a key set of discoveries. Tracking the term "genetics" would miss various turning points in the intellectual journey of the discipline. Tracking "human capital" might do the same.

Therefore, in tracking NBER research from its inception in 1920, we have searched for topics that are associated with human capital research. These include education, labor, health, migration, women, children, demography, fertility, marriage, the family, and economic inequality.

NBER research, today, is disseminated through working papers, seminars, conference volumes, and other books. In the past, NBER research was circulated mainly in volume form. The "occasional research paper" series was begun in December 1940 and was continued by "Explorations in Economic Research" in 1974, during John Meyer's tenure as NBER president.[23] Shorter pieces in collected volumes have existed from the 1920s with different sponsors and interests, including the Conference on Research in Income and Wealth and the Universities-National Bureau Committee for Economic Research.

The most convenient way to track the content of NBER volumes since 1920 is to use existing coding schemes, of which the most extensive is that of the Library of Congress (LoC). We have looked up codes for all 1,269 NBER published volumes (excluding working papers) from 1920 to 2019 listed on the NBER website.[24] Subtracting duplicates, internal documents, and other items that do not have LoC codes, results in 819 volumes. (These codes are not listed with NBER books, but *JEL* codes have recently been added.) We also used our knowledge of the volume content (see appendix). The results are shown in figure 7.2, part A. In figure 7.2, part B, we use the NBER website to search all NBER book chapters from 1958 to 2022 for the term "human capital."[25]

Therefore, we have two complementary measures of research on "human capital" in NBER volumes. The first gives the human capital content of NBER volumes from 1920 to 2019. The second gives the fraction of book chapters that reference human capital as a phrase. The first series is broad and covers a long period; the second is more directly focused on "human capital." Because of the small number of observations for NBER volumes, we use 10-year bins in part A but 5-year bins for part B.

About 37 percent of all NBER volumes today are concerned with material related to the human capital construct. The fraction was around 10 percent

23. The original "occasional paper" series appears to have ended with #119 in 1972.

24. The entire occasional working paper series has one LoC code and is numbered from 1 to 119.

25. Although most of the entries are actual book chapters, some items are front material and various portions of a volume. The NBER website calls them all "chapters." Most of the entries in the "monograph" series are not searchable since they are not posted as full text. We begin with 1958 because before then, the term "human capital" was rarely, if ever, used.

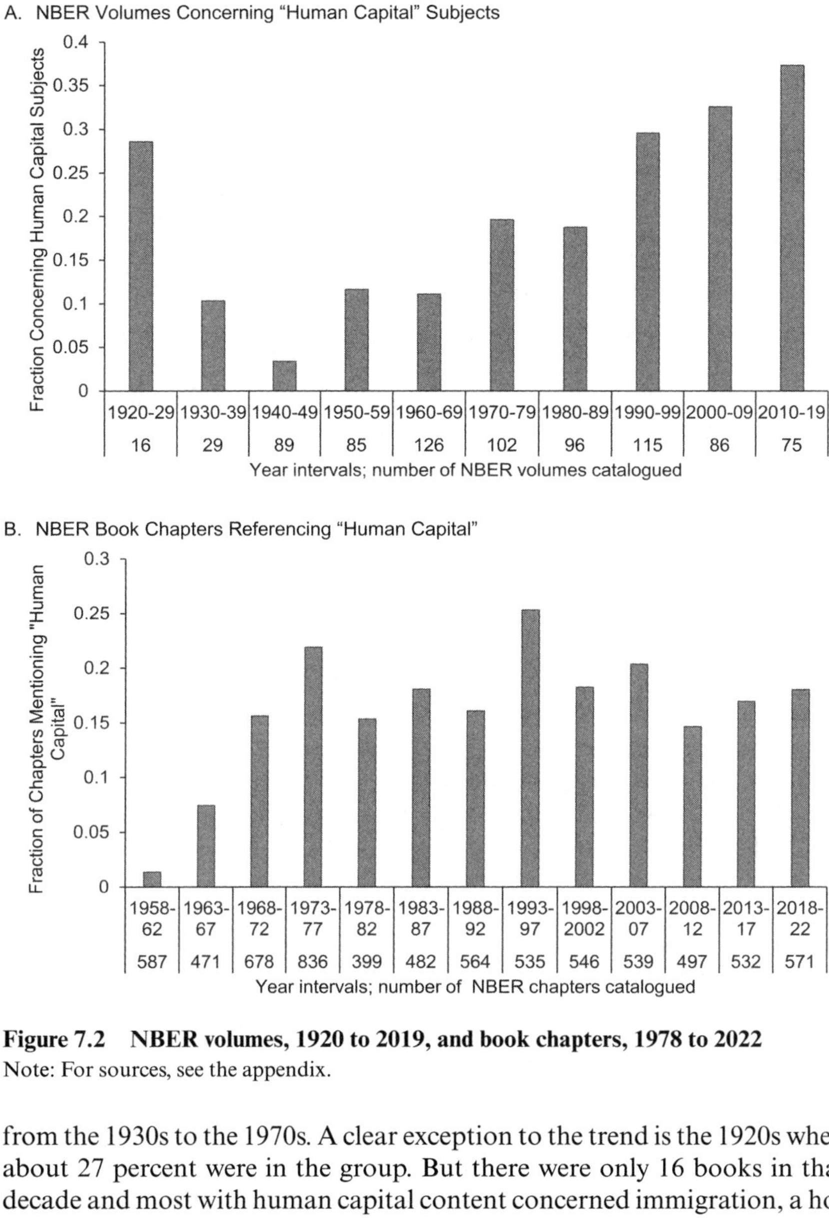

Figure 7.2 NBER volumes, 1920 to 2019, and book chapters, 1978 to 2022
Note: For sources, see the appendix.

from the 1930s to the 1970s. A clear exception to the trend is the 1920s when about 27 percent were in the group. But there were only 16 books in that decade and most with human capital content concerned immigration, a hot topic during the 1920s period of immigration restriction. Another break is with the 1940s when many volumes concerned subjects related to World War II. The main takeaway is that human capital topics were not high on NBER researchers' lists until the 1970s but then became so, especially in the 1990s.

The book chapters show a clear increase in the 1970s and then a slight decrease as the NBER established a large number of programs that would be only tangentially concerned with human capital. Somewhere between 15 percent and 20 percent of NBER book chapters have mentioned human capital ever since 1978 with an increase in the mid-1990s, similar to that seen in the Google Ngram with more research on inequality and the role of human capital. Interestingly, since the late 1990s about the same fraction of books in economics reference human capital as a phrase as do chapters in NBER volumes.

7.5.2 Articles, Working Papers, and "Human Capital"

NBER publications shifted decisively in favor of working papers after the 1970s. The official NBER working paper series was begun in June 1973 with Finis Welch's piece on "Education, Information, and Efficiency." Around 1977, with the transition from John Meyer to Martin Feldstein, new program names began to be attached to the working papers.

A direct comparison can be made between NBER working papers and all published articles using search routines in EconLit and JSTOR. We have categorized NBER working papers and all published articles two ways. In one, we use the EconLit search engine to categorize both NBER working papers and all published articles and working papers. Because EconLit does not have the full text, the search can only be done using the title, abstract, and the *Journal of Economic Literature* (*JEL*) code. The results for the search term "human capital" are given in figure 7.3 in five-year bins from 1990, when EconLit began to categorize NBER papers, to 2019.

We also use the NBER website and JSTOR to search across the full text for all published articles (in English in economics journals) from 1978 to 2022 and those results are shown in figure 7.4.

The fraction of all NBER working papers that use the term "human capital" in the title, abstract, or *JEL* code increased from just under 4 percent to 10 percent across the past three decades. The "human capital" phrase does not increase as much for all published articles and working papers, rising from around 3.5 percent to 6 percent. Working papers in the NBER series should have a higher fraction with the term "human capital" than all economics papers, since NBER working papers generally do not include pure theory pieces. The more rapid increase, however, is of interest.

The longer series in figure 7.4 that searches over the full text reveals, not surprisingly, a higher share using the term human capital. Interestingly, although the trend is similar to that in figure 7.3 for the period of overlap, figure 7.4 reveals that the NBER began operations in Cambridge in 1978 with a larger number of groups and associates in the human capital area but was then diversified, adding many associates in finance, productivity, and international finance, for example. The fraction of NBER working papers referencing "human capital" actually declined in the 1980s, while that for all published articles increased. Yet, by 2022 around 27 percent of all NBER

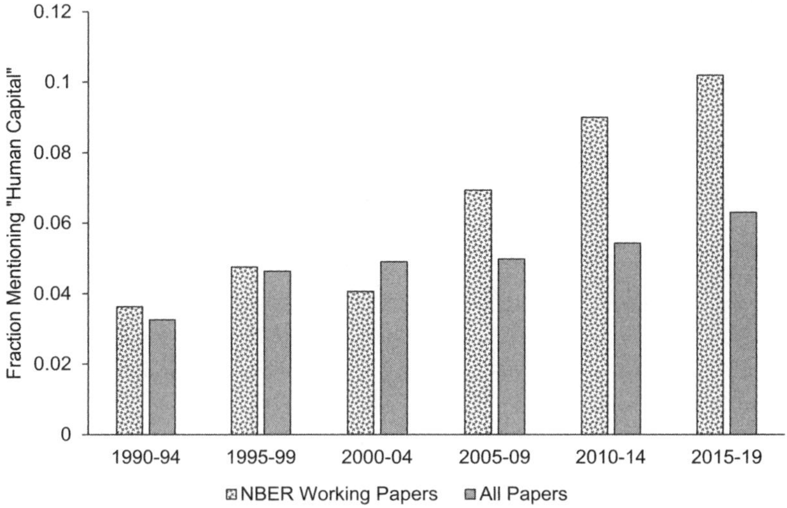

Figure 7.3 Fraction of NBER working papers and all EconLit papers (published articles and working papers) mentioning "human capital" (not full text), 1990 to 2019

Source: EconLit search engine. See the appendix.

Note: "NBER Working Papers" gives the results for ("Human Capital" + "NBER Working Paper") divided by ("the" + "NBER Working Paper") as words or phrases used in the title or abstract of the working paper. "All Papers" gives the results for ("Human Capital") divided by "the" as words/phrases used in the title or abstract of the paper and is computed for all published articles and working papers in EconLit. The number of NBER working papers from 1990 to 2019 is 23,036. The total number of economics journal articles and working papers catalogued by EconLit from 1990 to 2019 is 1,007,473. Information in EconLit on NBER publications is not available after 2019, at the time of this writing.

working papers referenced the term "human capital," whereas 20 percent of all economics articles did.

7.6 The Human Capital Takeoff at the NBER

What accounts for the takeoff in NBER human capital publications relative to all in economics? Is it due to a change in the composition of NBER researchers or have NBER researchers across fields turned their attention more to human capital? We believe it is the latter, but we do not yet have a full answer.

In 1977, the NBER relaunch in Cambridge, Massachusetts, under Martin Feldstein led to a reorganization with a focus on research programs, each with an ability to appoint NBER affiliates. The initial programs were in seven areas: Development of the American Economy, Economic Fluctuations and Growth, Health Economics, Labor Studies, Productivity, Monetary Economics, and Tax Policy (later renamed Public Economics). The

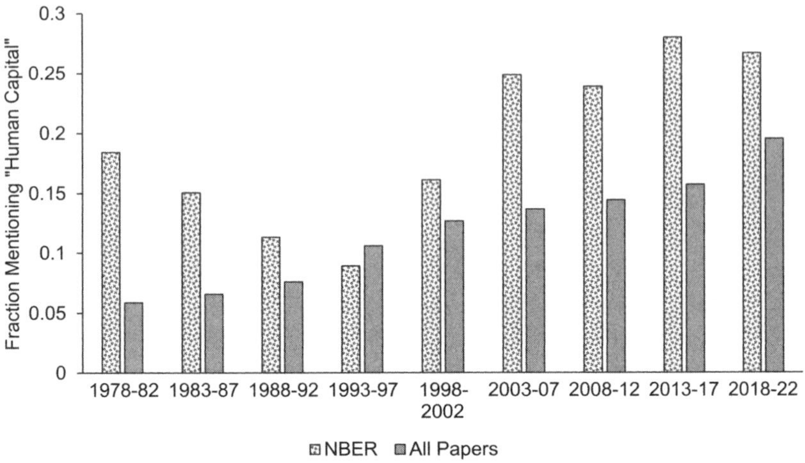

Figure 7.4 Fraction of NBER working papers and all published articles mentioning "human capital" (in full text), 1978 to 2022

Source: NBER website; JSTOR.

Note: All working papers on the NBER website were searched for the term "human capital" anywhere in the paper. All articles meeting certain criteria were searched on JSTOR for the term "human capital" anywhere in the paper. The criteria were: articles in English, in "content I can access," and searched only in the (183) economics journals.

rapidly growing network of NBER affiliates, NBER program meetings, conferences, working groups, and the NBER Summer Institute all served during the last 40 years to create stronger connections among empirically oriented scholars in economics and helped spread and foster advances in human capital research.

The NBER, today more than a century old, now has 20 formal research programs and 14 working groups, fostered first by Martin Feldstein and then by James Poterba. The Labor Studies, the Economics of Aging, Children, Development Economics, the Economics of Education, and Health Care programs helped catalyze research on core human capital issues. But these new program areas were also a way to attract federal research funding. NBER working groups in Behavioral Economics, Cohort Studies, Economics of Crime, Personnel Economics, and Urban Economics incorporated a broader range of scholars and human capital topics into the NBER network.

Increased federal research funding for economists through the National Institutes of Health (including the National Institute of Aging and National Institute of Child Health and Development) and the Institute for Education Sciences helped galvanize economic research on human capital that spanned the life cycle. Research flourished on the role of the in utero environment, early childhood education, health investments, K–12 and higher education, adult learning, retirement, aging, and life expectancy—human capital from womb to tomb.

NBER researchers, such as David Wise of the NBER Aging program, Caroline Hoxby of the NBER Economics of Education program, and Janet Currie of the NBER Children's program, have played key leadership roles in facilitating research expansions into new human capital areas.

7.7 Discussion and Conclusion

The human capital revolution incubated at the NBER in the mid-20th century by scholars such as Milton Friedman, Gary Becker, and Jacob Mincer has greatly influenced and enriched economic research and policy analysis in the late 20th and early 21st centuries. NBER-affiliated researchers have shown that shifts in the demand for skills stemming from technological change, combined with increased access to educational opportunities, have been central to shifts in the wage structure, earnings inequality, and cross-country differences in inequality (Autor 2014; Freeman and Katz 1995; Goldin and Katz 2008; Katz and Murphy 1992). They have studied the role of human capital and discrimination to understand racial inequalities (Bayer and Charles 2018; Card and Krueger 1992; Derenoncourt et al. 2022; Lang and Manove 2011; Margo 1990). They have, as well, been central players in debates over the role of signaling versus human capital in explaining educational investments and labor market returns to schooling (Angrist and Krueger 1991; Aryal et al. 2022; Weiss 1988).

Research has flourished on the importance of early childhood education and environments for long-run economic outcomes and broadened the human capital perspective to examine the development and returns to social and emotional skills (Cunha and Heckman 2007; Currie 2011; Deming 2017; Heckman 2008; Heckman et al. 2013).

Access to large administrative, linked longitudinal datasets from the Census Bureau and the Internal Revenue Service has enabled researchers to build on the conceptual insights of Becker and Tomes (1979). The result has been a better understanding of the determinants of, and geographical and racial variation in, intergenerational mobility (Chetty et al. 2014, 2020). These huge administrative datasets have also furthered the human capital revolution by permitting more compelling empirical analyses of the long-run causal impacts of educational interventions and childhood neighborhood environments (Chetty et al. 2011, 2016; Chetty and Hendren 2018).

The fruits of the human capital revolution are clear in the range of papers presented at the NBER's Summer Institute. One entire week of the Summer Institute in recent years has been devoted to research on labor markets, children, education, development economics, economics of crime, health economics, health care, gender in the economy, and aging.

Mainstream public economics research now engages with the implications of human capital investments for optimal tax policy (Stantcheva 2017) and for the welfare analysis of tax and expenditure policies. At the 2019 Summer

Institute, a paper by Hendren and Sprung-Keyser (2020) demonstrated that government programs that expand investments in children from low-income families provide the highest measured social return to public funds.

Macroeconomic research at the NBER has also been infused with human capital ideas. These include improvements in the measurement of the contribution of human capital investments to cross-country income differences (Jones 2016; Mankiw et al. 1992) and the central role of search models, building on Stigler (1962), for understanding unemployment and labor market fluctuations.

We have demonstrated the greatly increased importance of human capital research across all economics publications and its even greater increase for volumes and papers issued by the NBER. We have also indicated the ways that human capital research at the NBER was influenced by the dedication of NBER researchers to empirical research and how research on human capital brought the NBER into the modern age of economics.

At the end of NBER's first century, we can confidently say that *we are all human capitalists now*.

Appendix

A. NBER Volumes (Figure 7.2, parts A and B)

NBER volumes are not fully searchable on the NBER website. Chapters in conference and other volumes are searchable, and we use the NBER search routine to identify chapters that mention "human capital" (figure 7.2, part B). We have searched 4,665 chapters, which include front matter and references.

The classification of NBER volumes (figure 7.2, part A) was done differently. To categorize NBER volumes beginning with the first in 1920, we have collected all Library of Congress (LoC) catalog numbers for the volumes. (NBER staff have recently assigned JEL codes.) Note that NBER occasional papers are generally not coded under the LoC system.

We have coded 819 books. There were 1,270 books and occasional papers listed on the NBER site across the years shown to 2019 when we began the project. We eliminated repeat entries in the NBER system to the best of our ability.

The LoC coding scheme is a reasonable, but imperfect, device to code economics books. We have used the following LoC codes to indicate relevance to the concept of "human capital." The topics or words included are labor, labor force, employment, compensation, health and disability, demography, income inequality, marriage, the family, women, children, human physical growth, scientific personnel, time use, pensions (but not savings and Social Security separately), and unions. The LoC codes used are as follows:

Table 7A.1 Library of Congress codes relevant to the concept of "human capital"

LoC Number	Content for "human capital" designation
E1	History of the Americas, relevant portions
H11	Social Sciences, only if Labor Force, Employment, Servants, Compensation
HA	Health and disability, not Social Security; Health care, but not health costs
HB848–3697	Demography
HC106	Most listings, but not exclusively national income
HC110	Income inequality
HD4801–8943	Labor; not housing and not business cycles
HQ	Marriage and the family
HV	Items regarding women and children
GN	Anthropology (human physical growth)
JV6001–9480	Migration
L	Education
Q1	Scientific personnel
RA	Medicine and the state
TX	Home economics

Note: All other codes are treated as not having "Human Capital" content.

B. NBER Working Papers and All Published Articles (Figure 7.3)

The EconLit search engine was used to find mention of the phrase "human capital" and "NBER Working Paper" in all working papers deflated by the number of working papers that mention the "NBER Working Paper." EconLit uses a limited number of fields (articles are not available to the coders): title, abstract of the article, and the JEL codes for the article. Therefore, counts of the term "human capital" will be understated for articles that use the phrase if it was not mentioned in the title or abstract or JEL code. Note that just two JEL codes (E24 and J24) list the phrase "human capital," and any paper listing either of these codes will be included in the human capital group. EconLit provides JEL codes for NBER working papers only after 1990.

The fraction of all published articles referencing "human capital" is computed from EconLit by counting all articles with "the" in the abstract, title, or those having a JEL code (the presumption is that the number will be all articles). The numerator is the number that use the phrase "human capital" in the abstract, title, or JEL code and "the," to make certain that no articles omitted in the denominator are in the numerator.

C. NBER Working Papers and All Published Articles and Working Papers, Full Text Search, 1978 to 2022 (Figure 7.4)

All working papers on the NBER website were searched for the term "human capital" anywhere in the paper. All articles meeting certain criteria were searched on JSTOR for the term "human capital" anywhere in the paper. The criteria were: all articles in English, in "content I can access," and only in the (183) cataloged economics journals. There were 224,424 articles searched on JSTOR from 1978 to 2022. There were 31,066 NBER working papers searched on the NBER website.

References

Abraham, Katharine G., and Justine Mallatt. 2022. "Measuring Human Capital." *Journal of Economic Perspectives* 36 (3): 103–30.

Abramovitz, Moses. 1956. "Resource and Output Trends in the U.S. Since 1870." *American Economic Review* 46 (2): 5–23.

Angrist, Joshua D., and Alan B. Krueger. 1991. "Does Compulsory School Attendance Affect Schooling and Earnings?" *Quarterly Journal of Economics* 106 (4): 979–1014.

Aryal, Gaurab, Manudeep Bhuller, and Fabian Lange. 2022. "Signaling and Employer Learning with Instruments." *American Economic Review* 112 (5): 1669–702.

Autor, David H. 2014. "Skills, Education and the Rise of Earnings Inequality Among the 'Other 99 Percent.'" *Science* 344 (6186): 843–51.

Bayer, Patrick, and Kerwin Charles. 2018. "Divergent Paths: A New Perspective on Earnings Differences Between Black and White Men Since 1940." *Quarterly Journal of Economics* 133 (3): 1459–501.

Becker, Gary S. 1960. "An Economic Analysis of Fertility." In *Demographic and Economic Change in Developed Countries*, edited by George Roberts, 209–40. NBER. Columbia University Press.

Becker, Gary S. 1962. "Investment in Human Capital: A Theoretical Analysis." *Journal of Political Economy* 70 (5), pt. 2: 9–49.

Becker, Gary S. 1964. *Human Capital: A Theoretical and Empirical Analysis, with Special Reference to Education*. National Bureau of Economic Research. Columbia University Press.

Becker, Gary S. 1976. *The Economic Approach to Human Behavior*. University of Chicago Press.

Becker, Gary S. 1981. *A Treatise on the Family*. Harvard University Press.

Becker, Gary S. 1993. *Human Capital: A Theoretical and Empirical Analysis, with Special Reference to Education*. 3rd ed. NBER. University of Chicago Press.

Becker, Gary S., and H. Gregg Lewis. 1973. "On the Interaction Between the Quantity and Quality of Children." *Journal of Political Economy* 81 (2), pt. 2: S279–S288.

Becker, Gary S., and Nigel Tomes. 1979. "An Equilibrium Theory of the Distribution of Income and Intergenerational Mobility." *Journal of Political Economy* 87(6): 1153–89.

Bhuller, Manudeep, Magne Mogstad, and Kjell Salvanes. 2017. "Life-Cycle Earnings, Education Premiums, and Internal Rates of Return." *Journal of Labor Economics* 35 (4): 993–1040.

Blank, David M., and George J. Stigler. 1957. *The Demand and Supply of Scientific Personnel*. NBER.

Card, David. 2001. "Estimating the Return to Schooling: Progress on Some Persistent Econometric Problems." *Econometrica* 69 (5): 1127–60.

Card, David, and Alan B. Krueger. 1992. "School Quality and Black-White Relative Earnings: A Direct Approach." *Quarterly Journal of Economics* 107 (1): 151–200.

Chetty, Raj, John Friedman, Nathaniel Hilger, Emmanuel Saez, Diane Schanzenbach, and Danny Yagan. 2011. "How Does Your Kindergarten Classroom Affect Your Earnings? Evidence from Project Star." *Quarterly Journal of Economics* 126 (4): 1593–660.

Chetty, Raj, and Nathaniel Hendren. 2018. "The Impacts of Neighborhoods on Intergenerational Mobility I: Childhood Exposure Effects." *Quarterly Journal of Economics* 133 (3): 1107–62.

Chetty, Raj, Nathaniel Hendren, Maggie Jones, and Sonya Porter. 2020. "Race and Economic Opportunity in the United States: An Intergenerational Perspective." *Quarterly Journal of Economics* 135 (2): 711–83. https://doi.org/10.1093/qje/qjz042.

Chetty, Raj, Nathaniel Hendren, and Lawrence F. Katz. 2016. "The Effects of Exposure to Better Neighborhoods on Children: New Evidence from the Moving to Opportunity Experiment." *American Economic Review* 106 (4): 855–902.

Chetty, Raj, Nathaniel Hendren, Patrick Kline, and Emanuel Saez. 2014. "Where Is the Land of Opportunity? The Geography of Intergenerational Mobility in the United States." *Quarterly Journal of Economics* 129 (4): 1553–623.

Conrad, Alfred, and John Meyer. 1958. "The Economics of Slavery in the Ante Bellum South." *Journal of Political Economy* 66 (2): 95–130.

Copeland, Morris. 1937. "Concepts of National Income." In *Studies in Income and Wealth*, 1:3–63. NBER.

Corrado, Carol, Jonathan Haskel, Cecilia Jona-Lasinio, and Massimiliano Iommi. 2022. "Intangible Capital and Modern Economies." *Journal of Economic Perspectives* 36 (3): 3–28.

Corrado, Carol, Charles Hulten, and Daniel Sichel. 2009. "Intangible Capital and Economic Growth." *Review of Income and Wealth* 55 (3): 661–85.

Cunha, Flavio, and James Heckman. 2007. "The Technology of Skill Formation." *American Economic Review* 97 (2): 31–42.

Currie, Janet. 2011. "Inequality at Birth: Some Causes and Consequences." *American Economic Review: Papers and Proceedings* 101 (3): 1–22.

Deming, David. 2017. "The Growing Importance of Social Skills in the Labor Market." *Quarterly Journal of Economics* 132 (4): 1593–640.

Deming, David J. 2022. "Four Facts about Human Capital." *Journal of Economic Perspectives* 36 (3): 75–102.

Denison, Edward F. 1962. "Education, Economic Growth, and Gaps in Information." *Journal of Political Economy* 70 (5), pt. 2: 124–28.

Derenoncourt, Ellora, Chi Hyun Kim, Moritz Kuhn, and Moritz Shularick. 2022. "Wealth of Two Nations: The U.S. Racial Wealth Gap, 1860–2020." NBER Working Paper No. 30301. National Bureau of Economic Research.

Easterlin, Richard. 1962. "The American Baby Boom in Historical Perspective." NBER Occasional Paper No. 79. National Bureau of Economic Research.

Easterlin, Richard. 1968. *Population, Labor Force, and Long Swings in Economic Growth: The American Experience*. NBER. Columbia University Press.

Engerman, Stanley L. 1971. "Human Capital, Education, and Economic Growth."

In *The Reinterpretation of American Economic History*, edited by R. W. Fogel and S. L. Engerman, chap. 18. Harper & Row.

Fisher, Irving. 1897. "Senses of 'Capital.'" *Economic Journal* 7 (26): 199–213.

Freeman, Richard B., and Lawrence F. Katz, eds. 1995. *Differences and Changes in Wage Structures*. University of Chicago Press and NBER.

Friedman, Milton, and Simon Kuznets. 1945. *Income from Independent Professional Practice*. NBER.

Ghez, Gilbert R., and Gary S. Becker. 1975. *The Allocation of Time and Goods over the Life Cycle*. NBER. Columbia University Press.

Goldin, Claudia, and Lawrence F. Katz. 2008. *The Race Between Education and Technology*. Belknap Press of Harvard University Press.

Griliches, Zvi. 1995. "The Discovery of the Residual: An Historical Note." NBER Working Paper No. 5348 (November). National Bureau of Economic Research.

Heckman, James. 2008. "Schools, Skills, and Synapses." *Economic Inquiry* 46 (3): 289–324.

Heckman, James. 2015. "Introduction to *A Theory of the Allocation of Time* by Gary Becker." *Economic Journal* 125 (583): 403–9.

Heckman, James, Rodrigo Pinto, and Peter Savelyev. 2013. "Understanding the Mechanisms Through Which an Influential Early Childhood Education Program Boosted Adult Outcomes." *American Economic Review* 103 (6): 2052–86.

Hendren, Nathaniel, and Benjamin Sprung-Keyser. 2020. "A Unified Welfare Analysis of Government Policies." *Quarterly Journal of Economics* 135 (3): 1209–1318. https://doi.org/10.1093/qje/qjaa006.

Holden, Laura, and Jeff Biddle. 2017. "The Introduction of Human Capital Theory into Education Policy in the United States." *History of Political Economy* 49 (4): 537–74.

Jones, Charles I. 2016. "The Facts of Economic Growth." In *Handbook of Macroeconomics*, edited by John Taylor and Harald Uhlig, 2A:3–69.

Katz, Lawrence F., and Kevin M. Murphy. 1992. "Changes in Relative Wages, 1963–1987: Supply and Demand Factors." *Quarterly Journal of Economics* 107 (1): 35–78.

Kendrick, John, with Maude R. Pech. 1961. *Productivity Trends in the United States*. NBER. Princeton University Press.

Kiker, B. F. 1966. "The Historical Roots of the Concept of Human Capital." *Journal of Political Economy* 74 (5): 481–99.

Kuznets, Simon, with Elizabeth Jenks. 1961. *Capital in the American Economy: Its Formation and Financing*. Princeton University Press for the NBER.

Lang, Kevin, and Michael Manove. 2011. "Education and Labor Market Discrimination." *American Economic Review* 101 (4): 1467–96.

Mankiw, N. Gregory, David Romer, and David N. Weil. 1992. "A Contribution to the Empirics of Economic Growth." *Quarterly Journal of Economics* 107 (2): 407–38.

Margo, Robert A. 1990. *Race and Schooling in the South, 1880–1950: An Economic History*. University of Chicago Press and NBER.

Marshall, Alfred. 1890. *Principles of Economics: An Introductory Volume*. 8th ed. Macmillan and Co. Online Library of Liberty. https://oll.libertyfund.org/title/marshall-principles-of-economics-8th-ed.

Mincer, Jacob. 1958. "Investment in Human Capital and Personal Distribution of Income." *Journal of Political Economy* 66 (4): 281–302.

Mincer, Jacob. 1962. "On-the-Job Training: Costs, Returns, and Some Implications." *Journal of Political Economy* 70 (5), pt. 2: 50–79.

Mincer, Jacob. 1974. *Schooling, Experience, and Earnings*. Columbia University Press.

Mincer, Jacob, and Solomon Polachek. 1974. "Family Investments in Human Capital: The Earnings of Women." *Journal of Political Economy* 82 (2), pt. 2: S76–S110.
Mushkin, Selma. 1962. "Health as an Investment." *Journal of Political Economy* 70 (5), pt. 2: 129–57.
Nelson, Edward. 2020. *Milton Friedman and Economic Debate in the United States, 1932–1972*. Vol. 1. University of Chicago Press.
Schultz, Theodore W. 1961. "Investment in Human Capital" (presidential address). *American Economic Review* 51 (1): 1–17.
Schultz, Theodore W. 1962. "Reflections on Investment in Man." *Journal of Political Economy* 70 (5), pt. 2: 1–8.
Schultz, Theodore W. 1972. *Human Resources*. 50th anniversary, colloquium 6. National Bureau of Economic Research. Columbia University Press.
Schultz, Theodore W., ed. 1974. "Marriage, Family, Human Capital, and Fertility." *Journal of Political Economy* 82 (2), pt. 2.
Sjaastad, Larry A. 1962. "The Costs and Returns of Human Migration." *Journal of Political Economy* 70 (5), pt. 2: 80–93.
Smith, Adam. 1776. *An Inquiry into the Nature and Causes of the Wealth of Nations*. https://www.gutenberg.org/files/3300/3300-h/3300-h.htm.
Spengler, Joseph J. 1977. "Adam Smith on Human Capital." *American Economic Review: Papers and Proceedings* 67 (1): 32–36.
Stantcheva, Stefanie. 2017. "Optimal Taxation and Human Capital Policies over the Life Cycle." *Journal of Political Economy* 125 (6): 1931–90.
Stigler, George. 1947. *Trends in Output and Employment*. 25th anniversary ed. NBER.
Stigler, George. 1962. "Information in the Labor Market." *Journal of Political Economy* 70 (5), pt. 2: 94–105.
Universities-National Bureau Committee for Economic Research. 1962. *Aspects of Labor Economics*. NBER. Princeton University Press.
Weisbrod, Burton A. 1962. "Education and Investment in Human Capital." *Journal of Political Economy* 70 (5), pt. 2: 106–23.
Weiss, Andrew. 1988. "High School Graduation, Performance and Wages." *Journal of Political Economy* 96 (4): 785–820.

Author Index

Subject Index

Note: Page numbers followed by *f* or *t* refer to figures or tables, respectively.